Public Leadership

Perspectives and Practices

Public Leadership
Perspectives and Practices

Edited by Paul 't Hart and John Uhr

ANU
THE AUSTRALIAN NATIONAL UNIVERSITY

E PRESS

ANU
E PRESS

the Australia and New Zealand
School of Government

Published by ANU E Press
The Australian National University
Canberra ACT 0200, Australia
Email: anuepress@anu.edu.au
This title is also available online at:
        http://epress.anu.edu.au/public_leadership _citation.html

National Library of Australia
Cataloguing-in-Publication entry

Title: Public leadership pespectives and practices [electronic
                resource] / editors, Paul 't Hart, John Uhr.

ISBN: 9781921536304 (pbk.)
                9781921536311 (pdf)

Series: ANZSOG series

Subjects: Leadership
                Political leadership
                Civic leaders.
                Community leadership

Other Authors/Contributors:
                Hart, Paul 't.
                Uhr, John, 1951-

Dewey Number: 303.34

Cover design by John Butcher
Images comprising the cover graphic used by permission of:
Victorian Department of Planning and Community Development
Australian Associated Press
Australian Broadcasting Corporation
Scoop Media Group (www.scoop.co.nz)
Cover graphic based on M. C. Escher's Hand with Reflecting Sphere, 1935
(Lithograph).

Funding for this monograph series has been provided by the Australia and New
Zealand School of Government Research Program.

John Wanna, *Series Editor*

Professor John Wanna is the Sir John Bunting Chair of Public Administration at the Research School of Social Sciences at The Australian National University. He is the director of research for the Australian and New Zealand School of Government (ANZSOG). He is also a joint appointment with the Department of Politics and Public Policy at Griffith University and a principal researcher with two research centres: the Governance and Public Policy Research Centre and the nationally-funded Key Centre in Ethics, Law, Justice and Governance at Griffith University. Professor Wanna has produced around 17 books including two national text books on policy and public management. He has produced a number of research-based studies on budgeting and financial management including: *Budgetary Management and Control* (1990); *Managing Public Expenditure* (2000), *From Accounting to Accountability* (2001) and, most recently, *Controlling Public Expenditure* (2003). He has just completed a study of state level leadership covering all the state and territory leaders — entitled *Yes Premier: Labor leadership in Australia's states and territories* — and has edited a book on Westminster Legacies in Asia and the Pacific — *Westminster Legacies: Democracy and responsible government in Asia and the Pacific*. He was a chief investigator in a major Australian Research Council funded study of the Future of Governance in Australia (1999-2001) involving Griffith and the ANU. His research interests include Australian and comparative politics, public expenditure and budgeting, and government-business relations. He also writes on Australian politics in newspapers such as *The Australian*, *Courier-Mail* and *The Canberra Times* and has been a regular state political commentator on ABC radio and TV.

Table of Contents

Part IV: Australian Political Leadership

Part V: Political Leadership: New Zealand

Acknowledgements

This has been an ambitious project, and we are grateful to all our workshop participants and chapter authors for responding so enthusiastically to our call for 'joining up' scholars and practitioners from across Australia and New Zealand who shared an interest in understanding and improving public leadership. We would like to acknowledge financial support from ANZSOG, the Research School of Social Sciences at ANU and the Parliamentary Studies Centre at the Crawford school of Economics and Government at ANU for making the workshop possible. We are also grateful to Aaron Martin, Kathryn Kelly and Karen Tindall for their useful notes on the workshop discussions. Karen Tindall moreover played an invaluable role in organising the workshop. We intend to stage thematically focused workshops on public leadership annually, and we can only hope that future ones will be as engaging and productive as the first.

Paul 't Hart and John Uhr
Canberra, September 2008

Contributors

Editors

John Uhr is head of the Policy and Governance Program, Crawford School of Economics and Government, The Australian National University, where he teaches on leadership in the Masters of Public Policy degree. His research interests include ethics in the public sector, public policy and administration, public leadership, and democratic theory and practice. He is the author of *Terms of Trust: Arguments over Ethics in Australian Government* (Sydney: University of New South Wales Press, 2005).

Paul 't Hart is professor of political science at the Research School of Social Sciences, ANU, as well as professor of public administration, Utrecht School of Governance, Utrecht University. His major research interests include public leadership, political group dynamics, crisis management, policy evaluation and public accountability. Recent works include: *The Politics of Crisis Management: Public Leadership Under Pressure* (CUP 2005, with A. Boin *et al.*; winner of Herbert Simon Award, American Political Science Association), *Observing Government Elites* (Palgrave 2007, with R. Rhodes, M. Noordegraaf), *Governing After Crisis* (CUP 2008, with A. Boin, A. McConnell) and *The New Eurocrats* (Amsterdam University Press 2008, with K. Geuijen *et al.*).

Authors

Dr Norman Abjorensen teaches politics in the School of Social Sciences, Faculty of Arts, at the ANU, and is a prominent political commentator on radio, television and in print. His latest book, *Leadership and the Liberal Revival*, was published in 2007, and he is the author of studies of former Liberal leader John Hewson, former NSW premier Tom Lewis and the role of George Reid in federation. His new book, *John Howard and the Conservative Tradition*, will be published late 2008, as will two co-authored books, *Australia: The State of Democracy*, and a book dealing with the culture wars.

Dr Catherine Althaus is currently assistant professor in the School of Public Administration, University of Victoria, Canada and associate research fellow with the Centre for Governance and Public Policy, Griffith University. Previously she was ANZSOG Research Fellow at the Research School of Social Sciences at the ANU. Her research interests concern public policy processes, public sector leadership, political risk calculation, and the interaction between religion and politics. Catherine recently published *Calculating Political Risk* (University of New South Wales Press 2008) and co-authored the fourth edition of *The Australian Policy Handbook* with Glyn Davis and Peter Bridgman (Allen & Unwin 2007).

Paul W. B. Atkins is associate professor in leadership and organisational behaviour in the Crawford School of Economics and Government at the ANU. His research interests include leadership, perspective taking capacity, adult development, systems thinking, mindfulness and stress reduction. His recent publications include, 'Measuring systems thinking: Contributions from adult development', a paper presented at the Australia and New Zealand Systems Thinking Conference, Christchurch, NZ, December 5-7, 2005 (co-authored with K. Johnston); and 'Building better work places through individual perspective taking: A fresh look at a fundamental human process' *International Review of Industrial and Organizational Psychology*, 23 (co-authored with S. E. Parker and C. M. Axtell — forthcoming 2008).

Stuart Cunningham is professor of media and communications, and director of the ARC Centre of Excellence for Creative Industries and Innovation, Queensland University of Technology. Known for his contributions to media, communications and cultural studies, he works to promote their relevance to industry practice and government policy. He is the author or editor of several books and major reports, the most recent of which include *The Media and Communications in Australia* (with Graeme Turner, 4th ed, 2006) and *What Price a Creative Economy?* (2006). A collection of essays, 'In the Vernacular', is forthcoming in 2008 from UQP. Select recent publications are available at http://eprints.qut.edu.au/view/person/Cunningham,_Stuart.html

Dr Jennifer Curtin is a senior lecturer in the Political Studies Department, University of Auckland. Her research interests include the representation of women (cross-nationally) and rural Australians in politics and policy-making. She is the author of *Voicing the Vote of the Bush: Rural and Regional Representation in the Australian Federal Parliament* (2004), and co-author of *Rebels with a Cause: Independents in Australian Politics* (2004). She has published widely on women and politics, most recently in *Parliamentary Affairs*. She is guest co-editor of a 2006 issue of the *Australian Journal of Political Science* entitled 'Globalising the Antipodes?' and is currently working on a book entitled 'Gendering Political Leadership: comparative perspectives'.

Keith Dowding is professor and head of the Political Science Program at the Research School of Social Sciences, ANU. He has published extensively in comparative, urban and *beccabunga* politics, public administration and public policy, social and rational choice theory, and political philosophy. His recent research includes examining ministerial careers, and helped set up the Selection and De-Selection of Political Elites network of scholars co-editing a forthcoming volume, *The Selection of Ministers in Europe: Hiring and Firing* and is co-authoring *Accounting for Ministers*. He has been editor of the *Journal of Theoretical Politics* since 1996.

Wayne Errington is lecturer in political science and international relations in the School of Social Sciences, ANU. His research interests are in political leadership and communication. He is the author, with Peter van Onselen, of *John Winston Howard: The Definitive Biography* and, with Narelle Miragliotta, *Media and Politics: An Introduction.*

Jenny Fleming is research professor at the Tasmanian Institute of Law Enforcement Studies, University of Tasmania. Her research interests include police management, police leadership and public policy. Her recent publications include: 'Leading the Troops from the Top — The Role of Police Commissioner', *Public Administration (UK)*, 86:3, September 2008; *Fighting Crime Together: The Challenges of Policing and Security Networks* (co-edited with J. Wood) Sydney: University of New South Wales Press, 2006; and 'Les Liaisons Dangereuses: Relations between Police Commissioners and their Political Masters', *Australian Journal of Public Administration*, 63:3, September 2004, 60-74.

Barry Gustafson is emeritus professor of politics at the University of Auckland. His many publications include histories of the New Zealand Labour and National parties and biographies of three New Zealand prime ministers, Michael Joseph Savage (*From the Cradle to the Grave*, 1986), Robert Muldoon (*His Way*, 2000), and Keith Holyoake (*Kiwi Keith*, 2007). He also wrote essays on five other prime ministers for *The Dictionary of New Zealand Biography* and in the past three years has also published on populism and political leadership; New Zealand since 1945; New Zealand, Australia and the US; the Treaty of Waitangi; and New Zealand and the Cold War.

Dr Rob Hall, is a senior lecturer at the School of Government, University of Tasmania. His research interests include public policy, policy leadership, and Antarctic politics. His most recent publications include: 'Setting and Implementing the Agenda: Australian Antarctic Policy' (co-authored with M. Haward and A. Kellow); and 'Saving Seabirds', in *Looking South: Australia's Antarctic Agenda,* (edited by L. Kriwoken, J. Jabour and A. Hemmings), Federation Press 2007.

John Higley is professor of government and sociology and director of the Centre for Australian and New Zealand Studies, University of Texas at Austin. As chair of the Research Committee on Political Elites of the International Political Science Association, Professor Higley's interest is the theory of elites and politics. He is the co-author of *Elite Foundations of Liberal Democracy* (2006), *Elitism* (1980), *Elites in Australia* (1979), and co-editor of *Elites after State Socialism* (2000), *Elites, Crises and the Origins of Regimes* (1998), *Elites and Democratic Consolidation in Latin America and Southern Europe* (1992).

John Kane is professor in the Department of Politics and Public Policy and Deputy Director of the Research Centre for Governance and Public Policy at Griffith University. He works in political theory, political leadership and foreign policy. He was awarded (with Haig Patapan) the Mosher Award for best 2006 academic article in *Public Administration Review*. He is the author of *The Politics of Moral Capital* (Cambridge 2001), co-editor of *Rethinking Australian Citizenship* (Cambridge 2000) and *Dissenting Democrats* (Palgrave Macmillan 2008). His latest single-authored work is *Between Virtue and Power: The Persistent Moral Dilemma of US Foreign Policy* (Yale 2008).

David Kemp is a Vice-Chancellor's Fellow at the University of Melbourne and a Professorial Fellow of the Australia and New Zealand School of Government. He was professor of politics at Monash University 1979–1990, a member of Federal Parliament 1990–2004, and after 1996 held a number of Cabinet portfolios. He is the author of *Foundations for Australian Political Analysis* (OUP 1987); *The Reform of Schooling*, in J. Leeser (ed.) *State Policy Perspectives* (Menzies Research Centre, 2007); 'Advisers and Decisions 1976', *Australian Journal of Public Administration,* 66:1 (2007) pp. 1-9.

Raymond Miller is an associate professor and head of the Department of Politics at the University of Auckland, where he specialises in political parties, representation, electoral systems and elections, and leadership. He has collaborated on a number of election studies, including *Proportional Representation on Trial* (2002) and *Voters' Veto* (2004). His most recent publications include *Party Politics in New Zealand* (2005), *New Zealand Government and Politics* (2006), and *Political Leadership in New Zealand* (2006).

Jan Pakulski, MA (Warsaw), PhD (ANU), ASSA is Professor of Sociology and Dean of Arts at the University of Tasmania. He writes on elites, social inequality, social movements, and social change. He is the author of *Globalising Inequalities* (2004) and *Social Movements* (1991), co-author of *Postmodernisation: Change in Advanced Society* (1992) and *The Death of Class* (1996), and co-editor of *Postcommunist Elites in Eastern Europe* (1998).

Haig Patapan is professor in the Department of Politic and Public Policy and director of the Democracy Program, Centre for Governance and Public Policy, both at Griffith University. His research interests include political theory, leadership, and democratic governance. Professor Patapan is the author of *Judging Democracy* (Cambridge UP 2000) and *Machiavelli in Love: the Modern Politics of Love and Fear* (Lexington 2006); and co-editor of *Globalization and Equality* (Routledge 2004); *Westminster Legacies: Democracy and Responsible Government in Asia and the Pacific* (UNSW Press 2005); and most recently, *Dissident Democrats: the Challenge of Democratic Leadership in Asia* (Palgrave 2008).

Katherine J. Reynolds is an ARC Australian Research Fellow at the ANU. She has also held positions at the ANU as lecturer and senior lecturer teaching Introduction to Organisational Psychology and co-ordinating the postgraduate offerings in Applied Social and Organisational Psychology. Her research has mainly focused on the impact of social identification processes on stereotyping, prejudice and discrimination; group functioning (for example, motivation, productivity, leadership processes) as well as, more recently, individual psychological functioning (personality, well-being). She is co-editor of *Understanding Prejudice, Racism and Social Conflict* with Professor Augoustinos.

Will Sanders is a senior fellow at The Australian National University's Centre for Aboriginal Economic Policy Research. He previously worked in three other departments of the ANU, focusing his research on public policy towards Indigenous Australians. He has published numerous articles on various aspects of Indigenous affairs policy in the *Australian Journal of Public Administration*, the *Australian Journal of Political Science* and other journals over the last 25 years. His article 'Is home ownership the answer? Indigenous Australians and housing tenure in remote (and settled) areas' recently appeared in the journal *Housing Studies*.

Marian Simms is professor in political studies and served as chair of the politics department, University of Otago, New Zealand from 2002–2007. She recently held a visiting fellowship in the politics discipline, ANU. She has recently published on Australian and New Zealand politics: 'Australia and New Zealand: Separate paths but path dependent' *The Round Table*, 95:387, 2006, pp. 679-92 and *From the Hustings to Harbour Views* UNSW Press 2006 (distributed by University of Washington Press). Her forthcoming article 'Women's Politics and Leadership in Australia and New Zealand' will appear in the Autumn issue of *Signs: Journal of Women in Culture and Society*, and her forthcoming edited book *Kevin07: The 2007 Australian Election* will be published in Spring 2009.

Amanda Sinclair is foundation professor of management (diversity and change), Melbourne Business School, The University of Melbourne. Her research and teaching is in leadership and ethics, organisational culture and change, gender and diversity and she is the author of several books including *Doing Leadership Differently* (1998, 2004) *New Faces of Leadership* (2002) and *Leadership for the Disillusioned: Beyond Myths and Heroes to Leading that Liberates* (2007). In addition to her work at MBS, Amanda consults to organisations and coaches individuals and senior management teams, is a regular contributor to the business press and also teaches yoga.

Dr Paul Strangio is a senior lecturer in politics in the School of Political and Social Inquiry, Monash University. A biographer and political historian he has been the author and editor of several books on Australian politics, including writing on the areas of institutional change in governance, political leadership and political parties. His most recent books are *No, Prime Minister: Reclaiming Politics from Leaders* (co-authored with James Walter), UNSW Press, 2007; and *The Victorian Premiers, 1856–2006* (co-edited with Brian Costar), Federation Press, 2006.

Emina Subasic is a research fellow in the School of Psychology, ANU. She is also in the process of completing her PhD titled 'Political Solidarity as a Social Change Process: Dynamics of Self-Categorization in Intergroup Power Relations'. Her research focuses on the role of social identity and self-categorization processes in social change, influence and leadership.

John C. Turner is professor of psychology at the School of Psychology, ANU, educated at the University of Sussex and Bristol, he has held positions at the Universities of Bristol and Exeter, Macquarie University, UNSW, and the Institute of Advanced Study at Princeton, before coming to the ANU. Amongst his many publications as sole author, or with others, are the books *Intergroup Behaviour*, *Rediscovering the social group: A Self-Categorization Theory*, *Social Influence,* and *Stereotyping and Social Reality*. He delivered the Tajfel Memorial Lecture at the University of Oxford for the European Association of Experimental Social Psychology in 1999 and was the Freilich Foundation Eminent Lecturer for 2001.

James Walter is professor of political science and head of the School of Political and Social Inquiry at Monash University, and emeritus professor of Australian studies at Griffith University. His research interests include political leadership, biography, the history of ideas and institutional policy regimes. His recent works include: *The Citizens' Bargain* (UNSW Press 2002, with Margaret MacLeod), *Ideas and Influence: Social Science and Public Policy in Australia* (UNSW Press 2007, edited with Peter Saunders), and *No, Prime Minister: Reclaiming Politics From Leaders* (UNSW Press 2007, with Paul Strangio).

John Wanna is the ANZSOG Foundation Professor for the Sir John Bunting Chair of Public Administration. Formerly from Griffith University. His research interests include Australian and comparative politics, public expenditure and budgeting and government-business relations. Recent publications include: *Accounting to Accountability* (2001), *Controlling Public Expenditure* (2003) and *Yes Premier* (2005). He edits the Australian Journal of Public Administration, and is general editor of the successful ANZSOG monographs series at ANU E Press, for which he recently (co-)edited the volumes *Australian Political Lives* (2006) and *A Passion for Policy* (2008).

Dr David West is Reader in political science in the School of Social Sciences, ANU. His research and teaching interests include contemporary political theory; Hannah Arendt; Habermas and critical theory; theories of new social movements; and the politics of sexuality. His publications include 'New Social Movements' in *Handbook of Political Theory* (edited by G. F. Gaus and C. Kukathas, Sage Publications, 2004) and *Reason and Sexuality in Western Thought* (Cambridge and Malden, MA: Polity Press, 2005).

Hugh White is professor of strategic studies at the ANU and a visiting fellow at the Lowy Institute for International Policy. He has worked on strategic and defence issues in several different capacities: as an intelligence analyst, as a journalist, as a senior adviser on the staffs of Defence Minister Kim Beazley and Prime Minister Bob Hawke, as a senior official in the Department of Defence, and as the first director of the Australian Strategic Policy Institute (ASPI). In the 1970s he studied philosophy at Melbourne and Oxford Universities.

1. Understanding Public Leadership: An Introduction

Paul 't Hart and John Uhr

Aims of this book

'Leadership' often gets talked about in the world of politics and the public sphere at large. It is routinely admired, vilified, ridiculed, invoked, trivialised, explained and speculated about in media discourse and in everyday conversation. Yet, despite all this talk, there is surprisingly little consensus about how to answer some of the basic questions, for example, about the nature, place, role and impact of leadership in contemporary society. The idea of this project is to bring together academics from a broad array of social science disciplines in Australia and its near abroad who are interested in, and are contributing to, our understanding of (civic, political, bureaucratic) leadership in the public domain in Australia and beyond. We want to take stock of what we know and explore what we need to know about public leadership. In particular we want to explore — and put into a broader international perspective — the Australian 'state of the art' with regard to several key questions in the leadership perspective on social and political processes:

- Public leadership as an *object of study*: How do we know 'leadership' when we see it in different contexts? How we can conceptualise and study (public) leadership in a systematic fashion from the perspective of various social science disciplines and theories? What key questions ought to be addressed, what key insights have been obtained so far with regard to these questions, and which theories and methods have been employed to obtain them, and what research challenges lie ahead?
- Leadership as a *democratic design issue*: How can the three main forms of public leadership discerned here — civic, political, bureaucratic — be exercised, institutionalised and constrained in democratic polities? How do these various spheres of public leadership intersect, reinforce and/or conflict with one another and how can the 'creative tension' between them best be governed and utilised?
- Leadership as a *solution and a problem*: Pleas for 'more', 'better', 'genuine', 'transformational', 'authentic' or otherwise socially desirable public leadership are often heard in many different areas of politics and government. But what do people mean when they say that? How realistic are these pleas? Who should heed them? For example, what leadership philosophies and practices are able to accommodate the twin challenges of innovation and

conservation of public institutions, policies and values in an epoch of pervasive, yet complex, socio-technological changes and creeping crises? The widely perceived 'hollowing out' of classic nation state-centric politics under the twin forces of globalisation and individualisation implies that public leadership roles, such as agenda-setting and coalition-building, are increasingly being played by new, more fluid and boundary-less entities such as new social movements, think tanks, international government organisations and transnational alliances. What does this mean for the democratic accountability and legitimacy we have come to expect from those who ideas and actions govern our lives?

In the discussion that follows, we first demarcate the key phenomenon of interest: public leadership. We distinguish between political, administrative and civic spheres in which public leadership is exercised. Each of these spheres entails a number of specific leadership challenges awaiting holders of public offices as well as others aspiring to exercise leadership in the public sphere. Then we briefly survey different academic approaches to studying public leadership, identifying their general thrust and highlighting some key international as well as contributors to each. We conclude by asking some general questions about public leadership in Australia and beyond that we hope will stimulate further reflection as readers attend to the debates and discussion shaped by the contributors to this book.

The nature of public leadership

Aristotle is said to have originated the dictum that we want a government of laws not men. And, to an important extent, that is what we have got — the established democracies in particular. Yet men can never be factored out of the equation of governing. In fact, many contemporary commentators in Westminster style democracies such as Australia claim to observe an increasing 'personalisation' of politics (usually deemed due to the decline of ideologies, parties and the rise of television), or an increasing concentration of what once was dispersed and/or collegially shared power in the office of a single individual, for example, the head of government (Poguntke and Webb 2005).

People matter in governance, and some people matter a lot more than others. Perhaps because of this, the bulk of studies of public leadership are essentially studies of the lives and/or particular characteristics and behaviours of individuals occupying high public offices. These studies are part of a much broader effort to identify, describe, understand and evaluate the behaviour of elites — the few who exercise power and influence over the many. Elites can be studied in many different ways — by interviewing them, by ploughing through their speeches and writings, by administering surveys to them, by looking at their CVs and collating and comparing their demographic, social and professional characteristics, or by observing them up close as much as possible (cf. Rhodes, 't Hart and Noordegraaf 2007).

Yet while essential to our present endeavour, studying leadership by looking at individuals in positions of power is not sufficient for our purposes. We want to understand leader*ship,* which is a particular set of activities and interactions that people in position and power as well as other people engage in. Moreover, we want to explore the nature of a specific, self-conscious interest in *public* leadership as something distinctive, not as some derivative of corporate leadership, nor narrowed down to executive political leadership.

In order to do so, public leadership is conceptualised here in terms of a number of distinctive functions that need to be performed in order for a polity to govern itself effectively and democratically, but which are not performed spontaneously by a polity's public institutions, organisations and routines. Crucial though they are, institutions, organisations and routines constitute but a skeleton of the body politic. It is the people living in and with them that provide the flesh and the spirit that bring it to life. The answer to the classic question of 'who governs?' cannot be: 'nobody' — and not just for logical reasons. However elaborate and complex the institutional fabric of government is and, however overwhelming the situational pressures and contextual (historical, international, legal) constraints, at the end of the day it is down to individuals and groups taking up the strategic challenges and dilemmas of 'managing the public's business' (Lynn 1981) to give direction to governing. They do so by devising, deliberating, interpreting, challenging and changing the institutional rules and practices of government (and, increasingly, 'governance,' Rhodes 1997), which exist to deal predictably, reliably and efficiently with the much greater number and variety of routine tasks that day-to-day governance entails.

If we accept the general proposition that public leadership evolves as an adaptive response to the non-routine, strategic challenges in a society, we can begin to map out the specific challenges awaiting people whose jobs are primarily located in three constituent (and admittedly overlapping) spheres of public governance: the political, the administrative and the societal.

Political leadership

Political leadership tends to be exercised around a number of strategic, recurrent challenges facing societies and their governments.

Us and them: mediating identity, dealing with 'others'.

Leaders of government are also leaders of political parties. In most cases, they are leaders of parties well before they become leaders of government. Political parties perform many functions, one of which is to mobilise social and cultural partialities that support their cause. In this quite fundamental sense, leaders of governments promote an 'us and them' mentality, contrasting their own party against competing political parties. But this creative tension goes far beyond the polite forms of party competition: heads of government frequently define their government, their nation and indeed their society in terms of a set of differences between 'our world' and 'other worlds', trying to reinforce a sense of national or social identity by marking out differences or contrasts managed by competing leaders.

Attention and neglect: defining problems in/out, (re)directing institutional agendas.

Not only heads of government, but all political leaders are in the business of problem-definition, which is another way of saying that they are also in the business of problem-denial. This mode of leadership is illustrated in the competing postures of political leaders over threats posed by 'climate change', some of whom are deep in denial while others are high on fears for the immediate future. Immigration is another good example of a policy area which illustrates the way some leaders frame issues as 'problems' requiring 'solutions', while other leaders seize on the supposed 'solutions' as the real 'problems'. Another good illustration emerges when we look at a prominent public institution, such as a national public broadcaster, and note the remarkably divergent policy agendas devised as appropriate to the public management of that national broadcaster by competing political leaders. For some, the very existence of the public broadcaster is 'the problem', while for other leaders the urgent problem is the threat posed to the broadcaster's future by its opponents.

Stability and change: 'creative destruction' of public choices and policies.

Every aspiring political leader sees opportunities for policy change, even if they are persuaded that it is more fruitful to speak reassuringly of 'continuity' than of change. Conservative political leaders have mastered the art of disguising the extent of change that their party or government might be determined to effect. Sometimes conservative leaders are vulnerable to internal criticism from party members that the leadership team has 'sold out' the historic mission of the party. So too, many progressive parties and governments have leaders who draw attention away from the discontinuities that they have planned for their political organisation. Internal party squabbles over 'party policy' can reflect quite fundamental rifts over the manner and form of change being mobilised by the ruling group. Modernisers do battle with traditionalists, both of whom want change but often in different directions and for very different reasons.

Power and responsibility: insuring and embodying public accountability.

Political leaders are defined by power. At one extreme, there are leaders who so firmly adhere to the power of abstract doctrine that they can never quite embrace the power of mundane politics: in Gough Whitlam's immortal (if puzzling) words about his leadership rivals in the Australian Labor Party: 'only the impotent are pure'. At the other extreme, there are political leaders who embrace populism because that is the sure path to popular support and public power, regardless of what political doctrine to which they might have originally been attracted. In between, political leaders pursue the responsibilities of power with more or less acceptance of the burdens of public accountability. Leadership involves balancing the *responsibilities* of rule with the *accountabilities* of office: seizing the policy initiatives that come with the power of rule while knowing that a variety of pubic reckonings loom down the electoral track. And, of course, between elections there are plenty of opportunities for various accountability agencies to test, investigate, check, scrutinise or query the trustworthiness of those exercising the responsibilities of power.

Crisis and emergency: evoking and containing collective stress.

If crisis management is considered 'the big test' of leadership, then we should be prepared for the bad news that leaders are crisis-prone (Boin *et al.* 2005). It is not simply the case that 'great leaders' solve or resolve crises; some of the very greatest leaders provoke or at least seek to exploit crises (Boin *et al.* 2008). As Murray Edelman (1977: 43) argued: 'any regime that prides itself on its capacity to manage crises will find crises to manage'. Political leaders of the 'strong' type thrive in emergency conditions, as we have witnessed in the career of John Howard who sensed the enduring political value of yet another public crisis, including the self-proclaimed 'national emergency' in the Northern Territory and the crisis of national conscience associated with the unfinished business of the constitutional preamble. But they can also be destroyed by them, for example, Anthony Eden and the Suez crisis, Jimmy Carter and the hostage crisis and, less grandly, Malcolm Fraser and the economic crisis of the early eighties.

Administrative leadership

The most characteristic dilemma that senior public administrators ('bureaucrats') face is that of having to serve (their political masters, the democratic process, and the 'citizens as clients') and being expected to lead (namely big and complex public organisations) at the same time. In the American tradition in particular, the leadership expectations attached to senior administrative positions are strongly emphasised, and in part embedded in the Constitution. In other places — such as France and to some extent Germany — a remarkable degree of officially sanctioned 'hybridity' between political and administrative leadership roles and cadres exists. In the Westminster system, official doctrine almost exclusively, and sometimes quite narrowly, emphasises the 'servant' aspect of administrative roles ('the government of the day'), but the realities of modern governance are such that senior department and agency officials cannot help but also be exercising leadership — leaving them more vulnerable than their US counterparts to charges of being 'unresponsive'. Distinctive challenges of administrative leadership include the following:

Serving the government and the democratic process.

Classic civil bureaucracy derives from earlier military bureaucracy: a machine of state designed to carry out orders when managing and protecting political territory. Democracy is a late entry into this story, as we see in Max Weber's (1922) account of civil bureaucracy with its emphasis on the military precision of hierarchy and order, files and records. Administrative bureaucracy is consistent with democracy but it is not itself modelled on democracy: bureaucratic impartiality respects the political partiality of the government and, in its Weberian rendition, bureaucracy places its own hierarchical leadership at the service of the government. Or is it simply (but ominously) 'government', in the sense of 'the state' as distinct from the governing party? Following Eden (1983), we can interpret Woodrow Wilson's (1887) approach to this problem as a complement to Weber's approach by attempting to show how the public service can be democratic but not, in and of itself, political. What Wilson saw as 'the merit system' allowed the public service to look to its own internal leadership on issues of public administration but defer to political leadership on issues of public policy: the so-called separation of policy and administration. Having no legitimate power over the determination of policy, the public service leads the execution or implementation of government policy. Wilson (and remarkably few other theorists) attempted to 'constitutionalise' bureaucracy not by defining away its discretionary powers but by framing these considerable leadership powers in terms of business-like or entrepreneurial policy implementation: with tensions over responsibilities and accountabilities that we live with even to this day (Rohr 1978).

Crafting, sustaining and adapting public organisations.

Public servants manage public organisations. Managerialism is a doctrine that holds that the art of management has its own distinctive practices and values. When applied to public organisations, managerialism suggests that public servants have a set of distinctive managerial responsibilities that supplement the policy responsibilities of political officials. Below we will say more about the art of 'public management' that has overtaken the traditional art of public administration, but in this section we note an intermediate form of managerial organisation that attracted a leadership seal of approval from the likes of Philip

Selznick (1957). This intermediate form emerges historically later than the original validation of public service in the accounts of Weber and Wilson, and our reference to Selznick should be enough to suggest that mid-twentieth century experiments in quasi-autonomous public corporations like the Tennessee Valley Authority, the vast US public utility studied by Selznick, or the US Forest Service studied by Herbert Kaufman (1981). Of course, the public officials managing these valuable public enterprises exercised, writ large as it were, the family of administrative crafts also exercised in more modest profile by their bureaucratic cousins in the core public service. But the advantage of noting the scale of managerial mastery delegated by politicians to public managers in public corporations ('statutory authorities' in Australian parlance) is that we see all those business-like skills predicted by Wilson on public display by the original generation of public entrepreneurs, exercising leadership over the management of very large public assets placed by politicians in public trust beyond the immediate political interference of elected officials (Terry 1995).

Making government work: delivering public value.

Harvard scholar Mark Moore (1995) is credited with the slogan 'Creating Public Value' as a descriptor of the type of public leadership exercised by administrative officials. The emphasis in Moore's account is on the creative element, which can be seen as the contemporary restatement of the delegated discretionary power so valued by Wilson a century earlier. What is new in Moore's account is the explicit recognition that those who 'implement' the law have a legitimate role in shaping and forming the policy that supposedly informs the law. Even where the officials have had very limited input into the formal policy being authorised and implemented, they have substantial control over *how* the policy will be implemented, and that discretionary capacity over the mechanisms of implementation marks out the legitimate expectation of officials that they will 'create public value' out of the often incomprehensible, sometimes incoherent public law that is handed to them. Of special importance in Moore's framework is stakeholder negotiation: the many ways that public servants can lead the implementation process through their management of who gets to be heard when policy is translated into administrative practice. Crafting consultation is the name of this leadership game: and Moore has his gallery of exemplary public negotiators who can bring public legitimacy to policy implementation by exercising the sort of leadership that can be wielded through adept processes for public hearings. Environmental Protection Authorities at their best often illustrate these processes. There is robust debate on how applicable this interpretation of public service leadership is in Westminster settings (Rhodes and Wanna 2007; Alford 2008)

Civic leadership

The third sphere of public leadership focuses on actors/roles outside the governmental system. Most studies of political/public leadership ignore this sphere altogether, which is a gross omission since societal leadership is quite often what animates innovation, controversy and change in polities. It will be argued that societal leadership comes to life in explicit relation, and in opposition, to the power of governmental elites (Kane 2001). Three key leadership challenges on the societal side include:

Monitoring and evaluating politics/bureaucracy: the watchdog role.

Many interest groups act as watchdogs over government. What tends to be distinctive of the civil society role is the use of publicity as leverage over government. Many of the established commercial and policy interests prefer to operate 'behind closed doors' where they can try to extract concessions from governing authorities. They share with watchdogs the potential to bite, but they tend not to share the potential to bark. It is more the mark of civil society watchdogs that their public bark *is* their bite: such organisations contribute to public leadership by drawing public attention to the strengths or weaknesses of government action. These organisations also demand that politicians pay close attention to the electoral support that such organisations can mobilise for or against them. Public interest groups can do a lot to generate their own publicity but, ultimately, they are dependent on the power of the mass media to carry their message. So, the leadership available to public interest organisations comes down to the power over opinion formation: using publicity to shape and manage elite or public opinion in ways that support their cause.

Challenging and exhorting politics/bureaucracy: the advocate role.

Watchdogs are typically defensive, barking when they sense a threat to what is their own. But civil society organisations are often far more proactive, barking also when they sense that others might be awakened to help form a useful public coalition to generate a desired response from a cautious government or public authority. By definition, advocacy involves the use of 'voice', often to push the interests of quite vulnerable or marginal groups. Advocacy refers to many forms of policy leadership, only a few of which need have any public display or notice. That is, the voice exercised by effective advocacy groups need not be a voice heard in public. Many governments or public authorities will prefer to listen to external advocates in private 'behind closed doors'. This preference for secrecy is itself evidence of the power of those advocacy groups to get the ear of ruling powers and often rests on prior campaigns indicating the clear potential for wider public mobilisation of the sort feared by ruling authorities. But a common element on all effective advocacy by external groups is the threat of public leadership through the exercise of 'moral authority', typically involving the 'moral capital' (Kane 2001) — credibility and public trustworthiness — of the institution, organisation, or indeed the person (think of the recent spate of celebrity advocates such as Bono) engaged in advocacy.

Circumventing and replacing politics: the self-government role.

Civil society organisations have unusual capacity for 'forum-shopping': if they do not like the deal they are getting from government, then they tend to go in search of another government! This mode of authority-escalation occurs even in local or state levels of government, where effective social interests can circumvent a junior official and seek out the chief administrator or chief minister who has power to override the decisions of the officer or minister duly-authorised to manage the policy or issue in question. But this process does not stop there. At the national level, similar organisations can even bypass the national government and seek to enlist the aid of a relevant international authority, as Australian indigenous groups have done by entreating United Nations authorities to override Australian governments from time to time. At one level, this process is simply a form of 'forum-shopping', as when civil society interests move up the chain of public authority from local to national to international, seeking favourable treatment from any authority prepared to hear their case. But at another level, this same attitude can give rise to protests of autonomy and self-ownership, as when professional, or for that matter, religious (or confessional) groups contend that they are self-regulating and beyond the reach of governmental action and are prepared to 'lead from within'.

In our view, public leadership is what breathes life into the institutions that inhabit and constitute the world of Australian public governance: parliament and cabinet, state and federal levels, the courts, government departments and agencies, the Reserve Bank, the mass media, foreign governments, non-government organisations and international government organisations, and so on. These institutions run our lives, but leadership is involved in the (re)design, birth and termination of these institutions, critical choices that get made by them, and the policies they promulgate. Opportunities to exercise such leadership are vested particularly in the holders of certain pivotal public offices. *Inside government*, the key offices and their holders are readily discernible: they include heads of state, heads of government, leaders of parliamentary political parties, heads of the judiciary, and the top layers of the civil service. *Outside government*, the term office is less of a reliable torchlight, but it is clear that public leadership can be exercised by chief executives of non-government organisations, major corporations, social movements, organised interest groups, churches, trade unions — in short, key figures in 'civil society' who care about and/or have a clear stake in the course and outcomes of the political process, and whose formal or de facto position provides them with a following, a broad audience, and/or some degree of public authority to speak and act on behalf of significant segments of society. Note that this includes actors who, legally or technically, are commonly defined as 'private sector,' such as executives of firms, artists or journalists.

Given that they all act in the public sphere aiming to address social problems and public policy issues, there are more commonalities between politicians, senior bureaucrats and societal leaders than there are differences. Let us now examine the tools which we might use to examine public leadership.

Understanding public leadership: analytical perspectives

Leader-centred approaches

The bulk of publications about leadership worldwide comes from proponents of a leader-centred approach to leadership analysis most common in applied psychology, management studies, and — although in rather different guise — the field of history and (psycho)biography. Leaving the vast and rapidly expanding number of prescriptive, exhortative 'how-to' studies of (business) leadership aside, in the more empirical leader-centred studies, leadership is simply equated with whatever it is that people in high positions do: how they perceive the world and their role in it, and how they choose to use the latter to elaborate the former. Leadership is thus explained by looking at the personal characteristics and life histories of the individuals involved. The main source of variation and dispute in the field is: which characteristics and which parts of their histories? The number of leader-centred explanatory variables thrown up by decades of fundamental and applied research is quite staggering: personality traits, cognitive abilities/style, early childhood experiences, birth order, inner motivational drives, personal value systems, mental stability, interpersonal style, rhetorical skills, early career experiences, crucial mentor relationships and so on (Kellerman 1984; Blondel 1987; Ludwig 2002).

In the interdisciplinary field of political psychology, the behaviour of political office-holders has been described, compared, and explained with reference to psychological theories of personality and leadership style. Famous if controversial examples of this tradition include Harold D. Lasswell's (1930) and James David Barber's (1972) typologies of political leaders and leadership styles and Dean Simonton's (1987) work on explaining and predicting presidential 'greatness'. More recently, respected political psychologists such as Margaret Hermann (1980) and Jerrold Post (2003) have presented more empirically grounded clusters of personality traits which are said to be the basic components of a politician's leadership style, whereas Fred Greenstein (2003) has induced six key components of presidential leadership style that may explain the performance of different holders of that office. In Australia, various scholars associated with the so-called

Melbourne School of political psychology — notably A. F. Davies, Graham Little, James Walter and Judith Brett have produced innovative and internationally (if not locally) recognised typological and psychobiographic studies of Australian as well as foreign political leaders (cf. Brett 1997; 2007; Walter and 't Hart, forthcoming). Likewise in both Australia (cf. Arkley, Wanna and Nethercote 2006) and New Zealand (Clarke 1997; 2001; 2003; 2004; Gustafson 1986; 2000; 2007) there is a sustained interest in and pursuit of (auto)biography of political and to a lesser extent administrative and civic leaders.

Relational approaches

Secondly, from sociology and social psychology, a core contribution to leadership analysis lies in the idea that leadership is really, first of all, in the eye of the beholder, for example, those that 'follow' (comply with, believe in, support) leaders. Understanding public leadership thus requires a switch of the analytical lens away from the preoccupation with the leaders themselves and towards the nexus (the 'bond', the 'contract') between followers and leader, and, within that, the emphasis being more on the former than the latter. *The relational approach* — of which Max Weber's typology of authority and James McGregor Burns's (1978) distinction between transactional and transformational leadership form classic and enduringly relevant examples — is highly relevant to understand key forms of civic leadership such as social movement leaders. But it also goes deep within the executive branch of government to shed light on the nature of the vital yet delicate 'pact' that may or may not exist between political and administrative office-holders at any given time (Peters 1988). It is a much more productive way of understanding the special case of 'charismatic leadership' than any leader-centred approach can possibly be (cf. Tucker 1978; Bryman 1992).

If anything, the relational perspective shows that 'followers' in many cases do much more than just that. Followers are not mere 'sheep': they, in fact, often quite deliberately observe, weigh, test, choose and, indeed, 'deselect' leaders — thus determining the fate of leaders as much as leaders determine theirs. From this perspective, leadership, like any other feature of social life, emerges as a symbolic, negotiated order. When explaining the construction of this order, there is no prima-facie reason to privilege the words and deeds of leaders. In many ways, only those individuals who effectively mediate the ideas and feelings of the group or community they belong to, or seek to lead, will be 'attributed' the kind of authority necessary to lead. Political parties know this situation only too well: party leaders are prisoners of their followers. Patrick Weller has noted this when examining the comparative prominence of cabinet processes in Australian national government (Weller 2007). One reason is that Australian party leaders (Australian Democrats are an exception) are selected by a relatively small group: by their parliamentary colleagues and not, as in so many comparable nations, by a larger party convention. Australian party leaders can be dumped without notice or even ceremony. Heads of government like to keep cabinets in session as one way of managing their followers: keeping them at close range precisely because the power rests ultimately with the followers who can make and unmake the leaders.

Paradoxically, ruling elites rarely have the luxury of elitism. Elites have to manage relationships with their followers. They also have to manage relations with other competing elites, who can swing followers away from one elite guard to another. There is a long social science tradition of studying political organisations in terms of elite-mass relations. Elites get their reputation as wily rulers not because they take ruling for granted but because they know that their rule can only be sustained through careful organisation of their followers. Higley and Burton illustrate a contemporary version of this long tradition going back to Michels and Pareto examining the ways that competing elites manage both the vertical lines of support within their camp and the horizontal lines of opposition between competing camps (Higley and Burton 2006). Social structures matter: class, religion, region, ethnicity all influence the social composition of elite-follower relationships.

Institutional approaches

Thirdly, the institutional approach to public leadership analysis owes much to the fields of political science and public administration. Sets of rules and conventions are designed in every polity to somehow resolve the tension between democracy's need for holding the power of public officials in check and efficiency's need for strong executive and professional leadership at the heart of government. Different polities resolve that trade-off in different ways (and may change their ways of doing so in response to traumatic experiences, such as breakdown, crisis and war). They thus harbour different systems (structures and cultures) of public leadership. John Uhr's (2005a) work on the so-called 'lattice of leadership' (the institutionalised dispersal of leadership roles and opportunities throughout the political system) looks at the features of the institutionalised nature of the offices political and administrative leaders hold, and the formal and informal rules for acquiring, consolidating and losing public office and the authority that comes with it (Elgie 1995; Elcock 2001). Such an approach is clearly complementary to the two previous ones. It helps us understand, for example, similarities in leadership behaviour and leadership relations (for example ways of managing cabinet) of ostensibly rather different political personalities occupying the same office over time. It also documents how changes in the rules of office give rise to new patterns of behaviour in office-holders (cf. Weller 1985; Rose 2001; 2007). Examples include the move from parliamentary to presidential government in France in the fifties, and the oft-observed changes in senior civil servant behaviour (from 'mandarins' to 'managers') following the introduction of fixed-term contracts, output steering and performance pay in various countries (Weller 2001).

Contextual approaches

Fourthly, contextual approaches to understanding public leadership look at the role of situational and temporal factors. Leadership is often exercised most visibly and decisively at certain critical junctures ('occasions', 'crises' etc.). Political systems, with their routines and rhythms, typically throw up such occasions in patterned ways (electoral cycles, political business cycles), as do the ups and downs of national economies and fiscal positions. In addition, unscheduled events such as disasters, scandals, and so on, create the proverbial 'windows of opportunity' for 'policy entrepreneurs' inside and outside government to do business and exercise leadership, and at the same time may place severe, stress-inducing performance pressures on key office-holders (Holsti 1972; Janis 1989). Reading these various 'signs of the times' and acting upon them proactively, therefore, becomes an important leadership challenge. A key example of such a contextual approach is Stephen Skowronek's (1993) study of presidential leadership in the United States, which systematically uses a theory of political time to map out the leadership possibilities and constraints facing every holder of the US presidency since Adams, and to thus explain their success and failure from the (mis)match between this contextual opportunity structure and the individual's role conceptions and political stances.

Performative approaches

Leaders are actors. They need an audience. Some favour niche audiences tailored to their 'off-Broadway' versions of localised leadership. Others favour global audiences for their mission to mobilise transnational followers. Most operate in-between, playing to a national audience in a public theatre showcasing leaders' talent to appeal to audiences interested in issues of civic identity, sovereignty and national purpose. Carnes Lord's (2003) *The Modern Prince* is subtitled 'what leaders need to know': the chapter on communication traces the critical analysis of the stagecraft of public leadership back to Greece, taking Aristotle's *Rhetoric* as the most convenient point of analytical entry.

Uhr's *Terms of Trust* attempts to apply a similar framework of rhetorical analysis to Australian public leadership (Uhr 2005a: 65-78). Uhr draws on recent US scholarship on 'the rhetorical presidency' which investigates the careful and deliberate way that US national political leaders, like all good actors, manage through their mouths. This is echoed in the suggestive title of but one revealing US study: *Deeds done in words: presidential rhetoric and the genres of governance* (Campbell and Jamieson 1990). Despite considerable scepticism about rhetorical ruses (see for example, Edwards 1996), scholarship marches on. One of the latest publications deals with the hard reality of US economic policy: Wood's *The*

Politics of Economic Leadership which is subtitled: 'the causes and consequences of presidential rhetoric' (Wood 2007).

Researchers' interests in the 'cunning' of public speech matches public interest in the 'craft' of 'great public speeches'. This popular interest in 'great public speeches' is an important clue to the rhetorical construction of leadership. Leaders themselves frame their leadership in words addressed to followers, in a carefully orchestrated display of 'follow the *leider*' (apology for the pun). As with so many theatrical displays, the words alone do not tell the whole story: much depends on the setting, the scene, the show itself, including the body language of gesture and suggestion, often conveyed by silence as much as by explicit statement. Leaders have many tools at their disposal, many of which are forms of power and persuasion that are deployed only 'behind closed doors' out of public view. But one of the most valuable of their persuasive tools is their tongue, especially when used to provide a sustaining narrative to reassure followers that all are on the right path and heading in the right direction. This performative capacity does not have to come across in Oscar-winning polished routines: indeed, for all his lack of stage glamour, John Howard is a good working model of the effective public leader who knows the importance of his every word in holding his audience. In common with his predecessors Menzies, Whitlam, Hawke and Keating, he knows that his most important 'leider-script' is about the nature of citizenship, of Australian civic rights and responsibilities and of the place of Australia in a global world (cf. Uhr 2002).

Ethical approaches

Finally, there is the *ethical approach* to understanding public leadership. This asks the question if public leaders should, and can afford to, observe ethical standards, if not codes of conduct. This is an old question, harking back to Greek political philosophy and forever highlighted by the work of Niccolo Machiavelli. In this Machiavellian spirit, Lord Acton famously observed that power corrupts and absolute power corrupts absolutely, adding in the next line that 'great men are always bad men'. If that is the case, leadership in a democracy such as Australia becomes inherently problematic.

The primary task here is not to overlay a framework of ethics on top of leadership practice, as though we could clamp down on unethical leadership. Instead it is to try to reveal the ethical orientation of leaders themselves, to try as best we can to understand what leaders understand by 'the ethics of leadership'. Uhr suggests that Australian political leaders see their own role as inscribers of a civic ethic conveyed in the 'terms of trust' that leaders devise as a sort of contract between citizens and their political representatives (Uhr 2005a). In this approach, ethics emerge as an important element in the order of mutual obligation devised by political leaders who compete for the subscription and support of followers. Leaders are thus prepared to be judged according to the public estimate of their trustworthiness, which is among the most important of the ethical qualities requiring their constant political management.

As ever, Weber caught much of the meaning of this political management of ethics in his evocation of the calling or profession of politics (Weber 1994). Even democratic political leaders appreciate the value of excusing themselves from the ethical order properly accepted by their followers, and the value of abiding by a separate ethical order Weber termed 'the ethic of responsibility'. Under this leadership ethic, power holders put themselves forward for public judgment free from any constraint of traditional ethics of what Weber calls 'absolute conviction' or pure intention. The ethic of leadership responsibility is something of a call to arms: leaders do 'whatever it takes' in the knowledge that, if they have their way through their chosen terms of trust, they will be judged by the results of their rule, and not by their compliance with 'the rules' of any legal or ethical order. Call this a form of 'results-oriented ethics' if you want to place it in the content of new public management, where compliance with traditional rules of process is down-valued in favour of getting on with the job and delivering results.

Much of the recent surge in writing about political leadership is explicitly and self-consciously (neo-)Machiavellian (for example, Lord 2003; Keohane 2005), whilst at the same time there is a strand that is explicitly advocating moral fibre, public integrity and active responsibility as hallmarks of true leadership (Hargrove 1998; Dobel 1998; Uhr, 2005b). Clearly, there is a debate here that needs to be waged. The nature and terms of the debate vary markedly when it comes to political, bureaucratic and civic leadership. The tensions identified by Weber apply more generally: across the leadership scene, leaders manage the competing interests of the absolutist ethics of 'clean hands' and the relativist ethics of 'dirty hands'. There are many variations of these competing ethical obligations. Weber himself paints an image of decisive political leadership against a background of very dark and threatening colours: 'decisionism' becomes a privileged feature of this model of opaque leadership. Partly in response, Wilson changes the colours to convey a more democratic image of transparent leadership, working the system of dispersed constitutional powers by enlisting all the distinctive powers of what later scholars came to call 'the rhetorical presidency'.

A more measured version of this dialectic emerges in the classic Friedrich-Finer debate over democratic leadership, with Friedrich identifying the compelling ethic of executive leadership exercised by political and bureaucratic officials, and Finer defending the traditional ethic of legislative supremacy to rein in the leadership pretensions of 'big government' (Rosenthal 1990). This old debate continues to play out in contemporary governance where we see two opposed clusters of public ethics: one following the path of Friedrich in promoting the value of discretionary powers exercised by executive officials; and another rallying around the barricades erected by Finer to protect the rule of law from executive officials no longer overawed by traditional obligations of due process. The initiative clearly rests with the Friedrich cluster which sees leadership in terms of taking personal, as well as official, responsibility for public decision-making. The Finer cluster is more reactive but also, in some ways, more dutiful. They too have their distinctive take on leadership which they see in terms of an ethic of public accountability with duties to account to elected representatives for the manner, as well as the results of, the exercise of delegated public power (Uhr 2005a).

Australian public leadership in comparative perspective

Finally, a few questions about important unknowns in the Australian scene. What really is distinctive about the Australian setting of public leadership? Are there characteristic forms of leadership cultivated in Australia and not elsewhere? Do Australian leaders employ a particular range of leadership repertoires, or a particular blend of leadership strategies? How does the underlying political economy of Australia support some types of leadership and curb other types of leadership? Is Australia any different from other nations in its mix of institutional and individual leadership properties, and is our focus too biased in favour of 'great individuals' and blind to the greater role of institutions and social forces?

If institutions trump individuals, which institutions really matter? One place to begin an Australian audit is with the formal constitutional setting which is one of surprisingly dispersed leadership. The federal division of power between national, state and territory levels of government means that even the most powerful of the heads of government has to share many powers with competing heads of government. Similar divisions disperse public service leadership. Thus, there is no one governmental supreme. But even at the national level, there is a corresponding dispersal of powers: the separation of powers across the three formal branches of government: legislative, executive and judicial. Further, within the first or legislative branch, powers and hence potential leadership are distributed between the two houses of parliament. The 'lattice of leadership' (Uhr 2005a: 78-81) is alive and well, with a great many opportunities for a great many public leaders to contribute to, or try to undermine, co-ordinated national leadership. It is unrealistic to expect anything like 'joined-up' or consolidated or even cohesive public leadership. The governmental system blends elements of Westminster and Washington into a 'Washminster' mix, so that it is also unrealistic to expect Australian public leadership to match that of the UK or the USA, or any other prevailing model (Thompson 1981). It might be that this formal constitutional setting is compatible with more recent practices of 'networked governance', so that the public leadership from across Australian federalism can be seen as a valuable international case study of networked leadership.

The Australian polity has its own 'regime values' associated with public office and public trust. Leaders ply their trades in a particular social setting where, or so we are told, the grain runs against 'tall poppies'. Australia might stand out as a distinctively anti-leader society. But even if true, this distinction does not necessarily means that Australia is anti-leadership. Australian social values might locate leadership in unusual social spaces: think for example of how often the leadership of the Australian cricket team is described (often by prime ministers) as 'the second most important job in the country'. The facts about contemporary Australian social values are difficult to establish: is Australia as democratic as many of its early investigators thought or even feared; or is there a particular mode of elitism favoured in Australia that is compatible with popular acceptance of an egalitarian self-image, one perhaps floated by the very elites who exercise so much power behind the scenes? We really do need much more cross-national comparative analysis of Australian social values and what we here call 'regime values'.

And what about emerging modes of public leadership exhibited by younger Australians that break out of conventional institutional forms? Why focus so unrelentingly on the ways of the past when, for all we know, the ways of the future might expect different things from leadership: rewarding and punishing leaders according to a quite different scale of public honour? It is not all a matter of new social values, it is also a matter of new communications media. How will informational technologies transform tomorrow's landscape of leadership? This note of the unknown future is probably a good note on which to end this Introduction and turn the discussion over to the experts who have their own views about what really matters in the field of public leadership.

This volume

We will resist the temptation to preview each of the many individual chapters that follow. The authors can speak for themselves. Each chapter is relatively brief and accessible. It is important to note, however, that we have grouped the chapters purposefully in five parts. Part I 'Democracy and Public Leadership' tackles what is, perhaps, the central problem of public leadership analysis: the awkward place that 'leadership' takes in the wider fabric of democratic theory and practice. Three chapters explore the reasons behind this awkwardness, describe the *modus vivendi* that various theorists have tried to construct between the two, and signal trends in leadership thought and practice that challenge conventional wisdoms. All three chapters offer original takes on how to reconcile the need for leadership in politics with the equally deeply felt need to prevent leader dominance and dictatorship.

Part II 'Understanding Public Leadership: Emergent Approaches' consists of chapters that seek to make a contribution to leadership analysis. They do so in different ways, for example, by raising new questions for leadership research;

reviewing and/or challenging existing analytical traditions; and proposing and illustrating new frameworks and theories. This section highlights, in particular, the multi-disciplinary nature of leadership analysis, as it ties together contributions from an historian, a cognitive psychologist, a group of social psychologists, a student of business leaders and a political theorist working in the rational choice tradition.

Part III 'Spheres of Public Leadership Practices' contains empirical chapters that each move away from the often dominant preoccupation with political leadership. Taken together they display the 'lattice' of leadership at work, showcasing leadership in the public service, the police, the national security establishment, Indigenous communities, and the mass media. All of these chapters take a self-consciously critical and reflective approach to these various spheres of public leadership. Each of them asks if the key protagonists are up to the specific demands and dilemmas of leading in that particular sector.

Parts IV and V take us to the political science core of leadership analysis: trying to describe, understand, compare and assess the behaviour of senior political office-holders such as party leaders, prime ministers and premiers, as it takes shape in the nexus between individuals, institutional settings, cultural traditions and key issues of the day. In part IV the spotlight is on Australian political leadership, and in part V on political leadership in New Zealand, the latter following on from the recent Miller and Mintrom (2006) volume. In many ways, it is the combination of (and particularly the contrasts between) these two bundles of national practices chapters that cast light on the different sets of opportunities and constraints that both political systems offer to their senior political office-holders. Australian federalism and New Zealand's move to Mixed-member Proportional Representation in particular are key forces rendering generalised talk about 'Antipodean political leadership' rather useless.

In sum, this volume gives us a rich picture of current ways of understanding public leadership by scholars living and working in this part of the world. But much of what is being said here does not pertain exclusively to the two countries at all. Hopefully, therefore, this volume will find its way not just to Australians and New Zealanders studying or practicing leadership but also to leadership scholars and practitioners far beyond these shores.

References

Alford, J., 2008, 'The limits to traditional public administration, or: rescuing public value from misrepresentation', *Australian Journal of Public Administration*, 67, 3. 35-366/

Arkley, T., J. Wanna, and J. Nethercote (eds), 2006, *Australian political lives*, Canberra: ANU E Press.

Barber, J. D., 1972, *Presidential Character: Predicting Performance in the White House,* Englewood Cliffs, NJ: Prentice Hall.

Blondel, J., 1987, *Political Leadership: Towards a General Analysis*, London: Sage.

Boin, A., P. 't Hart, E. Stern and B. Sundelius, 2005, *The Politics of Crisis Management: Public Leadership Under Pressure*, New York: Cambridge University Press.

Boin, A., A. McConnell and P. 't Hart (eds), 2008, *Governing After Crisis: The Politics of Investigation, Accountability and Learning*, Cambridge: Cambridge University Press.

Brett, J. (ed.), 1997, *Political Lives*, Sydney: Allen & Unwin.

Brett, J., 2007, *Exit Right: The Unravelling of John Howard*, Melbourne: Black Inc.

Bryman, A., 1992, *Charisma and Leadership in Organizations*, Newbury Park, CA: Sage.

Campbell, K. K. and K. H. Jamieson, 1990, *Deeds Done in Words: Presidential Rhetoric and the Genres of Governance,* Chicago: University of Chicago Press.

Clarke, M. (ed.), 1997, *Keith Holyoake: Towards a Political Biography*, Palmerston North: Dunmore Press.

Clarke, M. (ed.), 2001, *Three Labour Leaders: Nordmeyer, Kirk and Rowling*, Palmerston North: Dunmore Press.

Clarke, M. (ed.), 2003, *Holyoake's Lieutenants*, Palmerston North: Dunmore Press.

Clarke, M. (ed.), 2004, *Muldoon Revisited*, Palmerston North: Dunmore Press.

Dobel, J. P., 1998, 'Political prudence and the ethics of leadership', *Public Administration Review*, 58:1, pp. 74-81.

Edelman, M., 1977, *Political Language: Words That Succeed and Policies That Fail,* San Diego: Academic Press.

Eden, R., 1983, *Political Leadership and Nihilism*. University Presses of Florida.

Edwards III, G. C., 1996, 'Presidential rhetoric: What difference does it make?', in M. J. Medhurst (ed.), *Beyond the Rhetorical Presidency*, College Station, TX: Texas A&M University Press, pp. 199-217.

Elcock, H., 2001, *Political Leadership*, Cheltenham: Edward Elgar.

Elgie, R., 1995, *Political Leadership in Liberal Democracies*, Basingstoke: Macmillan.

Greenstein, F. I., 2003, *The Presidential Difference: Leadership Styles from FDR to George W. Bush*, New Jersey: Princeton University Press.

Gustafson, B., 1986, *From the Cradle to the Grave: A Biography of Michael Joseph Savage*, Auckland: Reed Methuen.

Gustafson, B., 2000, *His Way: A Biography of Robert Muldoon*, Auckland: Auckland University Press.

Gustafson, B., 2007, *Kiwi Keith: A Biography of Keith Holyoake*, Auckland: Auckland University Press.

Hargrove, E. C., 1998, *The President as Leader: Appealing to the Better Angels of our Nature*, Lawrence: University of Kansas Press.

Hermann, M., 1980, 'Explaining Foreign Policy Behavior Using the Personal Characteristics of Political Leaders', *International Studies Quarterly*, 24:1, pp. 7-46.

Higley, J. and M. Burton, 2006, *Elite Foundations of Liberal Democracy*, Lanham, MD: Rowman and Littlefield.

Holsti, O., 1972, *Crisis, Escalation, War*, Montreal: McGill-Queens University Press.

Janis, I. L., 1989, *Crucial Decisions: Leadership in Policymaking and Crisis Management*, New York: Free Press.

Kane, J., 2001, *The Politics of Moral Capital*, New York: Cambridge University Press.

Kaufman, H., 1981, *The Administrative Behavior of Federal Bureau Chiefs*, Washington, DC: Brookings Institution.

Kellerman, B. (ed.), 1984, *Leadership: Multidisciplinary Perspectives*, Englewood Cliffs, NJ: Prentice Hall.

Keohane, N., 2005, 'On Leadership', *Perspectives on Politics*, 3, pp. 705-22.

Lasswell, H. D., 1930, *Psychopathology and Politics*, Chicago: University of Chicago Press.

Lord, C., 2003, *The Modern Prince: What Leaders Need to Know*, New Haven: Yale University Press.

Ludwig, A. M., 2002, *King of the Mountain: The Nature of Political Leadership*, Lexington: University Press of Kentucky.

Lynn, L., 1981, *Managing the Public's Business: The Job of the Government Executive*, New York: Basic Books.

McGregor Burns, J., 1978, *Leadership*, New York: Harper and Row.

Miller, R. and M. Mintrom (eds), 2006, *Political Leadership in New Zealand*, Auckland: Auckland University Press.

Moore, M., 1995, *Creating Public Value,* Cambridge, MA: Harvard University Press.

Peters, B. G., 1988, *Comparing Public Bureaucracies. Problems of Theory and Method*, Alabama: The University of Alabama Press.

Poguntke, T. and P. Webb (eds), 2005, *The Presidentialization of Politics. A Comparative Study of Modern Democracies,* Oxford: Oxford University Press.

Post, J. M., 2003, *The Psychological Assessment of Political Leaders: With Profiles of Saddam Hussein and Bill Clinton*, Ann Arbor: University of Michigan Press.

Rhodes, R.A.W., 1997, *Understanding Governance*, Buckingham and Philadelphia: Open University Press.

Rhodes, R.A.W., P. 't Hart and M. Noordegraaf (eds), 2007, *Observing Government Elites: Up Close and Personal*, Basingstoke: Palgrave Macmillan.

Rhodes, R.A.W. and J. Wanna, 2007, 'The Limits to Public Value, or Rescuing Responsible Government from the Platonic Guardians', *Australian Journal of Public Administration*, 66:4, pp. 406-21.

Rohr, J., 1978, *Ethics for Bureaucrats: An Essay on Law and Values*, New York: Marcel Dekker.

Rose, R., 2001, *The Prime Minister in a Shrinking World*, Oxford and Boston: Polity Press.

Rosenthal, U., 1990, 'Politics and administration: Max Weber and the quest for democratic order', in A. Kouzmin and N. Scott (eds), *Dynamics in Australian Public Management: Selected Essays*, Melbourne: MacMillan, pp. 392-408.

Selznick, P., 1957, *Leadership and Administration*, New York: Harper and Row.

Simonton, D. K., 1987, *Why Presidents Succeed: A Political Psychology of Leadership*, New Haven, CT: Yale University Press.

Skowronek, S., 1993, *The Politics Presidents Make: Leadership from John Adams to George Bush*, Cambridge, MA: Harvard University Press.

Terry, L. D., 1995, *Leadership of Public Bureaucracies: The Administrator as Conservator*, Thousand Oaks, CA: Sage.

Thompson, E., 1981, 'The "Washminster" mutation', in P. Weller, D. Jaensch (eds), *Responsible Government in Australia*, Melbourne: Drummond, pp. 32-40.

Tucker, R. C., 1978, *Politics as Leadership*, Colombia: University of Missouri Press.

Uhr, J., 2002, 'Political Leadership and Rhetoric', in H. G. Brennan and F. G. Castles (eds), *Australia Reshaped: 200 Years of Institutional Transformation*, University of Cambridge Press, pp. 261-94.

Uhr, J., 2005a, *Terms of Trust: Arguments Over Ethics in Australian Government*, Sydney: University of New South Wales Press.

Uhr, J., 2005b, 'Professional ethics for politicians?' *International Public Management Journal,* 8:2, pp. 247-61.

Walter, J. and P. 't Hart, 2009 (forthcoming), 'Political psychology', in R. A. W. Rhodes (ed.), *The Australian Study of Politics*.

Weber, M., 1922, *Wirtschaft und Gesellschaft*. Tubingen: J.C.B. Mohr.

Weber, M., 1994, The profession and vocation of politics, in M. Weber, *Political Writings (Cambridge Texts in the History of Political Thought)*, P. Lassman (ed.). Translated by R. Speirs.. Cambridge: Cambridge University Press, pp. 309-69.

Weller, P., 1985, *First Among Equals: Prime Ministers in Westminster Systems*, Sydney: Allen & Unwin.

Weller, P., 2001, *Australia's Mandarins: The Frank and the Fearless?* Sydney: Allen & Unwin.

Weller, P., 2007, *Cabinet Government in Australia, 1901-2006: Practice, Principles, Performance*, Sydney: University of New South Wales Press.

Wood, B. D., 2007, *The Politics of Economic Leadership*, Princeton, NJ: Princeton University Press.

PART I

Democracy and Public Leadership

2. The Neglected Problem of Democratic Leadership

John Kane and Haig Patapan

Introduction

Australia is usually regarded as one of the most *democratic* of countries. One of the signs of this is said to be the permanent, seemingly entrenched scepticism of Australians about politics in general and especially about the politicians they elect to lead them. Polls regularly show a curious disjunction between approval ratings for the political system itself, which are always high, and those for the politicians who inhabit it, which are invariably much lower. More than sceptical, Australians are often downright cynical about the motives and actions of their political leaders, even when they support the leader's party. If hope is occasionally vested in new leadership it is always subject to the lingering fear, or even expectation, that hope will inevitably be betrayed, sooner rather than later.

It is a mistake to think, however, that this is a peculiarly Australian phenomenon rather than a general feature of democratic government. The core animating principle of democracy is popular sovereignty, the idea that the people should rule. Yet democratic leaders inevitably exercise far more authority than ordinary citizens. This creates a permanent tension between the democratic leader and the sovereign people that engenders the kind of suspicion of leadership noted above. The fact that this tension is, in principle, irresolvable (as we would claim) gives democratic leadership its special character, explaining both its remarkable strengths and acknowledged weaknesses. Democratic leadership is, indeed, uniquely challenging because it must be most carefully exercised under conditions of peculiar constraint and constant distrust.

This is an important subject inadequately addressed in the scholarship. Indeed, the problem of democratic leadership constitutes a permanent blind spot for most modern students of democracy. Whole volumes dedicated to an appraisal of the state of democratic theory contain hardly a reference to the question (Held 1993; 1996; Shapiro and Hacker-Cordón 1999; Carter and Stokes 2002). Nor does it appear as a major (or even minor) theme in university teaching, at least according to a 2003 survey of American classes by Ronald Terchek (2003). Despite the modern flood of literature on leadership generally, the problem of specifically democratic leadership seldom appears. We argue that this strange silence is in fact symptomatic of the ambiguous place that leadership occupies in a democracy, being both essential to democratic government yet finding no secure justification within a theory resting on the concept of popular sovereignty.

With regard to this central ambiguity we may discern two fundamentally opposed tendencies. So-called elitist theorists resolve it in favour of leadership at the expense of popular sovereignty. The most famous formulation of their position asserts that oligarchic rule is an 'iron law' of politics. More democratically-inclined scholars, on the other hand, have reacted to the elitist challenge by trying to resolve the tension in favour of popular sovereignty. They do not so much solve the problem of democratic leadership as pass it over in embarrassed silence, typically pursuing more ideally 'democratic' political forms that envisage wider or even universal citizen participation in political processes and decisions. These strategies implicitly eschew the need for leadership altogether. A few scholars accept the importance of democratic leadership while recognising the tension between leadership and popular sovereignty, but they cannot resist the temptation to resolve it by prescriptively defining a type of leader who might guarantee good leadership while not betraying the promise of popular sovereignty.[1]

The present scholarship on democratic leadership is deficient precisely because it is unwilling to contemplate the possibility that the tension between leadership and popular sovereignty is incapable of resolution. We claim that this is not a political problem to be overcome but rather a theoretically invaluable starting point for understanding both the unique authority of democratic leaders and the perennial challenges they face. We have no space to pursue that argument here, but will clear the way for such a study by addressing the curious poverty of contemporary theoretical studies of democratic leadership.

The question ignored

The absence of scholarship on democratic leadership seems puzzling at a time when centres for leadership mushroom across the globe and when books on leadership pour off the presses at an alarming rate. There is hardly a problem or conflict anywhere in the world whose cause is not attributed, at least in part, to poor leadership, and for which the proposed solution is not more or better leadership. In the everyday discourse of liberal democracies, the quality of political leadership, whether to be lamented or celebrated, is a perennial theme.

Much of the extant literature on leadership is sociological, psychological, or organisational. Derivative from this, and highly repetitive, is a vast volume of material aimed at corporate CEOs looking for the secrets of business success. There is also a lesser quantity of material on specifically political leadership, much of it growing out of Weber's threefold division of authority into the customary, the charismatic, and the legal-rational. In this contemporary field, James McGregor Burns (1978; 2003) remains a dominant figure (as he does, indeed, in the business canon). But as the subject of political leadership encompasses figures like Napoleon, Stalin and Hitler, this work does not necessarily tell us much about the specific nature and distinctive challenges of democratic leadership. An even smaller literature on leadership in liberal democracies is mostly comparative and empirical, being either concerned with the institutional constraints and opportunities facing leaders in different democratic countries, or closely focused on particular historical figures (Mughan and Patterson 1988; Jones 1989; Elgie 1995).

What is lacking is a body of theory that provides, or attempts to provide, a reasoned explanation of, and foundation for, the role of leadership in representative democracies. This is despite the fact that the problem of democratic leadership is a prominent, if often only implicit, theme in historical and analytical studies of particular democratic leaders, both prime ministers and presidents.[2] It may be significant that such work, though voluminous, is somewhat ghettoised by hard-nosed political scientists who regard leadership as little more than an epiphenomenon overlying 'real' causal processes understood, usually, in economic, social-structural or institutional terms. Such positivistic attitudes, which regard leadership as not warranting serious theoretical investigation, might be thought, on their own, to explain the gap in democratic theory. But political science's principal disdain has not been for democratic theory as such (which it scarcely acknowledges), but rather for what it regards as the 'soft' empiricism of existing leadership studies. Though it is true that political and democratic theory in modern times has suffered from the cultural dominance of the natural sciences (see below), 'scientific' prejudice alone cannot explain the lack of theoretical reflection on democratic leadership. The real answer lies interestingly deeper.

We argue that this lack is no accident but itself tells us a lot about the problem. Democratic leadership is a blind spot for most democratic theorists and students of leadership because democrats have difficulty in articulating a proper democratic role for leadership. Democrats who feel the need for a leader must reconcile this with the belief that none among equals has any *innate* or *inherent* right to rule over others. On the one hand, democracy seems to require good leadership if it is to function effectively; on the other, the very idea of leadership seems to conflict with democracy's egalitarian ethos. The more strongly democratic leaders lead, the less democratic they appear; the more they act like good democrats, the less like true leaders they seem. Confronted with this dilemma, the general tendency among scholars has therefore been to accept the need for leadership in practice while overlooking it in theory.

The elitist flight from democracy

There is, however, another powerful reason why scholars ignore the problem of democratic leadership. The association of leadership with elites, and elites with hierarchy, subordination and exclusion, goes a long way toward explaining the failure of democratic theory to address clearly the issue of democratic leadership. Elite theorists of the early twentieth century powerfully reinforced the suspicions of egalitarian democrats by confirming the essential relationship between leaders and elites. They effectively resolved the core ambiguity between leadership and popular sovereignty by exalting the former over the latter.

William James (1912: 318) claimed that the problem of democracy could be reduced to a single question: What kinds of men are going to be charged with the responsibility of giving the cue to the masses? In more sociological mode, others argued that elite formation and rule by elites was unavoidable in the modern world (Pareto 1935; Mosca 1939). Elite control of decision-making and coordination was simply a functional necessity in complex organisations, including the political organisation of liberal democracy. Because these claims were couched in hard sociological terms, stamped with the authority of scientific fact, their impact on democratic theorists was profound. Indeed, democratic theory since 1915 can be interpreted as a variety of attempts to affirm, modify or transcend what Robert Michels (1962) then described as the 'iron law of oligarchy'.

Elite theorists who resolved the tension between leadership and popular sovereignty in favour of leadership, by affirming elitism, were compelled to redefine the classical conception of democracy as the rule of all (or at least of the many). Harold Lasswell claimed that a democracy could rightly express itself through just a few leaders provided those leaders remained accountable (Lasswell 1950: 201; Lasswell *et al*. 1952: 7). Joseph Schumpeter famously argued a revised version of representative democracy as free competition between elites for the people's vote. This was not government *by* the people, but government *approved* by the people (Schumpeter 1961: 246). In fact the less involvement people had with political processes and decision-making between elections the better. Liberty was preserved in such a democracy not by citizen engagement but by the balancing of autonomous, countervailing elites, none of which could concentrate all power in their hands (see also, Aron 1968; 1978; Kornhauser 1959; Etzioni-Halevy 1993). Openness to talent allowed the 'free circulation of elites' which was, according to Giovanni Sartori (1962: 85), what distinguished the democratic elite principle from others.

Sartori, however, even more emphatically than Schumpeter, confirmed the leadership function of the 'superior' few. Democracies, he said, have to reckon with 'minorities who count for much and lead, and with majorities who do not count for much and follow' (1962: 98). But on Sartori's view the main task of democratic leaders was to defend democracy against itself, or rather against its own excessive tendencies toward the 'perfectionistic' pursuit of the democratic ideal on the one hand, and demagogic mass manipulation on the other. Leaders were the necessary stabilisers of a potentially unstable system. 'And this is why adequate leadership is vital to democracy,' he declared, adding that eminent leadership was most necessary when pressure from below was (1962: 119). It was a sentiment echoed by the American V. O. Key Jr. (1961), who argued that only an elite leadership could shoulder the responsibility of forestalling a natural propensity in democracy toward indecision, decay and disaster.

As this revised model of democracy implied a deep distrust of the volatile masses and the need to exclude them from everyday political processes, it was little wonder that some democratic theorists felt extremely uncomfortable with it. Nor was it surprising, given that elite theory so closely identified itself with leadership, that theorists seeking to evade its logic should virtually ignore the question of democratic leadership. Pluralists, for example, sought to neutralise rather than to redefine the role of democratic leadership by arguing that power and influence were less concentrated in modern democracies than elite theory suggested. Power, they said, was dispersed among a plurality of civil groups to which individuals belonged, these groups competing for influence upon a 'neutral', interest-mediating state (Galbraith 1952; Dahl 1958; Truman 1971). Democracy might not work individualistically, as classical theory held, but it worked nevertheless. Fragmentation disallowed 'strong' versions of elite leadership and reinstated the possibility that democracy remained, at least in this reinterpreted sense, 'government by the people'.

The iron grip of elitism was not, however, so easily slipped. Critics of pluralism objected that modern democracy was neither as benign nor accessible as Dahl suggested. They confirmed the elitist picture if only to deplore it, often reinterpreting it in quasi-Marxist economic terms. They argued that the will of the people was systematically subverted by the hidden hand of a structural economic-political elite that established political agendas by suppressing issues threatening to its power (Bachrach and Baratz 1962; 1963; 1970; Crenson 1971; Lukes 1974; Gaventa 1980). Even Dahl, later in his career, accepted that tiny minorities in America made the key economic, political and social decisions, and that it could hardly be otherwise in a large political system (Dahl and Lindblom 1976). He would contend at last that the economic power of business elites contradicted the very essence of democracy (Dahl 1982; 1985).

These Marxist-influenced theories might seem to have implied the need for revolutionary change in both economic arrangements and people's consciousness, but most democratic theorists remained fundamentally liberal in temper. They were disinclined to hope, given the example of twentieth century revolutions, that socialistic egalitarianism would result in a truly democratic control of politics. In communist countries the nexus between leadership and elite had been not only reproduced but brutally reaffirmed, with the added disadvantage that accountability now travelled in a new, undemocratic direction — the people were accountable to the Leninist vanguard party and the party was accountable to no one. Yet anti-elitists' own prescriptive remedies tended to be weak. Peter Bachrach wrote a book stringently criticising democratic elitist theory which nevertheless asserted that '[t]he main thrust of the elitist argument is incontestable' (Bachrach 1967: 95). More contemporary theorists simply take this as a truism, using it as their starting point for their analyses of elite formation and change (Higley and Burton 2006).

What was notable about Bachrach's critique, however, was its defence of the classical view that democracy implied citizen participation in all aspects of public affairs as 'an essential means to the full development of individual capacities' (1967: 4). Dahl (1985) took up the same theme, arguing that 'real' democracy required that public participation be greatly enhanced in all spheres of life, implying an equalisation of the ownership and control of both economic production and the political agenda (McLennan 1989). This turn of argument was indicative of nearly all work on democratic theory in the latter part of the twentieth century whether it emphasised the economic dimension or not. Democrats sought in diverse ways for theoretical avenues that led away from elitism and toward what they hoped might be 'real' or 'strong' democracy.

The democratic flight from leadership

This flight from elitism in fact represented the modern theorists' resolution of the tension between leadership and popular sovereignty. Unable to refute the elite thesis, they hoped that strengthening democracy, through the widest possible participation by the totality of citizens in civil and political activity, would somehow disempower permanent elites. There was also the unstated belief that a reinvigorated democracy might solve the problem of democratic leadership by allowing all to lead. But because the mental association of leadership with elites was strong, the natural tendency was to avoid any explicit treatment of the question of leadership. The consequence of these theorists' preference for popular sovereignty over leadership was therefore a complete neglect of the problem of democratic leadership.

Attempts to redefine a 'truer' democracy took a number of forms. 'Inclusive democrats,' for example, were concerned to realise a democratic egalitarian ideal they claimed had been subverted in liberal democracies by the exclusion of certain disadvantaged groups (Young 1989; 1990; 1997; Taylor 1992; Honneth 1995). Iris Young (1997: 370) proposed special representation rights to 'women, blacks, native Americans, Chicanos, Puerto Ricans … Asian Americans, gay men. Lesbians, working-class people, poor people, old people, and mentally and physically disabled people' — in other words to a majority of the US population excluding, it seemed, only white, propertied males presumed still to be in control of the means of power and dominance (Young 1989: 261; see Kane 2002: 119). Other theorists were guided by an ideal of direct democracy (Pateman 1970;

Held 1996). Benjamin Barber argued for a ground-up development of direct democratic procedures starting from the local and progressing all the way to the national (Barber 1984). Associational democrats, by contrast, believed that the solution to the ills of the modern world lay in the devolution of economic and political power to various voluntary civil associations under the direct democratic control of their members (Hain 1983; Hirst 1994; Cohen and Rogers 1995; Giddens 1998).

Post-structural or 'post-modern' writing, by contrast, had rather unclear political theory implications, perhaps because of a radical tendency to decentre or reduce the citizen-self to some structural or discursive effect (Foucault 1983: 211-12; Lyotard 1977: 47; 1985: 36; Rorty 1989: 37-8). But when post-moderns did explicitly address the issue of democracy, it was typically to stress the need for *radicalisation,* meaning movement toward more direct and participative forms (Laclau and Mouffe 1985). For Jacques Derrida, this democratic impulse was tragically unfulfillable because of an inherent tendency to corruption in egalitarian institutions, a virtual acceptance of Michel's iron law, though Derrida's romantic prescription was that we nevertheless perpetually orient ourselves toward the unrealisable ideal (Derrida 1994). The so-called deliberative democrats, meanwhile, looked to establishing or reforming institutional and communicative means by which all citizens might play a part in political decision-making (Dryzek 1990; Habermas 1996; Guttman and Thompson 1996; Benhabib 1996; Cohen 1998; cf. Uhr 1998). The common commitment of theorists in this field was 'to the notion that political decisions are better made through deliberation than money or power, as well as to the ideal that participation in deliberative judgements should be as equal and widespread as possible' (Warren 2002: 196).

In all these non-elite democratic theories there was an assumption that greater democratisation could be recognised by how far decision-making was removed from the hands of an elite and distributed among 'the people'. The general tendency was clear. The theoretical landscape had become dominated by attempts to escape or overcome the problem of democratic leadership by annihilating the need for it.

Conclusion

Our intention here has been to clear the conceptual ground for a deeper study of democratic leadership as it actually exists.[3] Our orientation in approaching this study is to resist the common temptation to resolve the tension between leadership and popular sovereignty and to argue that it is in fact perennial and irresolvable. Not only that, we argue that this irresolvability is a good thing, democratically speaking. It is an essential motive force that helps to drive and sustain the highly flexible and dynamic system of government we call democracy.

We have argued here that one of the most striking consequences of the democratic leadership tension has been the relative neglect of the problem of democratic leadership as it is, and as it must be, practised in the real world. We believe that we will not properly understand the distinctive advantages and opportunities — nor the distinctive challenges and constraints — of democratic leaders if we continue to disparage them through an act of comprehensive, even if unconscious, oversight. Theory must engage with the in-built and unavoidable mistrust of leadership in democracies if it is to appreciate the perpetual question of legitimacy that hangs over the head of every democratic leader, and which he or she must continually negotiate. It is our contention that this perpetual demand to legitimise leadership is, in fact, the way that the principle of popular sovereignty manifests itself and is continuously realised in democratic government.

References

Aron, R., 1968, *Progress and Disillusion,* London: Pall Mall.

Aron, R., 1978, *Politics and History,* New York: Free Press.

Bachrach, P. S., 1967, *The Theory of Democratic Elitism,* Boston: Little, Brown.

Bachrach, P. S. and M. S. Baratz, 1962, 'Two faces of power', *American Political Science Review,* 56, pp. 1947-52.

Bachrach, P. S. and M. S. Baratz, 1963, 'Decisions and non-decisions: an analytic framework', *American Political Science Review,* 57, pp. 641-51.

Bachrach, P. S. and M. S. Baratz, 1970, *Power and Poverty, Theory and Practice,* New York: Oxford University Press.

Barber, B., 1984, *Strong Democracy,* Berkeley: University of California Press.

Burns, J. MacGregor, 1978, *Leadership,* New York: Harper Colophon.

Burns, J. MacGregor, 2003, *Transforming Leadership,* New York: Atlantic Monthly Press.

Carter, A. and G. Stokes (eds), 2002, *Democratic Theory Today,* Cambridge: Polity Press.

Cohen, J., 1989, 'The Economic Basis of Deliberative Democracy', *Social Philosophy and Policy,* 6:2, pp. 25-50.

Cohen, J. and J. Rogers, 1993, 'Associations and Democracy', *Social Philosophy and Policy,* 10, pp. 282-312.

Crenson, M. A., 1971, *The Unpolitics of Air Pollution: A Study of Non-decision Making in the Cities,* Maryland: Johns Hopkins University Press.

Cronin, Thomas E. and Michael A. Genovese, 1998, *The Paradoxes of the American Presidency*, New York: Oxford University Press.

Dahl, R. A., 1961, *Who Governs? Democracy and Power in an American City,* New Haven: Yale University Press.

Dahl, R. A., 1982, *Dilemmas of Pluralist Democracy,* New Haven: Yale University Press.

Dahl, R. A., 1985, *A Preface to Economic Democracy,* Cambridge: Polity Press.

Dahl, R. A. and C. E. Lindblom, 1976, *Politics, Economics and Welfare,* Chicago: University of Chicago Press.

Derrida, J., 1994, *Spectres of Marx: The State of the Debt, the Work of Mourning, and the New International,* trans. P. Kamuf. New York: Routledge.

Dryzek, John S., 1990, *Discursive Democracy: Politics, Policy, and Political Science,* New York: Cambridge University Press.

Edwards, G., J. H. Kessel and B. A. Rockman (eds), 1993, *Researching the Presidency: Vital Questions, New Approaches,* Pittsburgh: University of Pittsburgh Press.

Elgie, R., 1995, *Political Leadership in Liberal Democracies,* London: Macmillan.

Elster, J. (ed.), 1998, *Deliberative Democracy,* Cambridge: Cambridge University Press.

Etzioni-Halevy, E., 1993, *The Elite Connection: Problems and Potential of Western Democracy,* Cambridge: Polity Press

Fearon, J. D., 1998, 'Deliberation as Discussion', in J. Elster (ed.), *Deliberative Democracy*, pp. 44-68.

Foley, M., 2000, *The British Presidency: Tony Blair and the Politics of Public Leadership,* Manchester: Manchester University Press.

Galbraith, J. K., 1952, *American Capitalism,* Boston: Houghton Mifflin.

Gardner, John W., 1990, *On Leadership*, New York: Free Press.

Gaventa, J., 1980, *Power and Powerlessness: Quiescence and Rebellion in the Appalachian Valley,* Oxford: Clarendon Press.

Giddens, A., 1998, *The Third Way: The Renewal of Social Democracy,* Malden, MA.: Blackwell.

Greenstein, F. I. (ed.), 1988, *Leadership in the Modern Presidency,* Harvard: Harvard University Press.

Guttman, A., 1993, 'The Challenge of Multiculturalism in Political Ethics', *Philosophy and Public Affairs,* 22, pp. 171-206.

Hain, P., 1983, *The Democratic Alternative: A Socialist Response to Britain's Crisis,* Harmondsworth: Penguin.

Hargrove, E. C., 1998, *The President as Leader: Appealing to the Better Angels of Our Nature,* Lawrence: University of Kansas Press.

Heffernan, Richard, 2005, *Exploring (and Explaining) the British Prime Minister. British Journal of Politics and International Relations, vol. 7,* pp. 605-20.

Held, D. (ed.), 1993, *Prospects for Democracy,* Cambridge: Polity Press.

Held, D., 1996, *Models of Democracy,* Cambridge: Polity Press.

Hennessy, P., 2000, *The Prime Minister: The Office and its Holders Since 1945,* London: Allen Lane.

Higley, John and Michael Burton, 2006, *Elite Foundations of Liberal Democracy,* Lanham, MD: Rowman and Littlefield.

Hirst, P., 1994, *Associative Democracy: New Forms of Economic and Social Governance,* Cambridge: Polity Press.

Honneth, A., 1995, *The Struggle for Recognition: The Moral Grammar of Social Conflicts,* trans. Joel Anderson. Cambridge, MA.: Polity Press.

James, W., 1897, *The Will to Believe*, New York: Longmans, Green and Co.

James, W., 1912, *Memories and Studies,* New York: Longmans, Green and Co.

Jones, B. D., 1989, *Leadership and Politics: New Perspectives in Political Science.* Kansas: University Press of Kansas.

Kane, J., 2002, 'Democracy and Group Rights', in A. Carter and G. Stokes (eds), *Democratic Theory Today*, pp. 97-120.

Kane, John, Patapan, Haig and Benjamin Wong (eds), 2008, *Dissident Democrats: The Challenge of Democratic Leadership in Asia,* New York: Palgrave Macmillan.

Key Jr., V. O., 1961, *Public Opinion and American Democracy,* New York: Knopf.

Kornhauser, A. W., 1959, *Problems of Power in American Democracy,* Detroit: Wayne State University Press.

Laclau, E. and C. Mouffe, 1985, *Hegemony and Socialist Strategy: Towards a Radical Democratic Politics,* New York: Verso.

Lasswell, H. D, 1950, *Power and Society*: *A Framework for Political Inquiry*, New Haven: Yale University Press.

Lasswell, H. D., D. Lerner and C. E. Rothwell, 1952, *The Comparative Study of Elites: An Introduction and Bibliography,* Stanford: Stanford University Press.

Lijphart, A. (ed.), 1992, *Parliamentary Versus Presidential Government*, Oxford: Oxford University Press.

Lord, Carnes, 2003, *The Modern Prince: What Leaders Need to Know Now*, Yale: Yale University Press.

Lukes, S., 1974, *Power: A Radical View.* London: Macmillan.

Lyotard, J. F., 1997 [1976], *The Postmodern Condition: A Report on Knowledge* [including Appendix, 'What is Postmodernism?'] trans. G. Bennington and B. Massumi. Minneapolis: University of Minneapolis Press.

Lyotard, J. F., 1985, *Just Gaming*, trans. W. Godzich. Manchester: Manchester University Press.

Mackintosh, John P., 1977, *The British Cabinet, 3rd edition*, London: Stevens and Sons.

McLennan, G., 1989, *Marxism, Pluralism and Beyond*, Cambridge: Polity Press.

Miroff, Bruce, 2000, *Icons of Democracy: American Leaders as Heroes, Aristocrats, Dissenters, and Democrats*, Kansas: University Press of Kansas.

Mosca, G., 1939, *The Ruling Class*, trans. H.D. Kahn. New York: McGraw-Hill.

Mughan, A. and S. C. Patterson (eds), 1988, *Political Leadership in Democratic Societies*, Chicago: Nelson-Hall.

Neustadt, R. E., 1990, *Presidential Power and the Modern Presidents*, New York: Free Press.

Nevins, A., 1962, *The Statesmanship of the Civil War*, New York: Macmillan.

Novak, M., 1982, 'The Communitarian Individual in America', *The Public Interest*, 68, pp. 3-20.

Pareto, V., 1935, *Mind and Society*, trans. A. Livingston. New York: McGraw-Hill.

Pateman, C., 1970, *Participation and Democratic Theory*, Cambridge: Cambridge University Press.

Pennock, J., 1979, *Democratic Political Theory*, Princeton: Princeton University Press.

Putnam, R. D., 1993., *Making Democracy Work: Civic Traditions in Modern Italy*, Princeton: Princeton University Press.

Rawls, J., 1993, *Political Liberalism*, New York: Columbia University Press.

Rorty, R., 1989, *Contingency, Irony and Solidarity*, Cambridge: Cambridge University Press.

Ruscio, Kenneth Patrick, 2004, *The Leadership Dilemma in Modern Democracy*, Cheltenham, UK; Northampton, MA: Edward Elgar.

Sartori, G., 1962, *Democratic Theory*. Based on the author's translation of *Democrazia e definizione*, Detroit: Wayne State University Press.

Schumpeter, J., 1961 [originally 1942], *Capitalism, Socialism and Democracy,* London: Allen & Unwin.

Shapiro, I. and C. Hacker-Cordón (eds), 1999, *Democracy's Edges* and *Democracy's Value* (companion volumes), Cambridge: Cambridge University Press.

Shapiro, I., 1996, *Democracy's Place,* Ithaca, NY: Cornell University Press.

Shogan, R., 1998, *The Double Edged Sword: How Character Makes and Ruins Presidents,* Boulder, CO.: Westview Press.

Skowronek, S., 1997, *The Politics Presidents Make: Leadership from John Adams to Bill Clinton,* Cambridge, MA: Belknap.

Taylor, C., 1992, *Multiculturalism and the Politics of Recognition,* Princeton: Princeton University Press.

Terchek, R. J., 2003, 'Teaching Democracy: A Survey of Courses in Democratic Theory', *Perspectives on Politics (American Political Science Association),* 1:1, pp. 147-55.

Truman, D., 1971, *The Governmental Process, 2ⁿᵈ edition,* New York: Knopf.

Uhr, John, 1998, *Deliberative Democracy in Australia,* Cambridge: Cambridge University Press.

Warren, M., 2002, 'Deliberative Democracy', in Carter and Stokes (eds), *Democratic Theory Today,* pp. 173-202.

Woodhouse, D., 1994, *Ministers and Parliament: Accountability in Theory and Practice,* Oxford: Oxford University Press.

Young, I. M., 1989, 'Polity and Group Difference: A Critique of the Ideal of Universal Citizenship', *Ethics* 99:2 [Reprinted in S. Gershon (ed.), 1998, *The Citizenship Debates: A Reader,* Minnesota: University of Minnesota Press].

Young, I. M., 1997, 'Deferring Group Representation', in I. Shapiro and W. Kymlicka (eds), *NOMOS XXXIX: Ethnicity and Group Rights,* New York: New York University Press.

ENDNOTES

[1] We have not space to examine these in detail here, but see especially Pennock (1979); Miroff (2000); Lord (2003); and Ruscio (2004).

[2] On prime ministers consider, for example, Lijphart (1992); Woodhouse (1994); Mackintosh (1977); Hennessy (2000); and the recent scholarship on the 'presidentialisation' of the office of prime minister, for example, Foley (2000); Hargrove (2001). On US presidents see Neustadt (1990, 1997); Greenstein (1988); Edwards et al. (1993); Skowronek (1997); Hargrove (1998); Shogan (1998).

[3] For the usefulness of the concept of 'democratic leadership' in understanding the nature of dissent and democratic transitions in Asia see Kane *et al.* 2008.

3. Distributed Authority in a Democracy: The Lattice of Leadership Revisited

John Uhr

Introduction

Democratic regimes share with all regimes a source of rule and authority. This operational source of authority can be distinguished from the more distant sources of regime legitimacy (Kemp 1988). Public leadership in contemporary Australia broadly takes two forms. One form illustrates the theme of ruling by detailing the ways that different centres of authority (political, bureaucratic, civic) contribute to public leadership. The other form illustrates the theme of legitimacy by tracing out less direct ways that 'the public' or the people collectively contribute to leadership. To simplify: public authority generally reflects the leadership of elected rulers, while public legitimacy can be traced back to the electoral leadership exercised by the people as voters or, more particularly, the type of political leadership that voters are prepared to delegate to elected representatives or take on trust.

In this collection, some authors focus on public actors (politicians, bureaucrats, opinion shapers) exercising *authority leadership* and some focus on the space for delegated decision-making made available by the voting public as part of its own contribution to *legitimacy leadership*. For example, concepts of 'leader democracy' (see Pakulski, this volume) are dramatic sketches of the power of ruling authorities to manage contemporary democracies, often with the willing or at least trusting consent of the managed population. Similarly, concepts of 'democratic leadership' (see Kane and Patapan, this volume) remind us of the importance of the legitimacy theme and of the place of 'people power' to frame and reframe questions of the legitimacy of particular ruling authorities. In this chapter, I try to clarify the relationship between authority and legitimacy by reference to what I term 'the lattice of leadership'. This lattice concept conveys one picture of how authority can be distributed and legitimised in a democratic setting. Accordingly, this chapter links the discussion of legitimacy and indirect leadership in the chapter that precedes it and the discussion of authority and direct leadership in the chapter that follows it.

The concept of the lattice of leadership emerged in my book *Terms of Trust* as a way of trying to explain the character of dispersed leadership in a democracy (Uhr 2005: 78-81). The concept derives from the primary theme of democracy, or at least what I take to be contemporary democratic themes of power-sharing across many different locations of authority. I acknowledge that competing interpretations of democracy have alternative concepts of leadership. To take but one striking example: Schumpter's influential theory of democratic-elitism reinforces a concept of leadership resembling the classic pyramid shape, with the electorate at the base below an edifice that narrows as it ascends to a sharp point where peak leadership sits (Schumpter 1943). Leadership needs no unnecessary flattery and I contend that Schumpter's pyramid has provided more than enough flattery. Of course, I also acknowledge that Schumpter's modelling is more nuanced and subtle than this account conveys, and that even in his theory of elite-managed democracy there is quite some latitude for dispersed locations of leadership generated by competing political, social and business elites.

Leadership in all shapes and sizes

Schumpter's pyramid model is consistent with many conventional theories of public leadership. The pyramid shape might even be thought to favour democracy to the extent that the many who follow support the few who lead. Then there are other shapes favoured by leadership scholars, particularly the circle, which can describe an egalitarian distribution of power where influence is open to all, or even a device to share power equally among those making up the circle. Finally, in this brief gallery of leadership images, there are various constitutional sketches of the separation of powers which feature distinct 'veto points' where those in authority have opportunities for obstruction written into their job description. Think of Australian cartoonist Bruce Petty's many maps of misadventure where heads of government confront institutional opponents (for example, opposition parties in the Senate, or state governments, or international forces) with a recognised capacity to slow down or negate initiatives from the head of the governing party. In this sense, the lattice concept is not simply a story about power but also one of accountability: the points of intersection between vertical and horizontal laths resemble the reinforcement of vertical and horizontal forms of accountability frequently identified in democratic governance (see Mulgan 2003).

The lattice of leadership attempts to describe a style of dispersed public leadership based on a spread of locations where powers and influence intersect. The 'veto point' models play up the negative or obstructive potential. I wanted a version that allowed the flow of influence to go in both directions, positive as well as negative. As bad luck would have it, I came up with a wooden structure with few if any suggestions of two-way flows of influence. A lattice is exactly what you think it is: frequently wooden, it is a frame of intersecting laths designed either as a wall or as a screen to allow plants to grow aided by the support of the structure. Lattices are often longer than they are high, which suits my concept. They are often framed at the edges with quite heavy or substantial wood, but with thinner strips of wood used for the body of vertical and horizontal laths. The overall effect is of many intersecting points interspersed with many regular spaces, giving the structure considerable strength but also a degree of flexibility to cope with the growth patterns of the many plants benefiting from the lattice.

Where does trust enter this picture, and why does trust matter? My argument in *Terms of Trust* was that much of the leadership claimed by Australian governments took the form of delegations of trust according to terms and conditions established more by the trust-claimer than by the trust-granter. While democratic theory might assume that 'the people' delegate powers to their elected representatives, I suspect that Schumpter is closer to the mark when he argues that governing elites convince electors to give their consent to one or other of the competing elite groupings, not simply to 'hold office' but to rule as they see fit. The electorate's consent is a vote of confidence in the trustworthiness of the chosen party. Electoral contests come down to contests over which political grouping is fit to rule on the basis that they can be trusted to exercise public powers responsibly. Electorates might be more difficult to hoodwink than cynics fear, but electorates are also remarkably trusting, especially of fresh-elected governments. Sure enough, electorates can turn their back on any competing or even a governing party, and clearly do so, frequently. But this is simply the reverse side of their vesting of trust in a fresh party to govern, voters having persuaded themselves that the new party can be taken on trust to comply with its declared promises about how it will govern.

The Australian political system is a good example of how many contemporary democracies rely on popular trust in the capacity of ruling authorities to manage vast delegations of power, including considerable powers of self-regulation by governments over their conduct when leading, or allegedly misleading, public administration. But the system of trust and self-regulation is, or can be, quite dispersed, with important checks and balances to help manage misplaced public trust. And here we get to the political architecture of the lattice of leadership.

The constitution of public leadership

Is it feasible to think of the framework of Australian public leadership in terms of a lattice of leadership? My argument is that the formal framework of public power arising from the Australian constitutional design disperses political power. Leading power holders, such as prime ministers or, indeed, leaders of the opposition, see this dispersal as a traditional relic of the pre-democratic past (for example, the Senate, so the complaint often goes) and work to overcome its effects. But we can just as rightly argue that the constitutional design mixes dispersed along with concentrated powers, and that it is up to each generation of office-holders to set what they see as the appropriate balance between central and regional powers. In contrast to many conventional accounts of the centralising features of Australian responsible parliamentary government, I have tried to emphasise the misunderstood degree of dispersal of power and trust inherent in the design, if not the everyday operation, of Australian constitutionalism.

The Australian constitutional framework contains a variety of institutions (for example, written constitution, federalism, bicameralism, separation of powers with an independent judiciary) with many checks and balances which act as obstacles to the ambition of populist leaders intent on taking advantage of popular trust. The written constitutional order disperses public power across the system of government: across the federal divisions between Commonwealth and state; across the parliamentary divisions between House of Representatives and Senate; across the divisions between elected representatives and voters; and across the three branches of government, so that policy making requires considerable give and take among the political executive, the parliament and the judiciary. At each level there are plenty of opportunities for grandstanding, power-ploys and indeed trustworthy leadership. The leadership expected of the national government is not confined to any one site of power or authority, and it would be democracy at its worst to defer to the claims of any one set of political office-holders to act as 'the leaders'.

My image of the lattice of leadership is another way of conveying the message found in many traditional doctrines of 'ethics of office', where expectations about the right conduct of public figures derive from the nature of the specific office in question. One advantage of this type of so-called institutional or role ethics is that it helps officials avoid unnecessary abstraction in ethical thinking by keeping their focus on concrete circumstances and the practical responsibilities of role (Walzer 1983: 129-64; Hampshire 1993: 101-25; Appelbaum 1999; Sabl 2002).

Ethical discourse mirrors leadership language. Leadership responsibilities vary with the office of leadership. So too, ethical responsibilities vary with role. While general obligations to act honestly might be common, specific forms of honest ethical conduct can vary according to the role or office in question. This traditional orientation to public ethics undercuts expectations about a 'one size fits all' model of ethical conduct, deferring instead to a wide range of clusters of ethical priorities varying with different types of public office. Theories of ethics of office have survived so long precisely because they match the living realities of the public realm, where what is considered appropriate public conduct for officials derives substantially from the nature of the offices being occupied: take the occupant into another public office and you probably change most of their official ethical obligations. One striking example is the 'role-relative' ethics exhibited by leaders of the opposition and just as properly resisted by those performing the role of leader of a national government. When political leaders move between these two public offices, we are not surprised to see their public conduct change, consistent with the socially-valuable interests being protected by each office.

My model of the lattice of leadership reflects the prominent value placed on checks and balances in the tradition of liberal constitutionalism. Political power is dispersed along the vertical and horizontal axes so that it does not concentrate in any one spot, yet the overall structure is strengthened by this diversified arrangement. Admittedly, I know of no political entity neatly modelled on this lattice structure. But the lattice model serves a useful purpose in bringing to mind a mutually supportive arrangement of diversified leadership, consistent with the constitutional principles we associate with separation of powers doctrines. Much of the leadership literature rests on a political preference for strong government and the institutional supremacy of the executive branch. My countervailing orientation is towards legislative supremacy, but even this commitment to accountable government is only incompletely democratic compared to views supporting the supremacy of the people themselves.

All lattice, no leadership?

The case for dispersed leadership begins with doubts about the adequacy of executive supremacy and can then be taken as far as democratic commitments might warrant (Pennock 1979: 478-500). Democratic regimes vary greatly according to the degree of separation of legislative and executive power. The concentration of both powers in the hands of parliamentary executives flatters the leadership pretensions of heads of governments; just as formally separated powers invite chief executives to consider themselves singled out for greatness. Both types of democratic regime benefit from the checks and balances of dispersed leadership.

In the Australian case, the constitutional system contains other locations of leadership that are no less important than that potentially available through the chief political executive. For example, chief ministers do what they do in part because of the scrutiny exercised by their opposite number in the Leader of the Opposition which is a high public office that grows naturally out of institutional logic of the parliamentary system. So too the Senate provides plenty of opportunities for leadership to exercise itself when responding to executive initiatives or when stealing the initiative itself. Then there is the High Court where leadership is certainly not confined solely to the position of chief justice. And so on, across the system of constitutional government, including within the political parties which are vital public institutions that do so much to cultivate the leadership capacities of politicians (Uhr 1998: 213-49). The Australian constitutional system of governance provides many useful checks and balances against the worst excesses of executive self-interest.

The Australian political order as originally conceived one hundred years ago illustrates the preferred institutional path of nineteenth century liberal constitutionalism. Liberal constitutional doctrine was in two minds about the place of political leadership. This ambiguity is reflected in the Australian situation. The silence about the office of prime minister gives rise to two alternative accounts of ruling. One account says that this constitutional silence reflects the framers' commitment to the evolving norms of responsible party government which they were careful not to obstruct with legalese capable of impeding the progressive development of new and more effective forms of party government. That is, the constitutional reticence about the role of political parties and of the prime minister as leader of the major party grouping reflects a growing confidence in the rights of the prime minister as leader of the political executive and effective, if unspecified, ruler under the new constitution.

The alternative account is the one that I favour. This holds that the constitution is intended to protect the rule of law rather than the rights of any one claimant to the office of ruler in chief. The remarkable detail in the constitution about the composition and powers of the parliament specifies the procedures to be followed in the legislative process, thereby highlighting the basic importance of the norms of the rule of law subsequently reinforced by the constitutional provisions detailing the judicial powers. This alternative account is consistent with one version of liberal doctrine which holds that good government is the progressive replacement of arbitrary practices of ruling by impartial processes associated with the rule of law.

There are limits to the practical value of every leadership model. The lattice of leadership might be suggestive but perhaps it also carries the risk of enfeebling leadership through gridlock. Schumpter's followers would take that line on leadership. My preference is to retain the possibility of more openly democratic options for dispersed rather than concentrated leadership. The Schumpter pyramid privileges great and powerful leaders. Uninspiring at it might sound, properly constituted constitutional systems can supply valuable leadership even in the absence of great and powerful leaders. It is in our own interest as democrats to bring into play the leadership potential of many political offices scattered across the governmental system — not to mention those positions outside government in civil society, often closer to the conscience of a community.

The formal constitution of leadership limits the greatness that can be contributed by great prime ministers, but also protects the community against the weakness of the weakest prime ministers. This principle holds that Australian political leadership has to be explained in terms of the leadership framework found in the constitution rather than simply in terms of the passing parade of political leaders Australia has enjoyed. What is this leadership framework? Obviously, the term leadership is not mentioned in the Constitution; but neither is the prime ministership (ministers yes, but not the prime minister or cabinet), and that is my point. What makes the office of prime minister so fascinating is that its power rests on a mere convention or shared political understanding and not on any explicit constitutional provision. Yet from this convention or working assumption has grown the power and pre-eminence of our current system of prime ministerial, or as some would say, *presidential* government.

This rise in centralised political power would not take the original constitutional framers totally by surprise. Many of the most influential constitutional framers were themselves experienced heads of government before Federation and some went on to be heads of the national government in the early years of the Commonwealth. Just think of Barton, Deakin, Reid, and even the colourful Billy Hughes — not all of whom, I have to note, exercised leadership on a regular basis. But other framers went to be heads of other parts of the system of national governance. Think in turn of the leading High Court justices such as Griffith, O'Connor, Isaacs, and of H. B. Higgins as head of the Conciliation and Arbitration court. Think also of the many framers who went on to serve with distinction as members and senators who are only now coming to our attention in such works of rediscovery as the recently published *Biographical Dictionary of the Australian Senate* (Millar 2000; 2004).

Conclusion

I began by identifying two dimensions of public leadership, one drawing on perspectives of authority, and one on perspectives of legitimacy. The political health of a democracy requires both dimensions of public leadership: quite direct leadership over the public by ruling powers and indirect leadership from the public that helps to define the core legitimacy of the political order (Barber 1989). The concept of a lattice of leadership links both dimensions by sketching out the distribution of leadership positions. This pattern of distributed leadership maps points where different forms of power and accountability intersect. The concept is both normative and empirical, suggesting ways that a democracy such as Australia can build on (or indeed try to dismantle) promising constitutional foundations with potential to distribute public leadership in many institutional hands.

My argument relates to the diversity of leadership roles built in to the constitution. I contend that the intention of many of the constitutional framers was to reshape the institutions of responsible parliamentary government to counterbalance the inevitable power of the chief executive (the prime minister and cabinet). The framers countered the inevitable power of the political executive with the far from inevitable power of countervailing forces available in such institutions as federalism, with its vertical division of powers; the horizontal separation of powers between the political branches and the judiciary; the internal division of powers within the bicameral parliament; and so on. The system of governance provides for many leaders, but political leadership really comes about as the sum of the parts rather than the heroic work of any one part, party or party leader. This is what I mean by the lattice of leadership which I suggest is a model for organisational leadership more generally (Pennock 1979: 495-505).

References

Applbaum, A., 1999, *Ethics for Adversaries: The Morality of Roles in Public and Professional Life*, Princeton: Princeton University Press.

Barber, B. R., 1989, 'Neither Leaders nor Followers', in R. Beschloss and T. E. Cronin (eds) *Essays in Honor of James MacGregor Burns*, Prentice Hall, ch. 7.

Hampshire, S., 1993, *Morality and Conflict*, Blackwell.

Kemp, D. A., 1988, *Foundations for Australian Political Analysis: politics and authority*, Melbourne: Oxford University Press.

Millar, A. (ed.), 2002, *Biographical Dictionary of the Australian Senate*. Volume 1, Melbourne University Press.

Millar, A. (ed.), 2004, *Biographical Dictionary of the Australian Senate*. Volume 2, Melbourne University Press.

Mulgan, R., 2003, *Holding Power to Account: Accountability in Modern Democracies*, Palgrave Macmillan.

Pennock, J. R., 1979, *Democratic Political Theory*, Princeton University Press.

Sabl, A., 2002, *Ruling Passions: Political Offices and Democratic Ethics*, Princeton University Press.

Schumpter, J. A., 1943, *Capitalism, Socialism and Democracy*, London: George Allen & Unwin.

Uhr, J., 1998, *Deliberative Democracy in Australia*: *The Changing Place of Parliament*, Melbourne: Cambridge University Press.

Uhr, J., 2005, *Terms of Trust: Arguments Over Ethics in Australian Government*, Sydney: UNSW Press.

Walzer, M., 1983, *Spheres of Justice*, Blackwell.

4. Towards Leader Democracy?

Jan Pakulski and John Higley

Introduction

Three trends are apparent in today's liberal democracies: an ever more pronounced focus on political leaders; a heightening of this focus by electronic media; and more aggressive actions by leaders and the elites in which they are embedded. These trends reinforce each other and move the concrete physiognomy of liberal democracies to 'leader democracies'. This move prompts, in turn, a conceptual integration of leaders and elites, together with amendments to Max Weber's model of leader democracy (Weber 1978; Körösényi 2005).

Leaders and elites are clearly interdependent: leaders provide elites with political focus and direction; elites envelope leaders and give them the political muscle essential for effective action. Yet leaders and elites inhabit quite separate theoretical and research domains. Each is the subject of a distinct and large literature and major school of thought. Historians routinely focus on leaders in the guise of 'great men'. Outside the historians' province, analyses of leaders and leadership are anchored in social psychology and, as perusals of airport bookracks show, in the study of business organisation and management. In political sociology treatments of leaders typically centre on leader cults, populism, and authoritarianism, as well as Weber's thesis about charismatic authority. But Weber's concept of 'leader democracy' is seldom employed (Körösényi 2007). Elites, by contrast, are widely regarded as a critical variable in the founding and working of democracy (for example, Sartori 1987; Huntington 1991; Higley and Burton 2006). In this elite-oriented context, leaders are treated as the most prominent elite persons who provide policy direction to elites. Elite studies concentrate on groups and circles of power wielders and usually fold leaders into these configurations (for example, Higley *et al.* 1991).[1]

Leader democracy: Weber and beyond

Weber developed his concept of leader democracy (*Führerdemokratie*, also translated as 'leadership democracy') in the context of early twentieth-century trends toward professional politicians, bureaucratic states and mass democracies, trends that Weber observed mainly in Great Britain and the United States and that he anticipated in post-World War I Germany. He depicted leader democracy as a distinctive political order marked by the domination of charismatic leaders over professional parliamentary politicians, party machines, and state bureaucracies (1978: 241-71, 1111-55 and 1459-60). Domination by these leaders rests on the popular acclamation and public trust that they evoke through the use of demagogy during competitive electoral contests. Leader democracy is, thus, a representative political system in which charismatic leaders rule but citizens participate in their selection. The diffuse and highly personalised character of the mass support that such leaders obtain insulates them from public pressures once in office and this frees them to act responsibly in the public interest. They are able to rise above the sectional pressures and the crude horse-trading of narrow career interests in which professional politicians are immersed.

It is important to stress that for Weber leader democracy entails, above all, competitive elections that produce mandates to govern. Winning elections is the principal imperative, the main source of political power and the key test of political leadership. Parties, parliaments and leaders must cope with this electoral imperative and accept that their success depends vitally on winning votes. Parties do this by developing financial resources, professional staffs and strategies for persuading voters of their leader's personal superiority. Constituting forums in which leaders can display superior oratorical talents and personality traits, parliaments enable charismatic leaders to emerge and gain 'the confidence of the masses'. State bureaucracies — in Weber's eyes the 'completely indispensable' element of modern rule — submit to charismatic leaders backed by mass electoral support. In order for democracy to work effectively, in short, charismatic leaders who win the confidence of mass electorates are essential.

Weber held that charismatic leaders are individuals with 'great political instincts' who emerge only through political struggles, not through bureaucratic careers (1978: 1414). However, bureaucratic party and state hierarchies may prevent or at least hinder the emergence and the freedom of such leaders once they gain power because 'the whole nature of modern officialdom is most unfavourable to the development of *political* autonomy'. Effective leaders, in other words, are not only rare but also vulnerable to bureaucratic constraint. But ideally, charismatic leaders and high-ranking bureaucrats complement each other because they are located in different segments of political elites, and this is what a parliamentary democracy requires for success.[2]

Weber was adamant that charismatic leaders provide both parliamentary and mass leadership in the context of small political elites.

> The broad mass of deputies functions only as the following for the leader or few leaders who form the government, and it blindly follows them as long as they are successful. *This is the way it should be*. Political action is always determined by the 'principle of small numbers', that means, the superior political manoeuvrability of small leading groups. In mass states, this Caesarist element is 'ineradicable'. (1978:1414).

In Weber's view, however, charismatic leaders do not emerge ineluctably from masses, classes or even particular segments of elites. Charisma is rare, and those who possess it 'capture' audiences and impose themselves on followers. 'For it is not the politically passive "mass" that produces the leader from its midst, but the political leader recruits his following and wins the mass through "demagogy". This is true even under the most democratic form of the state.' (1978:1457). If the leader's charisma and determination are accompanied by accountability to parliament, this imposition enriches politics and assures its autonomy vis-à-vis party and state bureaucrats. But where this does not occur, there is either a 'passive' democracy controlled by professional politicians and bureaucrats or a volatile 'plebiscitary' democracy (1978:1460).

The dominance of leaders today

Weber's depiction of leader democracy accords with current trends in liberal democracies, whether parliamentary or presidential in form. One of their key features is the dominance of assertive leaders such as George W. Bush, Tony Blair, John Howard, Nicholas Sarkozy, Angela Merkel, Silvio Berlusconi and, more briefly, the Kaczynski twins in Poland. Voters focus almost exclusively on such leaders' likeability and other personality traits that inspire trust. Leaders' intellectual capacities, ideological and issue orientations, and policy-making experience and skill are of secondary importance at best. Leaders who inspire trust, project strength and gain wide appeal define issue agendas, overshadow party platforms and dominate elections. Elections are today mainly referendums on competing leaders' images.[3]

This dominance of leaders extends well beyond electoral contests. At international and national 'summit' meetings leaders fill the stage, their upbeat or downcast demeanours being most of what is reported about such gatherings. 'World leaders' are expected to tackle gigantic problems: economic globalisation, climate change, water shortages, energy supplies, WMD proliferation, terrorist threats, disease pandemics, criminal syndicates, and much more. One could be forgiven for thinking that world and national fates lie in the hands of a few leaders who are the foci of media and public attention.

This is a significant change from politics in liberal democracies during the decades before and after World War II. Then the role of leaders was to voice coherent ideologies, party programs and election platforms reflecting issues of broad public concern. Today, however, selecting a leader who is likeable, who has no skeletons in the closet, and for whom an attractive media image can be fashioned is seen as the key to success in democratic politics. Parties have become vehicles for leaders and governments are more and more synonymous with the prime ministers and presidents who head them. This change is particularly striking in parliamentary democracies that long emphasised party government and collective cabinet decision-making and responsibility. Most recent European electoral competitions — in Blair's Britain, Fogh Rasmussen's Denmark, Merkel's Germany, Berlusconi's Italy, Zapatero's Spain — have emulated the strongly leader-centred contests of the United States and the semi-presidential systems of France and Poland.

One cannot interpret this increased focus on leaders as simply the 'Americanisation' of parliamentary democracies or the necessary response to terrorism and threats to national security. American influence on parliamentary democracies has always been strong, but today's preponderant focus on leaders is of relatively recent vintage and it antedates the terrorist spectre, though there is no doubt that terrorism reinforces the concentration on leaders. Broader and deeper changes in democracies, both parliamentary and presidential, lie behind the change.

At the most general level, strong centripetal pressures are forcing the concentration of power at the apexes of political, business, and other key elites. Power is concentrated in prime ministers and opposition leaders who are clearly *above* rather than *primus inter pares* in cabinets and shadow cabinets. As shown by Donald Savoie (2008), Canada and Britain now approximate 'court governments' more than cabinet governments. Effective power in both countries rests with prime ministers and a small group of trusted courtiers.[4] Similarly, political observers in Australia (for example, McAllister 2003) note that cabinet ministers and their shadow counterparts operate increasingly as political conduits for leaders, while public service department secretaries are often political scapegoats who take the blame for policy failures.

This focus on leaders goes hand in hand, of course, with the waning of cleavage-based mass parties (*Volksparteien*). Jean Blondel (2005) observes that the structural bases of such parties have weakened greatly, and their ideological-programmatic competitions, which once addressed stable and loyal mass constituencies, especially class-based ones, have largely ended. Ideological blueprints for socialism, liberalism and conservatism have been abandoned as idioms for mobilising support, and they no longer serve as frameworks for policy-making. Instead, political leaders stitch together more or less ad hoc policy packages, parts of which are often copied from packages that leaders in other countries have marketed successfully. These assemblages are much more idiosyncratic than the programs of the earlier *Volksparteien*. Although they all assume a market economy, an electoral democracy and a national identity, the packages contain mixes of ideologically incongruous elements. Thus, a *laissez-fare* commitment to economic deregulation is packaged with collectivist commitments to environmental protections, new government health care programs or measures to alleviate the plights of home-owners. The packages are pieced together and presented by leaders and their coteries of close advisers and they are altered according to what incoming polling and focus group data suggest is most saleable.

Such manoeuvres attract the lion's share of media attention and leaders make their presentations media events. Leaders are portrayed as the key agents of change, especially when risky and painful policies have to be introduced and voters must be persuaded to accept them as bitter pills to be swallowed.[5]

Parties thus become 'leader parties' whose role is restricted to anointing leaders and financing campaigns in the hope of participating in the distribution of political spoils if their leader wins. In some cases (for example, Blair and Brown in the UK, Howard and Rudd in Australia), parties subordinate themselves to popular leaders and give them a free hand in reforming party programs and election strategies. In other cases (for example, Berlusconi in Italy, the Kaczynski brothers in Poland), leaders create their own political parties and use them as personal vehicles for gaining power. In general, leaders now bring parties to power rather than the other way round.[6]

The increasing focus on leaders is also a response to the growing complexity of political issues and sense of uncertainty and risk about unintended policy consequences. Ideologically robust parties and their programs were suited to times of greater certainty when policy choices were clear and policy outcomes were relatively predictable. But such certainties, which accompanied the organised superpower politics of the Cold War period and voters' innocence about environmental, globalisation and many other matters, have attenuated. As anticipated and detailed by Danilo Zolo (1992), in today's atmosphere of democratic complexity, voters fall back on leaders as guides and innovators who are ostensibly more capable of responding flexibly and rapidly to risks and uncertainties than the rigid party machines of yore. Leaders who grapple with 'issues whose complexities lie beyond the grasp of mass publics' (Zakaria 2003:241) offer vague visions that they articulate in charismatic ways. At this writing, the artfully presented vision of Senator Barrack Obama, the Democratic presidential candidate in the US, that 'change' from old to new politics is a matter of inspired leadership and collective will ('Yes we can!') is a case in point.

A public arena suffused by mass media facilitates much of this. The mass media, especially electronic media that create feelings of intimacy, are the natural allies of charismatic leaders. They accentuate the images of these leaders as mass persuaders, tone-setters, figures with whom voters can identify, and providers of reassurance. This media role is obviously great, especially during election campaigns that are now quite prolonged, even 'permanent campaigns'. The media cater to consumers' short attention spans and quickly grasped images, and this encourages hyperbole and spectacle. To suit the need for drama, brevity and simplicity, campaigns are framed as 'horse races' mostly devoid of policy detail and nuance (Denemark *et al.* 2007). Leaders' personalities, especially their quirks, are the core idiom and highlighting personal differences between leaders the *modus operandi*.

Leader-media relations are of course symbiotic. Leaders and aspiring leaders carefully cultivate relations with the media and work hard to buff their media images. Conscious of the impact that personalised media exposure has on voters, they comport themselves as celebrities. Indeed, growing numbers of leaders have previously been media celebrities with the advantages of 'recognition' and expertise in using the media. Leaders surround themselves with media-savvy advisers, PR experts and spin-doctors. Their image-shaping machines include public opinion pollsters and strategists who elbow aside advisers on substantive issues and ignore prosaic concerns of local party and faction bosses (Paisley and Ward 2001). Use of this image-shaping expertise strengthens leaders' positions vis-à-vis parliamentary and party colleagues, who, as background figures, see their political careers hinging on how leaders fare in voter approval ratings.

Voter-media relations are also symbiotic. Brief, dramatic and, above all, personality-focused media presentations suit voters well. This is because voters like to think of themselves as skilled in judging character, while few see themselves as capable of assessing complex and often-recondite policy issues and dilemmas. Forming an opinion about a leader as friendly, sympathetic, trustworthy, determined, committed, or as aloof, cold and uncaring is easily accomplished with the assistance of a few minutes of media exposure. Once formed, such voter judgments are relatively unshakeable, short of some scandalous revelation about a leader's personal behaviour.

Leonine leaders and elites

The strong focus on leaders and the influence of mass media coincide with a shift in the demeanours of political leaders. Starting in the 1980s more forceful, aggressive and peremptory leaders have become ascendant, displacing earlier generations of leaders who relied on quiet negotiation and compromise. The new type of leader indulges in demagogy more freely and makes clear a readiness to use coercion (Pakulski 2005; Higley and Pakulski 2007). In Weberian parlance, they are 'Caesarist' leaders; in the language of Machiavelli and Pareto, they exemplify the triumph of 'lions' over 'foxes'.

The two leaders who pioneered this more leonine style were Margaret Thatcher and Ronald Reagan (see for example, Little 1988). Each emerged out of a relatively uncompromising elite camp, Thatcher from the 'dry' Tory camp, Reagan from the 'anti-detente' camp of Republicans. While cultivating quite different images — Reagan as a humorous and warm man and Thatcher as the outspoken 'Iron Lady' — both reached the political pinnacle as determined 'anti-establishment' leaders and they became close confidants and friends. While differing from Thatcher and Reagan in party colorations, leaders who have subsequently emulated them display more or less the same demeanours: resolute, stubborn, uncompromising, determined, single-minded, nationalistic and fiercely loyal to close allies and staffs. These leaders tend to depict politics as approximating a zero-sum struggle between themselves and their enemies, and they justify themselves and actions by proclaiming their fidelity to 'values' that they say are held deeply by 'ordinary' citizens. The new brand of leonine leaders prefers confrontation rather than compromise and the use of force more than diplomatic stratagems. They often claim strong personal religious beliefs and anchor their political stands in morality and the condemnation of political vacillation.

If Pareto's theory of how political elites circulate, cyclically and endlessly, between foxes and lions is brought to bear, the recent ascendancy of leonine leaders reflects the failures of fox-like leaders who were prone to weakness, prevarication, compromise, surrender to sectional interests, opportunism and lack of fortitude. But if the theory of elite circulation is correct, today's more leonine leaders will alienate important allies, incur unacceptable costs in blood and treasure, and become embroiled in destructive conflicts. In path-dependency fashion, these leonine failures will pave the way for a return of more cunning and fox-like leaders who will outwit the lions in future political contests. It is plausible that the fates of George W. Bush, John Howard, Tony Blair and the tough-minded elites that followed them into executive power are a portent, though it is by no means certain that, amid the ominous circumstances facing the US, Australia, Great Britain and other Western countries today, successors will be any less determined and resolute.

Towards leader democracy?

What does the move to leader democracies imply conceptually? A first implication is that political theory and research must concentrate on leaders, the elites that surround them, and the outlooks and styles that distinguish them over time. This promises a better grip on contemporary political change, and it will revive an analytical and theoretical tradition that has been largely in eclipse since the beginning of the twentieth century. Neo-elite theorists who focus on leaders as key actors, and who analyze preponderant leader and elite outlooks and orientations, chart the direction in which political theory and research should go (Field and Higley 1980).

A second implication is that leadership studies must be unshackled from their excessive focus on pathological 'leader cults' and studies of authoritarianism. This unshackling will open the way to a reconciliation between democratic and elite theories — a reconciliation that is likely to strengthen both by injecting greater realism into democratic theory and discredit perceptions of elite theory as anti-democratic.

Third, the model of 'leader democracy' must be made more robust. One way to do this will be to add a conception of the 'political class' as a sub-elite stratum heavily involved in shaping leaders' images and mass-mediated political opinion. The electronic media's importance in leadership contests requires re-thinking the concept of 'political class' as consisting of public intellectuals and political activists — the traditional 'opinion-makers' The political class today has at its core 'image-makers' and 'spin-doctors' who are much more dependent on the patronage and success of leaders than traditional intellectuals and activists. Its members live off leaders, especially leaders of the leonine species.

Finally, the move toward leader democracy requires altering broad conceptions of political elites. The roles played by charismatic leaders as key shapers of elite integration must be brought to centre stage. The integration and normative consensus that distinguishes democratic elites are now affected strongly by the idiosyncratic behaviour of charismatic leaders. Even where elites are well integrated and share a tacit consensus, charismatic leaders are increasingly the key underwriters of this elite configuration and the main guardians and articulators of political game rules. Deep elite divisions that augur political warfare and democratic instability now typically start, first and foremost, among contending leaders and the power struggles in which they engage.

References

Blondel, Jean, 2005, 'The links between Western European Parties and their supporters. The role of personalization' Occasional Paper 16/2005, Centre for the Study of Political Change (CIRCaP), University of Siena.

Denemark, David, Ian Ward and Clive Bean, 2007, 'Election Campaigns and Television News Coverage: The Case of the 2001 Australian Election', *Australian Journal of Political Science*, 42:1, pp. 89-109.

Field, G. Lowell and John Higley, 1980, *Elitism*, London: Routledge & Kegan Paul.

Higley, John, Ursula Hoffmann-Lange, Charles Kadushin and Gwen Moore, 1991, 'Elite Integration in Stable Democracies: A Reconsideration'. *European Sociological Review* 7:1, pp. 35-53.

Higley, John and Michael Burton, 2006, *Elite Foundations of Liberal Democracy*. Lanham: Rowman and Littlefield.

Higley, John and Jan Pakulski, 2007, 'Elite and Leadership Change in Liberal Democracies', *Comparative Sociology*, 6:1-2, pp. 6-26.

Huntington, S. J., 1991, *The Third Wave*, Norman, Oklahoma: University of Oklahoma Press.

Körösényi, András, 2005, 'Political Representation in Leader Democracy,' *Government and Opposition*, 40:3, pp. 358-78.

Körösényi, András, 2007, 'Political leadership: Between Guardianship and Classical Democracy', Paper presented at ECPR Workshop on 'Political

Leadership: A Missing Element in Democratic Theory', Helsinki, Finland, 7-12 May.

Little, Graham, 1988, *Strong Leadership: Thatcher, Reagan and an Eminent Person*, Oxford University Press, Melbourne.

McAllister, Ian, 2003, 'Prime Ministers, Opposition Leaders and Government Popularity in Australia', *Australian Journal of Political Science,* 38:2, pp. 259-77.

Pakulski, Jan, 2005, 'Ascendant Lions? Changes in the Australian Political Elite'. Paper presented at the international conference on 'Changing Patterns of Elite Rule in Advanced Democracies', Ballestrand, Norway, 9-12 June.

Peisley, Michael and Ian Ward, 2001, 'Parties, Governments and Pollsters', *Australian Journal of Political Science,* 36:3, pp. 553-65.

Sartori, Giovanni, 1987, *The Theory of Democracy Revisited, Part I: The Contemporary Debate*, Chatham, NJ: Chatham House Publishers.

Savoie, Donald J., 2008, *Court Government and the Collapse of Accountability in Canada and the United Kingdom*, Toronto: IPAC Series in Public Management and Governance.

Weber, Max, 1978, *Economy and Society*, Berkeley: University of California Press.

Welsh, William, 1979, *Leaders and Elites*, New York: Holt, Rinehart, Winston.

Zakaria, Fareed, 2003, *The Future of Freedom*, New York: W. W. Norton.

Zolo, Danilo, 1992, *Democracy and Complexity*, University Park, PA: Pennsylvania University Press.

ENDNOTES

[1] Leaders and elites are sometimes yoked together under the all-purpose rubric of 'political leadership' (for example, Welsh 1979), but as analytic categories they remain mutually exclusive. The recent *Handbook of Political Sociology* contains one reference to leaders and none to leadership; the latest *Handbook of Leadership* makes no reference to elites at all. Scholars who study leaders and elites toil for the most part in separate vineyards.

[2] 'Neither the parties' *Caesarist* character and mass demagogy nor their bureaucratisation and stereotyped public image are in themselves a rigid barrier to the rise of leaders. Especially the well-organised parties that really want to exercise state power [and enjoy the spoils] must subordinate themselves to those who hold the confidence of the masses, if they are men with leadership abilities ... Particularly under the contemporary conditions of [mass democratic] selection, a strong parliament and responsible parliamentary parties, fulfilling their function as a recruiting and proving ground of mass leaders as statesmen, are basic conditions for maintaining continuous and consistent policies.' (1978: 1459).

[3] In the Australian context, see McAllister (2003) and Gallop (2005). As McAllister (2003: 259) notes: 'There is little doubt that political leaders have become more politically important over the past half century, in parliamentary as well as in presidential systems. Leaders' images are now as widespread as party symbols during election campaigns, and governments are routinely labelled after their leader, not the party ... Much of this change is attributed to the growth of the electronic media, which find it easier to disseminate visual and oral information through a familiar personality ... Parties, too, consider it advantageous to market political choices to voters through a personality. And for their part, voters prefer to hold an individual accountable for government performance, rather than an abstract institution

or a political ideal.' The centrality of leaders was apparent in the 2007 federal elections depicted in the media as a leadership contest between John Howard and Kevin Rudd.

[4] An analogous trend is observed in the corporate sector where power is concentrated in the hands of chief executive officers with bloated salaries and celebrity statuses akin to those of rock stars.

[5] According to Gallop (2007: 28) 'All governments (and Oppositions) need a centre from which generates the drive to gain, hold and use power. Leaders are that centre in a world of shifting loyalties and increased volatility.'

[6] In addition to those mentioned, leaders who significantly transformed their parties include Margaret Thatcher, Francois Mitterrand, Adoflo Soares, Helmut Kohl, and more recently Paul Keating, Felipe Gonzales, Jose Maria Aznar, Junichiro Koizumi, Helen Clarke, and Nicholas Sarkozy. In addition to Silvio Berlusconi, leaders who formed or transformed parties as personal power vehicles include Jörg Heider and almost all leaders in post-communist Eastern Europe.

PART II

Understanding Public Leadership:
Emergent Approaches

5. Identity Confers Power: The New View of Leadership in Social Psychology[1]

John C. Turner, Katherine J. Reynolds and Emina Subasic

Introduction

In this chapter we examine the question 'what is leadership?' and how it is understood from the perspective of social psychology. This field traditionally has been very interested in the question of leadership, with Kurt Lewin being one of the first to describe and empirically investigate the workings of authoritarian, democratic, and laissez-faire leaders (Lewin, Lippett and White 1939). Despite an encouraging start, in the post-war period the leadership question tended to disappear in social psychology, shifting into organisational psychology and other fields. The topic was approached largely implicitly in the 'group dynamics' tradition and through the study of 'group processes' – most fundamentally, of 'social influence' (Turner 1991). At the end of the 1970s, however, a new theory of the psychological group emerged — self-categorisation theory (for example, Turner, Oakes, Haslam and McGarty 1994; Turner, Hogg, Oakes, Reicher and Wetherell 1997). Over the last 20 or so years, research on self-categorisation theory (SCT) has produced a new way of understanding leadership in social psychology (for example, Turner and Haslam 2001).

This theory not only provides an integrated view of leadership, it also, importantly, offers an analysis of the dynamics of leadership — the ways in which leadership is gained, maintained, challenged and contested. Self-categorisation theory provides a new view of leadership that can speak as much to how an individual person within a group comes to have influence as to the way particular groups, elites, institutions, and authorities within society shape the system as a whole. It has been applied, for example, to better understand when the influence of certain leaders is likely to wane and new leaders will emerge within groups. In the same way, it speaks to issues of intergroup relations and examines when certain groups within a system are likely to accept or reject the status-quo (for example, the emergence of social movements, mobilisation and challenge — see Simon and Klandermans 2001; also West, this volume). As such, this view has been applied in the organisational domain to explain organisational functioning, to international relations and managing conflict between groups (for example, between Protestants and Catholics in Northern Ireland) and to the political contests within nations. The focus here, though, given space, will be on explaining in a very brief form the basic principles of the approach.

What is a social psychological perspective on leadership?

Social psychology is a social science, but a peculiar one. We are speaking here of the social psychology which is a major branch of modern psychology (not the field in sociology). It is a science devoted to the study of underlying causality, strongly oriented to abstract basic processes and the laboratory experiment. It does not seek primarily to describe or understand social interaction, institutions, or societies in their concrete specificity, but tries to understand the nature of the human mind (a mental system not a directly social one) at work in social life. What does social life tell us about the mind, how does the mind make society and social interaction possible, and how is the mind affected by its relationship to social life? Moreover, historically, there has been controversy about how to approach such questions. Social identity and self-categorisation theorists have been most vocal in arguing that social psychology must acknowledge the functional interdependence of mind and society in its theorising about the nature of mental processes (for example, Turner and Oakes 1997). This view contrasts with more individualistic approaches that reduce the working of the mental system to general (individual) psychological properties (for example, information processing and memory systems) or the nature of the individual perceiver (for example, personality, biology, socialisation experiences).

These same tensions concerning the appropriate level of explanation for behaviour exist very clearly in the leadership domain. Researchers, including social psychologists, have looked in an eclectic fashion at just about everything they could think of to do with leadership. The explanations offered often depend implicitly or explicitly on underlying theories of human behaviour. They have tried to define who will be leaders and who will not, what leaders do, what functions they serve, how they differ from non-leaders and what kinds of leaders produce what kinds of results in what kinds of situation. There has also been an attempt to identify the different kinds of psychological processes at work in different kinds of leadership and this attempt takes us into the realm of social psychology proper.

The social psychological perspective seeks to understand (in terms of general, abstract theoretical principles) the processes that enable individuals and group members to influence each other and develop shared norms and values and places leadership within this context. It has tended, since the emergence of the group dynamics tradition, based on the work of Kurt Lewin and others, to think of leadership in terms of relative influence within a group and the leader(s) as the person, role or subgroup which exerts more influence over the group than others. This statement of the leadership-influence connection is a summary of a huge field with many complicated areas (for example, group polarisation, minority influence, crowd behaviour, conformity, persuasion, power etc.).

Putting things more descriptively, we could say that social psychologists assume that leaders are group members who: exert more influence than others; tend to be seen as more trustworthy, prestigious, valued, credible and fair; and who play the most important role in the group in terms of directing it towards its goals, holding the group together socially and emotionally, and inspiring and motivating members to work towards and live up to a collective vision anchored in a common identity. The key point, however, is that we seek to understand the causal processes which produce such outcomes and judgements. It may or may not be the case, for example, that a particular kind of leader or leadership style is more effective than another in some situation but, irrespective of whether leaders are, or turn out to be, effective or not, why do group members follow some people and not others in the first place? What are the processes which lead members to find a person or authority persuasive, credible, legitimate, likely to prove right, etc.?

What have been the main ways in which leadership has been approached?

The *person-centred view* like the common lay conception argues that leadership reflects the personal qualities of individuals. These may be traits, behaviours, or behavioural styles. The implication is that certain individuals who differ from others in terms of their personal qualities relatively consistently across situations and time will tend to become leaders no matter the group or circumstance. In some sense leadership is driven by the person, flowing from the person to the group. If one has not got what it takes one will not become a leader and, if one has, then one can impose it on others. The evidence for this popular view is arguable at best and probably non-existent (for example, Mann 1959; also see Turner and Haslam 2001, and Haslam 2004 for more detailed overviews of approaches to leadership).

The *contingency view* also assumes that leaders have specific kinds of qualities but holds that these qualities will produce actual or effective leadership only in the right kinds of situation (for example, Fiedler 1964). Interpreted loosely this is fine, but the direction of work has focused on the stable individual qualities of the leader and defining situational features in a very static mechanic way (for example, group relations, high level of structure, and formal position of authority). There is no sense that a leader needs to be sensitive to the norms of a particular group and adapt to reflect these as the needs, interests and goals of the group change. In other words, there is no consideration of the dynamics of leadership.

In the post-war decades, social psychology focused on group dynamics and attitude change. A consensus emerged (still orthodox in textbooks) about the processes of social influence and persuasion. In these formulations it became assumed that conformity to and/or being persuaded by the group was a function of various kinds of dependence on the group (for approval, rewards, avoiding rejection, information, reducing uncertainty) to satisfy various kinds of personal needs. Leaders were implicitly understood as those upon whom others were dependent because they provided, or could provide, rewards. Gradually, then, leadership came to be seen as a form of *psychological or social exchange* in which, in return for the rewards provided by leaders, group members agreed to follow leaders thereby conferring respect, obedience and admiration (for example, Hollander 1958; French and Raven 1960). This transactional analysis focussed more on the leadership process than the particularities of the leader but still harked back to the person-centred view since it implied a process in which influence flows from specific capacities and personality of the leader which make him or her relatively less dependent on the group than vice versa. Influence flows from the less to the more dependent, but why some people are less dependent is never explored.

One response to the implausibility of the notion that we follow leaders on the basis of a careful, step-by-step, calculation of personal self-interest has been the reinvention of *charismatic or transformational leadership* (for example, Burns 1978; Bass 1990). Basically, where leaders are able to engender a sense of common purpose appealing to higher ideals and values, highlight the importance of the group's function and show concern for group members, positive outcomes are anticipated. These are themes that are familiar in management, political science, and organisational psychology but that, to some extent, re-describe certain forms of leadership rather than explain them. To the degree that transformational leaders are successful, it is not at all clear why this is so. There is discussion of leaders modelling behaviour, of fostering connections with the group and engaging members with the broader goals of the group, shifting and aligning personal self-interest with more collective interests. One of the issues is that the underlying processes at work have remained vague and unspecified, with the research literature being dominated by work on the constructs themselves (for example, how exactly is a transactional leader different from a transformational one? Are these leadership qualities mutually exclusive?), and confirming the validity and reliability of measurement tools. There is, however, a further move away from the personality view with a stronger emphasis on the fact that these leadership qualities can be acquired through experience, training and practice.

In the 1980s a new view of leadership began life, one still being developed. The central thesis is that leadership is a group process and depends on the existence of a shared social identity between the leader and other group members. This view offers an explanation of the underlying psychological processes that make leadership possible.

The new view of leadership: self-categorisation and the psychological group

What is the psychological basis of group membership? What leads a collection of individuals to perceive, feel, think and act as a group, in a collective, unitary manner pursuing common interests and goals? How does one rather than another of our group memberships become psychologically important or salient in a situation and affect behaviour? Which group member is likely to have most influence in the group? *Self-categorisation theory* (Turner *et al.* 1987), building on the insights from social identity theory (Tajfel and Turner 1979), provided a new set of answers to these questions and leads to a new view of leadership.

A central insight is that people can define themselves as individuals ('I' and 'me') and as group members ('we' and 'us'). Personal identity or the personal self is used to describe situations where individuals perceive themselves to be distinct and different from others and social identity or the social self refers to an individual's knowledge of belonging to a certain group that has some psychological significance to that individual. Within this approach the term 'group', then, does not refer to demographic, sociological or role groups (for example, women, those with low socio-economic status, or politicians). The term refers to psychological groups where an individual defines him- or herself as being a member because the group is self-relevant and self-defining. The group membership is psychologically or subjectively significant for members in that it shapes how they define and evaluate themselves, provides norms and values, and directly affects how they behave in specific situations when it is salient.

When people self-categorise or identify with a particular ingroup, the norms, values and beliefs that define the group are internalised and influence the attitudes and behaviour of group members. Social identity involves a process of *depersonalisation* where the self comes to be perceived as interchangeable with other ingroup members (Turner 1982; 1985). So, it is argued that when social identity is psychologically operative or salient, individuals come to see other ingroup members as part of the self (redefining the self as 'we' rather than 'I'). It proposes that it is where people shift from defining themselves at the level of their personal identities to categorising themselves at the level of shared social identity that group behaviour becomes possible. Group behaviour as opposed to individual or interpersonal behaviour is simply people acting in terms of a shared social identity rather than differing personal identities.

It is important to note that, at this point in the history of social psychology, the impact of the original group dynamics tradition had worn thin and the very idea of a psychological group process which actively transformed people's relationships to each other had gone missing. Self-categorisation theory reinstated this notion, arguing that shared social identity qualitatively changed the nature of people's relationships with each other, producing a distinctive psychology and making possible new kinds of group processes (of, for example, mutual attraction, cooperation and influence).

The idea that the self is multi-levelled, including the personal self and the social self, is central to the SCT analysis and explains how one's group memberships (for example, as Australians, conservatives, Catholics) can come to impact on the individual psychology of the person. It is possible to define oneself as an individual, as a member of particular groups in contrast to others and as a member of higher-order more inclusive 'ingroups'. At different times in different situations we define 'who we are' in different ways. Defining the self at a more inclusive level in term of some social category' in contrast to some other category, creates psychological interchangeability and can transform those who may be competitors and antagonists at one level (as individuals or sub-group members) to allies and as part of 'us' at another. The emergence of new identities and new ways of defining oneself can also affect lower-level identities. What it means to be a member of the Liberal versus the Labor party at a particular time, under a particular leadership, will affect the meaning of particular sub-groups within the parties (for example, what it means to be more left or right) and individual members attitudes towards certain issues and policies. One's higher-level self-categorisations as a party member may affect lower-level beliefs, values and opinions such as an individual's attitudes to various social and economic issues.

When there is a shared social identity there is a motivation to act in ways that advance the group's collective interests and goals and to ensure that one's own ingroup is positively distinct from other (out)groups . There are also greater opportunities for mutual influence and persuasion with the ingroup. Because other ingroup members are viewed as similar to oneself, they become a valid source of information and a testing ground for one's own views on relevant dimensions.

A shared social identity leads people to agree and to expect to agree where they confront a shared stimulus reality or object of judgement, and a consensual response to some identical situation subjectively validates the response as correct, right, appropriate and/or demanded by the objective situation (Turner 1987; 1991). Within any group it is the degree to which any response expresses the ingroup consensus or norm in relation to a stimulus that makes it persuasive, that defines it as likely to be true, valid, right and so on. Thus, within any group that shares a salient relevant identity, responses will differ in the degree to which they express, embody or represent that consensus and individuals will differ in the degree to which they embody that identity.

Relative influence within a psychological group reflects and is driven by these gradients of *relative prototypicality* (to use the term taken from self-categorisation theory to define the degree to which any member of a category is more or less defining of the category as a whole). Relative prototypicality is not given by closeness to the average judgement, but by a new theoretical principle which is assumed to apply to all categorising, the principle of *meta-contrast*. We seek to ensure that the differences perceived between categories are larger than the difference perceived within categories. Any group member is more prototypical to the degree that he or she differs more from outgroup members and less from ingroup members (for example, Hogg, Turner and Davidson 1990). Forgetting the technicalities, meta-contrast turns out to be fundamental because it tells us that identity is contrastive, flexible and relational. We are defined as much by *what we are not* as by *what we are* and the definition of both varies with the psychological and social context within which it is made.

There is no doubt that people have multiple ways of self-categorising available to them and are members of multiple, sometimes conflicting groups. Existing identities can shape the way new identities emerge and are created and new identities in some ways must serve to realign existing (potentially conflictual) identities and their meaning. A crucial idea is that self-categories vary in terms of level of inclusiveness, kind, defining dimensions (content or meaning) and internal structure (the relative prototypicality of instances/category members). All of these vary as different self-categories are created and become salient. In this way, self-categorising is assumed to be highly reality-oriented, dynamic and variable, but always tied to people's motives and goals, experience, knowledge and theories about the world. These are assumed to be interactive, not additive, factors in producing salient self-categories.

Thus far we are dealing with basic processes. Leadership is conceptualised as relative influence and power within a group where leaders are perceived as relatively more prototypical than others and hence more influential. People follow leaders because they embody 'us', and define what 'we' think is true and right, and do a better job than the rest of us of expressing what 'we' have in common. Often there are differences in roles, responsibilities, expertise, knowledge, and so on within a group (for example, a team, an organisation, an institution). What matters in relation to leadership and influence is whether or not these asymmetries are accepted as being legitimate and appropriate (i.e., the role of elites as leaders in a democratic system; see Kane and Patapan, this volume). To put these ideas to work in the context of all the many complexities of concrete life, it is useful to make some elaborations.

Leadership is not a product of personal factors but a group process

In self-categorisation theory, leadership does not flow from fixed, stable qualities of the individual, but from a person's perceived position within the nexus of intra-group and intergroup relations that define the identity of the group. Relative prototypicality and leadership are group properties of a person which change with the nature of the group as a whole and how it defines itself, as well as how a group defines itself varies (interacting with other things) with the context within which it is defined. Group identity is not defined simply by intra-group similarities, but by the meta-contrast between how we differ from each other compared to how we differ from them. A powerful illustration on which research has been done is group polarisation, showing how extremists within a group can gain or lose influence as a function of the outgroup, against which the ingroup defines itself. When thinking about a faction within the Labor party, the influence of this group over the views of more moderate party members will be affected by the comparative context. At a national party meeting, internal ingroup and outgroup divisions are likely to emerge within the Labor party itself (for example, left-wing extremists versus moderates). When the focus is on comparisons between the Labor party and the conservatives, however, the previous internal 'outgroup' will be re-defined as more 'ingroup' and become more prototypical, increasing opportunities for influence (for example, David and Turner 2001).

Leadership is distributed in that all psychological group members are perceived as more or less prototypical and exert more or less influence and all, even the least influential, contribute to the definition of the group as a whole. There is no strong absolute divide between leaders and followers in terms of some leadership 'essence'. At a given time a given group will define itself in light of its needs, goals, experience, situation, knowledge, ideology and other groups. Its identity will take on the special meaning derived from that interplay of perceiver factors and reality, and the member, role or subgroup which best embodies that identity by virtue of whatever factors and for whatever reason will acquire the force of credibility, the mantle of authority and the aura of power. As individuals or subgroups seek to shape, control, reinvent and define group identity ('who we are') in light of events, or fail to do these things, leadership may remain stable or change. Leadership being a group process means that changes in leadership depend on changes in group identity. This analysis offers a view of contingency that is more complex than previously believed and recognises the relationship between leaders and other group members in a broader context of individual and group dynamics.

Naturally, leaders have special qualities. All human beings have special qualities, but there is no one set of special qualities which ensure that one will be, become, or stay a leader. What matters for any particular set of personal factors to become leadership factors is that the group follows, is persuaded and sees those factors as being embodied in itself. There are individual factors, but they exert influence only insofar as they are seen at any time, by any given group, as representing its identity better than others do.

There is no question that leaders actively seek to embody, control and manipulate identity in order to maintain their place in the sun. Some leaders are 'identity entrepreneurs' who, through engaging in argumentation and political rhetoric, seek to maintain their relative prototypicality and their position (for example, Reicher and Hopkins 2001). Along these lines, work on political leadership in the UK has examined the ways in which politicians have canvassed the critical Scottish vote by trying to embody values that are deeply rooted in that group's history. Politicians attempt to portray themselves as being 'typically Scottish' and invoke this identity in their political communication. All leaders claim equally to represent Scotland but very different ideas of 'Scottishness' are crafted to suit the leader's and the party's policy platform (for example, Reicher, Drury, Hopkins and Stott 2001).

There is also evidence that leaders can attempt to restructure the social context and the definition of the group in ways that make their position more prototypical. Seeking conflict with an outgroup is one such response. A series of studies by Rabbie and Bekkers (1978) indicated that when the position of leaders becomes unstable they are more likely to engage in intergroup conflict rather than avoid it. It could be argued, for example, that the Tampa affair in 2001 was very much about what it meant to be 'Australian' and about Prime Minister John Howard as being best placed to lead such a nation (Marr and Wilkinson 2004). Thus, understanding leadership as a group process does not deny the capacity of leaders to make use of their insights into that process, conscious or otherwise.

Leadership is as much about being able to reflect and embody the group, as being able to create and shape 'who we are' in ways that are meaningful to the group. Conflict with an outgroup or minority can be used directly to create and or reshape ingroup identity and hence make oneself more representative of the ingroup and legitimate. The same is true when one demonises and discriminates against a minority group. Prejudice against a minority can be used to reshape the mainstream identity, place oneself at the core and increase one's power (Subasic, Turner and Reynolds 2007). Leading up to World War II, the Nazi portrayal of Jews as dangerous, shrewd, and evil was used not only to justify this group's harsh treatment, but also served to define a particular version of the national identity (i.e., what it meant to be German) in a way that most effectively mobilised support for the Nazi Party.

The point is that leadership is much more conferred than imposed. It flows from the nature of the group rather than the nature of the person leading and it is an outcome of group identity rather than being linked to the pre-ordained life trajectory of any one individual (for example, Turner 1991; Turner and Haslam 2001; Haslam 2004; Reicher, Haslam and Hopkins 2005). It is through defining 'who we are' that leader's are able to influence 'what we do'. Leadership stability or variability is tied to whether group identity varies or is stable. The universality of leadership derives from the social and psychological character of human groups.

Influence versus power: beyond leadership as resource control

So far we have talked of leadership in terms of influence – meaning persuasion – but what of power? Surely power based on authority and coercion can override influence? Can leaders with power ignore, suppress or deny the influences which flow from identity? To a degree certainly, but the new view underlines the limitations of force without legitimacy and authority without identification (Turner 2005). In the old view, power is the capacity to influence, to produce intended effects in others' attitudes and behaviours, based on various kinds of resources (capacities to provide positive and negative outcomes). This view draws on the most general way of understanding power, as the capacity to cause or have effects on things and people, but we think it is highly misleading as a conception of social power. It confuses power *over* people (a kind of social domination) with power *through* people. The theory of power which flows from self-categorisation theory argues that *social power* is the capacity to have effects on people and things *through people*, through being able to rely on, or get others to carry out one's will. Being able to stop somebody by shooting him or her is certainly power to have an effect, but social power is where one can get others to carry out the order. Social power also is being able to stop someone through influence and persuasion rather than coercion — through ideas rather than force.

There are three processes of power in the new view – *persuasion*, *authority* and *coercion* – and all three rest directly or indirectly on identity and the influence processes which flow from it. Persuasion directly reflects shared social identity, authority is leadership legitimated by ingroup norms, values and structure and the coercion of people against their will requires that there be coercive agents over whom the leader has influence and authority. Persuasion, authority and coercion flow from leaders, elites, institutions and authorities acting in line with the rules, laws, principles and beliefs that 'we are supposed to share'. Unlike in the traditional model of power, where control of resources leads to power and power leads to influence, this theory argues that group identity leads to influence, which in turn is the foundation of power (redefined as getting others to carry out one's will). Social power flows from group identity, organisation and ideology in this conception much more than from the control of resources desired by others. The implications of the two views are starkly different, as here we can only begin to explore.

The idea that 'resource control' is the basis of power tends to imply that differences in power between individuals and groups are relatively static and enduring. So long as one controls sufficient resources, it seems, one has power and those without resources have little option but to submit. It is difficult to see how power ever changes hands in this view. In practice there are many examples from real life of relatively rapid gains and losses in power where individuals and groups without initial resources become more powerful and those with overwhelming resources suddenly lose power. Turner (2005) gives an example of the New Model Army in the English Civil War that was created as a resource for the parliamentarians to oppose King Charles but then the resource itself turned on Parliament with certain factions taking control (Fraser 1997).

The new view of the dynamics of leadership outlined here makes sense in this context since it assumes that power reflects group identity and that all self-categorising is relational and dynamic, varying with social comparisons within and between groups, the specific social context, and the collective goals, values and beliefs of group members. Thus, for example, as intergroup relations change, so that cooperation between groups is replaced by conflict, then group identity is likely to polarise to emphasise differences from the conflicting outgroup and more extreme, conflictual members will tend to become more prototypical of each group than will more moderate members. Thus the more extreme members will gain in influence and authority over moderates. Stott, Adang, Livingstone and Shreiber (2007) have demonstrated the workings of these dynamics in the context of the policing of crowds and soccer hooliganism amongst English fans. Police actions that fail to recognise the differences between hooligans and more moderate fans (i.e., their use of coercive force in an indiscriminate way) serves to create an oppositional identity where resistance, conflict and violence against the police comes to be viewed as legitimate. As a function of police treatment the 'moderate' fan identity changes, so that they become empowered to resist the police and move more towards the position of the hooligans in opposition to the police. The emergence of such a confrontational 'English fan' identity may serve to recreate and escalate such conflict in future social contexts.

The idea of coercion by leaders evokes an image of control which cannot be resisted because it is based on overwhelming force. Far from being impossible to resist, however, coercion is often dangerously counter-productive. The coercion of a target tends to increase social distance from and dis-identification with the leader, undermines trust and feelings of control, and induces private rejection of the influence attempt. These are the kernels from which resistance and bloody-mindedness can grow with the goal of rejecting control and restoring freedom of action. Coercion persisted in, without the cloak of legitimacy, tends to produce private attitude change away from the leader, reactance, conflict and the emergence of a countervailing force. Authority is also undermined where a 'fifth column' sympathises with the enemy or where the conflict creates an ingroup identity in contrast, which marginalises the established leadership. Conflict and force therefore by no means necessarily strengthen established leadership, but it is still true that conflict can be used for such ends.

Is coercion always bad? No. Selective coercion can certainly be useful if the aim is to destroy, impede or constrain an enemy, but this is conflict rather than leadership through influence, and prevents the likelihood of influence in the future. The danger is that people assume that coercion provides a form of influence like any other. They ignore the fact that it undermines shared identity and so produces the very opposite of what they intended. Coercion, like all conflict, redefines identity and hence has direct implications for the power of leaders, but not necessarily as intended.

The implication is that power differences in society are constantly shifting and that power change is as normal as stability. The power of leaders and groups depends on identity, organisation and ideology and these foundations are always being built up or torn down, being developed creatively or deteriorating in indifference, as a function of partisan interests, collective experience, new tasks and problems and the endless battle between belief and reality. The power of leaders will rise or fall with any factor which makes them more or less representative of ingroup identity and authority. Changes in the collective goals, beliefs, attitudes, circumstances and even mood of the group, in fact any factor which leads the ingroup to define itself and its collective interests differently, can have implications for which members will have influence and power irrespective of the resources they control. A factor in radical change is often that some subordinate group develops a distinct identity through which to develop its own goals, values and beliefs, contest the power of the dominant group and reject as illegitimate the authority of the social order. Apart from what makes leaders, there is also the issue of how leaders lose or destroy their own authority and what damage is done as they seek to survive.

Conclusion: public leadership and organisational effectiveness

In sum, self-categorisation theory does not see power as fundamentally oppressive, divisive or tending to corruption. On the contrary, leadership is valuable and necessary. For a group to pursue its collective will there must be a power structure through which group identity and goals are realised. Organisations must solve the problems of power to function effectively since without effective leadership there cannot be unified, coordinated, cooperative action towards a common goal by large masses of people. Good leaders give people power rather than take it away, the power to pursue collective goals. Power flows to leaders who authentically embody the collective self. It is a free process, reflecting people's understanding of themselves and the world.

It is also true that authority can degenerate into coercion and lead to abuse. Authority provides the opportunity and temptation for reliance on coercion and at the same time may under certain conditions encourage those in authority to differentiate themselves from followers and develop partisan, separate interests. It is easy to see how the nature of coercion is likely to brutalise the authority that wields it and produce a cycle of conflict and even violence in which mutual hatred, delegitimation and self-justification thrive. It is also easy to see how a leader who has developed interests which conflict with those of subordinates will engage in deception, manipulation, coercion and terror to maintain his or her position, since by definition there can be no appeal to the common good other than dishonestly (for example, Pinochet's National Plebiscite of 1980). A leader may well believe their agenda for change is for the good of all and that time will vindicate their own and their supporters' actions. A failure to influence others about the future and that such trust is well placed, is an indicator of leadership failure.

Learning how to remove failed leaders efficiently is a problem that organisations and communities must solve to function effectively. Ineffective leaders do not merely fail to realise potential, they can be destructive as they seek to create an identity, culture and organisation, factions and divisions, which enable them to survive. We talk rarely of the huge damage done to organisations and institutions by leaders who are unable to meaningfully align identities and interests in ways that are of benefit to the group as a whole, in part because of our fixation on leadership as a set of personal traits.

The present view suggests a focus on organisational effectiveness in relation to the functioning of power structures might be timely. Education, transparency, and engagement need to be encouraged. The group having access to information that can be used to decide in whose interests certain decisions are being made is critical (for example, freedom of information, free media, a balanced judiciary, establishing, communicating and validating principles and procedures for decision-making). There has been little consideration of the ways to ensure leaders are judged in relation to the shared identity, aims and values and can be removed speedily where they fail to function as the group intended.

There is a challenge for those that at some level recognise the power of groups and are familiar with an analysis of group-based and constituent interests (for example, in the world of politics and public administration) to cease to perpetuate the person-centred view of leadership. There is a need to consider the dynamics of leadership and the way structures, conventions, policies, and values can create, shape, redefine, and modify identities, and the implications for leadership. These points speak to the heart of leadership as a group process and serve to locate public leadership not as being over the public or done to the public, but for and through the public.

References

Bass, B. M., 1990, 'Power and Leadership', *Bass & Stogdill's Handbook of Leadership: Theory, Research, and Managerial Applications, 3rd ed.*, New York: The Free Press, pp. 225-73.

Burns, J. M., 1978, *Leadership*, New York: Harper & Row.

David, B. and J. C. Turner, 2001, 'Self-categorization principles underlying majority and minority influence', in J. P. Forgas and K. D. Williams (eds), *Social influence: Direct and Indirect Processes*, Philadelphia, PA: Psychology Press.

Fielder, F. E., 1964, 'A contingency model of leader effectiveness', in L. Berkowitz (ed.), *Advances in Experimental Social Psychology, Volume 1*, New York: Academic Press, pp. 149-90.

Fraser, A., 1997, *Cromwell: Our Chief of Men*, London: Arrow Books.

French, J. P. R. Jr., and B. Raven, 1960, 'The bases of social power' in D. Cartwright and A. Zander (eds), *Group Dynamics*, New York: Harper and Row, pp. 607-23.

Haslam, S. A., 2004, *Psychology in Organizations: The Social Identity Approach, 2nd ed.*, London: Sage.

Hogg, M. A., J. C. Turner and B. Davidson, 1990, 'Polarised norms and social frames of reference: A tests of self-categorization theory of group polarisation', *Basic and Applied Social Psychology, 11*, pp. 77-100.

Hollander, E. P., 1958, 'Conformity, status, and idiosyncrasy credits', *Psychological Review, 65*, pp. 117-27.

Lewin, K., R. Lippett and R. White, 1939, 'Patterns of aggressive behaviour in experimentally created "social climates",' *Journal of Social Psychology, 10*, pp. 271-99.

Marr, D. and M. Wilkinson, 2004, *Dark Victory,* Crows Nest: Allen and Unwin.

Mann, R. D., 1959, 'A review of the relationship between personality and performance in small groups', *Psychological Bulletin, 56*, pp. 241-70.

Rabbie, J. M. and F. Bekkers, 1978, 'Threatened leadership and intergroup competition', *European Journal of Social Psychology, 8*, pp. 9-20.

Reicher, S. D. and N. Hopkins, 2001, *Self and Nation: Categorization, contestation and mobilisation*, London: Sage.

Reicher, S. D., J. Drury, N. Hopkins and C. Stott, 2001, 'A model of crowd prototypes and crowd leadership', in C. Barker, M. Lavaletee, and A. Johnson (eds), *Leadership and Social Movements*, Manchester: Manchester University Press.

Reicher, S., S. Haslam and N. Hopkins, 2005, 'Social identity and the dynamics of leadership: Leaders and followers as collaborative agents in the transformation of social reality', *Leadership Quarterly,* 16:4, pp. 547-68.

Reynolds, K. J., and J. C. Turner, 2006, 'Individuality and the prejudiced personality', *European Review of Social Psychology*, 17, pp. 233-70.

Simon, B. and B. Klandermans, 2001, 'Politicized collective identity: A social psychological analysis', *American Psychologist*, 56, pp. 319-31.

Stott, C. J., O. M. Adang, A. Livingstone and M. Shreiber, 2007, 'Variability in the collective behaviour of England fans at Euro2004: public order policing, social identity, intergroup dynamics and social change', *European Journal of Social Psychology*, 37, pp. 75-100.

Subasic, E., J. C. Turner and K. J. Reynolds, 2008, Creating a minority to create a shared identity: Dynamics of inclusion/exclusion and subordinate support for legitimate authorities, Manuscript in preparation, The Australian National University.

Tajfel, H. and J. C. Turner, 1979, 'An integrative theory of intergroup conflict', in W. G. Austin and S. Worchel (eds), *The Social Psychology of Intergroup Relations*, Monterey, CA: Brooks/Cole, pp. 33-47.

Turner, J. C., 1982, 'Towards a cognitive redefinition of the social group', in H. Tajfel (ed.), *Social Identity and Intergroup Relations*, Cambridge, England: Cambridge University Press; Paris: Éditions de la Maison des Sciences de l'Homme, pp. 15-40.

Turner, J. C., 1985, 'Social categorization and the self-concept: A social cognitive theory of group behaviour', *Advances in Group Processes*, 2, pp. 77-122.

Turner, J. C., 1987, 'The analysis of social influence', in J. C. Turner, M. A. Hogg, P. J. Oakes, S. D. Reicher, and M. S. Wetherell, *Rediscovering the Social Group: A Self-Categorization Theory*, Oxford: Blackwell.

Turner, J. C., 1991, *Social Influence*, Milton Keynes, UK: Open University Press.

Turner, J. C., 2005, 'Explaining the nature of power: A three-process theory', *European Journal of Social Psychology,* 35, pp. 1-22.

Turner, J. C., M. A. Hogg, P. J. Oakes, S. D. Reicher and M. S. Wetherell, 1987, *Rediscovering the Social Group: A Self-Categorization Theory*. Oxford and New York: Basil Blackwell.

Turner, J. C., P. J. Oakes, S. A. Haslam and C. McGarty, 1994, 'Self and collective: Cognition and social context', *Personality and Social Psychology Bulletin,* 20, pp. 454-63.

Turner, J. C., and P. J. Oakes, 1997, 'The socially structured mind', in C. McGarty and S. A. Haslam (eds), *The Message of Social Psychology: Perspectives on Mind in Society,* Malden, US: Blackwell Publishing, pp. 355-73.

Turner, J. C. and S. A. Haslam, 2001, 'Social identity, organizations and leadership', in M. E. Turner (ed.), *Groups at Work. Advances in Theory and Research*, Hillsdale, NJ: Erlbaum, pp. 25-65.

Turner, J. C., K. J. Reynolds, S. A. Haslam, and K. J. Veenstra, 2006, 'Reconceptualizing personality: Producing individuality through defining the personal self', in T. Postmes and J. Jetten (eds), *Individuality and the Group: Advances in Social Identity,* London: Sage, pp. 1-36.

ENDNOTES

[1] This research was supported by an Australian Research Council grant. We would like to thank Professor Paul 't Hart and Professor John Uhr, as well as the participants in the public leadership forum and Dr Chris Beer for helpful comments on this chapter.

6. Leadership as Response not Reaction: Wisdom and Mindfulness in Public Sector Leadership

Paul Atkins

Introduction

This chapter concerns the development of cognitive and emotional capabilities of leaders in the public sector; in particular, the capacity to respond rather than react automatically to challenging events, described herein as 'mindfulness'. The chapter aims to make the case:

a.   That key differences in the complexity of cognitive and emotional processing are not stylistic but developmental. Although difficult, it is possible for leaders to learn to think and feel in more complex ways; and

b.   That the cultivation of mindfulness in particular may well be associated with this development.

In essence, the chapter argues that the failure to think complexly is a problem for public sector and political leadership and that the cultivation of mindfulness may form part of the solution.

The chapter begins by outlining key theoretical beliefs embodied in the psychological perspective that informs this work, then outlines what mental complexity might look like in the context of a senior public servant. Two key developmental pathologies are then described (over and under-differentiation) and linked to senior leadership in Australia by considering Judith Brett's (2007) analysis of John Howard's term as prime minister. Finally, the possible implications of mindfulness training in the development of mental complexity are considered and related to leadership. The chapter concludes with a brief consideration of some key factors working against the development of mental complexity in public sector and political leaders.

The dynamics of mental development

In this section I present a set of theoretical assumptions underpinning the work to follow. Given space limitations, these assumptions are presented without great elaboration although each has supporting literature.

a.   Human beings must self-regulate physically, cognitively and emotionally in response to environmental challenge (Carver and Scheier 1998). For example, in the same way that a leader must physically self-regulate to maintain core temperature in the face of fluctuations in air temperature, she must mentally self-regulate in order to maintain a sense of coherence and well-being in the face of conflicts to her beliefs and attitudes. In practice, mental self-regulation involves striving to make sense of experience through fitting it to existing schemas or through the development of new schemas for conceptualising self and the external world.

b.   The active construction of meaning from one's interaction with the socio-physical surround develops across the lifespan such that more mature leaders are able to think, feel and respond (i.e. self-regulate) in more complex ways to environmental challenges (Fischer and Yan 2002; Torbert *et al*. 2004). While psychological development is most rapid in childhood, it can continue throughout adulthood given appropriate challenges and supports (Kegan 1982; 1994).

c.   The development of mental complexity can be seen as a dialectic process of ever more subtle and complex differentiations and integrations. For example, in the affective domain, wiser individuals are better able to differentiate between subtle emotions and their meanings, and are better able to integrate those emotions with situational demands to act effectively (Labouvie-Vief and Marquez-Gonzalez 2004).[1]

d.   Leaders, like all humans, strive for agency and communion. Agency refers to the need to act effectively to achieve desired ends and communion refers to the need to belong as a valued member of a community (McAdams 1997).

From this set of assumptions, the development of leader wisdom can be seen as the growth of capacity to respond in more complex ways such that the leader can maintain a stable sense of coherence and well-being in the face of increasingly complex challenges. This emphasis on maintaining well-being may seem excessively self-centred to those more accustomed to thinking about interpersonal, organisational, institutional and societal aspects of leadership. And indeed, it is a very partial perspective. However, the bridge from the micro-experience of leadership to more macro aspects arises particularly from assumption d). Coherence and well-being are the outcomes of effectively meeting the interpersonal, organisational and societal challenges of leadership. For the purposes of this chapter, it is useful to take the perspective of the leader looking out and acting at least partially from enlightened self-interest.

We know intuitively that leaders vary in mental complexity. When I ask people what makes a wise leader, they usually cite abilities like a deep understanding of the dynamics of the broader system (particularly the broader social system), a capacity to step back from experience to take a longer term or bigger perspective, an interest in people manifest in a capacity to listen, and a sense of their identity, values and limitations that preserves their integrity and humility through challenges that others might react to defensively. In short, wisdom, in common parlance, seems to mean a combination of good judgment, effective social action and a resilient sense of self.

Psychological processes underpinning mental complexity

What might mental complexity look like in terms of underlying psychological processes in the context of leadership? Let's use an example to illustrate. Mary is a leader of a major government department in the midst of a significant organisational cultural change effort to increase accountability and devolve decision making. Although generally supported, Mary is frequently engaged in heated disagreements with both her senior management team and her minister. Mary is confident in the direction she is taking, having successfully deputised during a similar organisational change in a different department. Her perception is that current criticisms of her arise from concerns among stakeholders about short-term costs of the change when her actions are designed to bring about long-term benefits.

Change happens (or not) through a series of conversations between Mary and key stakeholders including her senior management team, her minister, members of other departments, clients and so on. Many of these conversations are difficult, in the sense that they will directly challenge the way that Mary is seeing the world, potentially threatening her sense of her own capability to bring about the change and even her worth. Consider, for a moment, what emotional complexity might look like in the face of this situation. Mary must be able to:

- identify subtle differences between emotions and the informational signals these differences convey;
- predict the progression of emotions such that she can anticipate the effects of different actions;
- accept and regulate sometimes strong and painful emotions within herself to achieve desired ends;
- take the perspective of others, to anticipate and discern their emotional responses to her actions;
- modify her actions appropriately to facilitate others keeping their emotional responses at optimal levels for effective action;
- reconcile and integrate conflicting emotions arising from different aspects of the situation;[2]
- step back from her emotions enough to recognise that other emotional reactions might have also been possible given different interpretations of the situation; and
- even from this somewhat detached position, Mary must be able to honour and use the emotions to help move her in a valued direction, realising her commitments without being attached to her particular anticipation of the ways in which she might get there.

These are just some of the emotional capabilities required. There are also substantial cognitive demands of this situation. For example, as a leader, Mary must be able to disentangle her leadership role from her identity (Linsky and Heifetz 2002; Kets de Vries 2005). Not only does Mary require a finely tuned capacity to identify, predict and regulate different emotions within herself and others, she must also understand the motivations, values and world-views of others; anticipate the dynamics of conversations, patterns of influence and power that typically arise in conflict, and respond accordingly; understand her own strengths, needs and vulnerabilities; sustain herself in body, mind and spirit under stress and maintain a sense of who she is, what she stands for and what she hopes to achieve, not just for herself but for the bigger context in which she operates.

So, a wise leader is someone with sufficient cognitive and emotional complexity to consciously respond, as opposed to automatically react, to increasingly complex challenges. This amounts to a capacity to step back somewhat from experience, to see our experience in context. Rather than being swept up *in* experiences, to *have* experiences. In the terms introduced earlier, we must become more complex by differentiating our own reactions from the observable aspects of experience, allowing us to make choices as opposed to operating on automatic pilot. In simpler terms, to live wisely we must learn to watch our experience while living it.

Before we turn to a consideration of how we might help develop this mental complexity in public-sector leaders, it might be instructive to consider a couple of identifiable ways in which leaders might fail to develop or at least exhibit complexity in response to their experience. These can be seen as dead-ends branching off from the developmental pathway. I argued earlier that psychological development entails more complex forms of self-regulatory capacity such that we are able to maintain equanimity in the face of increasingly complex challenges. Another way to say this is that, faced with new and challenging experiences we must either integrate these with what we already know or we must differentiate new ways of knowing.

Developmental pathologies in leadership

The core processes of differentiation and integration suggest a couple of developmental 'pathologies' that seem highly relevant to leadership. First, it is possible to over-differentiate, such that a huge variety of perspectives and possibilities are perceived without the capacity to integrate these with past experience and context in a way that leads to effective action. This type of over-differentiation sees the nuances and relativities in everything but is effectively paralysed by this complexity. We perhaps see this in public sector leaders hamstrung between multiple conflicting points of view, seemingly unable to act in a world rich in context and nuance and, ultimately, electing the most timid courses of action. From a psychological perspective, this type of leader is complex but unable to self-regulate effectively to achieve positive affect and is prone to depression and stress. Such leaders are presumably rare in political leadership because they struggle to provide the clarity of message required to be elected.

Figure 6.1: Pathological leadership behaviours arising from over or under-differentiation relative to integration of cognitive-emotional experience (adapted from Labouvie-Vief 2005)

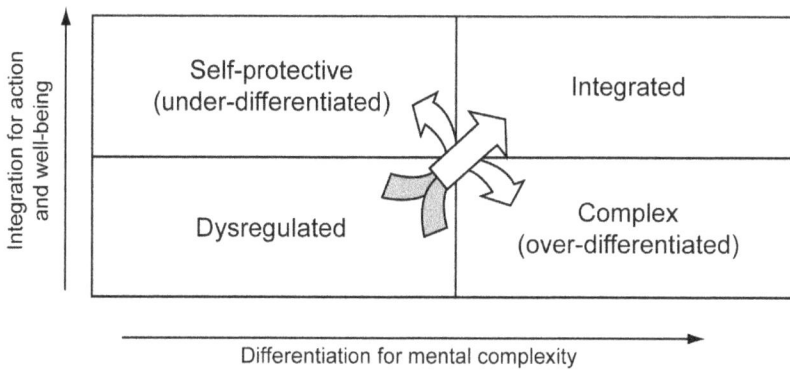

Differentiation for mental complexity

At the other end of the scale, leaders may fail to differentiate enough, prematurely foreclosing on complexity. We see this in examples of leaders who exhibit excessive certainty and confidence in their ability to control and predict the unfolding of events. Here the leader essentially ignores or denies complexity in order to protect threats to self and resorts to trusted and over-learned patterns of habitual response and categorisation. This sort of leader is able to maintain a high degree of positive affect (at least until change becomes undeniable) because uncertainty and complexity is either not considered or discounted as unimportant.

Judith Brett's (2007) fascinating analysis of the last year of John Howard's term as prime minister paints a picture of under-differentiated acts of leadership[3]. Brett (2007) drew upon Little's (1988) characterisation of 'Strong Leadership' to emphasise the way Howard reduced complexity by dichotomising issues:

> Howard thrived on division. After all, it is only with division that you can have a contest, show your strength and win. Whatever the issue, Howard turned it into a contest of opposites, in which there were only two possible positions, black and white, right and wrong, with him or against him. Under Howard's leadership, conversations about our national past, our present and our future were re-configured as 'The History

Wars' and 'The Culture Wars', all nuance and complexity reduced to a simplistic confrontation of claim, denial and counter-claim. Bipartisanship was rarely in his repertoire (Brett 2007: 11-12).

The simplistic approach of dichotomising may increase electability and speed up reaction times to urgent simple issues, but it has serious drawbacks in response to complex issues involving multiple stakeholders, long time frames and uncertainty. Again Brett (2007) illustrates these difficulties with respect to the way the Howard government responded to issues of climate change:

> The issue of global warming calls, above all, for co-operation, an open inquiring mind and new ideas. It does not lend itself to Strong Leadership's politics of conviction and control. As Graham Little put it, the Strong Leader prefers convictions to new ideas: 'A Strong Leader's philosophy must be simple and reliable ... Made to strike hard and stick. The intention is not to contribute to debate: the intention is to overcome and then marginalise contrary views out of existence.'

> The Strong Leader also wants to solve problems, but the more urgent demands of keeping control of the agenda, scoring points for one's own side and maintaining dominance keep getting in the way. Good policy making thus becomes hostage to the leader's reputation. The Howard government's record on climate change is a casebook study of the policy weaknesses of Strong Leadership: its propensity to construct policy problems in terms of friends and enemies, its lack of interest in new ideas, its imperative to control, and its vulnerability to seduction by special interests (Brett 2007: 56-7).

Brett (2007) discusses similar patterns in response to the release of a report into child abuse among indigenous communities:

> The Northern Territory intervention carried all the hallmarks of a Strong Leader's preferred way of operating. An emergency or a crisis requiring immediate and drastic intervention is declared. There is no time for doubt in the face of complexity, nor for talking, listening, consulting. What's needed is swift and decisive action, now! And the leader is convinced that they and only they can see what needs to be done. In response to critics, Howard declared, 'I don't care. I don't care what they say. They are wrong. I know what I am doing is right' (Brett 2007: 52).

Such under-differentiated leadership limits options because to change one's position in response to new information, or learn from others through consultation is cast in terms of weakness. To quote Peter Costello mocking Kevin Rudd, 'A leader doesn't go to committees, a leader knows what he wants and announces it!' (cited in Brett 2007: 56).

In summary, effective leadership must navigate between these two extremes: sufficient differentiation to be open to new information while recognising and understanding complexity, but sufficient integration with identity, experience and context to bound issues, maintain positive emotion and act effectively.

Having briefly painted a picture of what mental complexity might look like in leadership, and having identified two leadership pathologies that might arise, we are now in a position to return to the question of how this complexity might be developed in public-sector leaders.

The development of cognitive-affective complexity: the core capability of mindfulness

Earlier it was argued that an effective leader has the capacity to step back from experience, to see their experience in context, allowing them to make choices as opposed to operating on automatic pilot. Linsky and Heifetz (2002) refer to this capacity as 'getting up on the balcony', noting that it is also essential to be able to get down on the dance floor when appropriate. Indeed, mental complexity in leadership appears to involve being simultaneously on the dance floor *and* on the balcony, integrating action and reflection dynamically. In psychological terms, this ability has been referred to as 'mindfulness'. Mindfulness has been variously defined but two informative and complementary definitions are: '[p]aying attention on purpose, in the present moment, and non-judgmentally' (Kabat-Zinn 2005) and '[t]he continuous creation of new categories; openness to new information; and an implicit awareness of more than one perspective' (Langer 1997: 4).

Mindfulness, applied to leadership, implies a quality of openness to experience where the leader does not closely identify with their thoughts, feelings and sensations but, instead, fosters and maintains a moment-to-moment meta-awareness of the very process of their thinking and feeling. In other words, we are mindful when we are able to deliberately pay attention to what is actually happening without being swept up in patterns of judgment, evaluation, categorisation and reaction arising from past experience. Focusing on what '*is*' rather than our inferences allows us to discover new facets of our experience and act more creatively instead of being constrained by old habits of thinking. For example, most of the time, most of us are entirely unaware of the layers of judgment and evaluation we add to situations, thereby decreasing the possibility of perceiving from a different viewpoint or acting in a new way. The complex demands of public-sector leadership increasingly call for the capacity to creatively and consciously move between pure observation and judgment.

Mindfulness training is one pathway for cultivating a non-reactive self that is able to intelligently register multiple perspectives in ourselves and others. Mindfulness training allows participants to develop a broader perspective on themselves and their experience, often leading to both differentiation (of otherwise automatic thoughts and feelings) and integration (into patterns of thoughts and feelings, and their relationship to self). Of course, cultivating mindfulness is not the only aspect of enhancing mental complexity. Education, formal analytic techniques and techniques that foster creativity, or dialogue with diverse stakeholders can also be helpful. However, I believe mindfulness may be a *sine qua non* for the development of the highest levels of mental complexity. For example, even though consultation with others can foster mental complexity, it can only do so if the leader is willing and able to attend to multiple perspectives simultaneously instead of acting out of automatic judgment and evaluation.

So, cultivating mindfulness is cultivating cognitive and affective complexity by adopting a perspective that is somewhat outside the whole system of the self interacting with the world. Cultivating mindfulness allows us to self-regulate more effectively and, from a mindful vantage point, leaders are better able to respond rather than react, and to learn from, rather than avoid challenge.

How might mindfulness be developed? Cultivating mindfulness involves disrupting unconscious habits of automatic behaviour 'over-learned' across a lifetime. This disruption involves practice and so the standard intensive format for leadership development programs does not lend itself to mindfulness development. However, there is evidence that mindfulness can be enhanced in a relatively short time. The 'Mindfulness Based Stress Reduction' (MBSR) program yields demonstrable changes in brain structure and function (Davidson *et al.* 2003), as well as psychological changes associated with increased psychological flexibility and resilience in eight weeks – a time frame that is considerably shorter than the period within which leadership development coaching usually occurs. To date, such programs have been seen as interventions to improve psychological or physical health. However, my experience of teaching MBSR courses is that they can also improve performance at work through helping participants dis-identify with their thoughts and feelings, providing them with more options for response rather than reaction at work. Mindfulness is a mental ability that can be developed in any context and is not restricted to formal or meditative practices (for example, Hayes, Strosahl and Wilson 1999). Mindfulness based therapies are becoming increasingly popular for the treatment of depression, anxiety and a wide range of other psychological difficulties. These therapies tend to rely upon briefer exercises more akin to the sort of experience one might have in an intensive leadership development course. Together with colleagues from Sydney University, I am presently researching whether such brief interventions make any substantial difference to mindfulness and leadership capability.

In conclusion: awareness (perhaps) begets change

In this chapter I have presented a psychological perspective on wisdom in leadership by characterising it as mental complexity. In closing, I wish to broaden the focus from individual capability development to the systemic pressures operating against the development of mental complexity in leaders. First, in the context of public-sector leadership, mindfulness training might suffer by its association with somewhat esoteric or religious traditions. But mindfulness training can be entirely secular and is supported by an increasing body of scientific research showing improvements in psychological flexibility and performance. Second, the media, the oppositional political system and indeed public attitudes often work against the development of, or at least the expression of, mental complexity. For example, we need only to think back to the proposed 'Knowledge Nation' policy and the way in which Barry Jones' 'spaghetti and meatballs diagram' was received by the media and his opponents to see how expressions of uncertainty and complexity can come to be mindlessly evaluated, for example, by association with leader weakness.[4] It is my hope that, by relating mental complexity and leadership, and by highlighting the way in which leaders must integrate reflection and action — both 'getting up on the balcony' *and* 'being on the dance floor', that a more nuanced view of expressions of uncertainty and doubt might prevail.

It seems none of us are capable of designing systems of political interaction that capture the benefits of independent thinking and the generative power of a competition of ideas without degenerating into a simple competition of personalities that fosters premature foreclosure into simplistic and judgmental positions. If we are to have the sorts of dialogues and leaders we need, we must be able to tolerate enough uncertainty to allow more sophisticated integrations to emerge than what we already know. By definition, creativity involves a time when we don't know what to do and as leaders we must develop ways in which we can express this complexity and uncertainty in the very midst of acting.

References:

Brett, J., 2007, 'Exit Right: The unravelling of John Howard', *Quarterly Essay*, 28.

Carver, C. S. and M. F. Scheier, 1998, *On the Self-Regulation of Behavior*. Cambridge, UK: Cambridge University Press.

Davidson, R. J., J. Kabat-Zinn, J. Schumacher, M. Rosenkranz, D. Muller and S. F. Santorelli *et al.*, 2003, 'Alterations in Brain and Immune Function Produced by Mindfulness Meditation', *Psychosom Med*, 65:4, pp. 564-70.

Fischer, K. W., Z. Yan, and J. B. Stewart, 2002, 'Adult cognitive development: Dynamics in the development web', in J. Valsiner and K. Connolly (eds),

Handbook of Developmental Psychology, Thousand Oaks, CA: Sage. pp. 491-516.

Linsky, M. and R. A. Heifetz, 2002, *Leadership on the Line*, Harvard Business School.

Kabat-Zinn, J., 2005, *Coming to our Senses*, Hyperion.

Kegan, R., 1994, *In over Our Heads: The Mental Demands of Modern Life*, Cambridge, MA: Harvard University Press.

Kets de Vries, M. F. R., 2005, 'The Dangers of Feeling Like a Fake,' *Harvard Business Review*, 83:9, pp. 108-16.

Labouvie-Vief, G., and M. Marquez-Gonzalez, 2004, 'Dynamic integration: Affect optimization and differentiation in development', in D. Y. Dai and R. J. Sternberg (eds), *Motivation, Emotion, and Cognition: Integrative Perspectives on Intellectual Functioning and Development*, Mahwah, NJ: Erlbaum, pp. 237-72.

Labouvie-Vief, G. 2005, 'Self-with-other representations and the organization of the self', *Journal of Research in Personality*, 39:1, pp. 185-205.

Langer, E. J., 2005, *On Becoming an Artist: Reinventing Yourself Through Mindful Creativity*, Ballantine Books.

McAdams, D., 1997, *The Stories We Live By: Personal Myths and the Making of the Self*, Guilford Press.

Torbert, W., S. R. Cook-Greuter, *et al.*, 2004, *Action Inquiry: The Secret of Timely and Transforming Leadership*, San Franciso: Berrett-Koehler Publishers.

ENDNOTES

[1] Through this chapter I refer to more or less complex mental processes. The word 'mental' here refers to both cognitive and emotional (affective) processes. Contemporary neuroscience and psychology shows cognitions and emotions are inseparable: Our emotional experience is deeply informed by our conscious and unconscious cognitive interpretations of experience and, conversely, all mental events are infused with affective value.

[2] Even intrapersonally, conflicting emotions might arise at different times or at different levels of self-insight. For example, acting out of anger can be both disturbing and satisfying at the same time and each has different impacts upon action.

[3] With respect to John Howard, because I can only assess his mental complexity through the lens of the media, I must constrain any claims to qualities of acts of leadership rather than the qualities of Howard himself. It is of course possible that mentally complex leaders may choose simplistic rhetoric and action in order to persuade a disinterested or under-informed public or just to ensure they are given a 'sound-bite'. But for the climate change issue at least there is increasing objective evidence, irrespective or rhetorical demands, that Howard's rhetoric and policy was insufficiently differentiated and integrated at both the national and global levels.

[4] 'Knowledge Nation' was the ALP's education policy launched just before the 2001 federal election. See Barry Jones' explanation of the spaghetti diagram: 'How the Knowledge Nation diagram evolved' (July 6, 2001), *Sydney Morning Herald*, accessed 16 September 2008 at http://www.smh.com.au/articles/2003/11/24/1069522520574.html

7. Bodies and Identities in Constructing Leadership Capital

Amanda Sinclair

Identities, bodies and leadership capital

In this chapter, I explore two interrelated aspects of public leadership that have received little attention. The first is 'identity' and I argue that leaders are under new pressures to produce 'appropriate' leadership identities (Alvesson and Willmott 2002). Second, I draw attention to the importance of bodies and bodily performance in public calculations of leadership and who delivers it.

I begin by defining the concepts of identities and bodies and their importance in producing leadership capital. Drawing on the results of a pilot study into representations of leaders' bodies, I argue that leaders' identities and bodies are under new scrutiny.

Leadership is at least partially established by leaders giving an impression of (cerebral) intelligence, invincibility and invulnerability — of mind over body. The leadership of women, and potentially leaders of different racial and cultural backgrounds is undermined by their bodies being fore-grounded in public representations. Women leaders face particular challenges, expected to establish leadership in the context of stereotypical views that see them as women and bodies, not leaders. How should leaders react? One commonly-argued option is for women leaders to ensure their bodies are camouflaged. I conclude the challenge is a more complex task of identity work for leaders: acknowledging how one may be represented and scrutinised and seeking to choose how one reacts to these conventions in order to subvert them.

Producing leadership

People in all sorts of public roles are under new pressures to deliver leadership and produce a leadership persona, which I define here as a persona or projected sense of self that 'looks' like leadership. The expansion of leadership ideas into the corporate sectors and beyond has meant that now people working in for example, schools, community organisations, not-for-profit, sports and health sectors, are all subject to pressures to 'be' or 'become' leaders.

In the production of leadership identities, societies regulate the identities that may be taken up and individual leaders conform to, and struggle against, societal and organisational scripts of who they should be as leaders. Scholars have characterised this dynamic process as 'identity work' or 'forming, repairing, maintaining, strengthening or revising the constructions that may be productive of a sense of coherence and distinctiveness' (Sveningsson and Alvesson 2003: 1165). It is important to note that while leaders may have always been engaged in this process two trends may have magnified identity pressures. The first is proliferating media channels which increase scrutiny of and speculation about leaders' lives. Even those who formerly have been able to work inconspicuously such as bureaucrats or community leaders now often find themselves feted as role models and featured in magazines, websites and the like. The second trend is the measurement and management of leader performance that is now a pervasive aspect of organisational life. Appraisal processes, feedback instruments and other techniques of selection and promotion mean that most leaders are regularly tested against and expected to have their identities conform to, organisationally and societally-specified norms of success. Part of leadership work is producing a convincing leadership persona.

Bodies and bodily performances, including physical stature, physical features such as stance, gestures and facial characteristics and the way these are represented are also important to the construction of leadership personae. Here again there are new levels of visibility, scrutiny and management that apply to leaders and their bodies. The bodies of men and women, of indigenous and non-Anglo leaders, are often represented differently, activating unconscious processes and societal archetypes that reinforce or undermine authority, power and leadership capital (Sinclair 1998). For example, photographs of presidential campaigner Hilary Clinton capture large teeth and an appearance of desperation that are not present in photographs of her male rivals. Such representations are not accidental, according to feminist theorists who argue that they reflect a fear of female power or the 'monstrous feminine' (Creed 1993).

So, identities and bodies are important in the production of leadership and leadership capital. By adding the term 'capital' to leadership, I am following a tradition of usage to underline collective and complex processes of production. Leadership capital or an agreed reserve of leadership credibility is collectively negotiated and allocated to certain individuals by societal groups and norms. I also suggest with this notion of 'capital' that some groups and individuals may have access to more resources in creating leadership. We naturally expect certain individuals — native English speakers or well-educated men, for example — to be likely to provide leadership. Others, such as Indigenous or women leaders, cannot so easily draw from this established bank of expectations about where leadership will lie.

Pressures to produce a leadership persona

Political and corporate leaders are increasingly being encouraged to craft their personae, lives and their legacies to reinforce their status as leaders. From a leader's point of view, this may involve authoring a biographical narrative that helps establish and deliver one's credentials as a leader to followers.

Institutions, including corporations, political parties and governments gain an interest in monitoring leader identities and performances. Leaders are subject to image 'makeovers' and coached in communication styles. Corporate leaders cultivate personas that engender confidence among stakeholders and share-markets. They select the forums to which they lend their 'presence' while avoiding over-exposure. There are now, in Australia at least, 'beauty' pageants for business leaders in which panels select top leaders in particular categories, for example 'Young Entrepreneur' or 'Best Director'. These and other events are often photographed and stage-managed to convey the requisite levels of gravitas with a hint of 'quirkiness' or individuality.

The many pressures described above impinge on leaders who feel compelled to manage their personae (Collinson 2003; Thomas *et al*. 2004; Thomas and Graham 2005; Linstead 2006; Sveningsson and Larson 2006). New leadership discourses around asserting one's authenticity, for example, may heighten anxiety to demonstrably secure one's identity as a leader. Despite such efforts, there often remains an inescapable predictability about these representations of leadership, creating what Guthey and Jackson (2005) describe as an 'authenticity paradox': pressure to manufacture an 'authentic persona' which, by its very process renders that authenticity impossible.

Perceptions of leadership or greatness are always bestowed by followers. They are indelibly tied to a society's myths and history, which in the Australian case is interwoven with assumptions of masculinity, physical toughness and self-reliance (Sinclair 1994). A recent example of these gender effects in leadership identities occurred in the 2007 Australian Federal election campaign during which the then Leader of the Opposition, Kevin Rudd, described his eviction from his childhood home. This story about his identity was successfully used to establish his 'battler' credentials, and to show the roots of his claimed economic conservatism. In contrast, Rudd's Deputy, Julia Gillard, was featured in the media in her childless and partnerless home, symbolised by an empty fruit-bowl. This story of Gillard's identity — as a single, childless woman — was used in some parts of the media to question her status as 'normal' woman and in turn, her credentials for leadership.

As these and other examples show, how leaders go about their identity work reveals that it is rarely a process of simply crafting and projecting a self. Available leadership spaces and societal readiness to endow leadership capital are already deeply inscribed by gendered and cultural assumptions (Eagly and Karau 2002; Heilman *et al*. 2004). Women leaders in traditionally male dominated environments experience particular pressures to produce non-threatening leadership selves, to camouflage aspects of their gender, their children and sexualities (Thomas *et al*. 2004; Thomas and Graham 2005). Men also experience pressure to conform to often narrowly prescribed understandings of who a male leader should be.

Leadership bodies

The preceding discussion focused on pressures to project a successful identity but the bodily production of leadership is also a crucial and neglected aspect in leadership research.[1] What part do bodies, and public representations of bodies, play in producing or undermining leadership capital?

As part of my research in corporate leadership, I have studied photographs of corporate leaders in the business press. If they are male, leader images are of two main types: the large headshot or the shot of head and upper body. The upper body is presented as dark, without definition and often shading seamlessly into the background. Garments function to be uniform and camouflage with the occasional quirk: a bow tie, watch, or a freckled hand that allows a fleeting glimpse into age and vulnerability. If lower bodies are included in the photo they disappear into the background, groins and hips are shielded (sometimes literally with hands or arms) and bodies reduced to a silhouette. With full body shots, men are pictured against neutral or structural backdrops, rarely cluttered with objects or people. The overall effect is to render the body invisible or irrelevant. This leadership is without a body and therefore invincible and immortal (Sinclair 2005). All that's important is in the head, conveyed in a steely gaze or lines that function as reassuring badges of experience.

If we turn to look at representations of women leaders the photographs are very different. More of the body is included and more skin — in arms, legs, throats. Clothing, jewellery and other personal props give more away about the character of the leader. Colours are more evident in clothing, sometimes conveying frivolity or vanity. Backgrounds are more likely to also speak about this leader and can include photos or books, sometimes with a general sense of clutter that is rarely part of a male leader's photograph. Representations of male leaders of Indigenous or non-Anglo backgrounds are more likely to foreground body features, potentially reinforcing racial stereotypes (see also Sinclair 2007).

To more systematically explore these observations, we undertook a pilot study of the representation of leader's bodies in a selection of Australian newspapers and business magazines[2] over the week of 9-16 November 2007. We wanted to map how leaders' bodies were photographed and represented in the media, to explore which criteria emerged as important in the framing and imputation of power to some leadership bodies.

We chose four variables to explore: body composition or how much of leaders' bodies was included in the photograph (from head/neck, through the addition of shoulders or armpits, to waist, groin and below groin or full body); the amount of (non-facial) skin visible (from none to arms, legs, cleavage/upper chest, waist up and combinations of these); the clothing in which they were photographed as either 'neutral' (expected for their role, such as a business suit) or 'non-neutral' (unexpected or out-of-context clothing or garments); and backgrounds which we classified as 'neutral' (barely visible, predictable, bland, unimportant) or 'non-neutral' (leaders in surprising settings which changed the way they were viewed). The independent variables we mapped were type of leader (community, political, business or public sector professional), their sex and their ethnicity (Caucasian and non-Caucasian).[3] The sampling period was a couple of weeks before the Federal election and so political leaders were probably unusually well-represented in the media.

Many factors emerged as important considerations in how leadership bodies might be read and interpreted in this pilot study. One is the size of the picture and the positioning in the paper and on the page. Another is the important role of captions which change the way a pictured body is viewed. For example, in one of a media star and a woman who were involved in a dispute, the caption listed their names and added theirs was 'just a physical relationship'. We recorded in which newspapers and magazines leader portrayals occurred. The impact of editorial policy and media ownership on leader portrayals is also potentially a rich area for further analysis.

A criticism of our study might argue that we were capturing simply photographers' biases and conventions, perhaps in turn a reflection of editors' interests in selling papers. The media is manipulative in who and how it chooses to portray leaders, for example, closer to the election the soon-to-be deposed Government leader, John Howard, is pictured in funereal darkness and in another case, in darkness with an illuminated exit sign behind him. A related concern is the presence of our own biases. Others looking at the same photograph might make very different judgements about these leaders.

We acknowledge both concerns as limitations. Our study does not aim to capture an objective picture of how leaders' bodies are viewed, because no such unitary or final view is possible. Another study would be needed to systematically test people's responses to these representations of leaders. However, it is both possible and important to begin to systematically explore the multiplicity and features of representations.

Further, media gatekeepers of body representations play an important role in reflecting and shaping the public gaze about the nature of public leadership. Our intent is not to identify facts but discover more about the body as mediator in taken-for-granted processes of constructing leadership.

What did we find? Out of approximately 493 representations, there were 412 men and 81 women, including 76 leaders from community, 190 political, 161 business and 66 public sector professionals. There were only 17 non-Caucasians in our study (a number we judged too small to meaningfully analyse) but these were largely in the community and business sectors. These raw figures already show not just who is in leader positions, but who is regarded as embodying leadership worthy of news readership.

Turning to body composition, 20% of representations of male leaders were of head only and a further 15% with shoulders. For women, only 13% were head only and 9% with shoulders. In contrast, 37% of women (compared to only 20% of men) were portrayed with their whole body. The portrayal of whole-body was particularly noticeable with women community leaders (58%). 72% of community leaders were pictured with their waists, groins and/or full body showing. This contrasted with 63% of business leaders. Even where more of the bodies of business leaders were shown, they were likely to be rendered unimportant by clothing, lighting or situation.

On the skin exposed variable, 93% of male leaders had no skin apart from face exposed, while only 34% of women were in this category. Sex differences become more interesting by looking at what parts of the skin are captured and portrayed. While only 4% of men had arms, legs *or* cleavage/upper chest exposed, 33% of women were portrayed with one of these areas revealed. Looking at multiple combinations of skin exposure, only 2% of men (or eight out of 414) men were portrayed with two or more of the skin of arms, legs and cleavage/upper chest visible, compared to 33% of women (or 27 out of 82).

We also found sharp differences between the sexes in whether male and female leaders enjoyed neutral (for example offices or walls of buildings) or non-neutral backgrounds and clothing. 35% of women were presented against non-neutral backgrounds (for example, Queensland Premier Anna Bligh in an aeroplane), while only 21% of male leaders were photographed against novel or unpredictable backdrops. Looking at clothing, these differences were even more marked, with 40% of women leaders represented in non-conventional clothing (for example, not a business suit) whereas only six per cent of male leaders were portrayed in this way.

Although it can be argued that women have a wider range of acceptable clothing, these findings still seem to suggest that there are likely to be subtle – and less subtle – markers that are included in representations of women that may draw attention to, for example, idiosyncrasy or sexuality, which in turn may undermine their capacity to be seen as leaders. Even though social conventions, such as clothing, are different for men and women, it is important to understand the way these conventions are then exploited: for men it is to conceal and downplay bodies while highlighting intellect power; for women highlighting dress and bodies does the reverse.

What does this pilot study suggest about the role of bodies in the production of leadership? First, there is evidence here that leaders from some sectors experience more visibility but it is visibility of a certain kind. Political and business leaders are much more widely portrayed than community leaders (which might be expected given the selection of newspapers and magazines we chose). Among those commonly portrayed political and business leaders, men significantly outnumber women and men are many times more likely to be portrayed without bodies or other-than-facial skin. Such portrayals, we argue, reinforce an image of cerebral mastery and substance rather than bodily idiosyncrasy or frailty (Sinclair 2007).

How should leaders react?

Some leadership commentators argue that we are in a 'postheroic' leadership phase. Yet other evidence suggests followers continue to collude with the idea of leaders who are in some way above bodily matters, not vulnerable to bodily ailments and who can deliver mythic feats in maintaining share prices or keeping down interest rates. These leaders are 'above more ordinary men' in their powers (Sinclair 1994; 2005). We know that male leaders are at least as likely as women to experience serious ailments which will undermine their capacity to lead. Yet the findings above show that when we examine representations made available for the public gaze, we are being asked to believe that male leaders are less subject to the limitations of their bodies.

Through our pilot study we have documented a systematic bias in representations which portrays more of women leaders' bodies and skin, a tendency which potentially undermines their leadership. Feminist and other research affirms that power, gender and bodies are integrally connected (Butler 1993; Gatens 1996). Norms about leaders' bodies and their presentation are often interwoven into cultures. For example, in traditional Chinese cultures, a mandarin's status is signified by high collar and large sleeves that hide hands and foster inscrutability. In many Western cultures, young women perceive they have little power beyond the sexual power of their bodies. In showing off more of their bodies they gain fleeting power, but are simultaneously condemned to body-defined identities.

Representations of gendered bodies thus interact with likely attributions of power, authority and leadership. Women's bodies can be portrayed as frail (not stable or sound), elderly (cranky or 'past it', for example, particularly photographs of Indigenous women leaders), surrounded by distracting clutter (not focused on the job), or sufficiently generous to suggest a failure of self-discipline.

Critical and feminist scholarship has convincingly demonstrated how creating 'otherness' enables the norm to go unseen (Benjamin 1988). Further, dichotomies such as mind/body function alongside gender and racial dichotomies such as male/female and black/white to ensure that some people are defined and judged as bodies, without mind. Feminist theory also shows how the location of all that is sexual on women leaders prevents us from seeing the way sexualities are threaded through our appetites for leadership and the performances some male leaders deliver.

So how do, or might, leaders respond? There is a genre of literature and advice that encourages women leaders to conform — to dress professionally but innocuously, to be assertive but not aggressive in how they talk and negotiate, to steer an inoffensive path in the body language they adopt.

Yet, a now substantial body of research confirms that it is not what the woman leader does or even looks like that is important but how that behaviour is perceived and judged (see for example Heilman *et al*. 2004). Such judgements take place against a backdrop of gender-inscribed assumptions and stereotypes that are beyond the control of the leader. So, no amount of 'dressing-for-success' or finding the right height of shoe heel (too high=sexually available, too flat=lesbian or feminist) will necessarily imbue an image of leadership.

A different way forward may lie in leaders — of all genders and cultural backgrounds — being aware of the effects of these processes. By being aware, several things become possible. First, leaders can seek to influence the kinds of photographs and representations that are taken and used. Leaders may choose to downplay bodies in the clothing or type of shot that is taken. Alternatively they may choose to *not* do so, to make their bodies and their bodily performances a part of their leadership work. In other research, I have drawn on case studies of Chief Commissioner of Victorian Police, Christine Nixon, and Indigenous school principal, Chris Sarra, to show how paying attention to bodies can be a powerful addition to leadership work (Sinclair 2007).

Further, there is power for leaders in developing an understanding of the wider societal forces that shape how their leadership is seen. Being given the concepts to understand one's experiences as a product of structurally and socially determined forces alongside individual action is existentially empowering. In my own 'journey around leadership,' drawing on feminist research to help explain my experience enabled me to begin to see the 'bigger picture' of what was going on when I, as a woman, was working with predominantly male executive groups.

For the leader, such a deeper understanding and awareness may also enable the capacity to sit apart from the immediate need for acceptance, belonging or approval. This capability is explored in Paul Atkins' chapter in this volume under the title of 'Leadership as a Response not Reaction'. It involves developing the capacity to differentiate our reactions from the observed experience: to both watch our lives and leadership at the same time as living it.

In my experience working with leaders, most readily identify the societal and organisational identity 'scripts' that prescribe who they should be and how their bodies should conform. Once identified, there is the possibility of choosing how to react such as continuing to perform to win favour and recognition or to not conform to script for the moment or under these circumstances.

Conclusion

Leadership and leadership capital is constantly being negotiated and produced through the identities and bodily performances of leaders interacting with the responses of audiences. The high level of scrutiny experienced by many leaders in the political, business and community domains introduces new pressures on leaders to present convincing leadership identities and bodies. For some, the opportunities for performance and 'exposure' support claims to leadership while, for others, tacit but powerful norms in representation and stereotyping potentially undermine leadership.

Leaders have various ways of responding to these pressures, from active collusion through various strategies of camouflage, sense-making, interrogation, distancing and resistance. Because leadership capital is collectively produced, no strategy can ever be considered as individually successfully accomplished. It is rather a matter of navigating through the externally and internally-generated pressures and anxieties with insight and understanding of wider structural forces. The goals of this kind of identity work in leadership may be to argue for a deeper understanding about the way in which identities and bodies are interpreted and to exercise some choice about how, as a leader, to react.

References

Alvesson, M. and S. Sveningsson, 2003, 'Good visions, bad micromanagement and ugly ambiguity: contradictions of (non-) leadership in a knowledge intensive organisation', *Organization Studies*, 24:6, pp. 961-88.

Alvesson, M. and H. Willmott, 2002, 'Identity regulation as organizational control; Producing the "appropriate" individual', *Journal of Management Studies*, 39, p. 619-44.

Benjamin, J., 1998, *Shadow of the Other: Intersubjectivity and Gender in Psychoanalysis*, New York: Routledge.

Butler, J., 1993, *Bodies that Matter: On the Discursive Limits of Sex*, New York: Routledge.

Collinson, D., 2003, 'Identities and insecurities: selves at work', *Organization*, 10:3, pp. 527-47.

Creed, B., 1993, *The Monstrous Feminine; Film, feminism, Psychoanalysis*, London: Routledge.

Eagly, A. and S. Karau, 2002, 'Role congruity theory of prejudice toward female leaders', *Psychological Review*, 109, pp. 573-98.

Gatens, M., 1996, *Imaginary Bodies: Ethics, Power and Corporeality*. London: Routledge.

Guthey, E. and B. Jackson, 2005, 'CEO Portraits and the Authenticity Paradox', *Journal of Management Studies,* 42:5, pp. 1057-82.

Heaphy, E. and J. Dutton, 2008, 'Positive Social Interactions and the Human Body at Work: Linking organizations and physiology', *Academy of Management Review,* 33:1, pp. 137-62.

Heilman, M., A. Wallen, D. Fuchs and M. Tamkins, 2004, 'Penalties for success: Reactions to women who succeed at male gender-typed tasks', *Journal of Applied Psychology,* 89:3, pp. 416-27.

Linstead, A., 2006, *Managing Identity,* Basingstoke: Palgrave Macmillan.

Sinclair, A., 1994, *Trials at the Top,* Melbourne: The Australian Centre.

Sinclair, A., 1995, 'Sexuality in Leadership' *International Review of Women and Leadership,* 1:2, pp. 25-38.

Sinclair, A., 2005, 'Body possibilities in Leadership', *Leadership,* 1:4, pp. 387-406.

Sinclair, A., 2007, *Leadership for the Disillusioned: Beyond myths and heroes to leading that liberates,* Sydney: Allen & Unwin.

Sveningsson, S. and L. Larson, 2006, 'Fantasies of leadership: identity work', *Leadership,* 2:2, pp. 203-24.

Thomas, P. and J. Graham, 2005, *A Woman's Place is in the Boardroom*, New York: Palgrave.

Thomas, R., Mills, A. and J. Helms-Mills (eds), 2004, *Identity Politics at Work,* London: Routledge.

ENDNOTES

[1] There is a tradition of feminist research examining the role of bodies (for example, Butler 1993), work focusing on bodies in organisations and the production of masculinities in the workplace, yet very little of this has been taken up in the leadership literature. There is however, a new theme in the leadership advice genre which focuses on tuning the leadership body as a way of coping with stress and further research examining how the body may be a resource for leaders in mediating more positive work relations (see for example Heaphy and Dutton 2008).

[2] Data collection and analysis was undertaken independently by Dr Pat Seybolt. Decision criteria were discussed and refined as the study progressed. Eight newspapers and magazines were included: *The Age, The Age Weekly, The Australian, The Australian Weekly, The Financial Review, The Financial Review Weekly Magazine, Boss Magazine* (appears in *AFR*) and *Business Review Weekly.*

[3] With each of these dependent and independent variables, there were clear photographs which were hard to rate. We independently rated some and discussed others. Who constituted a leader was often a difficult decision and particularly who constituted a 'community leader', for example the wives of politicians were featured extensively in this period and also retired political leaders. We classified the former as 'community' and the latter as 'political'.

8. Perceptions of Leadership[1]

Keith Dowding

Introduction

There is a massive literature on leadership and leadership qualities (for some reviews see Grint 2000; Porter and McLoughlin 2006; Hunter *et al.* 2007; Mumford *et al.* 2008). Much of this literature concerns leadership in private sector organisations, but a great deal also concerns leadership in politics (Peele 2005; Morrel and Hartley 2006). There can be no doubt that personal psychological characteristics help some people to become leaders, and such characteristics can also help determine which leaders come to be seen as good or bad, strong or weak, progressive or regressive, and so on (Hogan and Kaiser 2005). Most accounts of leadership in the literature concentrate upon these qualities in the leader herself. It has frequently been remarked that accounts of good leadership often resemble a checklist of good qualities. As has also been noted, these lists are not always consistent and are sometimes contradictory. The reason, of course, is that qualities useful in some circumstances ('a good leader will show willingness to take a risk') might prove disastrous in other circumstances ('a good leader will be cautious where conditions dictate' (Boin *et al.* 2005: ch. 1)). Furthermore, whether a given risk was justified, or whether caution is later seen as the best course of action, is judged in retrospect, and so, is often not helpful as advice to a prospective leader.

It cannot be denied, of course, that personal qualities make up good leadership, though there can also be little doubt that structural or institutional features will also help select among those psychological factors who will get the top and succeed in different countries. What helps make a US President, might not be the same qualities that can enable someone to lead an Australian political party or succeed in the parliamentary arena. To succeed in the Australian Parliament a politician must be able to deal with the daily rough-and-tumble of parliamentary questions. To be sure, Australian premiers have had many different traits and personalities, but certainly over the last 50 years each, in his own way, was quick witted enough, or able enough to deflect criticisms, to be able to succeed in a parliamentary setting. The requirement for success as US President is somewhat different; Presidents receive much more protection from such hostile environments. The closest are the Presidential debates that candidates have faced, but these rule-bound occasions are very different from the parliamentary setting. Some US Presidents might have been wanting in the Australian context, just as some Australian prime ministers might have been found wanting in the rather different cultural context of a US Presidency. Thus from the outset we can see that whilst psychological attributes must play a role in who succeeds as a leader, it might not be the same psychological attributes in all institutional contexts. This fact demonstrates, at the very least, how important the individual and structural relationship is in any account of leadership.

The idea that both structure and agency are important in social outcomes is widely accepted in social science (Dowding 2008a). In leadership studies this view has been called the 'contingency approach' by Keith Grint (2000). It departs from what has been the dominant mode of analysis in leadership studies, which has tended to concentrate upon personal characteristics or 'traits' and so privileging individual over structure. However, leadership studies seem to be moving towards more contextualised accounts of leadership (Hunter *et al.* 2007; Yammarino and Dansereau 2008), taking into account the types of issues leaders face and the structures within which they operate. Grint identifies 'situational approaches' which draw attention to the fact that leaders emerge in certain types of circumstance and that leadership can be considered a niche that has to be filled. Through this literature there is a definitional issue over whether we see 'leaders' primarily as people who fulfil a role in an organisation or group, or whether the role is given an independent status, such that not all who hold such roles are 'leaders'. In other words, 'leadership' is defined by 'trait'. In this chapter I will assume that 'leader' means the role, but that we can talk of 'good' and 'bad' leaders in terms of their traits and the decisions they make *in the context* in which they make those decisions. I do not offer any objective definition of what constitutes good and bad leadership; there are plenty of claims in the literature (see for example Hogan and Kaiser 2005). Rather I offer some thoughts on how leadership is *perceived* by people and why some might be thought to be 'strong' or 'weak' given their actions in the context in which those actions take place. The argument is that how we view individual traits in terms of leadership characteristics is, in part, dependent upon the context in which those traits emerge. Furthermore, once those traits are perceived by people, including the subject themselves, they further develop as traits. Perceptions of someone as a strong leader can make that person a strong leader or, perhaps more pertinently, once someone is labelled as a weak leader there is little that they can do to lose that reputation or not be a weak leader.

This process occurs for two reasons. Firstly, actions that would have appeared strong if carried out by someone with a reputation for strength will be viewed as the actions of a weak person, perhaps trying to be strong. Secondly, the reactions of others to those actions will depend upon how they view the leader. Someone who is believed to be strong and shouts at a subordinate might lead that subordinate to quail and obey. The shouting leader the subordinate believes is weak might be laughed at, further weakening him. The analysis of strategic interaction through game theory has demonstrated how important reputation can be and the mere fact of a reputation for weakness can create (further) weakness (for example, Binmore 2007: 282-3). The literature on leadership has tended to ignore its interactive and strategic nature and, thus, misses an important aspect of contextual nature of leadership traits. In other words, as noted in other social science contexts (Dowding 2008a) traits and context (individual and structural) are not simply different sides of leadership but deeply implicate and transform each other.

I first explain how leadership qualities might emerge through luck and, then, informally model how patterns of relationships can lead observers to perceive some leaders as weak and others strong. It is through those external perceptions that the lead subject and those with whom they interact can believe those perceptions such that weakness and strength are realities.

Strength through luck

I first argue that a person's relative strength might occur through luck. I am not making the obvious point that, in retrospect, who we judge as a strong leader could be determined by luck. For example, two people in identical situations make the same risky decision: for one it pay off but for the other it fails and we judge (somewhat unfairly) that the one who was lucky is strong and the one who was unlucky is not. In other words, I am not making Napoleon's point that he preferred his generals to be lucky. Rather, I wish to suggest that the *actual* strength or determination of someone might occur through luck.[2]

Let us be clear. It might well be that there are individual traits that emerge in behaviour that are genetically determined. There might be a gene for 'determination', or 'stubbornness' or 'collegiality' such that those who have that gene are more likely to display the behavioural characteristics of determination, stubbornness, or collegiality. However, all geneticists are aware that 'genes for' some characteristics only get switched on in some environments. Not all who have the gene will display those behavioural characteristics, and those without the gene might display some of them. In other words, in context, those with the gene are more likely to display those behavioural qualities. My argument does not depend upon such an account of 'genes for' emerging in context. My argument can assume that two people with regard to any 'gene' for, say, determination, are identical. But for one, through sheer luck, the behavioural trait emerges, and so the person is at first 'perceived' to be more determined (though by other measures is no more so), but then, because of that perception, actually does become more determined (by those other measures). This is the luck through which leadership qualities might emerge. I will explain that possible emergence through a sporting analogy.

What is viewed as 'luck' depends upon the identification of a pattern associated with a reward (Dowding 2008b). Given a set of rewards (in a sporting contest, in a lottery, in the 'leadership stakes') luck is determined. If the winner of a lottery is lucky to have won, then we note that where there are lotteries there always will be *someone* who is lucky. Or with a nod to Napoleon, there will always be lucky generals. To the extent that life is a series of lotteries — that is, there are winners and losers — then there will always be some who are luckier than others. It might be responded that winners and losers are determined by their traits, but my argument here is that the emergence of traits also has an element of luck.

Imagine a simple Bournelli trial of coin tosses. In each trial we have a pattern of outcomes with probability p (success) and $1 - p$ (failure). What patterns do we describe as good/bad luck and what do we describe as 'to be expected'? For each trial we know the probability of heads is 0.5 and for tails is 0.5. Let us concentrate upon the probability of getting heads as success. Each time the coin comes down heads, we see this as success. If the coin comes down heads on a trial we can see this as good luck. Sometimes winning the toss can be very important to an outcome. In cricket, winning the toss can, at times, virtually decide the outcome of the match. But in any coin toss, with a fair coin, coming down heads has a probability of 0.5. We can see that how much luck we assign to any given coin toss is determined by the reward. Tossing a coin in a laboratory, to say, generate a random set of outcomes, involves no luck. Tossing the coin to see who gets the million dollars does.

Now consider a sequence of tosses. If we toss the coin 100 times, there will be sequences where it comes down heads more often than 50% of the time. Sequence 9-18 might have four heads; sequence 33-43 nine. Both *sequences* are expected in the sense that we can assign the same probability to each sequence. But if we are betting on the coin coming down heads, the second sequence is luckier than the first. But how much luck do we assign to each sequence? That depends on the bet. However, what if someone continually tossed heads 'more than expected' when they bet on it? At what point would we decide they had some skill in determining when the coin comes down heads?

We might need to use evidence independent of the result. The 'way' the person tosses the coin. Do they note whether the head or tail is on top before tossing, the flick of the thumb, the way they catch and so on. We have theories about 'looking right' in sport — the stroke of the golf player, the stance and movement of the cricketer when batting. In leadership terms certain types of behaviour are thought to correlate with good leadership, broadly those associated with competency (McClelland 1973). I will consider these as what I will call *temperament*. In sport, temperament both enables us to get down and work hard at training, and also affects the outcome of matches. Some players are thought to have the 'big match temperament' whilst others are seen as 'chokers' who play well but do not win as much and all-too-often lose the big games. Sometimes the player who appears less skilful wins because she seems to have the 'big match temperament'. She may be beaten more often than not by her opponent, until it comes to the big tournaments and then she seems to always prevail. We might think this 'big match temperament' is a type of skill. We might hope to find some material manifestation of this skill independently of the results one achieves due to it. For example, we might think it appears in some DNA sequence. However, given what we know about the manner in which genes are switched on and off by environmental conditions, this is likely to be a forlorn hope since the big match temperament is likely to be highly path dependent.

Greg Norman was a choker, but when did he become so? After Jack Niklaus' charge at the 1986 Masters; the following year after Larry Mize's lucky chip? Or was it during one of the playoffs at the other three grand slams? He was a choker for sure in final round at the Masters in 1996. What we might see in Norman's Grand Slam history is an outcome space that is typically patterned into different subsets and that Niklaus and Mize beat Norman, but the fact that the pattern matters to him affects his play in future final rounds which then alters future patterns of the outcome space. Future patterning would have its own luck without the past patterning affecting today's play. But players' behaviour has been altered by their perception of the past patterning. The patterning of a subspace of sequences of coin tosses gains significance depending upon what was riding on each sequence. Similar sequencing has occurred for Norman, but with the added difference that previous sequencing (by supposition caused through luck) has affected subsequent sequencing. Norman's choking traits were in part caused by luck.

Perceptions of leadership

The sporting analogy demonstrates how genuine traits might emerge through luck. Certain leadership traits are genuine — some people have them and others do not — but those traits might emerge through luck. They emerge because of the outcomes caused by certain decisions; how others viewed those outcomes; and how the leader subsequently made new decisions; and, how others responded to those decisions. I now want to give a very simple spatial analogy that suggests that perceptions of leadership quality might be determined by context.[3]

Imagine the lines in Figure 8.1 below represent some issue-dimension, left-right, or hawk-dove or similar. But the issue crosses the legitimate boundary of two different departments. We have three players: one minister from Department A, one from Department B, and the Premier (P). Their non-strategic (or 'naïve') preferred policy (their 'bliss point') is marked on the dimension. Cabinet government implies that there will be discussion across departments needing some bargain between the two. Furthermore, imagine, due to her greater institutional power, the leader can force her own bliss point, and does so. Our question is how do we view the leader in each situation?

Figure 8.1 Spatial Representation of Leader Reputation

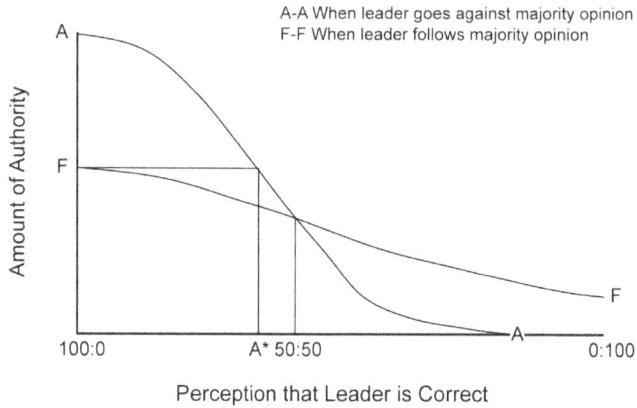

A-A When leader goes against majority opinion
F-F When leader follows majority opinion

A

Amount of Authority

F

F

A

100:0   A* 50:50   0:100

Perception that Leader is Correct

In 1(a) the leader gets her way (by assumption) and it is seen that this is so despite her being an outlier from her cabinet colleagues. She is determined and pushes her view. In 1(b) she is seen as concessionary since she forces policy through as a compromise between the two ministers. Indeed, if A and B were equal in power, this might well be the bargained compromise. We can note that, as drawn, the Prime Minster's bliss point has not changed, only the position of minister B. We can imagine that the qualities (personal characteristics of the Premier) are identical in each situation, although our views of those characteristics may vary, according to the situation. If the 'leadership prize' is 'dominance', then the Premier 1(a) is lucky. If 'getting what you want with least effort' is the prize, then the Premier 1(b) is lucky.

Of course, real life is more complex. We might know the bliss points prior to the situation arising, which might affect our judgement. Players have strategic as well as naïve preferences. Player A might pretend to be at the Premier bliss point in 1(a) hoping that the Premier would not want to be seen to favour A too much and so shift policy slightly towards B (and A's bliss point). The Premier might be very careful not to reveal her true preferences until very late in the game, and so on. But I want to make a very simple point. In the UK, Margaret Thatcher and Tony Blair have both been seen to have been strong British Premiers, and they were. But they also shared the feature that in their own cabinets they were preference outliers, both being further to the right than the median figure in their cabinets. John Major was perceived to be a weak leader, and he was, but he was also a median voter. He was perceived to be concessionary, giving way to one side on some issues, and the other side on others, and sometimes making compromises. But I would suggest he, just as often as Blair and Thatcher, forced his true bliss point.

If it is true that Thatcher, Major and Blair got what they wanted approximately equally as often, why do I also say that Thatcher and Blair were both strong leaders and Major a weak one, rather than claiming that is only our perception, and not the fact? I do so precisely because of the inter-activeness (and so 'path dependency') of perception and reality. Because Thatcher and Blair were seen to be strong leaders they were able to be so. Because Major was perceived to be weak, even when he forced the issues, which he did repeatedly, he was seen to be doing so from a weak position. And in each case their cabinet colleagues responded accordingly. Thatcher was not perceived as a strong leader in the first two years of her leadership (strident perhaps, not strong). Not concessionary certainly, but she was perceived as weak. She did not get her way on industrial relations, on Ireland, or on other matters.[4]

Success and strong leadership

Until the Falklands War, Margaret Thatcher was not seen as a strong leader. She was forced to concede in various areas of policy and whilst she held firm on the economy, the recession and mass unemployment her government seemed to do little to resolve did not make her seem a great leader. In her decision to send troops to win back the Falkland Islands she took a risk (against elite opinion) and it came off. She was seen to be a leader with authority. Furthermore, in retrospect economic decisions taken then have been viewed in a much better light by economists and public opinion. She was seen to be strong partly because she went against elite and public opinion and *has been viewed* as being right (whether or not she was 'really' correct is irrelevant to my argument). If you wish to be viewed as a great leader it is not enough to be thought to have done the right thing, but to have done the right thing against the odds of public opinion. I hypothesise, therefore, that how 'great', 'strong', or 'authoritative' we judge public leaders is based upon the relationship between their views and that of 'society' (say the majority or median voter); and *how often the leader was perceived to be right* (and since perceptions might vary, how strong a leader is viewed at time t_1 might change when t_1 is viewed at time t_2 — as indeed in retrospect has Thatcher's leadership qualities in her first two years). I illustrate this point in Figure 8.2.

Figure 8.2 Authority of Leader

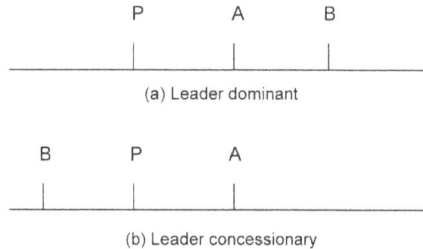

(a) Leader dominant

(b) Leader concessionary

The idea is that a leader who, let us say, is viewed as choosing correctly, but follows the median voter's views, is only given credit for following the median voter. The leader who is viewed as choosing correctly, against the wishes of the majority, is given extra credit, not only for being right, but being right against the odds. The leader who chooses wrongly but follows the median voter is perceived as weak. The leader who chooses wrongly against the prevailing opinion, is perceived as disastrous. She chose against the odds and lost.[5]

In Figure 2 we have a stylised picture of such a claim. I have suggested that when the perception that the leader is correct is about even, then both the leader following public opinion (represented by F-F) and the leader who opposes majority opinion (A-A) have the same authority. I have no evidence of that, but if the shapes of the 'authority curves' A-A and F-F are roughly correct, the figure illustrates the claim that with only a slight increase in the perception of the probability that the leader is correct, the leader who chooses against public opinion is given much greater authority.

Going wrong

Strong leaders often fall spectacularly: Thatcher is one example, John Howard another. Why does this happen? There are no easy answers, but the analysis here suggests one cause. Leaders can come to believe the perceptions – the myths of themselves – too readily and perhaps forget the important coalitions that were forged that helped make them appear strong. (Reading the autobiographies of former ministers in Thatcher's government, it appears that virtually all them invented the privatisation program. What this might show, is that there was a broad coalition in favour, no matter who actually *first* proposed *which* privatisations.) Specifically because they made tough decisions against majority decision that were later viewed as correct, they think that same trick can always be played. But it is the nature of risk that the odds are against you always winning. Arguably the Poll Tax did for Thatcher, Iraq did for Blair and WorkChoices did for Howard.

Conclusions

I have argued that we cannot understand leadership by looking at the qualities of any given leader, nor indeed all leaders outside of: (i) the issues they faced; (ii) whether the decisions they made were in line with what (a) elite opinion, and (b) public opinion thought correct; (iii) and how far, given the stochastic nature of the outcomes of public policy-making, those decisions were seen to be correct. Underlying all these judgements is luck. Luck that a leader is perceived in a given way given everything in (i-iii) and, secondly, how those perceptions caused the leader to view their own leadership credentials and, thus, make decisions in the future given everything in (i-iii), and so on. Leadership qualities and environment continually interact, and who becomes recognised as a great public leader depends as much upon the elements of luck I have identified as any potential leadership qualities they enjoy. Nothing in this analysis, however, denies that those perceived as great leaders actually were great, or that those who are perceived to be weak, actually were weak.

References

Binmore, K., 2007, *Playing for Real: A Text on Game Theory*, Oxford: Oxford University Press.

Boin, A., P. 't Hart, Stern, E. and B. Sundelius, 2005, *The Politics of Crisis Management: Public Leadership under Pressure*, Cambridge: Cambridge University Press.

Dowding, K., 2008a, 'Agency and Structure: Interpreting Power Relationships', *Journal of Power*, 1, pp. 21-36.

Dowding, K., 2008b, 'Luck and Responsibility', *Critical Review of International Social and Political Philosophy*, 11.

Dunleavy, P., 2007, *Leaders and Decision Delegates: A Rational Actor Approach*, unpublished manuscript, London School of Economics and Political Science.

Grint, K., 2000, *The Arts of Leadership*, Oxford: Oxford University Press.

Hogan, R. and R. B. Kaiser, 2005, 'What We Know About Leadership', *Review of General Psychology*, 9, pp. 169-80.

Hunter, S. T., K. E. Bedell-Avers and M. D. Mumford, 2007, 'The Typical Leadership Study: Assumptions, Implications and Potential Remedies', *Leadership Quarterly*, 18, pp. 435-46.

McClelland, D. C., 1973, 'Testing for Competence rather than Intelligence', *American Psychologist*, 28, pp. 1-14.

Morrell, K. and J. Hartley, 2006, 'A Model of Political Leadership', *Human Relations*, 59, pp. 483-504.

Mumford, M. D., A. L. Antes, J. J. Caughron and T. L. Friedrich, 2008, 'Charismatic, Ideological and Pragmatic Leadership: Multi-Level Influences on Emergence and Performance', *Leadership Quarterly*, 19, pp. 144-60.

Peele, G., 2005, 'Leadership and Politics: A Case for a Closer Relationship', *Leadership*, 1, pp. 187-204.

Porter, L. W. and G. B. McLoughlin, 2006, 'Leadership and the Organizational Context: Like the Weather?', *Leadership Quarterly*, 17, pp. 559-76.

Yammarino, F. J. and F. Dansereau, 2008, 'Multi-Level Nature of and Multi Level Approaches to Leadership', *Leadership Quarterly*, 19, pp. 135-41.

ENDNOTES

[1] I would like to thank participants at the 'Public Leadership in Australia and Beyond' conference, 29-30 November, 2007 at ANU for comments and Paul 't Hart for his written comments on the original memo contribution.

[2] The following six paragraphs are based on Dowding (2008b) though I use the example for a different purpose here.

[3] Dunleavy (2007) uses more complex spatial analyses in his account of leadership though in a very different way from that suggested here.

[4] Though in retrospect, tactically she got it right by getting her men into key economic roles, and that can be seen as a key leadership trait based on analysis rather than any form of luck or perception.

[5] The stochastic nature of most policy decisions means that 'getting it right' is often hard to judge. Therefore we often make judgements about people, and their leadership qualities based on issues where it is easy to judge. Thatcher won the Falklands war. Did she win education policy? Or civil service reform? Or even economic policy? These are much harder to judge. Lesson for leaders, win some easy-to-judge decisions against prevailing opinion. (Opinion in the UK was split over whether to fight or negotiate over the Falklands, but certainly prevailing elite opinion was to negotiate.)

9. History, Biography and Leadership: Grasping Public Lives

Barry Gustafson

Do leaders make a difference?

Historians have always been fascinated by leaders. Throughout recorded history, kings, generals, philosophers, prophets, dictators, presidents, prime ministers and captains of industry have been highlighted in accounts of public events. As one contemporary writer on leadership theory has suggested, 'From its infancy, the study of history has been the study of leaders — what they did and why they did it' (Bass 2007: 3).

One question that has persisted is the extent to which, on the one hand, an individual can create history compared to the extent to which, on the other hand, any individual, even a leader, is merely the product or prisoner of historical circumstances. Do leaders make history or does history make leaders? Certainly, some who became recognised as leaders owed much to the luck of being in the right place at the right time and responding successfully to a situation they had not initiated, while others on whom fortune did not smile faded from sight and never realised their potential (see Dowding, this volume).

Sidney Hook suggested some 60 years ago that individuals could make history but only when they had clear purposes and only when subject to a complex of conditions leading to 'a plausible balance' or even a symbiosis between the roles played by a leader and his or her context and culture. He concluded that 'if the great man had *not* existed the course of events in essential respects would in all likelihood have taken a *different* turn' (Hook 1945: 10 and 84).

Other historians, while recognising structural, situational and broader and more varied personal constellations at work, have also emphasised the causal role of great leaders in determining the politics of nations, economic and social changes within them, and wars and diplomacy among them. They assert that individual leaders made and still do make a difference, stressing what Peter Clarke has referred to as 'the crucial role of the individual in an appropriate historical context' (Clarke 1991: 7). As one historian has accurately suggested: 'The study of political leadership must acknowledge the interaction between the leader's resources, such as personal skills and political opportunities, and the constraints imposed by social, economic and political systems and historical circumstances' (Moon 1999: 81). Or as a political scientist has pointed out: 'Political leaders operate as wild cards between the realm of ideas and the material conditions which surround them' (Johannson 2004: 3).

The British historian Arnold Toynbee, in his 12-volume *A Study of History,* written between 1934 and 1961, suggested that there were broad general changes in history, specifically the rise and fall of civilisations and cultures, based to a large extent on religion, an approach that was not well regarded by most other historians of his generation, though the 'clash of civilisations' theory has been recently and also controversially revived by the American international relations specialist Samuel P. Huntington (1996). But Toynbee added that the rise or the fall was determined at least partly by the success or failure of leadership and the wise or unwise decisions leaders made and, in a discussion on leadership with the Japanese Buddhist leader and peace activist Daisaku Ikeda, suggested that 'personal leadership is needed for every collective enterprise of any kind, even for enterprises that are organised on the most democratic lines possible' (Toynbee 1976). Democratic leadership was 'a more delicate and difficult task than charismatic, dictatorial leadership', which often depended on coercion or emotionally exciting one's followers. The democratic leader had to steer a middle course between the populist pandering 'to the wishes of his constituents, even when he judges their wishes to be misguided', and tricking 'his constituents into voting for a policy that he judges to be right but that they would have rejected if it had been put to them candidly' (Toynbee 1976: 207).

Toynbee, incidentally, warned that the end did not justify the means and that leaders who follow such a course might reach ends quite different to what they intended. Robespierre and Lenin, for example, might have sincerely wanted what was best for most French or Russians but 'made the mistake (an ethical mistake as well as an intellectual one) of thinking that their aims were so good and the attainment of those aims was so important that violence was a justifiable means. Consequently, instead of creating earthly paradises, Robespierre produced the Terror and Lenin a totalitarian regime' (Toynbee 1976: 212). Hook also cautioned that in a democracy, because of the principle of majority rule, even when mistaken, people must be 'eternally on guard' against the heroic leader – 'an event-making individual who redirects the course of history' by choosing to impose his will against the wishes of the majority (Hook 1945: 157).

In recent years the role of leadership in history has been much more widely and radically questioned. It has been argued increasingly that, while leaders might well 'initiate action and play central roles' in a group's decision making, their followers and subsequent historians often incorrectly 'attribute effects that are due to historical, economic or social forces to leadership' As a result, although 'outcomes are determined primarily by other factors' the 'leaders are credited with what happens after the fact' (Evans 1997: 7 and 9). Certainly, society is always changing, if only by the process of birth and death. Generational, technological and attitudinal changes occur over time to a large extent irrespective of public leadership and, although the timing, pace and even direction of the change can certainly be affected by leadership, as I have noted elsewhere, that change may be inevitable not optional, organic not mimetic, complex not simple, and spontaneous not planned (Gustafson 2007: 143). For a fuller discussion of social and political transformation see Gustafson (1976).

Leaders, however, do have a significant impact on their own lives, their environment and on history. They may tend to merge into the organic life of their nation or organisation and certainly factors outside their control do provide both opportunities and impose limitations. Although context plays a key role, leaders should not be simply regarded as passive irrelevancies in a detailed analysis of context or buried in some collective mass. While they differ greatly, leaders can make a difference and can even substantially alter outcomes by the way they react to, facilitate or impede organisational, environmental and collective factors over which they may have only limited control and by which they may, in fact, be highly constrained. Evans is correct when he observes that, 'In the end, no one has managed to better Marx's dictum that people make their own history, but they do not do it under circumstances of their own choosing. It is precisely the interaction between the individual and his or her circumstances that makes the study of people in the past so fascinating' (Evans 1997: 189-90).

Understanding leaders: a biographical perspective

Biography or autobiography allows an individual to emerge more clearly from the context and be considered in much greater detail than he or she can be in general history. Many good biographies are intrinsically interesting and straightforward narratives that eschew generalised theory or sophisticated analysis and seek simply to recreate and evaluate, without necessarily judging, a person's life as accurately and fairly as possible. As Barbara Kellerman and Scott Webster believe, 'a well-told life story is leadership literature at its best. A good life history necessarily touches on a range of players, including, inevitably, followers, and it is embedded in context. So, in addition to being good yarns, first-rate biographies or autobiographies instruct' (Kellerman and Webster 2001: 490). Many such works, written when the subject is still alive or only recently deceased, may well provide sources for later more definitive studies that can draw on information, particularly documents and more candid interviews, not initially available.

A biographer, writing with the advantage of hindsight, must recognise that diverse sources may reflect subjective, value-laden perspectives, vested interests and even retrospective judgements and reinterpretations that do not reflect views held at the time. Despite extensive research, there may also be considerable gaps in knowledge of a leader's life, motives and relationships; gaps which either leave question marks or encourage contestable speculation on the author's part. As the New Zealand historian and biographer Keith Sinclair concluded, 'a biographer tries to tell the truth; to ensure that his facts are facts. But no biographer can tell the *whole* truth. There is a very real sense in which the biographer is inventing his subject. The writer decides what to put in and what to leave out' (Sinclair 1985: 36).

Another perennial question is whether leaders are born or bred, whether genetics or socialisation is the determining factor. Good biographies need to be more than just accounts of milestones in people's lives and their achievements and failures, virtues and vices, skills and relationships. As a result, many biographies study carefully a subject's early life and socialisation as the basis of an adult leader's personality, character, motivation, perceptions, values, and leadership style. They try to get inside the subject's mind and heart and assess that person's private life even though it can be argued that a biographer can never completely grasp or penetrate the inner reality of another person's life.

Leaders usually have intelligence, determination and energy but these are qualities shared by many others. The distinguishing marks of a successful leader are a compulsive, sometimes obsessive ambition and personal desire to lead, coupled with the luck of being in the right place at the right time and the decisiveness to take the risk and seize the opportunity. A powerful leader is one who, by the strength of personality, self-confidence, drive, ideas, knowledge and competence, inspires and mobilises others and influences the decisions and direction of an organisation in order to achieve results the leader desires. Gaining, exercising and retaining power is demanding and exhausting work and requires focus, a capacity to keep learning, adaptability and survival. To be able to do all that requires physical, mental and emotional strength, energy, perseverance, on occasion ruthlessness, and not a little luck. Power is achieved and maintained one transaction at a time and demands continuous success if it is not to be challenged.

There is always an element of psychopathology in leadership. As Hook has suggested, political leadership is

> a full-time activity. In political struggle, therefore, the integrated individual, who has a plurality of interests, which he [or she] is loathe to sacrifice on the sullied altars of politics, is always at a disadvantage. So is the sensitive and high-minded idealist who shrinks from the awful responsibility of deciding, quite literally, other people's lives, and from the moral compromises and occasional ruthlessness required even by statesmanship of the highest order (Hook 1945: 24).

Grasping leadership: types and styles

It is in trying to understand and explain all this that various comparative and theoretical approaches to public leadership are helpful. Bass has pointed out that, 'In modern psychology there is still a search for generalisations about leadership, built on the in-depth analysis of the development, motivation and competence of world leaders, living and dead'. Thus, one can look at the work of earlier writers such as Plato, with his model of the philosopher king, educated to rule with order and reason, and Machiavelli, whose prince was the ultimate pragmatist (Bass 2007: 4).

More recently, Margaret Hermann and others have argued that there are various categories of leadership: crusaders versus pragmatists; ideologues versus opportunists; directive versus consultative; task-oriented versus relations-oriented; transformational versus transactional (Hermann, Korany and Shaw 2001: 87 and 93). They suggest that the major distinction is between those, on the one hand, who are guided by ideals and ideas and who seek to effect change and those, on the other, who are more flexible and sensitive to the political context, respectful of constraints and relationships and who are less likely to engage in conflict.

Such a dichotomy is found also in James MacGregor Burns' division of leaders into 'moral transformational' and 'pragmatic transactional' (Burns 1978). All three biographies of New Zealand prime ministers that I have written (Gustafson 1986; 2000; 2007) drew, albeit not too ostentatiously, on Burns' presidential leadership theory. Michael Joseph Savage, I argued, was a transformational politician, Robert Muldoon and Keith Holyoake much more transactional. I cautioned, however, as do other writers, that in a democracy a successful transformational leader almost invariably is also a successful transactional one (See also, for example, Johansson 2005: 246). As Clarke has noted, 'If leadership is partly a question of vision about the direction in which policy ought to be developed it is also a matter of projecting electoral appeal and putting together a winning coalition of effective support' (Clarke 1991: 3). All three leaders believed that true leadership involved going with one's instincts, not just with one's informed intellect. They all accepted that leaders like themselves recognise, meet, manipulate and mobilise but do not initially create collective forces of social change or voter discontent or aspiration. They all sought to balance their ability to absorb, understand and utilise knowledge with their intuitive common sense and feel for public opinion. As leaders it was essential to understand people as well as policies and processes. As a result they tended towards populism and were anti-elitist. All were adept at using rhetoric, bargaining and manipulation. They were not averse to change, and in Savage's case avidly welcomed it, but all three valued security and stability and tried to minimise the radical upheaval of people's lives, although in Muldoon's case it can be argued that the means used proved counter-productive to the end sought.

The transformational model is also very similar to Erwin Hargrove's character analysis of the US president Jimmy Carter as a clear example of 'a policy politician: an elected politician who concentrates on policy work and who makes the achievement of good policy his main goal … his forte is issue leadership rather than the leadership of institutions or organisations' (Hargrove 1988: xix;

see also Hargrove and Nelson 1984; Hargrove 1998). Such a politician does 'what he thinks is right, whether it is popular or not' and may not last long in office as a result. One problem with such leaders is that they may be all substance and no style in contrast to more charismatic and symbolic leaders who may be all style and offer little, if any, substance but are more attractive to the electorate. Johanssen, has recently considered two former New Zealand prime ministers, Muldoon and David Lange, through the theoretical insights provided by Hargrove and another American political psychologist, Stanley Renshon, who also concluded that the different character, style and performance of US presidents have resulted in significant differences to the policy process and to the history of that nation (See Renshon 1996; Johansson 2005).

Other contemporary theoretical approaches to leadership have been based on studies of United States presidents: for example, the psychological approach, used by James Barber (1972); the institutional approach exemplified by Clinton Rossiter (1960); the power model approach of Richard Neustadt (1980); or Fred Greenstein's (1969) proposition that in unstable environments a leader's positions and skills could significantly determine the nature of outcomes. Barber's theories have been applied systematically over the past thirty years to New Zealand politicians by John Henderson, a political scientist and onetime head of the Prime Minister's Department (For example, Henderson 1978; 1980a; 1980b; 2006; Henderson and Gomibuchi 2006) and I also used Barber's typology to consider whether Muldoon was an active or passive, a positive or negative personality, leaning towards categorising him as active-negative (Gustafson 2000: 10-11).

One other particularly interesting theory is Aaron Wildavsky's suggestion that both leaders and citizens are guided and constrained by three competing cultural positions: individualism, which resists central authority and seeks equality of opportunity and the promotion of individual differences; hierarchy, which tends towards central authority and conservatism; and egalitarianism, which also resists central authority but seeks more equal outcomes and the diminishing of differences among people. Leadership, he suggests, derives its basic character from which of these it chooses to follow (Wildavsky and Ellis 1989: viii, 5 and 224 ff).

Are 'true' leaders necessarily radicals?

It can be contended that not all prominent public figures are 'leaders' and that those prominent in public office divide into moral, transformational *leaders;* pragmatic, transactional *managers;* and immoral, dictatorial *power-wielders.* Only the first of those three – who wish to inspire change, lead followers in a new direction and turn visions into reality – are true leaders.

Kellerman and Webster, for example, state categorically that 'we define "leader" as one who creates or strives to create change, large or small ... we consider leadership as a process — a dynamic process in which the leader(s) and followers interact in such a way as to generate change' (Kellerman and Webster 2001: 487; see also Kellerman 1984). And two other Americans repeatedly assert, the 'best' leaders make a difference because they challenge the process, inspire a shared vision, enable others to act, model the way, and encourage the heart (Kouzes and Possner 1995). Such definitions clearly favour radical leaders seeking systemic change and diminish the standing of more conservative leaders. Indeed, conservatives it is assumed, by their very resistance to radical change, are not really leaders but are instead good managers because, as John P. Kotter has suggested, 'Management is about coping with complexity … Good management brings a degree of order and consistency [but] … Leadership, by contrast, is about coping with change' as well as generating, inspiring and motivating a desire for that change among others (Kotter 2007: 24).

Many leaders do aspire to, inspire, and even effect significant change, but one cannot dismiss, as many writers do, 'conservative leadership' as an oxymoron (see Errington, this volume). Many pragmatic conservative leaders are not opposed to all change but believe it should be cautious and incremental and should follow a consensus and mandate that legitimises reform. They dislike change imposed against the will of the majority of the people by those they view as a dogmatic radical elite which regards itself as a meritocratic and paternalistic vanguard. Conservative leaders can leave significant marks when, as Clarke, has noted, 'their own outlook and gifts chimed in with the contemporary mood, anticipating rather than simply echoing it, because they were able literally to speak to the concerns of the people' (Clarke 1991: 2).

Leadership as co-production

Of course, one needs also to recognise that, while some leaders are more visible, more radical, more powerful and more efficacious than others, they do not act in isolation in either determining or implementing their policies. The most prominent in the halls and corridors of power are very much in the public eye and, today, projected by the media. But in an effort to get things done and objectives achieved they constantly interact with others, many of whom have always operated less openly in influencing the public policy agenda and determining outcomes. Leadership is about making choices and a good leader may not even personally initiate ideas for change but does recognise one when he hears it from a lieutenant, official adviser, lobbyist or even opponent. Hermann has observed that policy-making is usually the result of dynamic and often dialectic interaction among a powerful leader, a single dominant group, and various autonomous actors (Hermann 2001: 47). And Robert Dilenschneider reminded his readers that if a leader's 'power is the ability to get things done, it must usually — though not exclusively — be done through others … nearly all powerful people surround themselves with a formal or informal network which enables them to exert power' (Dilenschneider 1994: 2-3).

Recognising the complicity of others does not diminish the impact of leadership but it does acknowledge that although a president or prime minister may be the most influential person in a party or state, he or she is not solely responsible for either successes or failures. In a sense, power is conferred by allies and followers. Leaders in power, of course, have enhanced opportunities to control information and agendas, allocate resources, cultivate and reward allies and subordinates, sideline or punish critics and rivals, appeal directly to followers, build their formal authority and personal reputation, advance their own goals and programs, and thwart alternatives. But, as numerous historians and biographers have recorded, if power becomes too invested in a single public leader and that person's insight, judgement or communication skills begin to fail, then the government or political party he or she leads may well be gravely damaged and the leader's power also diminished, perhaps even fatally. A leader, at any level and in any organisation, who is trusted and whose power is seen to be growing, attracts followers. But when a leader is no longer trusted and when his or her power is perceived to be eroding, so also support dwindles as former supporters distance themselves. Onetime allies and sycophants may even make the embattled or rejected leader a scapegoat for policies and actions they once enthusiastically supported but which have failed or are no longer popular. For most leaders the loss of power is painful, even though nothing is surer than that those who acquire leadership and power will in time lose both in the organic process of continuing transformation.

History, biography and leadership studies: a two-way street

Historians and biographers have traditionally provided much of the material from which others, such as social scientists and more latterly business management specialists, have sought to discern patterns and develop categories of and theoretical generalisations on leadership. The disciplinary insights, however, work both ways. In biography, for example, where a writer seeks more than in a general history to penetrate the inner reality of a subject's life and his or her complex motivation, personality and character, and also seeks to ascertain and evaluate the skills and methods that distinguish the exceptional and successful leader from those less so, one can seek insights from a range of disciplines other than history: from psychology, sociology, political science, public administration, business management, economics, philosophy, or theology. The study of leadership has become, therefore, in recent years an intrinsically complex and disparate multidisciplinary field though, certainly, history and biography will continue to provide many of the case studies on which a more sophisticated interdisciplinary analysis is based.

References

Barber, James D., 1972, *The Presidential Character: Predicting Performance in the White House,* New Jersey: Englewood Cliffs.

Bass, Bernard, 2007, 'Concepts of Leadership', in Robert P. Vecchio (ed.) *Leadership. Understanding the Dynamics of Power and Influence in Organization*s, 2nd edition, Notre Dame: University of Notre Dame Press.

Burns, James MacGregor, 1978, *Leadership,* New York: Harper and Row.

Clarke, Peter, 1991, *A Question of Leadership. From Gladstone to Thatcher,* London: Penguin.

Dilenschneider, Robert, L., 1994, *On Power,* New York: Harper Business.

Evans, Richard, 1997, *In Defence of History,* London: Granta Books.

Greenstein, Fred I., 1969, *Personality and Politics: Problems of Evidence, Inference and Conceptualization*, New York: W. W. Norton.

Gustafson, Barry, 1976, *Social Change and Party Reorganization: The New Zealand Labour Party Since 1945*, London and Beverly Hills: Sage.

Gustafson, Barry, 1986, *From the Cradle to the Grave: A biography of Michael Joseph Savage*, Auckland: Reed Methuen.

Gustafson, Barry, 2000, *His Way: A biography of Robert Muldoon*, Auckland: Auckland University Press.

Gustafson, Barry, 2007, *Kiwi Keith: A biography of Keith Holyoake*, Auckland: Auckland University Press.

Hargrove, Erwin C., 1988, *Jimmy Carter as President: Leadership and the Politics of the Public Good*, Baton Rouge: Louisiana State University Press.

Hargrove, Erwin C., 1998, *The President as Leader: Appealing to the Better Angels in Our Nature*, Kansas: Kansas University Press.

Hargrove, Erwin C. and M. Nelson, 1984, *Presidents, Politics, and Policy*, Baltimore: Johns Hopkins Press.

Henderson, John, 1978, 'The Operational Code of Robert David Muldoon', in S. Levine (ed.) *Politics in New Zealand,* Sydney: Allen and Unwin, pp. 367-82.

Henderson, John, 1980a, 'Muldoon and Kirk: "Active Negative" Prime Ministers', in *Political Science,* 30:2, pp. 111-4.

Henderson, John, 1980b, 'Muldoon and Rowling: A Preliminary Analysis of Contrasting Personalities', *Political Science,* 32:1, pp. 26-46.

Henderson, John, 2006, 'Prime Minister: Personality and Style', in Raymond Miller (ed.) *New Zealand Government and Politics,* Melbourne: Oxford University Press, pp. 217-24.

Henderson, John and Seishi Gomibuchi, 2006, 'The Leadership Styles of Helen Clark and Don Brash', in Raymond Miller and Michael Mintrom (eds) *Political Leadership in New Zealand,* Auckland: Auckland University Press.

Hermann, Margaret G., 2001, 'How Decision Units Shape Foreign Policy: A Theoretical Framework', in *Leaders, Groups and Coalitions: Understanding the People and Processes in Foreign Policy Making,* Special Issue of *International Studies Review, pp.* 47-81.

Hermann, Margaret G., Baghat Korany and Timothy Shaw, 2001, 'Who Leads Matters: The Effects of Powerful Individuals', in M.G. Hermann (ed.), Leaders, Groups and Coalitions: Understanding the People and Processes in Foreign Policy Making, a Special Issue of *International Studies Review*, pp. 83-131.

Hook, Sydney, 1945, *The Hero in History: A Study in Limitation and Possibility*, London: Secker and Warburg.

Huntington, Samuel P., 1996, *The Clash of Civilizations and the Remaking of World Order*, New York: Simon and Schuster.

Johannson, Jon, 2004, 'Leadership in New Zealand', Special Issue of *Political Science.*

Johansson, Jon, 2005, *Two Titans: Muldoon, Lange and Leadership*, Wellington: Dunmore Publishing.

Kellerman, Barbara, 1984, *The Political Presidency: The Practice of Leadership from Kennedy through Reagan,* New York: Oxford University Press.

Kellerman, Barbara, and Scott W. Webster, 2001, 'The recent literature on public leadership reviewed and considered' in *The Leadership Quarterly,* 12, pp. 485-514.

Kotter, John P., 2007, 'What Leaders Really Do', in Robert P. Vecchio (ed) *Leadership: Understanding the Dynamics of Power and Influence in Organizations,* Notre Dame: University of Notre Dame Press, pp. 23-32.

Kouzes, James M., and Barry Z. Possner, 1995, *The Leadership Challenge: How to Keep Getting Extraordinary Things Done in Organizations*, San Francisco: Jossey-Bass Publishers.

Moon, Paul, 1999, *Muldoon: A Study in Public Leadership,* Wellington: Pacific Press.

Neustadt, Richard E., 1980, *Presidential Power: The Politics of Leadership*, New York: Wiley.

Renshon, Stanley, 1996, *The Psychological Assessment of Presidential Candidates*, New York: New York University Press.

Rossiter, Clinton, 1960, *The American Presidency,* New York: Harcourt, Brace and World.

Sinclair, Keith, 1985, 'Political Biography in New Zealand', in Jock Phillips (ed) *Biography in New Zealand,* Wellington: Allen and Unwin and Port Nicholson Press.

Toynbee, Arnold J. and Daisaku Ikeda, 1976, *The Toynbee-Ikeda Dialogue: Man Himself Must Choose,* Tokyo: Kodansha International Ltd, pp. 205-224.

Wildavsky, Aaron and Richard Ellis, 1989, *Dilemmas of Presidential Leadership: From Washington Through Lincoln,* New Brunswick, New Jersey: Transaction Publishers.

PART III

Spheres of Public Leadership Practices

10. The Institutionalisation of Leadership in the Australian Public Service

Catherine Althaus and John Wanna

Introduction

Public sector leadership is aspirational and contextual. It relies on a strange and complicated mix whereby politicians and bureaucrats are both meant to exhibit skills and outcomes emblematic of leaders whilst at the same time ensuring they respectively exercise their own responsibilities and duties without treading on each other's toes. Nevertheless, leadership is often a team or collaborative process where the various players combine their respective competencies to progress desired means or ends.

A traditional 'responsible government' view insists that politicians are the transformational leaders and bureaucrats simply the transactional managers. Administrative leadership according to this perspective is mundane and implementation-focused. Bureaucrats are risk-averse and lack vision; their task is simply to 'take the dreams of politicians and bring them gently to earth' (quoted in Ingraham 2005: 19). Hence, Bailey (2001: 80) insists:

> Between leaders and bureaucrats there is an inevitable dissonance; their styles and their values are discordant. Politicians are visionaries; they are bold, ready to take risks, and eager to venture into the unknown. The bureaucrat's task is to reduce the unknown to the known, to make the political process non-political by making it entirely predictable, so that it has a rule for every contingency and thus eliminates contingencies.

The converse view suggests that the administrative task is much more active and participatory. Bureaucrats contribute vision and policy ideas. In many ways they guide the minister towards certain goals and dominate their political masters by providing the brains behind the scenes.

According to Peter Edwards' (2006: 67) biography of Australian public servant Arthur Tange, by the 1950s and 1960s 'it was generally accepted that permanent heads were major contributors to policy-making'. Tange himself estimated at one point he spent 60% of his time on policy and 40% on administration (Edwards 2006: 67). This dominance of the bureaucrats in the policy making domain was explained by the relative endurance and focus of permanent heads compared to the transient tenure of ministers. Moreover, many ministers were seen to be weak and merely transactional in the federal arena during the 1940s-70s, preferring to rely on their bureaucratic advisers. Occasionally, strong ministers, such as McEwen, used their departmental head as strategic allies in forging a formidable alliance.

Today, however, the attributes and capacities of leadership are more formally articulated and instrumentally nurtured (Althaus and Wanna 2008). An interview survey of Australian Public Service (APS) senior executives showed that leadership is overwhelming viewed as an organisational management task (Althaus 2008). Executives defined leadership as a 'tool' for getting staff and resources to meet the goals and objectives of the organisation of which they had charge to a maximal extent. A typical definition of leadership was 'the capacity to develop goals, set programs to achieve them and encourage others to participate in reaching desired outcomes'. What was still striking from these interviews was that only two participants even mentioned the minister in reflecting on leadership in the public service. Either the relationship was assumed and taken for granted or contemporary public servants are more likely to view leadership as a component of management. Leadership was not a separate attribute (of 'leading') but enmeshed with the managerial aspects of their jobs and continually reconfigured because of the political context in which they worked. Leadership was not understood or discussed as charting or serving the public interest (indeed, the notion of the 'public interest' was mentioned only once), it was instead framed in the language of effectiveness and responsiveness to political imperatives.

This prominence given to the importance of leadership implies that it is now the 'latest big thing' in public sector reform. Rhetoric, at least, suggests that leadership now dominates the public sector agenda. It is a leading 'heading' in annual reports and corporate plans, and agencies report on their progress in this regard; it is a crucial part of the architecture of agency governance (often centred around internal 'boards of management' and executive team meetings); it is a developmental learning skill that ought to be taught to apprenticed executives. Top executives will regularly give speeches on the importance of leadership to public policy and the professional standing of the agency in the service.

The embrace of the discourse of leadership has occurred at the same time as governments have taken seriously the development of leadership skills more widely across the service. The APS has begun to institutionalise the concept of developmental leadership, especially since the inception of the Senior Executive Leadership Capability (SELC) framework in 1999, making it part of its senior executive recruitment, training and promotion framework. Officials undertaking managerial roles can be trained to display better leadership skills, and as a consequence huge investments are now being made in leadership training and development across the service (APSC 2008; Althaus 2008).

This chapter considers this evolving attempt to institutionalise leadership in the APS and reflects upon the various receptions of such endeavours among the target public servant population. It asks: how do changes in ideas about leadership relate to other forces shaping 'life at the top'? What does it matter if dominant conceptions of leadership within the APS shift? And, how has the institutionalisation of leadership been achieved in the APS and what has it achieved?

What this chapter suggests is that we need to take a closer look at the administrative-political interface before rushing to conclusions about the type of public sector leadership we should expect, or the best ways to encourage and improve leadership in practice. We argue that the institutionalisation of administrative leadership in the APS has been a bureaucratically-inspired initiative which, in part, reflects a need to reassert public service independence ('duty') amidst a more contestable world of policy advice and in an environment dominated by political frustrations concerning capacities of responsiveness and innovation in public sector agencies.

Separating indivisibility: from partner adviser to administrative secretary?

Referring to British experience, Kavanagh and Richards (2003) argue that there has been a radical change in the idea of the role to be played by officials in the British political system. The conventional understanding, perhaps best articulated in Lord Haldane's *Report of the Machinery of Government Committee* of 1918, believed that at the heart of the core executive rested a system of *advice* rather than rules. Just as cabinet ministers constitutionally advised the sovereign, so they, in turn, were advised by the senior practitioners of the civil service who were thought of as partners in the task of government. Central to this advisory relationship was the notion that officials-as-advisers maintained an 'indivisible relationship with their political masters' such that there was 'no requirement for the separation of powers between the two' (Kavanagh and Richards 2003: 178).

Kavanagh and Richards propose that British officials have experienced a shift in this 'indivisible relationship' over time, from a relationship of privileged *advice* and *partnership* to one of *assisting* ministers to carry out government policy. Kavanagh and Richards attribute the change in attitude and approach to a growth in bureaucratic power through to the 1970s. In turn, such an exercise of power caused a backlash from ministers who felt public officials were unhelpful and part of the 'governance problem'. During the Thatcher years there was a perception that ministers needed to gain greater political control over bureaucracy. Thatcher's attitudes to the civil service were influenced by her negative perception of the behaviour and attitude of officials. For instance, she was reputedly told by William Armstrong, Head of the Civil Service from 1968-74 that the role of civil servants was to 'manage the decline of Britain in an orderly fashion' — not a point of view she shared (Kavanagh and Richards 2003: 181).

Hence, Thatcher was determined to ensure that civil servants became specifically attentive to serving ministers rather than working to their own ideas of their historical role — or their own take on the public interest. Moreover, if ministers sought to become more proactive in policy making they had to turn to other sources of advice from outside the civil service. The monopoly of bureaucratic power was broken. According to Kavanagh and Richards, other factors contributed to the shift away from a dependency on the civil service, especially the heightened media scrutiny on ministers and expectations they could effect change.

This shift in the nature of relationship between minister and administrative official can also be identified in Australia. Althaus and Wanna (2008) argue that nomenclature change for departmental heads in the APS — from 'permanent head' to 'secretary' and sometimes to 'chief executive' — is an indicator of the shifts in attitude towards the roles of senior officials. The process of dismantling permanency and monopolistic advice was gradual and episodic (see Weller and Wanna 1997, Halligan 2007). Along with the introduction of fixed term contractual employment (or rather, 'letters of offer' with statements of expectations) and performance pay, politicians have used nomenclature to clarify the role expectations for their departmental heads (and, in doing so, for ministers as well). Today's secretaries became unsure how far they could sponsor new agendas or policy initiatives ahead of the government's immediate agenda — believing they were consigned to administering expediency (Wanna interviews 2005).

Such changes can also be discerned from the observations of reflective former long-serving departmental heads. For example, Tony Blunn argued (in Weller 2001: 201) that there has been a radical change in the concept of public service since the time of Fraser through to the Howard era:

> The whole concept of the public service as the partner of the government rather than the servant of the government changed … those reforms said, no, no, the minister is responsible. You didn't hear that the minister being responsible for the management of the department before the Dawkins reform; technically, and legally it was always the case but no one ever mouthed it. Dawkins really placed the responsibility for managing the department with the minister, with the secretary as his principal agent. That was a big shift.

The movement away from an adviser-partnership model to a more technocratic managerialist role is indicative of the type of leadership that is now expected from administrators, at least in the APS. Furthermore, the preferential elevation of the 'generic' mobile executive suggests an emphasis on administrative competence ('neutral competence') rather than policy or technical expertise (although some executives have challenged this orientation — see Henry 2007).

So is 'indivisibility' dead? Although traditionalists often articulate that ministers and departmental heads 'were on the same side' — at least for the life of the government — many public executives today dispute this cosy relationship, sensing they both have different interests and motivations which can conflict. Collaborative leadership between minister and bureaucrat then is highly contingent, it waxes and wanes not only according to the era but also according to personalities and differences or similarities in work practice and style. Many secretaries continue to refer to ministers as 'the Minister' even when speaking one-on-one or in informal settings — insisting on some degree of separation and role distinction. Speaking of his stint with Local Government minister, Tom Uren, Tony Blunn (in Weller 2001: 200) spoke of the uncertainty in relationship that he endured:

> You did not know if he was going to hit you or hug you, and I mean that's hard.

But it is not all down to personality. Collaborative leadership can vary according to the policy at hand and in particular who is, or was, involved in the trajectory the policy has followed to date. Leadership may be divisible or indivisible depending on who claims carriage and ownership of the policy and who disowns it. This can vary according to whether the policy problem is old and inherited or whether it is new and the creation of one of the player's own making (Loverd 1997: 24).

So, present debates over the roles and level of responsiveness of top public officials hints more at changes in the underlying Haldane model rather than at compromised independence or suspicions of politicisation. The subsequent emphasis upon public sector leadership suggests that the new model of technocratic management, contingent on the removal of tenure, has not yet resolved the tensions inherent in the key relationships at the centre of the policy making process.

Service-wide leadership: competition or cooperation?

There is also a wider notion of administrative leadership *across* the public service — a service-wide responsibility to assist and integrate government policy approaches. But how does administrative leadership manifest itself across the service as a whole? There have been competing patterns and expressions of leadership shown in the service in different eras, and vestiges remain to this day. We can think of these competing traditions as ranging from adversarial and pluralistic forms of competition for influence to orchestrated collaboration across and between agencies. Such patterns are significant in defining what administrative leadership means — it is a potent blend of individual careers, institutional power and policy ends.

In the early eras of the APS, Roland Wilson (in Edwards 2006: 83) made it clear to Arthur Tange that it was

> perfectly normal for departments to be as antagonistic to one another as two rival banks competing for market share and political influence. In short, what mattered for public servants was how their department was faring in a constant battle for influence. A truly successful public servant was one who led a department that was at or near the top of an imaginary league table. Standing in this table depended on perceptions of the department's strength and influence, particularly in the eyes of senior ministers and other departmental heads.

Departmental power and inter-agency rivalry, in other words, were the order of the day for earlier versions of the APS. Today, the leadership emphasis is on interdepartmental cooperation and whole-of-government collaboration. Departmental heads and senior executives are meant to operate as a team and to build trust and across-agency networks to facilitate smooth policy making. The APS with its largely graduate intake and generic responsibilities for facilitating and overseeing policies and programs is now far more homogenous than in former times, thereby making the service more amenable to a leadership focus than ever before (Gourley 2007). Competition is more about individual recognition and career progression than policy rivalry or institutional reputation. This is especially so given the move to enterprise bargaining which places the terms and conditions of employment with respective agency 'leaders' rather than with a centralised arbitration system (Henderson 2007).

The past internal rivalry between departments for the ear of government has also become superseded by the ability of ministers to source alternative policy advice from external parties. Nowadays, ministers have an amazing array of advisers ranging from their extensive political advice structures (Tiernan 2007) through to think tanks and direct contact with service providers, as well as sophisticated polling mechanisms that connect them to their constituencies (Stone 1996). The sharing of international experience and best practice as well as policy learning and the wide array of media sources has also heightened ministerial options and discretion. Public officials are no longer the sole purveyors of information or advice. Carving out a niche market in advice relevancy and usefulness is now a distinct aspect to the job of a public official rather than relying on monopoly positions once taken for granted.

The shift is a double-edge sword. Notions of generic administrative leadership have shifted in emphasis away from mere technical proficiency to greater attention to competence, managing to the bottom line, and operational fitness.

At the same time, however, officials are having to become more responsive to the (expedient) policy directives of the government of the day, making it challenging to contribute much in the way of strategy or vision without being seen to be 'interfering' (Gallop 2007). There are other paradoxes. Public officials appear now to pay more attention to interdepartmental cooperation and horizontal alignment. They are meant to work in dynamic partnership with private and non-governmental organisations, to show initiative and take calculated risks to achieve exemplary social outcomes (Shergold 2007; Kane 2007). All this at the same time as they are supposed to be responsive to community demands and have been placed under strict accountability regimes that demand almost excessive process requirements (Shergold 2004). Engaged in such complex intra and extra-governmental relationships, it is not surprising that secretaries find their relationship with ministers can be fraught with less trust.

The changing loci of leadership: top-down or bottom-up?

Leadership in the public sector was traditionally viewed as a top-down process governed by a command-and-control approach where strong individuals dominated through force of personality. According to Kavanagh and Richards (2003: 175-7), both ministers and civil servants operate on the basis of a 'leadership' conceptualisation of elite democracy premised on the core idea that 'government knows best'. Kavanagh and Richards see this as being a particular feature of British government which entrenches executive dominance over the legislature. As they see it, British — and by default Australian — members of the executive have a top-down view of representative democracy which downplays responsiveness to the populace or their participation in the policy process. Instead, the governing elite 'should be capable of taking decisive and necessary, even if unpopular, action' (2003: 177).

But as Broussine (2003) makes clear, this is not the focus that modern approaches to leadership adopt. The contemporary focus is to conceive of leadership as being at the core of what everyone does within an organisation; it is collective and team-based more than individual-reliant. Under the old autocratic model, leaders could expect to solve the problem, announce the decision and get compliance, based on their authority. But public sector leaders today must gain commitment, not just compliance and, therefore, a collaborative style is needed, built from the bottom-up. In the past, administrative leadership capacity and leadership practice was assessed according to perceived 'strength' of the departmental head and the results achieved in the 'departmental league table'. Now, according to the National Institute of Governance Report on Public Service Leadership (2004), public sector leadership capacity must be measured according to how well a government achieves horizontal and vertical alignment to connect policy intent with delivery and integrate organisational goals with performance.

These different approaches towards leadership have led Kavanagh and Richards (2003) to question whether leadership is genuinely being actualised or whether a smokescreen or mirage is occurring. As they see it, 'Ministers and civil servants have been adept at publicly pursuing a strategy of greater openness, inclusivity and flexibility, while privately being able to remain a homogenous elite with a tight hold on political power … British political elites have been successful at ensuring that there is plurality without pluralism in the political system' (2003: 175). Administrative leadership, in other words, may not really have changed at all. For Kavanagh and Richards, until participative policy making is a genuine reality, the call for leadership and the notion of a 'leadership gap' will remain. Continuing to situate the locus of administrative leadership within a top-down framework implies that while the rhetoric of leadership may have changed, the practice has not yet.

Expressing attributes of leadership: codification versus convention?

Competency-based leadership recruitment, promotion, and training are now the order of the day in public services across the globe (Hood and Lodge 2005). In Australia, the SELC framework ensures that senior executives are now selected and assessed on the basis of their abilities to match skills with five core competency criteria derived from public sector experiences. These are:

1. Achieves results;
2. Shapes strategic thinking;
3. Cultivates productive working relationships;
4. Communicates with influence; and
5. Exemplifies personal drive and integrity.

Aspiring public executives must address each of these competency criteria and outline their relevant experience in applications for promotion to the SES — and referees are asked to assess their performance in each category. Many agencies also use the framework to structure their own internal staff development programs and performance appraisal systems.

So, for some jurisdictions, this codification system of leadership provides a useful approach. It establishes a generic framework for the public service against which to nurture and judge leadership potential. It has thus helped focus attention both on the distinctiveness of public sector leadership from its private sector counterparts and on the requirements of agencies and executives to develop leadership attributes in their organisations (Page, Hood and Lodge 2005).

At the end of the day, however, it is worth asking the question of whether leadership needs to be defined and detailed with precision into taxonomic categories and have criteria fastidiously applied? John Uhr (2005: 82) points out that the term 'leadership' is not mentioned in the Australian Constitution. Yet again, neither is the term 'prime minister' nor 'cabinet'. That, according to Uhr, is the fascinating point and, in many ways, the beauty of the leadership concept. It rests on convention, on shared understandings that can shift and develop as times and people change. He prefers the notion of 'matrix leadership' contingent upon players, processes and structures, the public and personal, and the contextual circumstances.

Inevitably, the main problem with public service leadership as an object of study is that it is amorphous and obscure. While we tend to recognise leadership when it is both present and when it is lacking, either way we struggle to articulate exactly what it is. It is not clear whether public leadership is 'smart politics', 'good policy', 'strategic direction', or something 'well administered'. Serendipity and luck can play a big part — the 'right decision at the right time' — which is not something that can be learnt or taught in training programs.

There appear to be different underlying premises espoused by various proponents as to what is meant by public service leadership. Academics tend to conceptualise it in terms of the theory of democratic institutions, framing leadership according to concepts of politics, accountability, and power. Practitioners view it as an administrative responsibility — in organisational terms and part of the management task to which they have been assigned. According to the 'self-help literature' on the topic, organisational leadership is about intrinsic qualities and achieving change through persuasion and example, but also couched within organisational culture. Meanwhile the public tend to view administrative leadership as being in decline — they bemoan the absence of vision, integrity, and hard work on the part of public officials — yesterday's leaders tend to radiate with the passing of time!

It is an obvious but nevertheless important point to recall that leadership can be different things in different times and can be appreciated as different things to different people. Its malleability is simultaneously its usefulness and its bane. Who would not want great public leadership? But who knows exactly what this means? Codifiers can assist here and their criteria gain traction precisely because the bureaucracy adopts them, applies them in practice, and gives them cogency. Attempts to codify administrative leadership usually depend on formulating a number of 'competencies' which are then used extensively to develop training programs and skills development (Lodge and Hood 2005). If such competencies are mandated (or gain authoritative backing) then public servants must meet these criteria if they are to be recruited or promoted to senior ranks (APSC 2008). However, research undertaken on the Senior Executive Service by Althaus (2009) shows that links between leadership training and career progression remain weak. Senior executives themselves do not see a direct correlation between the undertaking of leadership training and promotion to executive positions. At the same time, these same executives *do* support a regime of leadership training although they tend to place greatest value in varied experience, on-the-job training and mentoring over formal training courses taught away from the workplace. As one participant observed: 'you can teach content, but not leadership'.

In many ways, the problem is that today's ordinary public servants, even if only implicitly, are being asked to deploy

> the acute political knowledge and instincts that had once been expected only of mandarins, even as they were admonished to remain strictly apolitical … The new generation of public servants soon learnt by experience the deeply political nature of their enterprise, but few of the extensive training programs they undertook made note of it or gave them the means, understanding of even permission to cope with it … (Kane 2007: 139).

This paradoxical demand for political passivity and responsivity mixed with finely honed appreciation for, and interaction with, the political dimension to policy making can be a volatile cocktail. Whereas the skills for navigating this delicate prudential site once rested within the leadership domain of the mandarins, now it is a widespread exercise given leadership has now been widely institutionalised within public service practice.

Parallel or complementary: the institutionalisation of leadership

These deeper dimensions to the public sector leadership conundrum are perhaps not yet fully appreciated and were hardly intended. Leadership was introduced into the public sector mantra in its most modern form because it was a 'safe agenda'. The concept of leadership is useful because it offers stories of inspiration as well as techniques and a focus on the laudable goals of enhanced ethics, due process, and integrity. When introducing the SELC framework, the APSC was acutely aware of trying to balance the introduction of substance in the leadership criteria at the same time as not wanting to impose too many rules into the system which might stifle recruitment flexibility (Podger 2007).

Many arguments can be found that might explain the rationale behind institutionalisation of the leadership agenda. The public service appropriated the leadership discourse not only because it was 'safe' but also because it found that the management jargon was not enough. The task of public service is not a simple matter of following commands blindly nor is it an endeavour where risk-taking and innovation can be employed at will or without boundaries. The public sector was facing competition in advice, was trying to define and delineate its unique nature from its private sector and NGO counterparts, and was trying to interpret and make sense of what politicians were demanding of it. Institutionalisation of leadership may not have provided the equivalent salaries to the corporate sector but it did offer a way of the public service reasserting itself and coherently reshaping its relevance in the new order of policy making. The concept of public sector leadership allows for public sector distinctions to be identified, it reinstates the notion that there is a sense of public duty to be performed and it gives a sense of professionalisation and meaning to the task of public service.

The drive to place leadership at the apex of the public sector mission (and its training regimes) was not a discourse introduced by politicians. Public servants have avidly embraced the language and appropriated the term. It provides a discourse and a malleable framework through which to understand their changing roles and negotiate changing expectations. Importantly, it also allows public executives to get onto the front foot and become conversant with the 'leader frameworks' of their political masters and private sector counterparts. Public service leaders are necessary (though not sufficient) for the success of political leaders and can be compared with the corporate leadership examples that dominate management texts. The concept of leadership offers a bridge to speak with the professionals in these other domains.

The leadership discourse sat neatly with the competing demands being made of the modern public service and gave public sector work a needed boost of legitimacy that coalesced with other agendas of the time such as the 'creating public value' model of Mark Moore (1995). Whereas the managerialist reforms of the 1980s relegated the public sector to mere imitation of private sector practice, the public value and leadership programs helped swing perceptions the other way, back towards the public sector contributing its own unique professional and technical skills. Leadership could be used to meet the demands of politicians for greater responsiveness from the public service at the same time as enhance the image of the public service task.

Hence, the institutionalisation of public sector leadership made a great deal of sense. It served multiple needs of the public service without causing any major political concerns. The language of leadership could creep seamlessly into the discourse of public service without a tremor. Managers across the public service could give added meaning to their work by becoming public sector leaders.

What we have suggested here, however, is that, in institutionalising leadership, public sector leadership doyens have perhaps introduced a parallel relationship with government rather than a complementary one. In many ways the role of a senior public servant can be likened to an experienced mountain guide. Without the expertise of the guide, the political climber is likely to get lost, hurt themselves, or fail to achieve their objectives while having a poor experience of the adventure. Both the guide and the climber provide leadership but it is of a different nature and both require each other if the goals of the exploration are to be achieved. This symbiotic relationship requires a particular form of cooperation to produce a successful partnership. In their laudable effort to highlight the unique contribution of public servants to the leadership task, proponents of the public sector leadership agenda may have, perhaps unhelpfully, gone off to climb their own mountain leaving their political leaders stranded at base camp.

So, is there a conclusion?

In this chapter we have examined some of the forces moulding the changing concept of administrative leadership in the modern era. Some aspects have changed markedly from former periods, others have remained the same. The significance of the term leadership has become more pronounced in current times but the same dilemmas challenge the executive; the relationship between officials and ministers remains one of complexity yet promise. The contemporary uptake of the leadership mantra might remain in place for some time in order to help practitioners and observers put some words and concepts around the need for greater panache in decision making at the top levels of government. Leadership by itself is not, however, a panacea for the policy making dilemmas facing the executive.

In one sense, it is easy to separate political from administrative leadership and to assume (wrongly) that responsible government provides for these respective leadership functions to be discharged simply and effectively. A raft of public sector leadership training programs now in place across the globe run the risk of embedding this naivety, even as they struggle to convey the complexity of the public sector leadership task.

In trying to establish a particular set of meanings for administrative leadership, modern public servants have perhaps sold themselves short. How accurately can public sector leadership be codified without limiting the understanding of what, exactly, it is that public servants contribute to the policy process? Public servants are not politicians, yet they do not simply carry out what politicians want. Public servants also provide strategic vision, policy expertise and innovative risk-taking flair, but not in isolation. They do so within a relationship with their political masters that cannot be neatly compartmentalised and which can vary from minister to minister and from government to government.

At the end of the day, any definition of administrative leadership runs the risk of being so vacuous that it is meaningless. Putting in place a rigorous leadership framework does not guarantee any change in the substance of leadership practice, and 'good leadership' could indeed potentially be the opposite of the attributes proposed given circumstances. Despite overwhelming support for the usefulness, rigor and rollout of the Integrated Leadership System and the SELC framework, the 2005/06 *State of the Service Report* reiterated the common longstanding view of lower level public servants who tend to rate lowly their supervisors' skills in strategic leadership capacities (Korac-Kakabadse and Korac-Kakabadse 1996; Burgess 2007). Moreover, shifting the mantle of leadership from senior mandarins to almost all public servants — even if the leadership skills are supposed to graduate the higher the level — potentially empties the leadership term of its potency.

What exactly is being sought when people demand public sector leadership? If it is *responsiveness*, then this term should be preferred and that agenda should be scrutinised. If it is *professionalisation* and greater meaning for public service work then using an institutionalised leadership framework can be a risky strategy as it plays into the arms of management gurus and threatens the delicate balance of the public service role.

Has the public sector leadership agenda made life easier for the public servants it affects? We would suggest not. To return to our climbing analogy: perhaps what we need from the public service is not so much greater leadership, but rather more attention be paid to addressing the challenging task of being a 'good guide' as the journey of good government is pursued through the myriad of tracks open to executive government.

References

Althaus, C., 2009, 'The Impact of Leadership Training on APS SES Career Trajectories', in C. Althaus (ed.), *Follow the Leader*, (forthcoming).

Althaus, C. and J. Wanna,, 2008, 'Why Leadership Now?', in C. Althaus (ed.), *Follow the Leader*, (forthcoming).

APSC Australian Public Service Commission, 2008, *Senior Executive Leadership Capability (SELC) Framework*, <http://www.apsc.gov.au/selc/index.html> [last accessed 19 February 2008].

Bailey, F. G., 2001, *Treasons, Stratagems, and Spoils: How Leaders Make Practical Use of Values and Beliefs*, Boulder Colorado: Westview Press.

Burgess, V., 2007, 'Skills and experience lacking', *The Australian Financial Review*, 30 March, p. 78.

Edwards, P., 2006, *Arthur Tange: Last of the Mandarins*, Sydney: Allen & Unwin.

Gallop, G., 2007, 'Towards a New Era of Strategic Government', in J. Wanna (ed.), *A Passion for Policy: Essays in Public Sector Reform*, ANU E Press, pp. 75-89.

Gourley, P., 2007, Interview with authors, Canberra, April.

Halligan, J., 2007, 'Repositioning Australian Public Governance: Three Generations of Management Reform at Commonwealth Level', in G. E. Caiden and T. T. Su (eds), *The Repositioning of Public Governance*, Taipei: Best-Wise Publishing.

Henderson, A., 2007, Interview with authors, Canberra, 29 November.

Ingraham, P. W., 2005, '"You Talking to Me?", Accountability and the Modern Public Service', *PS: Political Science and Politics*, 38:1, pp. 17-21.

Kane, J., 2007, 'The Problem of Politics: Public Governance and Leadership', in R. Koch and J. Dixon (eds), *Public Governance and Leadership: Political and Managerial Problems in Making Public Governance Changes the Driver for Re-Constituting Leadership*, Wiesbaden: Deutscher Universitats-Verlag.

Kavanagh, D. and D. Richards, 2003, 'Prime Ministers, Ministers and Civil Servants in Britain', in M. Dogan (ed.), *Elite Configurations at the Apex of Power*, Leiden: Brill.

Korac-Kakabadse, A. and N. Korac-Kakabadse, 1996, *Leadership in Government: Study of the Australian Public Service*, Canberra: Report for the Public Service and Merit Protection Commission.

Lodge, M. and C. Hood, 2005, 'Symposium Introduction: Competency and Higher Civil Servants', *Public Administration*, 83:4, pp. 779-87.

Moore, M. H., 1995, *Creating Public Value: Strategic Management in Government*, Boston: Harvard University Press.

National Institute for Governance, 2004, *Public Service Leadership: Emerging Issues — A Report for the Australian Public Service Commission*, Canberra: Commonwealth of Australia.

Podger, A., 2007, Interview with authors, Canberra.

Shergold, P., 2004, '"Lackies, Careerists, Political Stooges?" Personal Reflections on the Current State of Public Service Leadership', *Australian Journal of Public Administration*, 63:4, pp. 3-13.

Shergold, P., 2007, 'What really happens in the Australian Public Service: an alternative view', *Australian Journal of Public Administration,* 66:3, pp. 367-70.

Stone, D., 1996, *Capturing the Political Imagination: Think Tanks and the Policy Process*, New York: Routledge.

Tiernan, A., 2007, *Power Without Responsibility? Ministerial Staffers in Australian Governments from Whitlam to Howard*, Sydney: UNSW Press.

Uhr, J., 2005, *Terms of Trust: Arguments over Ethics in Australian Government*, Sydney: UNSW Press.

Weller, P., 2001, *Australia's Mandarins: The Frank and the Fearless*, Sydney: Allen & Unwin.

Weller, P. and J. Wanna, 1997 'Departmental Secretaries: Appointment, Termination and their Impact', *Australian Journal of Public Administration*, 56:4, December, pp 13-25.

11. Informal Public Leadership: The Case of Social Movements

David West

Introduction

One form of public leadership often overlooked by scholars is that of politically engaged parts of society, in particular, social movements. In fact, even within the social movement literature, the role of leaders(hip) is under-theorised. This chapter makes a small contribution to plugging these gaps. I focus on some of the *contrasts* between leadership in formal institutional or organisational contexts and leadership within the less organised, less institutionalised context of social movements (SMs). There is, however, considerable overlap between the nature of leaders and leadership in these different contexts. SM leadership is not entirely different from forms of leadership in more institutionalised contexts, if only because social movements do include organisations and often interact with political institutions. The distinctive nature of SM politics means, further, that SM contexts themselves cannot be demarcated as clearly institutional ones. The context of SM leadership always tends to extend beyond the movement and its membership to the broader public sphere and society. If anything, distinct constituencies of movement support, which might define the boundaries of 'a' movement, are products, rather than premises, of SM politics and leadership. For these reasons, the study of SM leadership cannot be isolated from the study of leadership more broadly.

Social movements as partially, non- or extra-institutional forms of politics

Social movements can be defined as non- or extra-institutional forms of politics, occurring within the sphere of 'civil society'. Jan Pakulski defines social movements as 'recurrent patterns of collective activities which are partially institutionalised, value oriented and anti-systemic in their form and symbolism'. (1991: xiv). Though they typically include, are associated with, or give rise to organised groups and formal organisations, SMs are both *broader* and *more diffuse* than their organisational manifestations. The green movement is, for example, more than the sum of associated organisations such as Greenpeace, the Australian Conservation Foundation, World Wildlife Fund or green electoral parties. Again, SMs often aim to bring about changes at the level of formal political institutions, but they need not be *exclusively* concerned with institutional changes and sometimes by-pass institutional politics altogether.

Although it is difficult to characterise the relationship between SMs and institutional politics in general, yet still precise, terms, it is intuitively helpful to understand that SMs as primarily concerned with the *formative dimension* of politics. Where institutions and organisations reflect existing interests and social divisions, SMs are typically concerned with *emerging* issues, values, identities and constituencies. Institutional reforms and new organisations may come about as a result, but the movement as such cannot be reduced to its institutional manifestations and consequences. Alain Touraine describes social movements in quasi-volcanic terms: 'Men make their own history: social life is produced by cultural achievements and social conflicts, and at the heart of society burns the fire of social movements.' (Touraine 1981: 1)

Imagery apart, it is significant that social movements imply conflict. Social movements are not only *extra*-institutional, they are also *anti-systemic*, challenging current institutions or 'the system' from outside. SMs typically occur where institutions are judged to have failed, or to stand in need of reform or even revolutionary change. At the same time, SMs are not necessarily *anti-institutional* in the sense of being opposed to all (rather than just existing) institutions. However, an anti-institutional or quasi-anarchist orientation has been a significant element in some recent movements. Further complications arise from the fact that anti-systemic movements often provoke 'conservative' or 'reactionary' movements, which defend the status quo against these 'radical' or 'progressive' challengers.

The complex relationship between SMs, organisations and institutional politics results in a similarly complex relationship between what I shall refer to as 'formal' and 'informal' models or, in Weberian terms, 'ideal types' of leadership. *Formal* leadership occurs within conventionally institutionalised political contexts — government, public service, judiciary — as well as in formally constituted organisations — political parties, interest groups, lobby groups, trade unions etc. The formal model of leadership is compatible with an overall view of a hierarchy of levels of leadership from smaller and more local to larger regional, national and global contexts. By contrast, *informal* leadership occurs essentially outside of such contexts. It is particularly relevant to SMs, although it should be clear that issues of formal leadership still arise both within movement organisations and in their relations with political institutions.

This chapter concentrates on some consequences of the informal nature of (much) social movement leadership. As a secondary issue, it will consider some implications of the actual situation of SMs, which involves a complex interaction between institutional and extra-institutional, formal and informal, fully constituted and formative dimensions of politics.

Extra-institutional sources of leadership

Institutional leaders have whatever power and authority they have, at least in part, by virtue of their office. In contrast, SM leadership involves acting without a recognised institutional position or office. In Weber's terms, SM leaders cannot rely on either 'traditional' or 'legal-rational' authority, but have to *create* their authority by means of *charisma* (Weber 1947: part III, 324 ff). Charisma refers to those personal qualities of a leader that inspire loyalty and recognition from followers: 'It is recognition on the part of those subject to authority which is decisive for the validity of charisma' (Weber 1947: 359). In the absence of traditional, routinised or rule-based institutions and obligations, charisma has the capacity to generate 'new obligations' (361). Charismatic leadership has often been based on religious, mystical, emotional and other seemingly 'irrational' forms of appeal. This is particularly clear for religious and religio-political leaders (of particular interest to Weber) such as the Jewish 'Messiah', Muslim 'Mahdi' or Christian revivalist. Unlimited by either traditional, legal or rational constraints, charismatic leadership readily assumes authoritarian form and is associated with violent social upheaval and, in the twentieth century, fascism.

However, more pertinent to the *recent* experience of SMs is a variant of charismatic authority qualified by *moral* constraints. Although the category of 'new' social movement (NSM) is contested and problematic, it does serve to highlight prominent features of the upsurge of SM activity from the 1960s (for example, Jennett and Steward 1989, Dalton and Kuechler 1990). SMs, like second-wave feminism, gay and lesbian liberation, environmentalism and the peace and anti-nuclear movements largely avoided violence and revolutionary insurrection. In place of a conflictual and state-centred politics of class interest and material advantage, they pursued an 'identity politics' of moral and cultural contestation. They favoured a 'pre-figurative' politics, which seeks to align present political means with future political goals. Accordingly, traditions of non-violent direct action and civil disobedience, which involves violating current norms of *institutional* legitimacy (i.e. laws) by means that are yet *morally* defensible (Singer 1973), played an important role.

The morally constrained variant of charisma appropriate to NSMs is illuminated with the help of John Kane's notion of moral capital, which refers to 'the part played in political contexts by people's moral perceptions of political actors, causes, institutions and organisations' (2001: 4). Moral capital is an important political resource of *formal* leaders, 'one that in combination with other familiar political resources enables political processes, supports political contestants and creates political opportunities' (Kane 2001: 2). But moral capital is something that also originates, and can be created outside of existing political institutions in *informal* leadership contexts. Kane discusses Nelson Mandela and Aung San Suu Kyi as two leaders who deployed moral capital in the cause of dissident politics. Moral capital is also a key resource of the movement as a whole in its promotion of new identities, communities of interest and, ultimately, social and cultural change.

Crucially, a dissident politics of moral challenge and moral capital implies corresponding limits on the goals and tactics that can be adopted by the movement — a feature, as already noted, of pre-figurative styles of politics favoured by NSMs. Of course, any moral limits will depend on prevailing moral norms and on the public's *perceptions* and *judgments*. But although moral norms may be culturally and historically variable, they are not infinitely malleable or meaningless. At the same time, a significant goal of SMs is the reinterpretation and transformation of prevailing values and norms. For example, the gay movement seeks to extend liberal values of privacy and freedom concerning self-regarding actions to sexual conduct. Anti-racism and feminism advocate more consistent and inclusive values of equality and fairness. The politics of moral capital seem particularly suited to such goals.

NSMs have succeeded in transforming broader norms of legitimate political conduct as well. Before the 1960s, liberal democrats routinely denied legitimacy to all extra-institutional movements and challengers, maintaining that advocates of change should vote in elections, petition leaders and officials, form new political parties or put forward their arguments in the public domain. From this perspective, SMs were regarded as disorderly threats to political stability along with mobs, riots and panics — examples of what was derogatively termed *collective behaviour*. The rise of the 'new' movements rehabilitated extra-institutional forms of politics so that SMs can now studied as potentially rational forms of collective *action* (Della Porta and Diani 1999). SMs can be understood, not as irrational 'outbursts' or 'eruptions' of pent-up frustration, but as the *rational achievement* of collective action on behalf of previously neglected or excluded issues and groups. This understanding of SMs provides the context for the following discussion of informal leadership.

Three dimensions of social movement leadership

The following explores three salient features of ideal-typical SM leadership.

Leaders, followers, actors

It has been widely observed that leadership depends on the correlative role of followers or 'followership'. Particular leadership qualities reflect complementary tendencies of followers to approve or respond appropriately to those qualities (Burns 1978; Little 1985). But the relationship between leaders and followers is significantly qualified in the *informal* context of social movement politics. In part, this results from what we have described as the formative nature of social movement politics. Since a SM does not have a *pre-existing* constituency or membership, the first task of SM leadership is to encourage people to *become* followers, to *identify* themselves as members of a movement (cf. B below).

The recent context of 'new' social movements further qualifies the leader-follower relationship through the widespread suspicion of leadership associated with the 'new' politics. Of course, formal and even strikingly hierarchical organisations have played a prominent role in some contemporary movements — Greenpeace is an example familiar from the green movement. But more distinctive of NSMs is a suspicion or even hostility toward hierarchy and leadership. The 'affinity' groups of the May 1968 Events in Paris, the 'consciousness raising' groups of second-wave feminism and anarchist elements of the anti-globalisation movement limit or dispense altogether with leadership roles on principled grounds (Bookchin 1974; Rowbotham 1979). Also influential was the New Left, which canvassed criticisms of Soviet 'democratic centralism', bureaucratic labour organisations and Leninist parties of 'activists' charged with 'organising' the masses of workers and peasants. Strong leadership and hierarchical organisations were, in other words, implicated in the authoritarian politics of 'actually existing socialism'.

The 'new' movements sought to avoid the authoritarian fate of the Old Left by encouraging more active and widespread involvement of members. A fully active membership will better be able to control leading figures of the movement. Active members will also be 'empowered' — gaining confidence as well as technical and political skills — through their involvement (West 1990). Rather than being a passive 'constituency' or interest group 'represented' by its leaders, members of SMs are therefore more accurately described as *actors* or *agents*. Not passive 'followers', these actors are the true bearers of the movement. Indeed, in contrast to formal organisations and institutions, a social *movement* can only be said to exist at all to the extent that there is an ongoing and widespread pattern of collective activities. 'Subject group' may be a more appropriate term to refer to the collectivity of actors constituting the movement (Laclau and Mouffe 1985).

The more active role of movement participants has implications for the relationship between leadership and *representation*. If the representative acts not only *on behalf* but also *instead of* those she represents, representation *substitutes* for, rather than complements the active involvement of movement actors. Deleuze and Foucault speak in this context of the 'indignity of speaking for others' (Foucault and Deleuze 1977). In fact, SM leaders (and organisations) have been criticised, because they are unable to make binding commitments on behalf of their 'followers' (Offe 1985). But this is to misunderstand the relationship between movement leaders and participants in terms more appropriate to the context of formal representative organisations. What is more, the strength of a movement may be increased, when its actions cannot be easily controlled or predicted. Movement leaders may be co-opted by the 'system', but they are less able than their institutional counterparts to 'deliver' the movement as their part of any bargain.

It follows that informal leadership will require different qualities (or a different weighting of qualities) than is the case in formal leadership contexts. SM leadership implies, for example, the ability to 'inspire', 'activate' and 'empower' rather than qualities of decisiveness or authoritative command. Military qualities and corresponding metaphors of 'militants' and 'mobilisation' are inappropriate. The institutional leader may be able to decide when to order his followers to act; electoral parties are only periodically concerned with attracting and 'getting out' votes in electoral contests. By contrast, SM leadership is always concerned, first and foremost, with generating and maintaining participant activity.

Significantly, SM leaders also aim to inspire actions with a greater degree of *autonomy* and *initiative* than in formal contexts. Hierarchical organisations have typically valued obedience, loyalty, solidarity and, at the extreme, the sacrifice of individuality and autonomy for the sake of the cause (cf. Arendt 1952/1958; Koestler 1950). The strength of movement, on the other hand, is increased when actions proliferate both numerically and qualitatively as a result of the plurality of relatively independent centres of thought and decision. Change may occur less through a unified course of action imposed from above than from a 'contagion' of actions and reactions (Guattari 1984). On the other hand, this contagious quality also represents a challenge for SM leaders. Cascading political actions may violate the moral norms — and so diminish the moral capital — on which the broader authority and impact of the movement relies (Philp 2007: ch. 8).

A deeper investigation might consider how the to-us-familiar opposition of 'leader' and 'followers' serves to distort our understanding of political action. According to Hannah Arendt, the ancient Greek understanding of action acknowledged the differing roles of 'leader' and 'followers' without obscuring their interdependence in an essentially cooperative enterprise. This recognition has been lost in the subsequent evolution of our political vocabularies (Arendt 1958: 189; 2005: 45). Something like Arendt's more cooperative understanding of action is particularly relevant to the experience of contemporary social movements. Indeed, renewed focus on social movements brings us closer to the 'original' understanding of action.

Moral, cultural and ideological innovation

The nature of SM leadership is further qualified by the role of creativity and innovation in social movements. Social movements, as we have seen, are not concerned so much with the pursuit of *existing* interests or issues as with the emergence of *new* interests and issues, new political identities and cultural patterns.

There is a problem, therefore, with theoretical approaches premised on *fixed* assumptions about interests and motivation. For example, rational choice approaches such as 'resource mobilisation theory' portray the task of SM leadership as predominantly concerned with the organisation of political resources and incentives in order to mobilise self-interested utility-maximisers with a given array of interests. The leader is a political 'entrepreneur' searching for new (political) market opportunities (Taylor 1982). Whilst their conclusions may be valid within the limits of their own assumptions, such approaches neglect the essentially *creative* role of SM leadership. Rather than simply 'packaging' existing interests and resources into more politically potent combinations, SMs succeed by *transforming* interests and identities.

The creative demands of SM leadership require a different range of leadership qualities. Ideological and cultural innovators play a significant role in SMs. SMs leaders flourish, accordingly, on the basis of rhetorical skills, moral suasion and cultural inspiration as much as organisational skills or decision-making. By implication, too, there are diffuse boundaries between SM politics and other areas of social life, such as the arts, cultural activities and even science. A work of literature or philosophy may make a crucial contribution to the emergence of a SM. This helps to explain the acknowledgement of a writer like Oscar Wilde as a leading figure of the gay movement, Frantz Fanon as an icon of anti-colonialism, or Germaine Greer and Shulamith Firestone as leading feminists. Scientific ecology and other sciences have played a similarly important role in the rise of 'green' and environmental movements. The porous boundaries of politics and the political reflect the particular role of SMs as significant agents of *politicisation*, which involves transgressing these boundaries.

Social movements and the public sphere

The porous borders of politics are also manifested in the relationship of social movements and SM leaders to the public sphere. SMs obviously have an important relationship to the emergence of the modern 'public sphere' in western societies. Both SMs and the public sphere rely on and reflect key dimensions of 'modernity' — including industrialisation and urbanisation, expansion of printing and news media, improving means of transportation and communication. Both develop in complex interaction with parliamentary politics and broader processes of democratisation (Tilly 1978).

But SMs should also be recognised as *active agents* in the formation of the public sphere, not simply as players within it. The democracy movements in communist Eastern Europe before 1989 can be understood, in this way, as laying the foundations of a previously non-existent (or fragmentary) public sphere and civil society (Keane 1988). Even in liberal democracies with established civil societies, NSMs have broadened the agenda of public discussion along a number of dimensions. Previously neglected issues and constituencies — relating to gender, sexuality, racism, peace and the environment — have been introduced to the public sphere as a result of their activities since the 1960s. NSMs have contributed to the increasing *complexity* and *responsiveness* of the public sphere — or, more accurately perhaps, they have contributed to the *proliferation* of a plurality of public spheres (Habermas 1981; Fraser 1997).

The relationship of social movement and public sphere(s) has implications for informal leadership. The public role of SMs means that they and their leaders never simply address a confined constituency of 'members' or 'supporters'. They must always strive to reach across the boundaries of their 'subject group' to a wider public of potential participants and supporters. Even *opponents* are an important 'counter-constituency', especially when movements represent nominally minority interests and so must depend on their support or, at least, acquiescence. The complexity and heterogeneity of the 'audience' of SM leaders means there will often be tensions between public and 'movement' responses to particular statements or actions. The public context of SMs means, finally, that the movement *as a whole* itself exercises a kind of leadership role within the wider society.

Interactions between institutional and social movement leadership

It has already been noted that informal SM leadership will rarely exist in 'pure' or 'ideal typical' form, because SMs are almost always involved with movement organisations and political institutions. But if SM leadership rarely occurs in pure form, it is also true that formal institutional leadership, in its turn, seldom lacks a 'social movement dimension' entirely. The following are a few relevant observations on interactions between formal and informal leadership contexts.

Social movements are, in practice, more or less closely related to the broader institutional and organisational terrain. Leaders sometimes derive their initial authority within the movement in part, at least, from their pre-existing *institutional* leadership positions. A perhaps minor formal or institutional position can sometimes be translated into a much expanded role within the movement. Religious office often plays this role: Martin Luther King, for example, was a minister of the church before he rose to a position of leadership in the Civil Rights Movement. Conversely, of course, SM leaders often take up positions within the institutional sphere. In Australia, Peter Garrett and Bob Brown offer contrasting lessons of the difficulties and opportunities involved in the transition from the green movement and its associated organisations to formal positions of leadership.

More generally, formal institutional leaders will also depend on qualities associated here with informal leadership. We have already mentioned Kane's exploration of ways in which institutional leaders are reinforced or undermined by their moral capital or lack thereof. He considers the contrasting cases of Nelson Mandela, John F. Kennedy and Richard Nixon (2001). The 'Machiavellian' dilemmas faced by political leaders, who try to reconcile effectiveness in the 'real world' (or 'realism') with moral principles ('idealism'), inevitably tend to erode their moral capital in the long run. In contrast to *social* capital which, according to Robert Putnam, *increases* the more it is used (Putnam 1993: 169), the use of *moral* capital does tend to use it up. The durability of formal leaders, their ability to maintain appeal and authority over time, therefore depends on their ability to manage this problem. To achieve this may require qualities more often associated with *informal* leadership — qualities, for example, enabling formal leaders to revive their support and/or extend their appeal beyond existing constituencies.

Evidently, the same Machiavellian dilemmas also afflict social movements and informal leadership. Partly as a result, the successful institutionalisation of a movement — the translation of its demands and values into political influence, legal and institutional recognition, party formation and even government — is not infrequently associated with the decline or disappearance of the movement *as a movement*. Institutional manifestations of a SM readily fall victim to the same contradictions between ideal values and political expediency besetting conventionally institutionalised politics. Leaders faced with difficult policy dilemmas are tempted to sacrifice long-term movement ideals for the sake of immediate practical gains. Drawn into the orbit of institutional politics and tempted by the rewards of office, leaders may be 'co-opted' by the 'system'. Movement participants may feel 'betrayed' by their co-opted leaders. Perceptions of institutional recognition and satisfied demands may, in any case, encourage participants to withdraw from active involvement in the movement.

A prominent example of the price paid by a SM for institutional success is the nineteenth-century working-class movement, which gave rise to, but then was effectively *replaced* by its institutional offspring of trade unions, labour and social democratic parties and welfare state. The demise of the working-class movement in its revolutionary incarnations has been even more stark. Of course, some substantive gains resulted from the institutional successes of the movement — the welfare state in capitalist liberal democracies and some equivalent social protections in the former communists states. But since the 1970s at least, the welfare state has, in the absence of a strongly persisting social movement, proved vulnerable to neo-liberal counterattack. The dramatic collapse of 'actually existing socialism' after 1989 led, by an even more direct route, to harsher versions of liberal capitalism.

The mixed outcome of the working-class movement's 'successful' institutionalisation provided important, formative lessons for 'new' social movements. One of the most distinctive features of NSMs has been their self-consciously critical or cautious orientation towards institutional politics and the attempt to avoid such negative outcomes. NSMs have sought to achieve changes beyond and, to some extent, independently of the institutional political sphere — changes in identity, culture, consciousness, consumption and so on. When these movements *have* nevertheless sought institutional reforms, they have done so with the intention of preserving high levels of movement activity. The German Green Party is the most well known example of an organisation designed to pursue the benefits of institutionalisation without exhausting the transformative force of the underlying movement. The Greens were formed, in this sense, self-consciously as an 'anti-party' or 'movement' party. Their qualified successes in this regard only confirm the difficulties involved in truly achieving this goal (Hülsberg 1988).

More broadly, the *fragility* and *enduring value* of social movements are important themes in the renaissance of SM studies since the 1970s. These studies support the view of social movements and civil society as permanent and essential elements of any genuine, as opposed to merely formal or nominal, democracy (Keane 1988; Cohen and Arato 1992). By the same token, leaders and movements attempting to satisfy the 'hybrid' demands of both formal and informal political contexts face a complex and daunting task.

References

Arendt, H., 1952, *The Origins of Totalitarianism*, London: Allen & Unwin.

Arendt, H., 1958, *The Human Condition*, Chicago and London: University of Chicago Press.

Arendt, H., 2005, *The Promise of Politics* (ed. Jerome Kohn), New York: Schocken Books.

Bookchin, M., 1974, *Post-Scarcity Anarchism*, London: Wildwood House.

Burns, J. M., 1978, *Leadership*, New York and London: Harper & Row.

Cohen, J. and A. Arato, 1992, *Civil Society and Political Theory*, Cambridge, MA: MIT Press.

Dalton, R. J. and M. Kuechler, 1990, *Challenging the Political Order: New Social and Political Movements in Western Democracies*, New York and Oxford: Oxford University Press.

Della Port, D. and M. Diani, 1999, *Social Movements: An Introduction*, Oxford and Malden, MA: Blackwell.

Foucault, M. and G. Deleuze, 1977, 'Intellectuals and Power' in *Language, Counter-memory, Practice*, trans. D. F. Bouchard and S. Simon, Ithaca, NY: Cornell University Press.

Fraser, N., 1997, *Justice Interruptus: Critical Reflections on the 'Postsocialist' Condition*, London and New York: Routledge.

Guattari, F., 1984, *Molecular Revolution: Psychiatry and Politics*, trans. R. Sheed, Harmondsworth: Penguin.

Habermas, J., 1981, 'New Social Movements', *Telos*, 49, pp. 33-7.

Hülsberg, W., 1988, *The German Greens*, trans. G. Fagan, London and New York: Verso.

Jennett, C. and R. G. Stewart, 1989, *Politics of the Future: The Role of Social Movements*, Melbourne: Macmillan.

Kane, J., 2001, *The Politics of Moral Capital*, Cambridge and New York: Cambridge University Press.

Keane, J. (ed.) 1988, *Civil Society and the State: New European Perspectives*, London and New York: Verso.

Koestler, A., 1950, *Darkness at Noon*, trans. D. Hardy, London: Cape.

Laclau, E. and C. Mouffe, 1985, *Hegemony and Socialist Strategy: Towards a Radical Democratic Politics*, London and New York: Verso, 1985.

Little, G., 1985, *Political Ensembles: A Psychosocial Approach to Politics and Leadership*, Oxford and New York: Oxford University Press.

Offe, C., 1985, 'New Social Movements: Challenging the boundaries of institutional politics', *Social Research*, 52:4, pp. 817-68.

Pakulski, J., 1991, *Social Movements: The Politics of Moral Protest*, Melbourne: Longman Cheshire.

Philp, M., 2007, *Political Conduct*, Cambridge, MA and London: Harvard University Press.

Putnam, R. D., 1993, *Making Democracy Work: Civic Traditions in Modern Italy*, Princeton, NJ: Princeton University Press.

Rowbotham, S., 1979, 'The Women's Movement and Organizing for Socialism', in S. Rowbotham, L. Segal and H. Wainwright (eds), *Beyond the Fragments*, London: Merlin Press.

Singer, P., 1973, *Democracy and Disobedience*, Oxford: Clarendon Press.

Taylor, M., 1982, *Community, Anarchy and Liberty*, Cambridge and New York: Cambridge University Press.

Tilly, C, 1978, *From Mobilization to Revolution*, Reading, MA and London: Addison-Wesley.

Touraine, A., 1981, *The Voice and the Eye: An Analysis of Social Movements*, Cambridge and New York: Cambridge University Press.

Weber, M., 1947, *The Theory of Social and Economic Organization*, New York: Free Press.

West, D., 1990, *Authenticity and Empowerment: A Theory of Liberation*, Hemel Hempstead: Harvester Wheatsheaf.

12. Outsiders or Insiders? Strategic Choices for Australian Indigenous Leadership

Will Sanders

The outsider-insider conundrum

In the last couple of years, Cape York Aboriginal leader, Noel Pearson, has taken to writing regular columns in *The Weekend Australian* newspaper. On 7-8 July 2007, he wrote a column in which he reflected on the reactions of Indigenous leaders to the then recently announced Commonwealth 'intervention' in Northern Territory Aboriginal communities, following the Northern Territory Government's *Little Children are Sacred* report (BIPACSA 2007). Pearson was critical of Indigenous leaders, such as the Northern Territory Government minister Marion Scrymgour and the former Chief Executive Officer of ATSIC and now head of National Indigenous Television (NITV), Pat Turner, who were 'nay-saying' the intervention. He suggested that there was a 'psychological incapacity' among many Indigenous leaders 'to step up to politics in mainstream Australia' and that this was 'one of the reasons' why Indigenous people 'continue to lose in this country'. Indigenous leaders, he argued, 'have to deal with the Government and the politics of the day and devote our maximum energies and talents towards making good of things that otherwise seem bad' (Pearson 2007a).

Pearson seems to be arguing that more Indigenous leaders need to become 'insiders' of Australian political processes who engage strategically with whatever political circumstances emerge and whoever is in government. Conversely he seems to suggest that, psychologically, many Indigenous leaders are locked into an 'outsider' position of inflexible stand-taking, on the basis of history, identity or philosophical commitment. The terms 'insider' and 'outsider', as descriptors of Australian Indigenous leadership styles, are my own rather than Pearson's. But I do think they are a convenient way to capture Pearson's argument. My aim in this chapter is not specifically to agree or disagree with Pearson's argument and judgment about the psychology of most Indigenous leaders, but rather just to think some more about the ins and outs of Australian Indigenous leadership: how, when and why Indigenous leaders use insider and outsides stances. My own, more analytic, argument is that these leadership styles are complementary, that they entail and feed off each other systemically in public life, rather than existing as clear alternatives between which individual Indigenous leaders can always be clearly allocated. I will begin, however, by making a few comments about the apparent relative numbers of Indigenous leaders in three constituent and overlapping spheres of 'public leadership' the political, administrative and civic.

Forms of indigenous leadership: political, administrative and civic

At first glance there is a dearth of Indigenous *political* leaders in Australia. There have only ever been two Indigenous Commonwealth parliamentarians — Queensland Liberal Senator Neville Bonner from 1971 to 1983 and New South Wales Australian Democrats Senator Aden Ridgeway from 1999 to 2005. At the state and territory level, there have historically also been very few Indigenous parliamentarians, although currently there is something of a bumper crop — two in Western Australia, one each in Tasmania and New South Wales and six in the Northern Territory, all representing the Australian Labor Party. Indeed in 2007, very unusually, there were three Indigenous ministers in Australian state and territory governments, Linda Burney in New South Wales and Marion Scrymgour and Elliot McAdam in the Northern Territory. Prior to these three however, there have, to my knowledge, only ever been two other Indigenous ministers in state and territory governments — Ernie Bridge in Western Australia in the 1990s and John Ah Kit in the Northern Territory in the early 2000s.

There is, however, another way to count Indigenous political leaders which, by definition, leads to greater numbers. This is to include members of the elected national Indigenous representatives bodies which existed from 1973 to 2005, the National Aboriginal Consultative Committee from 1973 to 1977, the National Aboriginal Conference from 1977 to 1985 and the Aboriginal and Torres Strait Islander Commission (ATSIC) from 1990 to 2005. ATSIC had some hundreds of elected regional councillors who in turn elected seventeen national Commissioners, and from 1999 these Commissioners *elected* their own Chairperson. While the first elected ATSIC Chairperson, Geoff Clark from Victoria, enjoyed some national public prominence, the position was abolished before it became institutionalised. Interestingly, one of the national ATSIC Commissioners from 1999 to 2004, Alison Anderson from Central Australia, has gone on to become a Northern Territory parliamentarian. But I am unaware of any other ATSIC Commissioners, or regional council members, who have made the transition from elected national Indigenous representative body to parliamentarian.

There is also a dearth, at first glance, of Indigenous *administrative* leaders. Perhaps the most prominent of recent years has been Pat Turner, the CEO of ATSIC from 1994 to 1997, who later went on to become a deputy CEO of Centrelink before retiring from the public service and becoming the head of National Indigenous Television. A little earlier, Lois (now Lowitja) O'Donoghue enjoyed some public prominence as ATSIC's *appointed* Chairperson from 1990 to late 1996, followed by Gatjil Djerrkura to late 1999. Another administrative position of public prominence for Indigenous people in recent years has been that of Aboriginal and Torres Strait Islander Social Justice Commissioner within the Human Rights and Equal Opportunity Commission (HREOC), filled by Mick Dodson from 1993 to 1998, Bill Jonas from 1999 to 2004 and Tom Calma since 2004. As five-year statutory appointees, these HREOC Commissioners have considerable autonomy to reflect critically on what other parts of government are doing. However having done so, their position seems to be more that of passing Indigenous advocate than career public servant. Both Dodson and Jonas moved outside the public service at the end of their five-year statutory appointment. And the same pattern can be observed with the two Indigenous Chairpersons of the Commonwealth-appointed Council for Aboriginal Reconciliation, Pat Dodson from 1991 to 1997 and Evelyn Scott from 1998 to 2000.

In an earlier generation, back in the 1970s and 1980s, the most prominent Indigenous career public servant was Charles Perkins, who joined the new Commonwealth Office of Aboriginal Affairs in the late 1960s and rose through the ranks of the Department of Aboriginal Affairs established in 1972 to become its Secretary from 1984 to 1988, as well as being the inaugural chairperson of its statutory off-shoot the Aboriginal Development Commission from 1980 to 1984. Perkins commanded far greater public attention than most Australian administrative leaders, even before he was a statutory officer. This could possibly be attributed to him having worked in leadership roles in Indigenous community organisations before becoming a career public servant, but also to his strong sense of being an advocate for Indigenous interests within the public service. Indeed, Perkins' public service career came to a slightly premature end in 1988 when his advocacy of the interests of an Indigenous community sector organisation for Commonwealth funding became unacceptable to his minister, Gerry Hand, who saw it as a conflict of interest with his role as departmental secretary (Read 1990: 290-301). However, Perkins re-emerged in the 1990s as an elected ATSIC Commissioner, so his career in national Indigenous public leadership simply shifted, quite quickly, from the administrative to the (quasi-) political sphere.

Charles Perkins' career illustrates the way in which Australian Indigenous public leaders can move between the administrative, political and societal spheres over time, all the time maintaining their identity-based commitment to Aboriginal interests. Another example of this is John Ah Kit, who became the first Aboriginal minister in the Northern Territory Legislative Assembly in the Martin Labor Government elected in 2001. In the early 1980s, Ah Kit worked for the Commonwealth Department of Social Security assisting Indigenous people in the Katherine region of the Northern Territory to gain access to their recently-won income support entitlements. He then became the manager of an Indigenous community-sector organisation providing accommodation and related services to Aboriginal town campers in Katherine. Ah Kit then moved to Darwin to become the Director of the Northern Land Council, a Commonwealth statutory creation which has a high degree of operational autonomy to work in the interests of Aboriginal traditional owners of land, but is still ultimately a part of Commonwealth administration. In the early 1990s, Ah Kit returned to Katherine and the Indigenous community sector as Executive Director of the Jawoyn Association, an organisation working with the Aboriginal land owners of the Katherine region. In this role he helped negotiate one of the first post-Mabo native title agreements with a mining company at Mt Todd in 1993. In 1995, Ah Kit became the member for Arnhem in the Northern Territory Legislative Assembly and so began his career as an elected politician. In retirement since 2005, Ah Kit has also occasionally re-emerged as a public leader. For example, in 2007, he stood beside Pat Turner as a critic of some of the land aspects of the Commonwealth's intervention in the Northern Territory (Turner and Watson 2007).

Both Charles Perkin's and John Ah Kit's stories illustrate the way in which Indigenous leaders can move between the administrative, political and societal spheres in the course of a public leadership career. They also suggest that a conventional administrative career alone might be somewhat too constraining for many Aboriginal public leaders who see their primary task as the promotion of Aboriginal interests. Without ATSIC's elected arm, the options for a political career based on Indigenous votes are also limited to a few parliamentary seats in the Northern Territory and one or two in Western Australia. Beyond this, there is, theoretically, the possibility of building an Indigenous political career on party service and non-Indigenous votes, as some of the current small crop of Indigenous Labor members in the more southern state parliaments would appear to have done. But there is still no easy, or clear, path for Indigenous political careers. So, in many ways the most obvious and most likely path for Indigenous public leadership is through societal leadership, with occasional opportunistic forays into political and administrative spheres.

In many ways this emphasis on the civic sphere among Indigenous leaders is entirely understandable. As 't Hart and Uhr (this volume) note, leaders tend to monitor and challenge the political and administrative spheres, rather than defend or endorse them. This is a very comfortable position for Indigenous leaders, who wish to assert the distinctiveness of their identity and historical perspectives. This is, in many ways, Noel Pearson's point in the *Weekend Australian* article quoted above: that being on the outside monitoring and challenging politics and administration is the psychologically comfortable position for Indigenous public leaders. In terms of positions occupied, Noel Pearson's own career bears out this point. Over the 15 years since he rose to prominence as the Cape York representative in the 1993 Indigenous team negotiating the passage of the Commonwealth's Native Title legislation, Pearson has, to my knowledge, always remained outside direct public sector employment. He has worked for a variety of community-sector or societal bodies, like the Cape York Land Council and the Cape York Institute for Policy and Leadership, which accept government money to undertake certain tasks but which, ultimately, guard their independence and autonomy from governments quite strongly.

Many other Aboriginal leaders also seem most at home in the societal sphere. Pat Dodson, for example, since retiring from being Chair of the Commonwealth-appointed Council for Aboriginal Reconciliation in 1997, has worked in a private capacity for the Lingiari Foundation. While brother Mick Dodson, since finishing as HREOC's Aboriginal and Torres Strait Islander Social Justice Commissioner, has become a professor at The Australian National University and, internationally, a member of the United Nations Permanent Forum on Indigenous Issues. Two other prominent Indigenous public leaders in the university sector are professors Marcia Langton at the University of Melbourne and Larissa Behrendt at the University of Technology Sydney.

However, Pearson's criticism of his fellow Aboriginal leaders is not so much about the *positions* they occupy in the system of public leadership as in the *strategies* they pursue. Pearson is an advocate of Indigenous leaders pursuing more 'insider' strategies, even though they might do so predominantly from 'outsider' positions of societal leadership within the community sector. To illustrate and develop this idea further I will return to some earlier events.

Insider and outsider strategies of indigenous leadership

After the 2001 expiry of the Commonwealth-appointed Council for Aboriginal Reconciliation, a new body, Reconciliation Australia, took over the reconciliation cause at a somewhat greater distance from government. In May 2005, Reconciliation Australia organised a National Reconciliation Planning Workshop, in an attempt to re-invigorate the idea of reconciliation between Indigenous and settler Australians in the lead up to the 40th anniversary of the famous 1967 Aborigines constitutional alteration referendum. Reconciliation had, in their view, become somewhat stalled under the Howard government's focus on 'practical' measures in Indigenous affairs and its hesitancy both about endorsing Indigenous rights and about revisiting past wrongs. Prime Minister Howard was invited to speak fairly early in the May 2005 Workshop and there was a strong reaction among his audience when he uttered the following words:

> Reconciliation is about rights as well as responsibilities. It is about symbols as well as practical achievement. It is about the past as well as being about the present and the future (Howard 2005)

After the Prime Minister had left the workshop, Noel Pearson reminded others of those words. He encouraged a strategy among those assembled of accepting these words in good faith, repeating them back to the Prime Minister and trying to hold him to them. Others, however, were more sceptical, focusing on some of the surrounding words which suggested more continuity in the Howard government's approach to reconciliation. A difference of opinion developed among the Indigenous delegates, in which Pearson occupied something of a minority position. The majority distrusted Howard and were inclined to continue doing so, despite his words.

In retrospect this was, perhaps, just one of many instances in which Pearson was advocating the adoption of an 'insider' strategy — in which the best possible construction is put on what people currently say, or what is currently written in official documents, and then using this to push as hard as possible for people to deliver on that best possible construction of their words. The 'outsider' strategy, by contrast, is to hold onto previous events which suggest less empathy and opportunity and to distrust new, more sympathetic words and actions until they are built on and proven.

Another instance of Pearson advocating an 'insider' strategy can be seen right back at the beginning of his public leadership career in his 1993 Boyer Lecture. Native Title had just been recognised by the Australian High Court as a common law right and the Commonwealth government was in the throws of developing legislation to statutorily recognise and deal with it. Pearson concluded his lecture as follows:

> The test of credibility of a strategy is not whether the approach is radical or conservative, but whether it is smart or dumb, and whether it enhances or jeopardises the rights and interests of one's people.

> The politics of victims asserts that unless the dominating State accepts us on our own terms, any complicity, any dealing constitutes an unacceptable relinquishment of our power. For a long time, the only political currency which Aboriginal people could use was their refusal to be involved. Now that the non-Aboriginal legal system has offered something in the way of rights, however narrow, to refuse to engage in the game and fail to appreciate the rules and its limitations — even if our purpose be to disrupt the game — no longer seems smart. The challenge is to negotiate the expansion of those rights without losing ground and without surrendering the chances of future advances in a struggle which has incrementally advanced and whose destination is still long in arriving (Pearson 1994: 101).

Again we see Pearson encouraging his fellow Indigenous leaders to engage with and put a positive construction on emerging political circumstances in order to extract the best opportunities from them for Aboriginal interests. And again we see him judging quite harshly his Aboriginal leadership colleagues who find more comfort in 'outsider' stances of principle.

Among Indigenous societal leaders perhaps one of the most well known takers of 'outsider' stances over the last three decades has been Tasmanian Aboriginal, Michael Mansell, who is a lawyer working for the Tasmanian Aboriginal Centre and a long time Secretary of the self-proclaimed Aboriginal Provisional Government. Mansell has long maintained that Aboriginal people have never recognised the sovereignty of the settler state and, hence, have maintained their own sovereignty. His Provisional Government once produced passports for Aboriginal people and in 1987 he and some colleagues doubly confronted Australian authorities by attempting to use these passports while travelling to and from the then pariah state of Libya. In the 1990s Mansell refused to participate in elections for the Aboriginal and Torres Strait Islander Commission because doing so required Indigenous people to be on the Commonwealth Electoral Roll and hence, as Mansell saw it, to recognise settler sovereignty. Effectively, this also stopped Mansell, and others who followed him, from participating in other elections as well.

In more recent times, Mansell has also explicitly criticised Noel Pearson for his more insider approach to government. In a recent article in a book focused on the Howard government's intervention in Northern Territory Aboriginal communities from mid-2007, Mansell wistfully recalled the more enlightened days of the 1970s and 1980s, before lambasting the Howard government and those who have worked with it. He criticised Pearson both for being 'too close' to the Keating Labor government in the Native Title negotiations of 1993, and of 'courting the conservatives' and 'slamming the left' after Howard came to power in 1996. He suggested that Pearson had 'replaced a national Aboriginal political voice' with his own, and that while most Aboriginal leaders had been 'sacked' or 'went home' after the election of the Howard Government, Pearson had regrouped and courted 'the new, extreme conservatism'. Mansell also argued that there was a 'contradiction' in Pearson's position, in that 'relying on the coercive powers of government' to implement his desired welfare reform agenda, Pearson was denying Aboriginal 'people the right to choose' (Mansell 2007: 79-80).

These are harsh words, to which, Noel Pearson has not, to my knowledge, responded directly. However, Pearson has at times made some more general comments about Aboriginal leadership, which could be seen as indirectly critical of Mansell, and others of his strategic inclinations. In a more substantial article published in 2007, Pearson wrote the following:

> In my (relatively) short experience, I have endured my fair share of fanciful separatist rhetoric — and plenty of inane stunts and speeches — founded on vague and insufficiently grasped theories. As long as some key words and concepts are sprinkled amidst the denunciations, then any lunatic can be a leader. I've often had the sense that we are

playing delusional games in our own little sandpits. We want our sovereignty recognised by the International Court of Justice, and in the meantime I'm off to the TAB and the pub (Pearson 2007b: 20-1).

Exclusive or complementary roles?

Pearson and Mansell, it seems to me, are each rather harsh in their judgments of those who adopt opposing strategies to their own preferred mode of operation in Australian public life. In many ways their insider and outsider strategies play complementary roles in relation to each other. This was evident back in 1993 in negotiations around Native Title legislation, when Pearson worked more closely with the Labor Government and Mansell with the Senate crossbenches. And it may be similarly the case in more recent times, when Pearson has engaged with a Coalition government over welfare reform while Mansell and other Indigenous leaders have kept other agendas alive more on the margins of public debate, such as the demand for Indigenous-specific rights.

Analytically, we need to recognise that insider and outsider roles and strategies feed off each other in public life, with each reinforcing and complementing the other as much as being directly opposing alternatives. Insider strategies, and strategists, need outsiders also to be present in the public realm in order for their 'insidedness' to be effective while outsiders also rely on insiders to carry at least some part of their principled cause into practice. Perhaps Pearson's complaint about his fellow Indigenous leaders is more one of numbers. He sees more Indigenous leaders pursuing strategies at odds with government than working in partnership with government like himself. And yet, interestingly, among those of whom Pearson has been most critical in recent times are some, like Marion Scrymgour —in 2008 the Deputy Chief Minister in Northern Territory Labor Government – who positionally, are far more insiders than Pearson. Their experience over the last few years, in particular, would seem to be worthy of further study for what it can tell us about the insider and outsider roles and strategies of Indigenous public leaders.

References

Board of Inquiry into the Protection of Aboriginal Children from Sexual Abuse (BIPACSA), 2007, *Ampe Akelyernemane Meke Mekarle: 'Little Children are Sacred',* (Rex Wild and Pat Anderson, Inquiry Co-Chairs), Northern Territory Government, Darwin.

Howard, J., 2005, ' Transcript of the Prime Minister The Hon. John Howard MP Address at the National Reconciliation Planning Workshop', Old Parliament House, Canberra, 30 May.

Mansell, M., 2007, 'The Political Vulnerability of the Unrepresented', in J. Altman and M. Hinkson (eds), *Coercive Reconciliation: Stabilise,*

Normalise, Exit Aboriginal Australia, Carlton: Arena Publications, pp. 73-84.

Pearson, N., 1994, 'Mabo: Towards Respecting Equality and Difference', in M. Yununipingu, D. West, I. Anderson, J. Bell, G. Lui, H. Corbett and N. Pearson, *Voices from the Land: 1993 Boyer Lectures,* Sydney: ABC Books, pp. 89-101.

Pearson, N., 2007a, 'Action only way forward', *The Weekend Australian,* 7-8 July.

Pearson, N., 2007b, 'White guilt, victimhood and the quest for a radical centre', *Griffith Review,* Edition 16, Brisbane: Griffith University.

Read, P., 1990, *Charles Perkins: A Biography,* Ringwood Victoria: Viking.

Turner, P. and N. Watson, 2007, 'The Trojan Horse Unrepresented' in J. Altman and M. Hinkson (eds), *Coercive Reconciliation: Stabilise, Normalise, Exit Aboriginal Australia,* Carlton: Arena Publications, pp. 205-12.

13. From Bean-Counter to War Leader: National Security and Australian Public Leadership

Hugh White

Introduction

This chapter aims to do two things.[1] First, it explores how national security issues have recently shaped the styles and practices of public leadership in Australia. Second, very briefly, it looks at how, and how well, public leadership on these issues has been exercised. It will thus try to approach the interaction between public leadership and national security from both ends — how each affects the other. The essay will focus on political leadership: that is, on how national security issues shape the leadership of our politicians and how they lead on national security issues. There is much to be said about other kinds of public leadership in the national security field, of course. Taking a broader sense of 'public leadership' to include leadership on public issues but not necessarily in the public eye, Australia has a rich tradition of national security leadership encompassing civilian figures like Sir Fredrick Shedden (see Horner 2000) and Sir Arthur Tange (see Edwards 2006). There are also important military figures like Sir John Wilton, who profoundly shaped Australian policy and approaches, to say nothing of military leadership in the narrower sense — command — in which we have had our fair share of remarkable personalities, and one figure, Monash, of truly exceptional stature (see Serle 1982). But this study has a contemporary focus and I believe that, at present, in the light of recent history, political leadership offers the most interesting area for consideration of the nature of public leadership on national security questions.[2]

I will focus primarily on the role of the Prime Minister, and specifically on the leadership that the Prime Minister provides in what are seen to be times of national security crisis. Briefly, I will be suggesting that in times of perceived crisis, prime ministers have the opportunity to project a kind of leadership that differs significantly from more normal patterns of political leadership in a country like Australia. Although, as we shall see, other leaders may try to hop aboard, this opportunity seems most to be available to the Prime Minister because it involves a transcendence of, or regression from, the collaborative and consultative styles of political leadership embodied in collective cabinet models of government, in favour of a more direct and individual model of leadership focused on the person of the Prime Minister. I will argue that this model of national security leadership has recently exercised a sharply increased influence on the way national security issues have been considered in Australia and that it has also influenced the way the Prime Minister has projected his political leadership more broadly. At the same time, the quality of political leadership on national security issues – and perhaps more broadly – has declined. Finally, I will suggest that there may be a link between these two: the more leaders strive to project a certain image of the 'national security leader', the worse leadership they are likely to be providing.

Inevitably I will give most attention to the national security leadership of John Howard. I hope that I might contribute to assessments of Howard's achievements in the field of national security and to evaluations of his style as a political leader. It may be that there is scope to go further and draw more general theoretical conclusions about the nature of national-security leadership, but my expertise in the field is not equal to that task. Instead I will offer more modest suggestions about the implications of the issues addressed here for other leaders, especially Kevin Rudd.

A word on definitions: 'National Security' is a notoriously loaded and contested concept (see for example, Buzan, Weaver, and de Wilde 1998) and, as we shall see, the manipulation of its meanings is central to our topic. We can roughly delineate what we mean by it here along two axes. First, a security issue is regarded as a *national* security issue when it is seen to threaten not just the lives or welfare of individuals but of the national community as a whole. Hence, ordinary murder and motor accidents are not seen to be national security issues because, although in aggregate they cause death and injury on a large scale, they are factored into the way society operates and we do not feel that society as a whole is threatened by them. Conversely, by identifying terrorism or global warming as national security issues we are saying that they do threaten society as a whole. Second, while threats to national security can be seen in many forms, including such impersonal factors as climate change or a meteor strike, most discussion of national security seems to focus back onto violence deliberately inflicted by other people. More inclusive conceptions of national security have obvious conceptual appeal but, at the visceral level at which national security debates tend to operate, they never quite seem to draw attention away from the narrower concepts that centre on concerns about what other *people* might do to us. In particular, national security threats tend to be seen as coming from other people who are, or are seen to be, outside the national community. Hence, in the US, it apparently seems natural to see Al Qaeda as a threat to national security but not the Oklahoma Bomber.

National security and models of leadership

To understand the way national security leadership has functioned in Australia recently, we need to draw a contrast with other, more typical modes of political leadership in modern democratic societies. On most issues, these societies appear to seek political leaders who are cautious, prudent, analytical and accommodating: good at examining evidence, weighing all sides of an argument, persuading others of their view, and reaching sensible compromises with those they cannot persuade. In the Australian context this model of political leadership is exemplified by Bob Hawke and, for the first four years of his time as PM, by John Howard; in the UK by Tony Blair in his domestic guise; and in the US by Bill Clinton. Even leaders with a less accommodating manner — think of Reagan, Thatcher, and Keating — still owed much to this model of political leadership. It is apparently well adapted to the actual demands of running modern liberal market democracies in a globalised world. It is the model of their own leadership that political leaders seek to project when they address most domestic and many international issues — indeed, almost any issue except national security.

But surviving alongside this collective, domesticated model of leadership is a very different one; an atavistic concept that seems to owe more to society's tribal past than the urbane present, and which seems to come into play when national security issues move to the centre of the public agenda. This 'national security model' of leadership in many ways inverts the characteristic virtues of the domesticated, managerial model. Boldness is preferred to prudence; analysis is devalued in favour of intuition; inspiration is preferred to persuasion; accommodation and compromise are sacrificed to steadfastness and determination; and a sense of proportion is devalued and displaced by a willingness to persevere 'whatever the cost may be'. The overriding virtue in this national security model of leadership is a characteristic which is often called 'strength', but is often better seen as a kind of a determined, single-minded stubbornness.[3] Other leadership virtues — caution, agility, wisdom, inclusiveness, persuasiveness — are discounted. The outstanding exemplar of this national security leadership style is the Churchill of World War II. Careful historical analysis might sow doubts that Churchill was really like that as a war leader, but this image of Churchill remains perhaps the most potent model of national security leadership in the world today.

This model of leadership is reflected in the way that issues are discussed, and decisions made. Issues are presented as being simple, rather than complex. The essential features of the situation are considered to be beyond doubt or debate, and often cast in terms of often tendentious) historical metaphors like 'Pearl Harbour' or 'Munich'. There are no realistic alternative courses of action to the one selected by the leader. The issue under consideration is the most important the society now faces, and other priorities must make way for it. Costs in money, international standing, political freedoms, and even lives are not to be considered. Bureaucratic policy-development processes are discarded in favour of quick decisions made by the leader himself and a willingness to ignore advice and defy different opinions becomes virtues in their own right.[4] Dissent is considered tantamount to disloyalty to the country.

It is easy enough to see how this style of leadership has been at work in Australia, the UK, and the US in recent years, exemplified by George W. Bush, Tony Blair, and John Winston Howard. Since 9/11, these leaders have adopted a series of policies under the banner of the 'war on terror' that have had little or no coherent relationship with the threat of terrorist attacks per se, from granting additional powers to police and security services to invading Iraq. In each case it has been notable that normal standards of transparent, evidence-based, contestable public policy consideration and debate have been discarded in favour of unexamined, and frequently mistaken, assertions by national leaders about the nature of a threat and the appropriateness of a response.

It may be that we can see in this national security model of leadership a reversion to what we might think of us a more tribal concept in which the roles of political leader and military leader were merged — the ruler as war leader. In actual combat, this model of war leadership makes sense; because of the pressure for instant and decisive action to achieve immediate and overriding objectives do not favour more analytic and consultative models. But leading a complex modern society, even in a major war, is very different from leading an infantry company in combat. There may be times — in total national emergencies like those faced by Churchill in 1940 or by Curtin in late 1941 — when even for modern societies the war leader model works best. But such circumstances are extremely rare.

How and why, then, have some modern democratic leaders like Howard found themselves adopting this leadership model, in the absence of the kind of extreme security threats which might justify them in doing so? I think the answer is simply this: leaders such as Howard, Blair and Bush[5] have actively sought to interpret events and fashion policy agendas which have allowed them to project themselves as war leaders to their constituents. They have wanted to be seen as war leaders, and they have willingly promoted an interpretation of the policy challenges they faced as a war in order to allow them to do that. The rhetorical mechanisms at work here are pretty simple: by magnifying our enemy, we magnify ourselves; by identifying our struggle with the great struggles of the past, we identify ourselves with the great leaders of the past. The willingness of leaders to do this tells us something about them, but the political success they have enjoyed as a result tells us something also about ourselves as citizens. Leadership is, after all, transactional — it has to be not just given but received. It is hard to escape the conclusion that Howard, Bush, and Blair have projected themselves as war leaders because that is what they think voters think and, for a while, it seemed they did. It is, therefore, hard to escape the suspicion that within the modern citizen there lurks some kind of nostalgia for the strong, simple, primarily xenophobic leadership of a more primitive and immediately violent age.

The political appeal of war leadership, and the temptations this provides to politicians, is hardly new. Even highly managerial leaders like Bob Hawke could occasionally benefit from it. In 1990-91 Bob Hawke's standing was boosted by his role in leading Australia in the Iraq-Kuwait crisis, and in the early 1980s Thatcher's leadership in Britain was boosted, and even rescued, by the Falklands. Barry Buzan and others have written extensively on the way in which political leaders and systems use the emotive and political potency of 'security' to garner power and authority — a process they call 'securitisation' (Buzan, Weaver, and de Wilde 1998). But I think that over the past few years — since 9/11, in fact — national security issues and national security models of leadership have been used to frame and project political leadership to a much greater degree, and for much longer periods, than we have seen in comparable societies for a long time.

Of course, there would be nothing surprising in this if it were true that since 9/11 we have been facing a threat to national security greater than any we have seen for a very long time. A central premise of the projection of war leadership over the past six years has been the assertion that terrorism poses a mortal threat to our nation, our society, the global order and our way of life: as big a threat, it is often said, as did the challenges from Fascism and Communism in the twentieth century. So it is central to my argument here that I do not believe that to be the case. This is not the place to present an extended argument on that, so let me simply offer my hunch that in a decade's time we will look back and wonder how a statement so obviously false could have been believed by so many people for so long with such conviction. Terrorism is a serious problem and the risk of nuclear terrorism is especially grave. But to compare the consequences of even a nuclear terrorist attack with World War II suggests a major collective lapse of historical perspective and common sense.

'We live in a time of war'

If that is right, then the way that national security has intruded into our concepts and practices of political leadership seems to require serious attention. The fact that Howard, like Bush and Blair, so comprehensively projected himself as a war leader, and was — at least for a while — so successful in doing so, in the absence of a genuine war, seems to tell us something interesting and perhaps disheartening, about the nature of political leadership in Australia. It is especially striking in Australia's case because we have little or no tradition of war leadership. Britain, of course, has Churchill himself, as well as long traditions stretching back through Wellington to Henry V. The US has Washington, Lincoln, Grant, Teddy Roosevelt and Eisenhower. But for Australia, World War I threw up no enduring figure of war leadership and World War II produced, after Menzies' failure in the role, only the curious, complex, and ambivalent figure of John Curtin. So Howard was, in a sense, trying something new in the annals of Australian political leadership.

It would be interesting to catalogue in some detail exactly how this has been done over the years since 9/11. Here there is only space to identify the main themes through which Howard projected himself as a war leader. It started with the characterisation of the response to the original attacks as a 'war', from which a great deal else has flowed: the magnification of the threat to existential proportions; the characterisation of the adversary as inhumanly evil; the repeated affirmation that we will never surrender to terrorists; the call to the nation for a contribution to the common defence by each citizen, uniting the nation in a mighty collective effort to safeguard all we hold precious. Perhaps most tellingly, when the question of his retirement came on the agenda around his 64th birthday, Howard declared that he was determined to remain to lead Australia through this immensely challenging period. As late as March 2007, Howard was still saying, 'We live in a time of war'.

We can probably trace the origins of Howard's model of war leadership back before 9/11 to the East Timor Crisis of 1999. I think it can be argued that his role in that crisis transformed Howard's view of himself, and encouraged him to think that he could recast his identity as leader away from the rather drab bean-counting persona that had stuck with him since his time as Treasurer to something more glamorous and compelling. But it was not until the war on terror after 9/11 that the opportunity arose to reprise that role and embed it in his core leadership style. After 9/11 it can be argued that Howard's whole approach to leadership was reformed on the 'war leader' model.

One critical factor in Howard's national-security leadership after 9/11 was the apparent collapse of processes of advice from the bureaucracy concerning key assessments and decisions being made. Much has been made of the failure of Australia's intelligence agencies to provide better advice on the state of Iraq's WMD programs, but far more important is the failure of the Government's foreign and strategic policy-advising institutions to provide advice on whether, even assuming Iraq had WMD, invasion of the country was a good idea. Some may suspect that this failure reflected the erosion of policy-advising capacities in key Commonwealth departments, but there is no doubt that such advice — and good quality advice – would have been available if ministers had wanted it. The fact that it was not suggests to me that ministers — and especially the Prime Minister — conveyed a clear impression that such advice was not needed or wanted.[6]

How calculated was Howard's adoption of the war leader's persona? Some will be tempted to see his approach to the war on terror as a cynical exploitation of popular fears after the shock of 9/11 to bolster his own electoral standing. But I am not sure it was that simple. Clearly he was following where others led: almost all the elements of his projection as war leader were appropriated from Bush and Blair. Like Bush and Blair, he was following, or at least sailing in convoy with, wider intellectual fashions. At first, at least, many people inside and outside government — especially in the US — argued forcefully that the West was at war and needed a war leader. I think in Howard's case, as in many others, he was happy enough to accept what so many were saying, without bothering much to work out if it was true, because it suited him. We cannot say that Howard deliberately concocted the war on terror as a political artefact, but we can perhaps surmise that he self-consciously exploited it to project an image of his leadership which had evident popular appeal, and that he did so without reflecting on the real national interests at stake and how they might be affected.

For Howard, moreover, war leadership dovetailed with a broader political agenda. The past, and management of the way people view the past, was always central to Howard's political strategy. In this respect he differs from Blair, and even from Bush. Projecting himself as a war leader gave Howard firmer ownership of Australia's core national stories, because those stories revolve so much around our military exploits. Howard is hardly the first leader to try this: the appropriation of the ANZAC story for political purposes can be said to have entered its current phase with Paul Keating's repatriation of the Australian Unknown Soldier. But under Howard the political management of history became a central concern, and the projection of himself as war leader did much to promote his appropriation of Australia's military past for contemporary political benefit.

Finally, and notwithstanding the focus on John Howard in the preceding paragraphs, it is important to note that he was not the only political leader who sought to project himself as a war leader in the years since 9/11. State premiers were often enthusiastic to identify themselves with national security issues which arguably went beyond the traditional state concerns with law and order. One of Morris Iemma's first actions after assuming the Premiership of NSW was to announce a highly questionable scheme for the evacuation of Sydney's CBD in the event of a terrorist attack, and state premiers were quick to call for new tougher measures against terrorism after the London bombings of 7 July 2005. At the Commonwealth level, other ministers also echoed the Prime Minister's focus on national security. In May 2002, for example, Peter Costello devoted almost half of his Budget Speech to national security questions before turning to the economy — an emphasis unprecedented since World War II.

Proof of the pudding

From a policy maker's perspective, leadership is most naturally judged instrumentally: does it produce good outcomes? We, therefore, need to ask how well national security policy has been done under Howard's war leadership. There are four brief observations we might make.

First, so far as we can tell the most effective policy responses to the threat posed by terrorism since 9/11 were essentially bureaucratic. The high-profile leadership decisions about major military deployments and additional police powers have probably done little if anything to reduce the likelihood of a terrorist attack and may have been counterproductive. More effective measures such as increased funding and numbers for intelligence agencies and police forces have been relatively low-key. The natural conclusion to draw is that the high-profile 'tough decisions' that would-be war leaders feel called upon to make may have little to do with meeting real threats and much more to do with projecting an impression of the leader's determination and strength than with achieving an effective response to the threat.

Second, some of the policies that have been presented as central to political leadership in the war on terror have in fact been empty. Howard, for example, like Bush and Blair, often made much of his policy of refusing to give in to or negotiate with terrorists. This kind of talk conveys an agreeably Churchillian aroma, but it means nothing. There has been no occasion since 9/11 in which negotiating with terrorists has seriously been an option and there is no likelihood that it will be. Such statements have been pure posturing.

Third, some of the policies and approaches that have been adopted have been evidently counterproductive — and these are especially the higher-profile polices and rhetoric that have been adopted to give substance to the national security leadership model. The characterisation of terrorism as a threat to our way of life and the international order has almost certainly helped encourage terrorism by exaggerating the damage that can be done to society by these random acts of pointless violence which, in reality, achieve nothing except what we do to ourselves through our own exaggerated responses to them. Potential terrorists believe our leaders when they say that terrorism poses an existential threat and are encouraged by it. Some of the expansions of police and surveillance powers have arguably helped to build a sense of alienation between Islamic communities and others, which also helps the terrorist recruiters. And the decision to invade Iraq was, to put it mildly, a misconceived response to the threat we face from terrorists. Indeed the strange failures of decision making that led into Iraq provide a caution about the dangers that arise when war leadership models are adopted by those who face much more modest problems. When the full story is written it may appear that one of the potent factors leading to the American decision to invade was the need to meet public expectations of decisive action which had been fanned by the rhetoric of war leadership. It may be not so much that Bush, followed by Blair and Howard, talked up the war on terror in order to invade Iraq as it was that they found they had to invade Iraq in order to justify the posture of war leadership they had adopted after 9/11.

Finally, while Howard was posing as a war leader in the war on terror, some more serious security issues — ones that really might pose a fundamental risk to our well being — were allowed to languish without serious policy attention.

One could mention, for example, global warming, avian influenza and the immense questions posed about Asia's stability by the rise of China and what it means for the future of American primacy. What this list suggests, is that when we face serious security issues the last thing we need is the atavistically appealing, but often-dysfunctional, leadership provided under the war leadership model. We need quite the opposite, in fact: attention to evidence, careful consideration of alternatives, balance, inclusiveness and a real grasp of our long-term trends and interests. And, where needed, a willingness to take unpopular decisions that serve those long-term interests.

Conclusion: beyond Howard

This analysis carries interesting implications for the way the present Prime Minister, Kevin Rudd, and his successors might approach the task of national security leadership. It suggests, first, that they should resist the temptation to see national security crises as opportunities to recast their leadership in a more heroic mould and instead aim to bring to the making and presentation of decisions in the national security field the same kinds of rigour, discipline and due diligence that should characterise good public policy and good democratic leadership in any other field of government. After the first six months of the Rudd Government, the signs are not especially encouraging. The new Government's first 'strategic crisis' was the shooting of Jose Ramos Horta in East Timor in February 2008. The first reaction was immediately to send additional Australian soldiers and police to East Timor without waiting to learn what had actually occurred and without any clear idea of what the additional forces might do. This response suggested an overwhelming desire to be seen to do something decisive, and not to be seen to be reluctant to deploy forces — in short, a desire to be seen to follow Howard's example. A better response would have been to make a point of assessing the situation a little more carefully, and to send forces only if there was a clear requirement for them.

This early experience suggests, secondly, that a new government needs to start building a different, more robust and effective model of national security leadership early, before crises emerge. The essence of that model is quite simple: that national security issues, including national security crises, need to be approached with the same model of leadership as any other major policy question. The standards of good public policy and effective political leadership are the same. And indeed, we look at the great democratic war leaders of history, we can see this at work. Lincoln, perhaps the greatest of them, never oversimplified or glorified the issues, never ceased to explore the options, and went out of his way to avoid glamorising his own role as leader. Rudd's challenge is to build a new model of national security leadership which genuinely supports our national security.

References

Blair, T., 2006, 'Global Alliance for Global Values,' Speech to a joint sitting of the Australian Parliament, 27 March, <http://www.number-10.gov.uk/output/Page9245.asp> [Accessed 30 May 2008].

Buzan, B., O. Weaver and J. de Wilde, 1998, *Security: A New Framework for Analysis*, Boulder: Lynne Rienner.

Cohen, E., 2002, *Supreme Command: Soldiers, Statesmen and Leadership in Wartime,* New York: Free Press.

Cosgrove, P., 2006, *My Story*, Syndey: Harper Collins..

Edwards, P., 2006, *Arthur Tange: Last of the Mandarins*, Sydney: Allen & Unwin.

Horner, D., 2000, *Defence Supremo: Sir Frederick Shedden and the Making of Australian Defence Policy*, Sydney: Allen & Unwin.

Serle, G., 1982, *John Monash: A Biography,* Melbourne: Melbourne University Press.

ENDNOTES

[1] I should perhaps point out at the start that I am not a political scientist, but rather a student of strategic policy. My credentials to contribute to debates on leadership are therefore limited to my knowledge of and reflections about how leadership has been exercised in the policy area which I study. I trust that readers with more expertise will make allowances accordingly.

[2] There is one important exception to this proposition. In the years after the East Timor intervention of 1999 a military officer — Peter Cosgrove — became identified as a national leader in a way perhaps unprecedented in Australian history. How and why this happened, and how it related to the developments in national-security leadership I will explore in this essay, would be a fruitful focus for further work. A starting point would be Cosgrove's own memoir (2006).

[3] It can be argued that both Bush and Howard won re-election in 2004 despite the evident failure of their policies in Iraq because of their ability to portray their willingness to stick out the problems there as evidence of firm resolve.

[4] Apparently this was the unfortunate implication drawn from George Bush's reading in 2002 of Eliot Cohen's excellent book on war leadership, which has much to say of interest in the current context.

[5] The literature on the leadership of these three leaders in the war on terror is vast, but the patterns we are studying here are best seen in their own speeches. Perhaps the clearest and starkest, because the best drafted, examples are to be found in a series of speeches Tony Blair gave in 2006. See for example his Speech to a joint sitting of the Australian Parliament: *Global Alliance for Global Values.*

[6] There is some anecdotal evidence that from the start of the war on terror attempts to convey reservations about the directions of US policy from officials to ministers met strong resistance.

14. Police Leadership in Australia: Managing Networks

Jenny Fleming and Rob Hall

> Organisations are bound up with the conditions of their environment. Indeed, it has been said that all organisations engage in activities which have as their logical conclusion adjustment to the environment (Hawley 1950: 3).

Introduction

There is a tendency in the police literature to attribute organisational activity and outcomes to individual action and specific internal factors (see, for example, Reiner 1991; Etter and Palmer 1995; Adlam 1998a, 1998b; Adlam and Villiers 2003; Haberfeld 2006). Relatively little of the police leadership literature focuses on the environmental context of organisations. Indeed, a recent entry in an international dictionary of policing on 'police leadership' refers to 'the varied nature of the interpersonal relationships between police managers and supervisors and the impact of these upon organisational performance'. The management of external environments is not considered in the entry (Bradley 2009). Such texts neglect the importance of political and social context and the external environment in which police leaders operate. No organisation operates in a vacuum. Perhaps we should not be surprised — the environment within which police work has changed significantly. Other studies of police leadership have also largely assumed the internal perspective with little reference to external activity. In 1991, Reiner's seminal work on police leaders in the UK identified leaders' 'main management problems' as relating to budgeting issues, internal communications, the increasing size of their organisations and the difficulties associated with meeting a variety of internal expectations (1991: 227-8). Similarly in Bradley, Walker and Wilkies' *Managing the Police* the emphasis is on 'managing within the police service' and there is no discussion at all of 'leadership' (1986: 3).

Today, internal issues are still important, but police organisations in Australia and elsewhere recognise that, to operate effectively, organisations must interact with their external environment and manage and steer the networks and the relationships successfully (Mitchell and Casey 2007: 201ff). As much of the public administration literature shows, a successful organisational leader is one that demonstrates 'the ability to cope with environmental contingencies; negotiating changes to ensure the continuation of needed resources'. Dealing only with internal adjustments, however effectively, will not guarantee 'survival of the organisation' (Pfeffer and Salancik 1978: 258). Police leadership now requires, in Rhodes' terms (1997: 57), a 'distinctive managerial style based on facilitation, accommodation and bargaining'.

This chapter considers these observations in the context of police leadership in Australia. It suggests that while internal management is important, strong and effective police leadership is increasingly about negotiating and managing the external and, in Emery and Trist's terms (1969), the often 'turbulent' and 'relatively uncertain' environment. It is about recognising the changing and dynamic nature of that environment, identifying the important actors and successfully interacting with those actors in an effort to maximise the control the leader has over his/her organisation and its resources. As well, it acknowledges the diverse nature of the governing structures within police organisations. After all, policing is also still about command and control regardless of the push for network activity (Fleming and Rhodes 2005). Creating the right balance within the organisation and minimising the impact of any potentially negative external elements on the organisation's resource base will be key roles for the police leader in the 21st century.

We begin by providing a brief historical and institutional context for policing in Australia, demonstrating the traditional role of the police leader as working with and through their organisation with an emphasis on internal management. In the absence of any theoretical frameworks for police leadership we don public administration spectacles and draw on public administration literature to discuss public leadership and the management of external constituencies. Drawing on resource dependency theory, the chapter identifies a number of strategies open to organisations to manage inter-organisational dependence and the power of external environmental elements. We provide illustrative examples. The chapter argues that a critical role for police leaders is to identify and pursue strategies that allow them to negotiate and manage the overlapping networks that make up their external constituency as well manage the internal dynamics of the organisation.

The Australian context of policing

Australia comprises six States — Queensland; New South Wales (NSW); Victoria; Tasmania; South Australia (SA); and Western Australia (WA) and, for the purposes of policing, two Territories, the Australian Capital Territory (ACT) and the Northern Territory (NT). Each jurisdiction has a Police Commissioner (or in the case of the ACT, a Chief Police Officer) and its own government-administered police agency. The Australian Federal Police (AFP) is Australia's federal law enforcement agency. It provides a community policing service to the ACT government. With a national total of approximately 52,000 officers, the eight police forces range in size from NSW with almost 15,000 officers to the ACT with approximately 621.

Australian police organisations were shaped and consolidated in the mid-1850s in a colonial context, 'which gave them a specific political and administrative role' involved in a variety of duties. Over time police were formed into 'substantial bureaucratic organisations'. These highly centralised organisations were 'subject to the powerful authority of a single [Police] Commissioner, subject *de jure* to the direction of a responsible minister' (Finnane 1994: 29-30, 34). The following decades were characterised by the growing importance and political influence of the Police Commissioner, 'sustained by judicial and political affirmation of the relative independence and autonomy of police administrations in police affairs' (Finnane 1994: 31).

Over time, the formation of police unions (Finnane 1994: 44-51; Fleming and Marks 2004) and the increasing involvement of political figures in police operations (Fleming 2004) curtailed the Commissioner's autonomy and forced him to look beyond the four walls of his organisation. Prior to the 1980s, police organisations were structured on authoritarian, paramilitary lines and regulated through strict organisational rules and legislation. Recruitment, training, promotion and disciplinary processes were conducted internally and in line with administrative trends elsewhere. Police organisations were hierarchical, inwardly focused and conducted their business through the relevant police departments and their attendant bureaucracies (Fleming and Lafferty 2000).

New management techniques derived primarily from the private sector were introduced in the 1980s to restructure public sector agencies along broadly corporate lines. Administrative and police reform became a continuing activity for police organisations. Performance management regimes, new accountability mechanisms, external civilian review bodies, budgetary concerns and recruitment and retention strategies became central issues for the police leader. The external environment had also changed. A new focus on community policing, with its emphasis on working with communities to identify problems and solutions, was an example of such change. Communities were now consumers or clients and educated to expect a particular level of service. A number of mechanisms were put in place whereby community satisfaction with police services was monitored regularly, resulting in a more outwardly focused pro-active emphasis on police practice (Fleming and O'Reilly 2007).

The political salience of domestic law and order issues and the perceived threat of terrorism activities have become part of the everyday discourse of politics (and indeed the media). Once part of every bureaucratic decision and change, police commissioners are now part of a rapidly changing world where delegation is the order of the day and they are assessed as much for their ability to manage their external constituencies — and to operate effectively in a public arena — as they are for their internal management skills.

Slowly, Australian police organisations have broadened their horizons and have acknowledged the changing environment in which they are now expected to operate. The traditional closed and insular nature of police organisations, committed essentially to managing the internal components of the organisation, has given way to a stronger focus on external constituencies. The 'tell 'em nothing era' (Munday 1995) has faltered under the gaze of an increasingly intrusive media and self-aware communities who demand to be informed and consulted about the way police do business. Every jurisdiction now has a media director and media department. As MacDonald has commented, such a level of scrutiny ensures that every comment or decision made by a police leader has the potential to become part of a public debate. As he points out, 'Today, policing is everybody's business' (1995: 220-1). The police leadership role is shaped accordingly. The following section turns to the issue of leadership and the increasing need to interact with other organisations in an effort to manage resources and minimise the impact of external elements.

Public leadership and external constituencies

Storey (2004: 23-5) cites the importance of big picture sense-making (i.e. the ability to scan and interpret the environment; to identify threats to and opportunities for the organisation; and to assess the strengths and weaknesses of the organisation); the ability to deliver change and inter-organisational representation (involving skills such as coalition-building, understanding others' perspectives, persuasion and the assessment of client needs) as crucial elements of good leadership.

While we acknowledge the significance of these capabilities, we would add that such behavioural attributes are much broader than he sketches and more literally embodies Allison's (1982: 17) 'external constituencies'. These include, dealing with external units of the organisation and dealing with independent organisations such as other public sector agencies, interest groups, the private and voluntary sectors, the public, and the media. In other words, engaging in external network activity and developing strategies to steer and manage those networks. Ferlie and Pettigrew's work has shown that public sector managers are increasingly looking to the external environment. In their study of network management in the British National Health System (1996: 88-9), Ferlie and Pettigrew's CEOs felt themselves to be highly 'outward facing' and believed that it was crucial to institutionalise strategic alliances by fostering a shift from reliance on interpersonal trust to a deeper inter-organisational trust (Ferlie and Pettigrew 1996: 88-9). How then to achieve such focus?

A resource dependence perspective, based on the seminal work of Thompson (1967), Elkin (1975), Pfeffer and Salancik (1978) and Rhodes (1997) provides insights into what this 'outward facing' leadership of network management entails. This perspective starts from the premise that, to survive, organisations require resources. The acquisition of these resources typically means that the organisation must interact with others who control them. Control over required resources provides those who control them with power over the organisation. It follows, then, that managing relations with networks of interdependence is the focus of much organisational attention and activity. In the following section we identify a number of strategies available to organisations to manage dependence: the development and maintenance of alternative sources of needed resources; the acquisition of prestige; contracting or bargaining; penetration; knowledge-driven strategies; and the socialisation of conflict. It is not an exhaustive list. It provides a context for us to frame the increasingly outward focus of Australian police leaders

Network management by Australian police leaders

Managers and, for our purpose, police leaders can seek to minimise the power of external environmental elements over them by adopting a number of strategies (see for example, Kickert *et al*. 1997; Perri 6 *et al*. 2002). Thompson (1967: 32-3) refers to competitive strategies, one example of which is the development and maintenance of alternative sources of needed resources. The recruitment of police officers from a relatively small pool has meant that finding alternative sources has been a preoccupation for Australian police leaders.

In the face of unusually high attrition rates, many Australian police organisations have, in recent years, needed to negotiate the difficulties of recruiting police officers. The lack of suitable applicants has been compounded by a number of issues. The AFP's continued involvement with international deployment activity has seen the secondment of several state and territory officers to overseas postings indefinitely. The growth of the AFP's national counter-terrorism activities in Australia has required a significant increase in specialist personnel. It is common knowledge that the AFP is successfully enticing such specialist staff from the States and Territories. Rather than relying on poaching officers from other Australian jurisdictions and/or hoping for an increase in interested parties, many States are now competing against each other in the quest for recruits. Most jurisdictions are looking carefully at alternative recruitment sources. Strong economic booms in Queensland and Western Australia (WA) have seen many officers abandon policing for lucrative jobs in the States' mining industries. At the present time, WA Police is competing with jurisdictions, not only in Australia but also in the United Kingdom, to recruit British police officers. In the past year, South Australian police leaders have successfully recruited over 200 trained officers from Britain.

Acquiring prestige is another important competitive strategy. As Thompson notes (1967: 33), 'Acquiring prestige is the "cheapest" way of acquiring power'. It is a strategy whereby organisations create and maintain a 'favourable image of the organisation in its salient publics'. This is crucial when support from external constituencies is required to control, or reduce dependency. Prestige is acquired in a number of ways, most obviously in the representative role of the Commissioner.

The representative role of police leaders is now an accepted part of a police leader's portfolio. An examination of one police leader's diaries reveal that the external representative role in the years 2001-05 took up almost 60% of the Commissioner's working time. Apart from extensive engagement with the media over this period the interactive role includes formal meetings with the Police Minister, meetings with other government figures (including opposition members), meetings with the Ombudsman, working on external committees, parliamentary estimate hearings, liaising with the police union and various other activities that involve working closely with a variety of external organisations and networks. By far the more time-consuming work is the Commissioner's 'community role'. Official ceremonies, invited speeches and attending social gatherings as 'Commissioner' takes up the bulk of the external constituency work. The work is regarded as crucial in maintaining the organisation's positive and prestigious profile in the community. [1]

Cooperative strategies — or tactics as Perri 6 *et al.* (2002: 126) refer to them — are increasingly utilised by police leaders. Thomson talks about contracting or bargaining (Thompson 1967: 34-6). Elkin (1975: 175) refers to 'exchange' whereby an organisation may negotiate a deal with another organisation on which it may depend for resources. In Australia, the police union movement is active, politically manipulative and not reluctant to flex its industrial muscle where necessary (Fleming and Marks 2004). The organisations are staffed by professional industrial advocates and non-police personnel. Working police officers form an executive which oversees activities. The organisations have significant amounts of money and are a formidable external presence for Australian police organisations. In most jurisdictions the unions enjoy almost 100% membership. Most police leaders have, in recent years, been required to bargain either in a formal industrial relations context with their respective unions or in a more public setting where unions are threatening to withdraw resources if their needs or demands are not met. Such scenarios have, in recent years, become quite common in specific States. The degree to which the police organisation has been able to develop 'a favourable image … in its salient publics' is often important in the context of community support and also when bargaining situations have to be negotiated by third parties (Fleming and Lafferty 2001).

Another cooperative strategy is that of penetration (Elkin 1975: 175), whereby an organisation places its own personnel into the organisation in which it is dependent. Two short examples illustrate the point. As national security and technological crime become a central focus for police organisations, knowledge becomes an important commodity. Many organisations seek out the information by placing their own personnel into organisations that have this information. So for example, senior officers in Australia have been seconded to the nation's airline in order to understand and develop strategies around aviation security. Similarly, technological challenges for police have meant close ties with computer technology organisations as together they seek to curtail the rising levels of cybercrime.

Knowledge-driven strategies or tactics are defined by Perri *et al*. (2002: 127) as those which seek to create a 'specialist structure for knowledge creating and sharing'. In Elkin's terms this could also be referred to as 'penetration'. The emphasis in Australia on police professionalism, tertiary education and the importance of evidence-based research in policing has led to all jurisdictions collaborating with universities and other knowledge based institutions to deliver education and training services and to engage in research that will inform police policy and practice. We now talk about 'police research networks' (Bradley *et al* 2006).

Illustrating this strategy further is the recent establishment of the Australia and New Zealand Policing Advisory Agency (ANZPAA). In an effort to provide stronger support to police commissioners and collaborate effectively across the jurisdictions, Australian police commissioners have brought together 17 agencies previously committed to research, policy advice, training and education initiatives and a variety of police advisory forums to form a cross-jurisdictional organisation. ANZPAA is staffed by police personnel and trained researchers and the emphasis is on knowledge-management and information sharing. ANZPAA's role will be to develop research and policy and provide strategic advice and support to the Australian and New Zealand Police Commissioners. This knowledge-driven strategy allows for a range of occupational experts, researchers and consultants to engage in advocacy to build an environment and culture, in which police commissioners can direct their resources to attaining knowledge they require and in the format they prefer, rather than relying solely on university researchers, monitoring databases and official state statistics for their information. Such a prestigious organisation will assist in facilitating information sharing across a variety of organisations and will assist in building and sharing information with those among whom they seek integration (Perri 6 *et al*. 2002: 126-7). Such a structure has created a 'specialist structure for knowledge creating and sharing'. It also allows police commissioners to identify their favoured research areas and control the dissemination of the findings.

A final example can be identified using Elkin's discussion of the 'socialisation of conflict' whereby the focal organisation attempts to involve other actors in a particular issue in order to broaden the scope of discussion and/or possibilities in an attempt to alter the balance of opinion and resources confronting the organisation (Elkin 1975: 173-5).

In July 2007, following a suicide attack at Glasgow airport in Scotland, the AFP apprehended Dr Haneef trying to leave Australia. He was held without charge under new laws that allowed terrorism suspects to be detained indefinitely without questioning. The charges were dropped soon after, although his working visa was revoked on 'character grounds'. A political controversy arose around immigration policy and the extent to which the AFP had played into the hands of a government seeking to impose its anti-terrorist policies ahead of an imminent federal election. The media focus compelled everyone involved to seek mitigating circumstances for their actions.

The Director of Public Prosecutions (DPP) admitted to mistakes, blaming an 'over-worked prosecutor for undue haste'. The AFP Commissioner's strategy was to deflect effectively the onus of responsibility by pointing the finger elsewhere. Despite discrepancies in the interview process (the transcript of which was made public by Haneef's lawyers) and a court affidavit, and despite the British authorities disputing the AFP's account of the affair, the AFP response was to widen the scope of conflict.

In the first instance, the AFP Commissioner made formal complaints to the Legal Services Commission about Haneef's legal team releasing information to the media during an inquiry. Effectively such an action meant that the lawyer in question could be struck off the Register of Barristers. Such a strategy ensured front-page headlines and high profile debate. The Commissioner publicly refuted the way in which Australian courts operated, arguing that, 'The courts ... are going to need to change the way they view evidence, witnesses and forensics'. His railing against the 'court of public opinion' and the irresponsible media 'hampering the efforts of police' was widely reported in the media. The Commissioner's allegations that he had advised the DPP that the evidence was weak, but that 'the police were obliged to charge Haneef on the prosecutor's advice' was also widely reported. Despite the obvious blunderings of the organisation, his assertions to a Senate Committee hearing that there was no need for the AFP to 'alter our policies or alter our approaches' compounded the organisation's efforts to widen the scope of conflict in the political arena.

By altering the balance of opinion in the public arena and diluting the onus of responsibility, the AFP Commissioner had effectively in, Elkin's terms, 'socialised the conflict'. While many media outlets commented on the Commissioner's attitude that 'everyone was to blame but him,' the strategy was successful. At one point it looked like the Commissioner would lose his job but the moment passed as 'ongoing inquiries' have served to defer a conclusion to the affair.

These examples have sought to demonstrate the way in which police organisations can manage dependence and minimise the power of external environmental elements. Such strategies are not mutually exclusive. For example, the AFP and its standing in the community (a standing that the AFP and its public relations department work on fervently) was frequently commented on in the media at the same time it was vilifying the organisation's behaviour in the Haneef case. The prestige of the organisation became a mitigating factor that the AFP could fall back on in the face of a barrage of external criticism.

Conclusions

Elkin notes (1975: 175-6) that while one actor in the network may be engaged in one or more of these strategies, others are similarly engaged. As a result there is a complex dynamic at work, 'there are multiple, overlapping relationships, each one of which is, to a greater or lesser degree, dependent on the state of the others'. It is in recognising this complex dynamic and identifying the most appropriate strategy to achieve a specific objective that the police leader will demonstrate to what extent he/she has developed a skill set for managing networks. And the stakes can be high. Coping with external contingencies and constraints is critical to organisational effectiveness and, in many cases, survival. As Pfeffer and Salancik (1978: 137) succinctly put it, when external demands cannot be met because of constraints on the organisation, the leader can be removed: the replacement of the leader, who has come to symbolise the organisation to various groups, may well be sufficient to relieve pressures on the organisation. Or, as noted above, strategies to manage dependence and conflict may well save the day.

Police leadership is fraught with difficulty. The modern Australasian policing environment is increasingly complex and challenging. Changing demographic, social, and economic conditions; transnational crime, terrorism, peacekeeping and international deployments have served to broaden the focus of police leaders. Law and order was always a political minefield and continues to be so. New and emerging technologies have transformed the nature of crime and the manner in which police respond to it. Traditional police tasks such as finger printing and escorting prisoners to court are now outsourced by many organisations. Meeting community expectations, providing a visible presence and working with a variety of stakeholders to identify and solve problems is resource intensive. Such complex changes require police leaders to look forward and outward to ensure that they have the capacity to anticipate and manage resource dependency and the external environment.

This complex and ever changing environment raises a number of issues for police governance. Traditionally, police leaders in Australia were autonomous and answerable only to the department. They ran tight, authoritarian organisations that were essentially inwardly focused. Today, command and control is still the dominant governing structure in police organisations but the external environment requires more flexibility than this structure allows. The importance of working with communities and connecting with external constituencies is crucial. In doing so new governing structures with an emphasis on networks and partnerships have come to shape and determine many aspects of the police leader's role. But, as Fleming and Rhodes have noted (2005: 203), 'the cooperative behaviour of a network can collapse under the impact of competition or of changed priorities'. Ensuring the capacity of the organisation for command and control responses while at the same time maintaining the fine balance of an inter-dependent network, managing dependence and the external influence of organisations is a primary focus for today's police leader. In some ways it may well be regarded as what Mark Moore has termed an 'impossible job' (1990: 72).

References

Adlam, R., 1998a, 'Uncovering the "ethical profile" of police managers and the "moral ethos" of police organisations: A preliminary study', *International Journal of Police Science and Management*, 1:2, pp. 162-83.

Adlam, R., 1998b, 'What should we expect from police leaders?' *Police Research and Management*, Spring, pp. 17-30.

Adlam, R. and P. Villiers, 2002, *Police Leadership in the Twenty-first Century: Philosophy, Doctrine and Developments*, Winchester: Waterside Press.

Allison,Jr. G. T., 1982, 'Public and Private Management: Are they fundamentally alike in all unimportant respects?', in F. S. Lane (ed) *Current Issues in Public Administration*, 2nd edition, New: York: St Martin's Press, pp. 13-33

Bradley, D., 2009, 'Police Leadership', in A. Wakefield and J. Fleming (eds), *The Sage Dictionary of Policing*, London: Sage Publishing (forthcoming).

Bradley, D., C. Nixon and M. Marks, 2006, 'What works, what doesn't work and what looks promising in police research networks', in J. Fleming and J. Wood (eds) *Fighting Crime Together: The Challenges of Policing and Security Networks*, Sydney: University of New South Wales Press, pp. 170-94.

Bradley, D., N. Walker and R. Wilkie, 1986, *Managing the Police: Law, Organisation and Democracy*, Sussex: Harvester Press.

Elkin, S. L., 1975, 'Comparative urban politics and interorganisational behaviour', in K. Young (ed) *Essays on the Study of Urban Politics*, London: MacMillan Press, pp. 158-184.

Emery, F. E. and E. L. Trist, 1969, 'The causal texture of organizational environments', in F. E. Emery (ed) *Systems Thinking*, Harmondsworth: Penguin, pp. 241-57.

Etter, B. and M. Palmer, 1995, *Police Leadership in Australasia*, Leichhardt: Federation Press.

Ferlie, E. and A. Pettigrew, 1996, 'Managing through networks: Some issues and implications for the NHS', *British Journal of Management*, 7, pp. 81-99.

Finnane, M., 1994, *Police and Government: Histories of Policing and in Australia*, Oxford: Oxford University Press.

Fleming, J., 2004a, 'Les liaisons dangereuses: Relations between police commissioners and their political masters', *Australian Journal of Public Administration*, 63:3, pp. 60-74.

Fleming, J., 2004b, 'Commissioner Mick Keelty, Australian Federal Police', *Police Practice and Research, an International Journal*, 5:4/5, pp. 317-26.

Fleming, J. and G. Lafferty, 2000, 'New management techniques and restructuring in police organisations', *Policing: An International Journal of Police Strategy and Management*, 23:2, pp. 154-168.

Fleming, J. and G. Lafferty, 2001, 'Police Unions, Industrial Strategies and Political Influence: Some Recent History', *International Journal of Employment Studies*, 9:2, pp. 131-40.

Fleming, J. and M. Marks, 2004, 'Reformers or Resisters? The State of Police Unionism in Australia', *Employment Relations Record*, 4:1, pp.

Fleming, J. and J. O'Reilly, 2007, 'The small-scale initiative: The rhetoric and the reality of community policing in Australia', *Policing: A Journal of Policy and Practice*, 1:2, pp. 1-8.

Fleming, J. and R. A. W. Rhodes, 2005, 'Bureaucracy, Contracts and Networks: The Unholy Trinity and the Police', *Australian and New Zealand Journal of Criminology*, 38:2, pp. 192-205.

Haberfeld, M. R., 2006, *Police Leadership*, New Jersey: Pearson Prentice Hall.

Hawley, A. H., 1950, *Human Ecology*, New York: Ronald Press.

Kickert, W. J. M., Klijn, E. H. and J. F. M. Koppenjan (eds), 1997, *Managing Complex Nnetworks: Strategies for the Public Sector*, London: Sage Publications.

MacDonald, R., 1995, 'Skills and Qualities required of police leaders, now and in the future', in B. Etter and M. Palmer (eds), *Police Leadership in Australasia*, Leichhardt, Federation Press, pp. 208-233.

Mitchell, M. and J. Casey (eds), 2007, *Police Leadership and Management*, Leichhardt: Federation Press.

Moore, M. H., 1990, 'Police leadership: The impossible dream?' in E. C. Hargrove and J. C. Glidewell (eds) *Impossible Jobs in Public Management*, Kansas: University Press of Kansas, pp. 72-102.

Munday, J., 1995, 'You can run, but you can't hide — dealing with the media, for chief executives' in B. Etter and M. Palmer (eds), *Police Leadership in Australasia*, Leichhardt, Federation Press, pp. 256-77.

Perri 6, D. Leat, K. Seltzer and G. Stoker, 2002, *Towards Holistic Governance: The New Reform Agenda*, Hampshire: Palgrave.

Pfeffer, J and G. Salancik, 1978, The External Control of Organisations: A Resource Dependence Perspective, New York: Harper and Row.

Reiner, R., 1991, *Chief Constables — Bosses, Bobbies or Bureaucrats?* Oxford: Oxford University Press.

Rhodes, R. A. W., 1997, *Understanding Governance*. Buckingham: Open University Press.

Storey, J., 2004, 'Changing theories of leadership and leadership development', in J. Storey (ed), *Leadership in Organisations: Current Issues and Key Trends*, London: Routledge, pp. 11-37.

Thompson, J. D, 1967, *Organisations in Action*, New York: McGraw Hill.

ENDNOTES
[1] Research in progress by Fleming.

15. Political and Media Leadership in the Age of YouTube

Stuart Cunningham

Introduction

In this chapter, I will track the key academic traditions that inform the field of media-politics relations. I will then argue that the way in which both political science and media and communications academic traditions approach the politics-media relationship — an 'inter-elite' account — is being eroded by contemporary developments in internet affordances, especially around the blogosphere, citizen journalism and the extent of 'virtual' public communication. The implications of these trends for political leadership and the media-politics relationship, focusing on some relevant developments during the 2007 Australian Federal election campaign, are then briefly explored.

Understanding the media-politics nexus: academic traditions

The media and politics literature has a venerable tradition. It dates from Harold Lasswell in the 1930s and his fundamental model of public communication as 'who says what, in which channel, to whom, and with what effect?' This highly influential model, psychologistic, individualistic and linear, was complicated by the work of Paul Lazarsfeld and his colleagues (Lazarsfeld *et al.* 1944[1969]) at the Bureau of Applied Social Research when they hypothesised a 'two step' flow between influencers like politicians — and the media in general — and the public. The role of opinion leaders became crucial in a less deterministic and complex model of public communication.

This forms part of a broader media and politics-effects studies tradition. It can be characterised as politico-centric (rather than media-centric) and focussed on political 'management' — the modernist assumption of political leaders' management of media in a close but controlled symbiosis. I would characterise this tradition as political science based on an 'inter-elite' model, which finds accomplished proponents in Australia in the work of, for example, Ian Ward (1994), Rod Tiffen (1989; 1999; 2001) and Murray Goot (Goot and Tiffen 1992).

A canonical work in this tradition is Tiffen's *News and Power* (1989). *News and Power* follows this tradition even as it complicates it. While the power of media to directly influence public opinion, and the power of media owners to control media content, are both overstated according to Tiffen (2006: 41), the analytical attention is on those ways, systemic as well as highly personal, that political and media elites interact for mutual advantage, deal making and power-assertion and, where necessary, power-sharing.

News and Power analyses the mechanism of inter-elite power and concentrates on the clashes of the elites — where elite interests do not align. In a contemporary setting, this would explain the government's inactions over more than a decade on media ownership changes — mooted twice and abandoned before there was finally some change in 2006-7. Another good example would be pay television policy in Australia, where the interests of the media elites clashed directly (Murdoch wanting it, Packer opposing it) such that political decision making was stymied for many years.

In the media and communication studies tradition, there is also a modernist school. Works such as Julianne Schultz's *Reviving the Fourth Estate* (1998) and Graeme Turner's *Ending the Affair* (2005) are good examples in this tradition. Turner's *Ending the Affair* is a history of current affairs television in Australia which decries the loss of its fourth estate function and argues that the only way forward for this media format is to recover such a function. Political leadership is able to escape close, sceptical scrutiny as a result of this decline, and the Australian polity and the intellectual and ethical provenance of Australian journalism is the poorer for it.

There is also a post-modernist tradition in media and communications studies which finds its partial mirror in varieties of post-modernist political science. Whereas the modernists see the contemporary Western public sphere having been tarnished or even fatally compromised by the encroachment of commercial media and communications, the postmodernists see the media having become the main, if not the only, vehicle for whatever can be held to exist of the public sphere in such societies. Such 'media-centric' theorists within these fields can hold that the media actually envelop the public sphere. For John Hartley (1999: 217-8):

> The 'mediasphere' is the whole universe of media … in all languages in all countries. It therefore completely encloses and contains as a differentiated part of itself the (Habermasian) public sphere (or the many pubic spheres), and it is itself contained by the much larger semiosphere … which is the whole universe of sense-making by whatever means, including speech … [It] is clear that television is a crucial site of the mediasphere and a crucial mediator between general cultural sense-making systems (the semiosphere) and specialist components of social sense-making like the public sphere. Hence the public sphere can be rethought not as a category binarily contrasted with its implied opposite, the private sphere, but as a 'Russian doll' enclosed within a larger mediasphere, itself enclosed within the semiosphere. And within 'the' public sphere, there may equally be found, Russian-doll style, further counter-cultural, oppositional or minoritarian public spheres.

Hartley's topography has the virtue of clarity, scope and heuristic utility, even while it remains provocatively media-centric. This is mostly due to Hartley's commitment to the strictly textual provenance of public communication, and to his interest in Lotman's notion of the semiosphere, more so than Habermas's modernist understanding of the public sphere standing outside of and even over and against its 'mediatisation'.

Such programmatic postmodernism comes to appear quite prescient when set against contemporary accounts of the *realpolitik* of political leadership. Tony Blair's seventh and final plenary address in the 'Our Nation's Future' series just before he stepped down (http://www.number-10.gov.uk/output/Page11923.asp) was about politics and the media. He lamented that no matter how available and open government/leadership is today, it doesn't matter, because of the way politics is reported — with exponentially increasing rhetorics of conflict, suspicion and cover up. The necessity for the modern political leader to lead *through and for* the media interface, aligning their style or persona with the protocols of 'politicotainment' (Riegert 2007), is the stuff of contemporary journalistic accounts of the modern political leader.

An Australian political leader who exemplified this approach was Queensland Premier Peter Beattie. Rather than a command-and-control 'management' of media through the calculated soundbite and the photo opportunity and carefully orchestrated rounds of the AM talk radio stations (a practice once thought mandatory and indeed cutting-edge in the 1990s and brought to temporary perfection by Prime Minister Howard), Beattie embodied the idea that 'you get to know your pollies in roughly the same fashion you get to know TV personalities' (Burchell 2007). This meant a focus on FM youth radio and light entertainment TV formats and 'politicians-as-everyday people' interactions demonstrating that they had a life outside politics. 'All this casualness and nonchalance, needless to say, took a fearsome amount of training and self-discipline' (Burchell 2007).

One of the important works of political science in the postmodernist tradition is Stephen Coleman's *A Tale of Two Houses* (2003[1]), which compares unflatteringly 'political junkies' with 'Big Brother' watchers. The former group, the 'PJs', exhibited more hierarchical and traditional attitudes to political participation, scorning the relevance of reality television's take on plebiscitary democracy (for example, audience voting on Big Brother evictees), while the BBs were more accepting of the relevance of PJ culture while typically not sharing it themselves. Coleman argues that mainstream politics could learn a great deal from the plebiscitary provenance of popular reality shows for the light they shed on contemporary forms of engagement with audiences, fans, communities, and constituencies.

Essentially, though, the modernist and postmodernist traditions are in broad agreement about the *objects* of analysis: mainstream media and its representational power in relation to the prospects for political leadership and political management. Their differences: on the one hand the modernists seek to countervail or balance the power of the state with the power of the media, and on the other the postmodernists analyze the subsumption of the political domain by a more media-centric focus than is traditional.

The dilemma for politics and media

Today we find that, even as the media's capacity to countervail or subsume political reality is either decried or extolled, the media's capacity to deliver this representational envelope is being eroded by the rise to political prominence of the blogosphere, citizen journalism and the burgeoning extent of 'virtual' public communication. The now irresistible array of new communicative activity engendered by new digital technologies has reached a stage where mainstream media and political leadership can no longer deny or avoid it, or indeed operate effectively without engaging with it.

The power bases — on both sides of the elite equation — are changing. As Charles Leadbeater (2007) puts it:

> … formal party politics is an industry in decline. In the late 19th century, people campaigned in their millions to be allowed into political processes that were dominated by elites. Little more than a century later and the disenchanted great-grandchildren of those campaigners are flooding out of the political realm as fast as they can … people talk of their political representatives as invisible, alien, partisan, arrogant, untrustworthy, irrelevant and disconnected. Industrial-era mass media — newspapers

and television — suffer from serious weaknesses as vehicles for democratic life. They have high fixed costs (printing plants and television studios) so they have to reach mass markets to earn their keep. As a consequence they treat people as an audience to be titillated rather than citizens who have a responsibility to engage in debate.

The dilemma is that contemporary political leadership must deal with the broad trends away from political engagement through embracing new means of socially-networked communication which are largely unable to be controlled in the time-honoured way of conventional politics.

The irony is that, as Westminster politics becomes more presidential, with its concentration of power in the executive and election campaigns more and more obsessively focussing on the leaders alone, the more new social media platforms are opening up the hyperlocal and the 'neo-demos'. And these are driving each other, as the mainstream media power base is being challenged by reader decline, the blogosphere and the blurring of the line between professional and citizen journalism. The inter-elite model, on which both media and communications studies and political science traditions have relied for decades, is coming into question.

The mainstream media (dubbed 'MSM' in the blogosphere) seek to speed up the political cycle, and ratchet up the 'politicotainment', in good part because of the competition they face from a wellspring of user-generated content and communication that is beginning to shoulder aside the traditional professional sources of public communication together with the commercial business models 'big' media are built on. Big media are especially sensitive to this perceived incursion onto its own turf and react, in general, very badly to it. In play and at stake are time-honoured notions of professionalism, the fourth estate function and centralised, one-to-many communication paradigms versus networked, planar, paradigms, to say nothing of their bottom lines. During the long pre-campaign period in 2007, the 'July 12' incident (when *The Australian* blew its stack over the blogosphere's better analysis of its own Newspoll data) stood out as the low point of a simmering stand-off between MSM and its bothersome 'other' (see Flew 2008).

But of course, leaders, governments and bureaucracies also react badly. The litany of missed opportunities, wrongheaded schemes and just plain failures to engage positively with online worlds and the dynamics they unleash speak fulsomely: Howard Dean's rise and fell on the back of online opinion in the last US Presidential campaign, Mark Latham's failed experiment in localism through e-democracy, and top-down communication strategies by bureaucracies using online simply as another linear 'consultation' medium, are a few examples.

Margaret Simons' *The Content Makers* (2007), and her regular Crikey and other posts, are an important response to these trends. Her starting point is this erosion of media power (the end of the 'imperial age'), but what is different is the practicality of her response, which is to lead hyperlocal initiatives such as The Map in Flemington and to warn that good quality journalism never paid its way and that the 'creative destruction' of news organisations' business model may bring about the demise of adequately paid, quality journalism.

Professional journalism and the internet have existed peaceably for more than a decade but now it is very hard to do so. There is an erosion of inter-elite symbiosis and, while these changes are never as abrupt and revolutionary as the utopian or dystopian rhetoric would suggest, and shifts in the balance are more in evidence in US politics than in Australia, there is a more planar sense of the distribution of influence than previously. The blogosphere lays claim that they are the true inheritors of the fourth estate function, as they are increasingly, and competently, critical of the degree to which mainstream media performs this function.

But the fact is that there is a great degree of porosity between citizen journalism and mainstream journalism. It is still the case that to become well known in the blogosphere you must break stories and breaking stories involves strategic and successful interactions with mainstream media. At this stage there has been greater impact registered by the new social media and the blogosphere in mainstream media than in politics. However, this is changing, as the 2007 Federal election campaign began to demonstrate clearly.

The 2007 Federal election campaign: contrasts in leader projection

While the 2007 Federal election campaign was 'not yet the internet election' (Flew 2008), it may have constituted an intriguing confluence of the 'coming of age' of the Australian blogosphere (Simons 2008) and evidence of the relative success and failure of the opposing campaigns — and especially their leaderships — in developing a 'politics 2.0' (which takes account of both the threats and affordances of web 2.0).

The incumbent Howard government went into the almost year-long pre-campaign as well as the campaign proper without a developed strategy to engage with online and web 2.0 platforms and services. This was exemplified in Howard's initial foray into the world of YouTube as he appeared in prime ministerial stand-and-deliver style behind his office desk with the flag as backdrop and addressed his 'audience' with a TV-radio real time-based 'Good Morning'. This was to deliver a speech on climate change — the issue which many Howard ministers and commentators believed was the single most important issue that changed votes, especially amongst younger voters. It might not have been possible to choose a more difficult topic to start one's YouTube career!

The received wisdom is that political communicators 'use' social networking and other web 2.0 sites not primarily because they want to reach the main users of those sites, but because journalists pay attention to them and this is a way of securing *their* attention. But this too-clever-by-half strategy was undercut by the deluge of criticism, savage satire and — perhaps worst of all when set against the original intent — mainstream media reportage of what had become a minor *cause celebre* within a few days.

On the Labor side, the relative success of the Labor online strategy stands in stark contrast. Matthew Hindman's (2007: 12) argument is that the largest impact of the internet on politics has been, to date, on the 'backend' of politics. While there has been great emphasis placed on the breakthrough business models of online retailers such as Amazon and eBay, most businesses have 'quietly used the internet and related information technologies to streamline operational logistics and generally make business processes more efficient'. He suggests that political practice is likely to mirror this process, with the internet being more important in the 'campaign for resources' than the 'campaign for votes'.

The Kevin07 campaign exemplified this, and more.[2] The campaign motto, Kevin07, with its simultaneously self-mocking and self-bolstering allusions to 'James Bond 007' (given the image of Rudd as a nerd and bureaucrat), and its marginalisation of the party in favour of presidential 'New Leadership', both centred the campaign on the leader and, in Camilla Cooke's term, 'humanised' him. Cooke, media manager of the Kevin07 campaign website, has a commercial digital marketing background and brought this experience to the campaign. The ALP, she argued, 'embraced' online campaigning, 'seeing it as an opportunity to communicate and have a dialogue'. They 'broke new ground', dealing with the more open space of blogging, MySpace, and YouTube. The backend use of the website was critical, but it was not only about the campaign for resources but as much if not more about reinforcing those already disposed to vote for Rudd that this side of politics was more on their wavelength than was the other side.

The Kevin07 campaign has been compared (by, for example, George Megalogenis on his blog Meganomics) to Barack Obama's Presidential campaign in two key aspects. First is the ability to generate resources built up from small contributions accessed by 'long tail' (Anderson 2006) principles of aggregation that the internet facilitates. Second is that Rudd, like Obama, had been able to secure the youth vote and this, more than any other single demographic, may have been determinative in winning the 2007 election.

Camilla Cooke reports that the Kevin07 website was not prepared for the amount of backend traffic the campaign generated. The sales of Kevin07 T-shirts and associated paraphernalia were far more successful than anyone had planned. The vast majority of website traffic up to the last weeks of the campaign was from those under forty, and who were confirmed in their voting intentions. The experience provided by the website was to 'make them excited, feel part of the campaign'. A large and growing body of online supporters had a 'ripple effect', reinforcing the image of youth vote turning to Rudd and bolstering the campaign coffers on the long tail model.

But there was also a major upswing in traffic to the site in the final weeks of the campaign (see Alexa 2007), far greater than any other campaign website. These were not decided voters and visited for far less time. What they were presented with upfront, at that stage, were short web camera coverage of ALP leaders – 'something more charming than a policy document' – which made 'the whole thing seem more domestic', according to Cooke.

The online political culture during the long campaign period also featured some highly creative and popular art and commentary screening on YouTube that underlines the extent to which alternative, informal arenas have opened up outside television and live performance venues. Hugh Atkin's 'Chinese Propaganda' online video, a brilliant satire of Mandarin-speaking Rudd's rapid rise to power, was reputedly accessed by a quarter of a million viewers in the lead up to the election. Stefan Sojka's 'Bennelong Time Since I Rocked and Rolled' satirises Howard to the tune of the Led Zeppelin classic. Killerspudly's series 'John Howard: Search for a Scapegoat', followed a puppet figure Howard seeking 'something special to scare the people into voting for me'. For Atkin, 'the internet is a far better barometer of generation Y's engagement with politics than a head count at a rally' (Wilson 2008).

Final remarks

What does this presage for notions of political and media leadership? The new social media and the arena of light entertainment favoured by younger citizens, and the blogosphere (which is much more a sphere which skews older and professional than the general population), are not unitary phenomenon. They present opportunities for formal political leadership but these opportunities can only be grasped if traditional command-and-control strategies are rethought. They both facilitate access to a hard-to-reach younger demographic and can enhance their exposure as they make themselves more accessible, and constrain standard issue politics by upsetting the old inter-elite modes of engagement. They also have facilitated emergent, alternative, forms of political communication and leadership.

What of media leadership? Mainstream media will need to work with the blogosphere rather than attempting to stand over against it as the primary authoritative source of news and information. In Margaret Simon's estimation:

… the media model of the future will be pro-am a small core of media professionals surrounded by, supported and critiqued by a swarm of amateurs who will be both audience and colleagues. If professional journalists are 'gatekeepers', able to decide what gets reported and how, they are now going to have to learn to live with increasingly active 'gatewatchers' (Bruns 2007), who will both critique what journalists do, and generate their own, different, material.

References

Alexa, 2007, 'Traffic History Graph for kevin07.com.au', Alexa The Web Information Company, http://www.alexa.com/data/details/traffic_details/kevin07.com.au?site0=kevin07.com.au&site1=liberal.org.au&site2=nationals.org.au&site3=greens.org.au&site4=democrats.org.au&y=r&z=3&h=400&w=700&u%5B%5D=kevin07.com.au&u%5B%5D=liberal.org.au&u%5B%5D=nationals.org.au&u%5B%5D=greens.org.au&u%5B%5D=democrats.org.au&x=2008-03-25T06%3A26%3A25.000Z&check=www.alexa.com&signature=VWlowMl%2FThwUfzPOY5uEOLy3l%2Fk%3D&range=6m&size=Large (last accessed November 2007).

Anderson, Chris, 2006, *The Long Tail: Why the Future of Business Is Selling Less of More*, New York: Hyperion.

Bruns, Axel, 2007, *Gatewatching: Collaborative Online News Production*, New York: Peter Lang.

Coleman, Stephen, 2003, 'A Tale of Two Houses: The House of Commons, the Big Brother House and the People at Home', *Parliamentary Affairs,* 56:4, pp. 733-58. See also *A Tale of Two Houses* http://www.hansardsociety.org.uk/publications/recent/bigbrother

Cooke, Camilla, 2007, Interview conducted by Jason Wilson, 17 December 2007.

Flew, Terry, 2008, 'Not Yet the Internet Election: Online Media, Political Commentary and the 2007 Australian Federal Election', *Media International Australia,* 126, pp. 5-13.

Goot, Murray and Rodney Tiffen, 1992, (eds), *Australia's Gulf War*, Carlton, Vic.: Melbourne University Press.

Hartley, John, 1999, *Uses of television*, London: Routledge.

Hindman, Matthew, 2007, *Voice, Equality and the Internet* (draft ms) http://www.matthewhindman.com/ (last accessed 11 April 2008).

Lazarsfeld, Paul F., Bernard Berelson and Hazel Gaudet, 1944 [1969], *The People's Choice: How the Voter Makes Up His Mind in a Presidential Campaign*, 3rd ed, New York and London: Columbia University Press.

Leadbeater, Charles, 2008, 'Democracy in the network age: time to WeThink', http://www.opendemocracy.net/article/charles_leadbeater/WeThink (accessed 10 April).

Leadbeater, Charles, 2007, *We-Think: Mass Innovation not Mass Production*, Profile Books.

Riegert, Kristina (ed.), 2007, *Politicotainment: Television's Take on the Real*, New York, Peter Lang.

Schultz, Julianne, 1998, *Reviving the Fourth Estate: Democracy, Accountability and the Media*, Melbourne: Cambridge University Press.

Simons, Margaret, 2007, *The Content Makers: Understanding the Media in Australia*, Camberwell: Penguin Books.

Simons, Margaret, 2008, 'New Media Lessons from Election 07', http://www.crikey.com.au/Media-Arts-and-Sports/20080410-New-media-lessons-from-Election-07.html 10th April (accessed 10 April 2008).

Coleman, Stephen, 2006, 'How the other half votes: Big Brother viewers and the 2005 general election', *International Journal of Cultural Studies*, 9:4, 457-79.

Tiffen, Rodney, 1989, *News and Power*, Sydney: Allen & Unwin.

Tiffen, Rodney, 1999, *Scandals: Media, Politics and Corruption in Contemporary Australia*, Sydney: UNSW.

Tiffen, Rodney, 2001, *Diplomatic Deceits: Government, Media and East Timor*, Sydney: UNSW Press.

Tiffen, Rodney, 2006, 'Political economy and news', in S. Cunningham ans G. Turner (eds) *The Media and Communications in Australia*, Sydney: Allen and Unwin, pp. 28-42.

Turner, Graeme, 1998, *Ending the Affair: The Decline of Television Current Affairs in Australia,* Sydney: UNSW Press.

Ward, Ian, 1994, *Politics of the Media*, South Melbourne: Macmillan Education Australia.

Wilson, Lauren, 2008, 'Mouse clique that roars', *The Weekend Australian Review*, 5-6 April, p. 6.

ENDNOTES

[1] Coleman (2006) has extended his analysis to cover the latest UK general election in 2005.

[2] Some of the following analysis is taken from an interview conducted by Jason Wilson with Camilla Cooke, online campaign consultant for the ALP, and manager of the Kevin07 website, 17 December 2007.

PART IV

Australian Political Leadership

16. Is There a Command Culture in Politics? The Canberra Case

James Walter

The rise of the command culture

My recent concern has been with the conditions that encourage political leaders to 'go too far', that is, to override the constraints that not only reinforce democracy by diffusing power, but also that contribute to good policy-making by enforcing recurrent reality checks (Walter 2006). Part of the story is about the proclivities within leaders themselves, but part, too, is about the historical, sociological and cultural changes that have eroded the institutional barriers to leadership caprice. Studies of leadership psychology have alerted us to predictable patterns of leadership behaviour (Walter 2007a; Walter 2007b), but these must be seen in conjunction with institutional transformations. I want here to explore a proposition: that recent institutional change has been conducive to the evolution of a 'command culture' that is potentially anti-democratic.

Such a proposition is not peculiar to Australia: it is part of a wider debate about the consolidation of executive power, sometimes discussed in terms of 'presidentialisation' (Poguntke and Webb 2005). Nor is the personalisation of politics around commanding leaders without parallels elsewhere: it is much discussed, for instance, in the literature on Tony Blair (Kampfner 2003; Coates and Krieger 2004; Hennessy 2005). Yet both institutional factors and the proclivities of individual leaders endow every instance with uniqueness and my argument is that the Australian case has not been closely enough studied.

While I will focus here on John Howard's government, similarities can be seen in the practices of state premiers (see Wanna and Williams 2005). As Paul Strangio and I argue in a recent book, *No, prime minister* (Walter and Strangio 2007), the underlying trend long predates Howard; the phenomenon is much more widespread and it will continue – Howard is simply a convenient exemplar. The demise of his government prompts the question: does a new government presage a new approach? My analysis suggests: not necessarily.

From dispersed to concentrated leadership

Democracy is premised upon avoidance of leadership dominance. It assumes that individuals will be driven by self-interest and that elites will emerge, but the *demos* will be protected by countering power with power —the checks and balances of countervailing institutions. John Uhr's concept of 'the lattice of leadership' is a useful gloss on this point — leadership diffused *across* institutional spheres, but constrained to work collectively for the common good, with each elite challenged to do its best by being held to account by leaders in another sphere (Uhr 2005: 78-81). When one element becomes too dominant, the ethical constraint of the lattice breaks down. The counterpoint is that when power is allowed to aggregate, democracy is threatened.

Many have noted the tendency towards the aggregation of executive power. Uhr himself provides a valuable chapter on national security initiatives as a war *against* ethics and an assault on 'the lattice of leadership' (Uhr 2005: ch. 7). Ian McAllister has carefully plotted the trends accentuating prime ministerial leadership, while noting that particular personalities tend to accelerate or to contain those trends (McAllister 2008). Jenny Hocking provocatively claims that we are witnessing the emergence of post-democratic leadership, with closed and secretive decision-making depending on an assertion that contemporary government is dealing with matters of such moment and urgency that an elision conflating its interests with those of the state can be taken for granted, at the expense of community consultation, parliamentary oversight and judicial review (Hocking 2005). At the national level, this also justifies overriding federal devolution and local government.

Such arguments can be related to cumulative institutional changes in our political system. These include the conduct of prime ministers over at least the past three decades; reforms to the public service to make the bureaucracy more responsive to incumbent governments (with the centralisation of policy co-ordination and authority in the Department of the Prime Minister and Cabinet and through it the Prime Minister); the development of dense and highly centralised political advisory structures; the evolution of media conventions that draw attention to leaders and the 'story' of personality conflicts rather than to policy debate; and the hollowing out of political parties which once acted as a brake on politicians, including leaders (Walter and Strangio 2007).

The dynamic is illuminated in the patterns of decision making relating to the commitment to war and the response to terrorism, as Uhr (2005), Hocking (2005), Walter (2006) and many others have argued. It is not surprising that, for decision-makers, crisis situations provoke concern about the security of information, inhibit open communication, reinforce 'inner circle' interaction, and are conducive to 'groupthink'. It is for these reasons that war and foreign policy are favoured by theorists such as Irving Janis (1982) and Graeme Allison (1971). Recently, others (for example, Preston and 't Hart 1999) have shown the broader potential for groupthink, where the leader's needs demonstrably affect the organisation and operation of advisory systems in bureaucratic politics. Taking this lead, Strangio and I concentrated on domestic policy making, arguing that, with the erosion of institutional constraints, leader-centric policy making has become more and more the norm across the policy terrain, and not just in relation to war, terrorism and foreign policy.

In broad terms, this might be seen as an incremental progression in the case of the Howard government. Howard did not, in the main, by-pass cabinet. He was both committed to, and respectful of, cabinet government (Weller 2007: ch. 10); he listened to colleagues and exerted discipline effectively, but cabinet became an instrument of his dominance (Kelly 2005). Yet, what was once the exception, when Howard by-passed cabinet to work with a small inner circle — such as in the 'exceptional' circumstance of the 'children overboard affair' (Weller 2002), or the secretive decision-making surrounding the Iraq commitment (Walter 2006) — became, increasingly, the tactic of choice the longer he was in power.

This syndrome was particularly evident in 2007, when there was what amounted to a year-long election campaign. In the theatre of campaigning, politicians' minds were concentrated on the battle for power and, suddenly, social problems of lengthy duration were starkly revealed as now being urgent and so challenging that only an experienced government (the Coalition) could manage, or that only 'new leadership' (Labor) could break through.

Dramatic responses in such cases as described below have revealed a style of decision-making that should concern us. Initiatives were driven by leaders (to the detriment of community consultation), tactics were fundamentally illiberal (the urgency of action used as a licence to break down the 'normal' checks and balances), and the strategy was essentially undemocratic (as power aggregated at the top).

The characteristic pattern was to transform a matter that might normally be seen as subject to routine processes of policy deliberation into a crisis, giving discretion to the leader to override the usual (democratic) provisions (cf. Marrs 2001: 25) and, incidentally, legitimating extreme centralisation of decision making ('t Hart, Rosenthal and Kouzmin 1993; Kouzmin 2008). Thus, a number of crises were identified — social breakdown in Indigenous communities, the states' administration of hospitals, water management, for instance — and it was argued that only central government intervention and strong leadership could serve as the circuit breaker. The government would make a forceful statement (such as, 'the army will arrive next week') in advance of community consultation. Labor occasionally engaged in its own pre-emption, trying to second guess government intentions, and announcing its position — usually no less top-down, no less leader-centric — in advance of government action.

Other authorities (local and state governments especially) were overridden or attacked as barriers to the resolution of national problems. Liberal institutions (the federal devolution of power, parliamentary scrutiny, the courts), whose purpose is to guard against capricious government, were diminished. There was a devaluation of local knowledge and of the wisdom of those with hands-on experience of those areas the policy community now determined to take over. Despite rhetorical gestures towards community engagement, there was rarely any commitment to co-operative management regimes.

Command in action: the NT intervention case

I will use one case to illustrate the argument: the Howard government's intervention into Indigenous communities in mid-2007. It exemplified a pattern of policy making said to be driven by the dimensions of the crisis it sought to address, but which is indicative of a broader tendency in the domestic policy arena — the command culture. I do not gainsay the extent of the problem: none could doubt the social dysfunction in some of the Indigenous communities targeted, or the failure of prevailing policy regimes. Nor do I question the intentions of the advocates of the intervention policy, or concentrate upon its alleged ideological subtexts. Instead, I explore those things the policy community seems to accept as 'givens' in such an approach.

The catalyst for intervention was *Little Children are Sacred*, a report by Rex Wild and Pat Anderson on the sexual abuse of children in Indigenous communities (Wild and Anderson 2007), and the failure of the Northern Territory government to act decisively when it was released. In fact, a series of reports, stretching back at least 18 years to Judy Atkinson's report on the Northern Territory in a national inquiry on violence, had come to similar conclusions without eliciting such a response. It was significant, however, that Wild and Anderson again dealt with the Northern Territory — the sole jurisdiction in which the Commonwealth government had the power to act more or less unilaterally. To summarise, the government plan encompassed:

- increased police numbers, with support from the army;
- government acquisition of Aboriginal townships for at least five years;
- imposition of community management;
- clean up and repair of community facilities;
- compulsory child health checks;
- school attendance to be enforced;
- welfare payments to be quarantined to 'responsible' families (i.e., those whose children attended school and who complied with hygiene protocols);
- scrapping permits for outsider access to Aboriginal land;
- alcohol bans to be imposed on Northern Territory Aboriginal land; and
- X-rated pornography to be banned (with publicly funded computers to be audited).

The Minister for Indigenous Affairs, Mal Brough, was a former army officer and was widely interpreted as believing that, to quote Tim Rowse, 'if people are behaving in a problematic way, you create a more rigorous framework of rules and enforce that … [N]o doubt it works in a military setting' (Grattan and

Chandler 2007). A perceptive newspaper profile described Brough as pursuing 'a frantic quest for swift results in the quagmire of Indigenous affairs':

> ... everything about him screams haste ... [H]e has been a whirlwind of activity — racing into and out of remote communities, reorganising the bureaucracy and demanding answers and solutions from everyone in his path. The former army officer appears to have internalised the military doctrine that momentum is everything, and this week seized the opportunity of another devastating report to launch a 'shock and awe' blitz ... at speed and with scant consultation with Indigenous leaders — hallmarks of the evolving style of the man (Schubert and Murdoch 2007a).

Some in those remote communities concluded, 'he talks, but he doesn't listen'.

Undoubtedly Brough's frantic activity during the year prior to this initiative fed into the policy outcome and cabinet was deeply troubled by the Wild and Anderson report, endorsing the idea that this was an emergency to which the government must respond. An inner group, Howard, Brough, Peter Shergold (the secretary of the Department of the Prime Minister and Cabinet, or PM&C) and Jeff Harmer (secretary of the then Department of Families, Community Services and Indigenous Affairs, or FaCSIA) then decided that a blueprint for wide-scale intervention was needed. A small team from PM&C and FaCSIA was told to draw up a plan, (the usual interdepartmental policy process was abandoned), 'and within 72 hours of the ... cabinet meeting the Government unveiled the boldest Aboriginal policy in 40 years' (Karvelas 2007a).

The shadow framework was that provided by Cape York indigenous leader (and public intellectual) Noel Pearson in his long-running campaign against 'passive welfare' (Karvelas 2007a; Rothwell 2007). Pearson has illuminated the destructive effects of entitlement without responsibility. The 'entitlement' to welfare support, he argued, excluded Indigenous people from the real economy and the lack of any expectation of reciprocity defined its recipients as 'hapless and helpless' (Pearson 2000). Helplessness, disillusion and, above all, 'rivers of grog' were seen by Pearson as integral to community dysfunction and child abuse. Thus, he was to endorse the government's intervention: these were, he said, 'cut-through' measures (Schubert and Murdoch 2007b), needed because 'we must stop the suffering straight away' (Pearson 2007). Howard mirrored this view, saying: 'It is interventionist. It does push aside the role of the territory ... But what matters more: the constitutional niceties, or the care and protection of young children?' (*The Age*, 22 June 2007: 5). Howard was to advance a similar proposition in a number of other cases, for instance, in justifying the take-over of Tasmania's Mersey Hospital. The point to note is that 'constitutional niceties' are what sustain the lattice of leadership.

Nonetheless, while giving the government credence in its response to this emergency, Pearson had argued for seven years about the necessity for government to *engage* with the community — progress could only be achieved through state-community partnerships. The harsh welfare crackdown, he said, should apply only in the case of 'responsibility failure' (Schubert and Murdoch 2007b). In relation to the NT intervention, he also argued from its inception that 'as well as policing, there must be a strategy for building Indigenous social and cultural ownership' (Pearson 2007).

No such strategy was evident at any point in the policy process. The consistent defence when this was articulated was (as expressed by Sue Gordon, Chair of the NT Emergency Response Taskforce): 'this was an emergency, and if you have an emergency … you don't have time to consult people in the initial phases. Every day that there's a delay, that means there's another child at risk' (Karvelas 2007b). Yet the authors of *Little Children are Sacred* themselves were to condemn the intervention for its failure to engage with target communities. Rex Wild said:

> We need long-term strategic work with people, building up trust. We were able to do that in a very short time by, we think, sitting down with people under the trees in the gymnasiums or equivalents and talking with them. That doesn't seem to happen when the bureaucrats arrive (Wild 2007)

The acclaimed reform in Cape York, said Pat Anderson, had been achieved in consultation with Indigenous people: 'There needs to be a radical change in the way government and non-government organisations consult, engage with and support Aboriginal people' (Chaney 2007).

It was a point increasingly strongly argued by those with lengthy experience in these domains. Pearson himself argued: 'The difference between disaster and success will depend on whether Brough and Howard will engage with … the traditional leaders of the NT on a way forward' (Chaney 2007). Fiona Stanley suggested that 'measures that exclude the views and involvement of Aborigines will serve only to further diminish their capacity, exacerbate marginalisation and add to the damage in these vulnerable communities' (Chaney 2007). Howard was quoted as rejecting criticism that the power structures in Aboriginal communities should be respected, saying they were 'part of the problem'. Implicitly, then, all Indigenous communities (and community leaders) were identified as suffering 'responsibility failure'.

Not only was an approach that would build community capacity (and state community-partnership) fudged, but there was also considerable doubt about the capacity of Commonwealth authorities. 'There is a huge implementation challenge', said Pearson, 'I am not confident they are up to it' (Pearson 2007).

The legislation, said Fred Chaney, 'authorises an absurd and unobtainable level of micro-management of Aboriginal lives far beyond the capacity of the federal bureaucracy that would permit the notorious protector, Mr Neville, to ride again' (Chaney 2007). A medical anthropologist argued that there is no evidence that micro-management — enforcing compliance with rules and regulations — induces long-term behavioural change. Instead, it demands on-going policing and surveillance. 'Has government got the stomach for this in the long-term?' Chaney later asked (Grattan and Chandler 2007).

In many respects, the way policy was developed in the case of the Northern Territory intervention seems, perversely, as if modelled on the case studies of what produces 'policy fiasco' (Janis 1982; Preston and 't Hart 1999). Decisions were made in haste by a small inner circle, on the advice of a minister who 'talks, but does not listen'. Routine practices of inter-departmental policy consultation were abandoned in the interests of speed. There was no provision for robust debate about alternatives — nor is it clear that expert advice (from economists, medical anthropologists, health professionals, social workers) was sought. Such practices are commonly thought to encourage 'groupthink'. Once legislation was developed, it was pushed through Parliament at speed, making nonsense of the notion of appropriate legislative scrutiny. The explicit concerns of the authors of the report taken as the catalyst for intervention were overlooked. Breaking the cycle seemed to be seen as an end in itself, so there was no apparent thought about the post-intervention phase. Community leaders were defined as 'part of the problem' and so there was no effective community engagement. Yet, without such engagement, there was no prospect of building community capacity or responsibility.

The chance factor — that Brough had an army background and appeared to favour a military approach to policy intervention — alerted commentators to the 'command culture' aspect of the Northern Territory intervention (for example, Schubert and Murdoch 2007a). Several evoked an Iraq parallel by referring to the 'shock and awe' blitz at the core of the government's approach (for example, Grattan and Chandler 2007). Pat Dodson made the connection explicit: 'This is an Iraq style of intervention with no exit strategy or plans for long-term economic and social development' (Dodson 2007). Indeed, just as the invasion of Iraq was premised on the fallacious notion that overthrowing a dictator would unleash the forces of 'freedom' and democracy would follow, the Northern Territory intervention seemed to hinge on equally unfounded assumptions that rules and regulations alone (without attention to the dynamics of dysfunction) would change behaviour and that breaking down the impediments (customary law, collective ownership, etc.) between remote communities and the 'mainstream' would encourage Indigenous people to integrate into the national economy. Given the Howard government's defeat, we can only speculate about how management of the Northern Territory intervention would have progressed, but it is probable that the failure of community engagement would have subverted the capacity-building that could be the only foundation for a long-term plan and a viable economy. This missing element — community engagement — appears now to be the principal task of the Rudd Labor government.

As suggested earlier, the Northern Territory intervention is far from the only instance where a command culture appeared to operate. I have written elsewhere about 'groupthink' and the Iraq commitment (Walter 2006). With Strangio (Walter and Strangio 2007), I have drawn attention to other instances, such as Howard's unilateral 2002 decision to circumvent defence procurement processes by committing Australia to the hugely expensive US Joint Strike Fighter program, the bypassing of cabinet the same year when announcing Australia would not ratify the Kyoto Protocol, and the 2007 Murray Darling Plan that was originally concocted without reference to cabinet or relevant departments. What we also now know is that Howard brushed aside concerns some ministers raised about WorkChoices, as well as having marginalised alternative viewpoints within government circles on global warming, and blocking proposals for investigating carbon trading schemes in the late 1990s and 2003. As Strangio and I have argued, the trend towards leadership centrality predates Howard, but his practices were integral to the evolution of a command culture in domestic policy making and the increasing resort to crisis techniques indicated it was becoming routinised rather than emerging only in exceptional cases.

Counter-tendencies

Paradoxically, an antithetical trend was gaining ground in policy circles. Increasingly, the solution to 'wicked' policy problems of the sort that Indigenous community dysfunction represents, has been taken to be devolution of authority and community engagement. A bringing together of the policy community, engaged experts and community representatives in 'learning networks', together with a transfer of authority to act to local levels, was a recurrent topic within debates about contemporary governance (see Head 2005). But such approaches take time and care and will always be denied if, as Howard said about the Northern Territory intervention, 'the time for talking is past'. Yet exercises of this sort have been successfully trialled: local governments in some US jurisdictions have adopted deliberative democracy techniques to determine the allocation of services. Another leading example has been the linking of public agencies, activists, researchers and community groups in restorative (or community) justice initiatives. Are there ways not only of embedding such practices more generally in policy-determination but, also, of carrying such deliberative processes into the parliamentary forum, so that majority consensus is built on key issues rather than being simply asserted by a minister in a hurry, or by a domineering leader?

In the end, I suspect, there are conflicting cultural tendencies at work. On the one hand, in some policy deliberations there is, as Brian Head shows, an increasing emphasis on community engagement; on dialogue between government and citizens (Head 2007). Gven the declining trust in liberal institutions, it may be only through such engagement that democracy can be rejuvenated, by encouraging processes that allow citizens to 'discover their preferences' (Dahl 1961). Yet it will always be difficult, since the socialisation of policy-makers makes it difficult for them to relinquish control. On the other hand, in a context where old certainties and established institutions are under siege, there is a contradictory current, an atavistic belief that heroic leadership can break through just those 'wicked' issues that seem to be at the base of our difficulties. All, then, depends upon belief — belief in the leader and the leader's self-belief. Policy is judged only on whether the leader believes it is right: the death knell of evidence-based deliberation. In fact, the style of leadership this encourages is good for one purpose only: combat. Yet, as one US army researcher observed, 'a command culture, indispensable in combat, is an impediment to open discussion of fundamental issues at all levels'. In other words, not only does it undermine 'the lattice of leadership', but it is also a style that is inimical to good policy making.

The 'leader as solution' is an assumption evident in many fields, and not just in politics. How else can one explain the astronomical salaries paid to CEOs, the ferocity with which — when any weakness is revealed — they are dispatched, and the recklessness with which we accept their assurances that they are 'the smartest guys in the room' and leave them alone to trigger enormous market failures (such as the corporate collapses of Enron, HIH and Barings)? (see Khurana 2002). Leaders acting unilaterally, closed decision making, and the failure of accountability lead to policy fiasco in every field. When power aggregates at the top, we break democratic connections, losing the capacity to connect the individual to the group, the group to the community, and the community to the state. (These were precisely the connections that were denied in the Northern Territory intervention). The challenge now is how can we develop appropriate channels of community engagement that re-institutionalise liberal constraints, dispel magical thinking about heroic leadership, encourage humility in public officials and devolve power?

Towards the end of the command culture?

Can a new government overthrow what is described here as a trend, albeit one given powerful impetus by the Howard government's practices and which became more entrenched the longer it held power? Evidently, changes to the machinery of government — enhanced parliamentary scrutiny, the imposition of restraint and accountability on ministerial staff, and restoration of a degree of independence in the public service (Walter and Strangio 2007: ch. 4; Walter

2008) — would contribute to restoring the 'lattice of leadership' and the Rudd government initially made promising moves on all of these fronts. The appointment of Senator John Faulkner as Special Minister of State to oversee such reform was positive. He was, in opposition, a notable defender of Senate powers of inquiry to ensure proper scrutiny of government. (But, one recalls, Howard also made promises about opening up government on first assuming power). The Rudd team's search for alternative ideas provoked Coalition derision during the 2007 election campaign (Peter Costello's dismissive comment — an exemplary statement of the command culture — was, 'A leader doesn't go to committees, a leader knows what he wants and announces it!'). Yet Rudd's tactics in broadening the scope of policy input (for example, initiating the 2020 summit), committing to community engagement (the community cabinets), and installing representatives of all points of view (for example, appointing Howard's chief of staff and principal adviser, Arthur Sinodinis, to a review of Defence) all seem designed to broaden options, to step back from the leader principle and to hedge against the inner-circle thinking that leads to groupthink. Are they a decisive counter to the command culture?

The other side of the coin is that, on early indications, neither Labor nor Rudd are immune to the cult of leadership. The ALP projected 'Kevin07' as the harbinger of 'new leadership', but tellingly the slogan was personalised and the party gave its fortunes into his hands as completely as it had in the disastrous Latham experiment. Rudd soon gave us a clue to what that might mean by single-handedly overriding Labor's organisational tradition, not with the goal of devolving authority, but centralising it in his hands. Notwithstanding the ALP's expressed intention of addressing the problem of consolidated executive power, some questioned Rudd's ability to do so. A former Foreign affairs colleague of Rudd, for instance, predicted he would be a 'nightmare, an obsessive who would micromanage everything' (*The Age,* 6 November 2007: 6), and seasoned observers canvassed the indications that he would 'seize more power as PM' (Kelly 2007). Once in power, the commentary on Rudd's predilection for micro-management and his tendency towards a controlling centralisation became more detailed and more persuasive (Taylor 2007; Grattan 2008, Murphy 2008). Yet, at the time of writing, it remained an open question: was the mantra of Rudd's dominance the media feeding on itself (and on an inclination to cast him as Howard in another guise)? Is Rudd clever enough to see the limitations of his penchant for control and to establish countervailing measures? Or is he yet another leader 'steering by power chances' (Davies 1980: 5), for whom the erosion of institutional constraints will prove an irresistible inducement to exercise the command imperative; stalling democratic reform?

References

Allison, G., 1971, *Essence of Decision: Explaining the Cuban Missile Crisis*, Boston: Brown.

Chaney, F., 2007, 'Give Aborigines hope' *The Age,* 15 August.

Coates, D. and J. Krieger, 2004, *Blair's War*, Cambridge: Polity Press.

Dahl, R. A., 1961, *Who Governs? Democracy and Power in an American City*, New Haven: Yale University Press.

Davies, A. F., 1980, *Skills, Outlooks and Passions: A Psychoanalytic Contribution to the Study of Politics*, Cambridge: Cambridge University Press.

Dodson, P., 2007, 'An entire culture is at stake', *The Age,* 14 July.

Grattan, M. and J. Chandler, 2007, 'A new dawn?' *The Age,* 23 June.

Grattan, M., 2008, 'Much to do and to care about,' *The Age,* 14 March.

Head, B., 2005, 'Governance', in P. Saunders and J. Walter (eds), *Ideas and Influence: Social Science and Public Policy in Australia,* Sydney: UNSW Press, pp. 44-63.

Head, B., 2007, 'Community engagement: participation on whose terms?' *Australian Journal of Political Science,* 42:3, pp. 441-54.

Hennessy, P., 2005, 'Rulers and servants of the state: the Blair style of government', *Parliamentary Affairs,* 58:1, pp. 6-16.

Hocking, J., 2005, 'Liberty, security and the state', in P. Saunders and J. Walter (eds) *Ideas and Influence: Social science and public policy in Australia,* Sydney: UNSW Press, pp. 178-197.

Janis, I., 1982, *Groupthink: Psychological Studies of Policy Decisions and Fiascos,* Boston: Houghton Mifflin.

Kampfner, J., 2003, *Blair's Wars*, London: The Free Press.

Karvelas, P., 2007b, 'Tactic a backward step, say authors', *The Australian,* 11 August.

Karvelas, P., 2007a, 'Moved by Pearson's passion, *The Australian,* 23-24 June.

Kelly, P., 2005, *Re-thinking Australian Governance: The Howard Legacy,* Cunningham Lecture 2005, Occasional paper series 4/2005, Academy of the Social Sciences in Australia, Canberra.

Kelly, P., 2007, 'Rudd would seize more power as PM', *The Australian,* 7 November.

Khurana, 2002, *Searching for a Corporate Savoir*, Princeton: Princeton University Press.

Kouzmin, A., 2008, 'Crisis management in crisis?' *Administrative Theory and Praxis,* 30:2 (forthcoming).

Marrs, J., 2001, *Rule by secrecy,* New York: Perennial.

McAllister, I., 2008, 'Political Leaders in Westminster Systems', in K. Aarts, A. Blais and H. Schmitt (eds) *Political Leaders and Democratic Elections,* Oxford: Oxford University Press, (forthcoming).

Murphy, K., 2008, 'Rudd's will to power', *The Age,* 29 March.

Pearson, N., 2000, *Our Right to Take Responsibility,* Cairns: Noel Pearson and Associates.

Pearson, N., 2007, 'An end to the tears', *The Australian,* 23-24 June.

Poguntke, T. and P. Webb (eds), 2005, *The Presidentialization of Politics: A Comparative Study of Modern Democracies,* Oxford: Oxford University Press.

Preston, T. and P. 't Hart, 1999, 'Understanding and Evaluating Bureaucratic Politics: The Nexus Between Political Leaders and Advisory Groups', *Political Psychology,* 20:1, 49-98.

Rothwell, N., 2007 'Desert sweep', *The Australian,* 11-12 August.

Schubert, M. and L. Murdoch, 2007a, 'Cyclone Mal rips through Territory troubles', *The Age,* 23 June.

Schubert, M. and L. Murdoch, 2007b, 'Child abuse crackdown on benefits', *The Age,* 23 June.

't Hart, P., U. Rosenthal and A. Kouzmin, 1993, 'Crisis decision-making: the centralization thesis revisited', *Administration and Society,* 25:1, pp. 12-45.

Taylor, L., 2007, 'Method man', *AFR Magazine,* 23 February.

Uhr, J., 2005, *Terms of Trust: Arguments over Ethics in Australian Government,* Sydney: UNSW Press.

Walter, J., and P. Strangio, 2007, *No, Prime Minister: Reclaiming Politics from Leaders,* Sydney: UNSW Press.

Walter, J., 2006, 'Why prime ministers go too far', in D. McDougall and P. Shearman (eds) *Australian Security After 9/11: New and Old Agendas,* London: Ashgate, pp. 189-206.

Walter, J., 2007a, 'Political Leadership', in B. Galligan and W. Roberts (eds) *Oxford Companion to Australian Politics,* Melbourne: Oxford University Press, pp. 428-30.

Walter, J., 2007b, 'Political Leadership', in G. Rizer (ed.), *The Blackwell Encyclopedia of Sociology Vol VII,* Oxford: Blackwell, pp. 3441-5.

Walter, J., 2008, 'Neither fear nor favour', *The Age*, 25 March.

Wanna, J. and P. Williams, 2005, *Yes, Premier: Labor leadership in Australia's States and Territories*, UNSW Press.

Weller, P., 2002, *Don't Tell the Prime Minister*, Melbourne: Scribe Publications.

Weller, P., 2007, *Cabinet Government in Australia, 1901-2006: Practices and Principles*, Sydney: UNSW Press.

Wild, R. and P. Anderson, 2007, *Ampe Akelyernemane Meke Mekarle: 'Little Children are Sacred'*, Report of the Northern Territory Board of Inquiry into the Protection of Aboriginal Children from Sexual Abuse, Northern Territory Government, Darwin.

Wild, R., 2007, 'Child abuse inquiry head criticises Govt reponse', *Lateline Business*, Australian Broadcasting Corporation, 27/06/2007, at http://www.abc.net.au/lateline/content/2007/s1964086.htm, accessed 18 March 2008.

17. Leadership Practices: Reflections on Australian Political Leadership

David Kemp

Political leadership: the larger story

This chapter provides some reflections on political leadership in Australia from the perspective of one who has been involved both as an academic studying politics and leadership and as an active participant in national politics for a number of years.

The growing body of literature on political leadership points to many aspects of public leadership that could be (and are) readily illustrated from Australian examples. Paul 't Hart and John Uhr (this volume) usefully bring many of these together in a way that has considerable resonance for one who has been an active practitioner: the close interdependence of leaders and 'followers'; the way in which leaders through their rhetoric present their cases and mobilise support; the significance of the institutional framework within which leadership is offered; and different approaches that may be adopted to political and policy change. Others, of whom Walter and Strangio (2007; see also Walter, this volume) are an example, point to the increasing centralisation of power around prime ministers and wonder how far this is eroding traditional checks and balances within the system of government.

My reaction, as a practitioner, to these useful studies and observations is that there is a need for the larger story to which they contribute to be articulated. As we disaggregate public leadership for analysis we should not lose sight of the larger purposes that have motivated it. There is a macro- as well as a micro-story about political leadership. The larger story has to do with what 't Hart and Uhr call strategic challenges.

The core concern of political leadership is policy. It is by their policy successes and failures that leaders are judged, and on which they ultimately win or lose elections. Voters want leaders to solve problems and policies are the way they do that. It is not just administrative leaders who attempt to 'create public value', to use Mark Moore's term (Moore 1995) and, in the effort to do so, political leaders reorganise government to suit their needs, taking advantage of the opportunities provided by the constitutional arrangements. Whether, in doing so in Australia, they have eroded the checks and balances of the system, or the principal mechanisms of accountability, is an important question but, to understand why the question arises, the larger context of the changing character of Australian political leadership needs to be brought into focus.

From this perspective, there is a story to be told about Australian political leadership and national policy outcomes over the last four decades. It is a story that transcends political party, though each major party has played a distinctive role in the story, and leaders in each have had to deal with unique internal challenges arising from the distinctive character of their party.

The larger story linking leadership and policy suggests, in turn, a research agenda to do with the relation between a leader and a set of policies: how leaders have approached and dealt with the dominant policy ideas, why they have made the choices they have, why they have organised the advisory process in the way they have, and so forth. Why the agenda transcends party is one of the most interesting questions of all.

I will outline my version of the larger 'macro' story, and then indicate some of the research directions it suggests.

Leadership and public policy

In recent decades Australia has been through an extraordinary period of policy dynamism that has transformed the national policy framework and Australia's character both as a society and as a component of the global economy. Debates about further national reform dominated the recent election campaign. The journalist Paul Kelly recently suggested (*The Australian Literary Review, Oct. 3, 2007*) that Australia had been blessed with first class political leaders over this period who, through their leadership, had wrought this transformation and, as a consequence, positioned Australia as an exceptionally successful nation on the global scene.

I believe that, on the whole, this is a valid assessment. To achieve this transformation our political leaders have reorganised the central government of the country; including a radical reinvention of the framework within which the Australian Public Service operates. The reform drive continues to put great pressure for change on the Federal system itself. This reorganisation has occurred to facilitate policy innovation and it has achieved its objective, though it has provoked a debate about the effectiveness of traditional accountability mechanisms.

This is not the place to detail all the components of the policy revolution of the last few decades, but it will be useful to record some of the major elements. Central has been a change in the role of government. Government has largely withdrawn from its role as an active participant in the economy through government owned enterprises (usually monopolies). The economy has been opened to international competition and efforts to protect Australian industry (with few exceptions) have been abandoned. The tax system (principally through the consumption tax) has become much more neutral in its sectoral impact. Domestic regulation to protect major industry sectors from competitive entrants has largely disappeared. Market forces have been given a greatly expanded role in initiating innovation and determining enterprise success and failure. There has been a significant devolution of the management of workplace relations to the enterprise level. The movement away from the politically managed economy was symbolised by the floating of the Australian dollar and financial deregulation. Monetary policy has been handed to an independent Reserve Bank, and Keynesian efforts at demand management have largely been set aside.

Policy innovation has reached deeply into many areas of social policy. Consumer choice has been given an expanded role in social areas such as employment services, education, and health, and market mechanisms are increasingly being used to manage formerly public environmental goods such as water (and greenhouse gases). Private funding and investment in areas formerly regarded as public goods (education, training, health, roads and infrastructure) has greatly expanded. The welfare system has moved from one based simply on payment of benefits to one based on training and incentives to participate through principles of 'mutual obligation'. The overturning of the decades old framework for aboriginal policy in the Northern Territory is but the latest example. Perhaps most fundamentally, in family and gender relations, government has withdrawn from the attempt to define distinct roles for men and women by law and has attempted to outlaw employment and other discrimination based on gender, race or religion.

In seeking a comparative perspective 't Hart and Uhr (this volume) pose the question: is there something distinctive about Australian political leadership? Do Australian political leaders employ distinctive strategies? Does the political economy support some types of leadership and not others? If we pursue the focus on the policy transformation, a further set of questions is suggested: have Australian leaders been more successful than leaders in other countries in responding to globalisation through policy and institutional reform? If so, why has this been the case? What is it about Australian political leadership that has led to Australia's improved international ranking on measures of competitiveness, real per capita income, and even freedom?

Political leadership has obviously been at the centre of these changes, and the identification of the main elements of 'the Australian model' that has produced this change becomes a research focus. What have been the features of the political system and culture that have contributed to Australian leaders' innovative capacity? Equally significant in a comparative framework, while Australia has been very successful in pursuing a reform agenda to change the relationship between government and the marketplace, it has not been alone. Indeed, key elements of the program have been copied or adapted from leaders in other countries, and urged on Australia by policy leaders from elsewhere. It is clear that Australian political leaders are a sub-group of a wider category of Western political leaders (or is it Anglo-sphere leaders?) and that the Australian case is but one example of a wider shift in Western policy.

Leadership credos: engines of policy change

Why did this policy revolution occur? Indeed, it is still continuing. What is the most fruitful starting point to try to unravel the intertwined causes of the change? Let us now step back from the big picture and turn the focus to the leaders themselves. If these policy changes have transcended political parties, what is it that has provided the linkage between our political leaders that gives us the most explanatory traction?

I suggest that the most useful starting point is not the personalities of our leaders nor their rhetoric, nor the advisory structures with which they have surrounded themselves, nor the pattern of lobby group pressures they have faced, nor the inexorable challenges of the international economy, but what our political leaders have believed, and what their purposes and values have been: their credos. Certainly they have responded to circumstances, but circumstances only create the opportunity for action. After several decades of involvement as a practitioner I still believe that the most powerful factor in political life is ideas, and I suggest that it is the way in which ideas have been mobilised that should be our starting point. What these ideas are; where they have come from; and more especially how they have been understood by, and mobilised by, political leaders is a central part of the story.

I offer four propositions:

1. The policy dynamism of Australian political leadership in recent decades is a consequence of leaders with developed political credos, committed to policy reform.
2. The driving ideas of this policy program have been largely derived from Australia's unusually homogenous, individualistic, egalitarian and rational democratic culture, mediated in various ways through the requirements of leading one of the major political parties.
3. In developing their policy programs these leaders have been able to draw on a substantial growth in the policy capacity of government arising from expanded knowledge of policy impacts and improved issue analysis. It is this feature that largely explains the major change in policy direction from earlier decades.
4. In implementing policy change Australian leaders have been able to draw upon executive authority of broad scope, including the authority to reorganise the central government apparatus to achieve improved strategic capacity and flexibility in implementation.

The value of the concept of the leadership credo is that it puts the focus on the explicit and formulated ideas of political leaders as they face the choices that will lead to policy action. It is a key to understanding the meaning leaders give to the circumstances in which they find themselves, and their efforts to reconstruct these circumstances. It is the leader's credo that will be a key factor in determining whether an opportunity or pressure created by circumstances leads to a particular course of action. As someone who, as a practitioner, has worked with a number of our political leaders in the development and statement of their political credos and who, as a minister, was aware of the ideas driving my own efforts at policy innovation, I am conscious of the significance of these idea sets to the decisions leaders make.

A credo comprises a set of values and beliefs about what is important; what governments can and should do; and how they can be most effective. Over the last 35 years Australian political leaders have worked hard to establish policy agendas; and defining for voters the reality with which they claim politics must deal. Whitlam's mixed offering of big government egalitarianism and liberal tariff reform; Fraser's critique of big government and his social liberalism; Hawke's promotion of consensus; Keating's championing of competition; reconciliation and republicanism; and Howard's explicit avowal of a policy package based on social conservatism and economic liberalism — none of these were 'inevitable' agendas, all were expressions of the leadership credo of the Prime Minister of the day. All were contingent, in the sense that other leaders would probably have pursued other purposes and policies. Their contingent character is emphasised by the fact that we have clear examples of conflicts between political leaders and their principal official advisers (for example, Whitlam and Fraser with Treasury).

In the development of their political credos, Australian political leaders over this period were both 'sellers' and 'purchasers' of ideas. Whitlam's policy program developed over a number of years but, as Prime Minister, he established a policy 'think tank' – the Priorities Review Staff – and actively sought and adopted ideas on economic reform such as tariff reduction. Fraser's speeches over many years reveal a deeply thoughtful approach, drawing on liberal political thinkers he had first met as an undergraduate at Oxford. In office, Fraser assiduously recruited policy thinkers and experts to his political office. Hawke, a former Rhodes Scholar, brought a sharp intellect to a prime ministership that actively sought ideas and political compromise through summits of national business, union and other leaders. Keating's biographer described the ethos of a leadership and advisory structure in which virtue was to be 'at once economically sound and politically clever' (Watson 2002: 89). Howard had worked at ideas for 'future directions' over many years, even if, as his recent biographers suggest, he had no deep interest in political philosophy (Errington and van Onselen 2007: 216). Nevertheless he surrounded himself with the most developed strategic, policy and political staff of any of these leaders, and was comfortable characterising himself along the liberal-conservative dimensions.

The recognition of the importance of credos is to some extent an antidote to easy cynicism about politics, because it points to the fact that our leaders have deeper purposes and beliefs, and that there is a linkage between these purposes and beliefs and those of the people they claim to represent, and to whom they are accountable.

Leaders, as we know, are not free (if they seek support) simply to advocate whatever public philosophy randomly takes their fancy. They are constrained by the cultural context in which they appeal for support, by the intellectual world of ideas, and by the institutional setting within which they will seek to lead. Their party's policy traditions influence the direction of innovation. How Australians think about their country becomes a constraint and an opportunity. The constraining influence of popular values on leadership credos is a key mechanism by which the values of the Australian people are translated into political action.

Beyond leaders: culture and policy continuity

Given the differences in political party, personality, background and style of top Australian political leaders during the period of the policy revolution, the continuities over the period require explanation. Circumstances that pushed/encouraged leaders to act are not difficult to find. The Australian policy revolution occurred in an international historical context: the post-World War II world, where much had been learnt about the dangers of protectionism and of the decline of trade for both prosperity and peace, and in which post-war institutions were overseeing an accelerating economic globalisation. It was a context in which the policy survivals of pre-war and war time economic planning in Europe in the pursuit of growth and social justice were increasingly being seen to fail. Australia was experiencing a relative decline in its standard of living and an eroding competitiveness in global markets. The attempt to understand and learn from these failures through policy analysis — located in Australia in the universities, in the central departments of government (Treasury, Finance and Prime Minister and Cabinet), in the central bank and in advisory authorities such as the Industries Assistance Commission — was gathering pace.

But why did Australian leaders come to share a particular set of policy goals and objectives and even policy solutions in response to this situation? In a largely shared context, political leaders in Europe and elsewhere came to different conclusions. In looking for an explanation of the commonalities among the credos of political leaders in Australia, I offer the following proposition. Unlike Europe, the United States or Canada, Australia has a homogenous culture in which two ideas have a dominating role in our political life, and indeed our academic evaluations of politics: democracy and rationality. Australian political leaders argue and debate with each other so strongly – at times bitterly – that it is easy to overlook the very large area of agreement between them on the guiding values of policy.

Democratic values are the most powerful drivers and motivators in Australian politics and these values transcend party political differences. The political core of the democratic idea is 'government with the consent of the governed'. A foundation concept, since at least the eighteenth century, has been the idea of the equality of all people, including the equal entitlement of every person to be heard and to pursue their individual values in life. This revolutionary idea has been at work now for over two centuries in our political systems. Policies as disparate as tax neutrality, free market entry, gender equality, educational opportunity, non-discriminatory immigration and accountability of our political leaders, all find justification in the democratic idea. In *Democracy in America,* Alexis de Tocqueville wrote about the inexorable march of the democratic idea through societal institutions (de Tocqueville 1991: 5-6; see also Rae 1981; Kemp 1987); and we are living in an era when the process is as evident as ever.

Again, the idea of rationality means that action should be justifiable as a rational means of pursuing an objective. Commonsense understandings of the world can be extended by professional experts who attempt to understand more deeply how human beings and human society function and, therefore, how certain ends can be best achieved (for a fascinating analysis of different rationalities see Diesing 1962)

These two concepts — democracy and rationality — link the credos of Whitlam, Fraser, Hawke, Keating, Howard and now Rudd. While there are many differences to which one might point between the public philosophies of these leaders, the continuities are obvious in relation to key aspects of economic reform, gender and racial equality, education, immigration policy and the use of policy analysis, to name but a few.

How can a policy revolution be explained, even in part, by cultural elements which have been around for a long time? The basic answer is again de Tocqueville's: the democratic idea is inherently revolutionary because the search for institutions and policies that will best acknowledge human equality still continues. Australia's rationalist democratic culture sets objectives and points to methods to achieve them. Australian leaders on all sides of politics are deeply imbued with the democratic project. The intensifying process of study, research and learning from experience ensures that it maintains momentum. As a result, the recent policy revolution is only the latest in a series of such phenomena.

Australia has known policy revolutions before. At least two stand out: the initial policy settings of the newly established representative colonial governments in the mid to late nineteenth century and the post-Federation protectionist settlement. The policy revolution of the last three and a half decades is at least the third Australia has experienced since the transportation era. In each era circumstances have produced a different policy expression of democratic values.

What is it that has given democratic ideas their particular policy form in the current period? The current Australian policy revolution reflects deep learning about the consequences of different policy frameworks, especially learning about what governments can and cannot do effectively. The failures of protectionism (in Australia and elsewhere) and of government monopolies (in Australia) and central planning (elsewhere) to meet individuals' values revived interest in market-based approaches that can better accommodate diverse wants. The policy analysis that expresses this learning has become a preoccupation of leaders and has led to the establishment of many public agencies and private consultancies. The key central departments — Treasury, Finance and Prime Minister and Cabinet — have played a key role in bringing this policy analysis to the political leadership. The increase in policy analysis has, in turn, led to a weakening of the effectiveness of special interest lobbying and empowered the wider public demand for non-discriminatory policies in all walks of life.

In 1929, Keith Hancock pointed out that Australians were using the collective power of the state in the pursuit of their individual values. He presciently observed:

> These policies … yield diminishing returns, until at last they may become a positive danger to the national purpose that has called them into existence. We have already seen that the increased costs of Protection are endangering the essential purpose of Protection. We shall observe the same tendencies at work in Australian State Socialism (Hancock [1929]1961: 106).

In the 1970s, Australians began to realise, with assistance from a growing army of policy analysts, that important public interests were being sacrificed by the way in which they were trying to achieve their values, especially interests in the economic efficiency and industry competitiveness required to underpin economic growth.

Political parties and policy differences

Given the level of agreement on the content of the policy revolution, what then have our leaders been debating with each other about? What are the differences in their political credos and what is the significance of these differences? Some of the differences have undoubtedly been rhetorical, prompted by the requirement in election campaigns to highlight real or perceived weaknesses in the other side. Keating's crusade against the horrors of the consumption tax in 1993 falls into this category. At the other extreme some have been, in part, genuine differences in principle or differences that arise from the way in which political parties organise values and impose additional constraints on leaders beyond those arising from voters themselves.

Liberal leaders, for example, have been constrained by their party's traditional commitment to the federal system. Fraser, indeed, sacrificed votes in the 1983 election in part because of his commitment to the Federal system despite the *Dams Case* decision. Howard later sought to move these boundaries in a centralist direction. Again, tariff reform was more straightforward for Whitlam than for a Liberal Party for which protected manufacturing interests were more influential. Conversely, Labor leaders have been constrained by their party's organisational links to the trade union movement and even the economic liberalism of Paul Keating was modified by the corporatism of the Hawke approach. Because of these constraints on Labor, Liberals have pressed further on labour market reform over the years. The effect of the debate between the parties has been to explore and clarify where the strength of the argument lies, and what the relative power of interests will permit.

Have the constraints imposed by the institutionalised values and interests of political party organisations weakened over the years? Labor leaders for many decades have been freer in their policy-making capacity than their party's formal rules might suggest. The constitutional authority granted prime ministers seems largely to have outweighed contradictory party rules. Liberal leaders have always been formally accorded policy autonomy by the rules of the party. In practice therefore, there seems little to differentiate the parties on this dimension. Nevertheless, the constraint imposed on leaders by their need to maintain unity in the party, and to acknowledge the strength of its constituent interests remains even for policy-empowered leaders. The changing social character of the parties' bases means that the nature of these constraints has evolved over time, but the dependence of leaders on the party organisation and on their voting bases means that the constraints continue.

Australian parties seek to embrace large proportions of the electorate and, therefore have incentives to avoid narrow ideological positions. Within the parties, however, ideologies and philosophies are continually debated. Leaders have strong incentives to become proficient in handling the ideas that power the intra-party debates and, hence, to develop their political credos. A common interpretation of the current policy revolution is that it is a victory of liberal over socialist or individualist over collectivist ideas. Certainly a central feature is the search by governments for solutions to problems which allow individual people greater choice and scope in expressing their values.

Divergent philosophical policy frameworks are important for a number of reasons. One is that they provide terms and concepts for leaders. Second, they enable leaders to orient themselves in the historic debates and to take advantage of learning about the functioning of society as the behavioural, social and physical sciences develop and elaborate concepts and knowledge in these debates. Political parties provide forums and arenas within which these debates are often crystallised. It is in part through linkages to these debates that researchers and theorists come to impact on the credos of leaders in a changing society. An awareness of these linkages in particular requires us to recognise that the competition between public leaders is, in significant part, a competition of ideas which is not adequately embraced by treating ideas just through their expression as rhetorical devices.

How do the 'grand debates' between liberalism and socialism, individualism and collectivism, over the role of government, and the linkage between human society and the environment relate to the credos of Australian political leaders? The Labor Party has provided the main institutional basis for romantic ideas conflating government and community, and for socialist concepts of government control over the means of production, distribution and exchange. The failure of central planning and the collapse of the socialist states of Eastern Europe had a profound effect on the internal Labor debate and weakened the constraints on leaders from pursuing more market oriented policies. The decisive policy defeat of the socialist Left began under Whitlam, accelerated under Hawke and Keating and has become almost irrelevant under Rudd. A major constraint on Labor leaders thus disappeared.

Over the last century we have been through an era of upheaval in political ideologies and behavioural studies. Our age has been one in which there has been a great contest of ideas over the extent to which policy should and can acknowledge the diversity of individual people, their values and ambitions and be directed to their empowerment, and the extent to which policy should be directed to advancing collective agendas based on nation, class, race, religion and gender. Debates around these ideas between competing public leaders constitute crucial continuities in our political life.

Do all political leaders have credos?

It has been important in Australian politics for leaders to articulate a credo. The nature of Australian political parties has encouraged a level of expertise in the handling of ideas and offering incentives to find those that will maintain the unity of their party while seeking the middle ground in the wider electorate. To the extent that leaders have been unable, or fail, to do so, their leadership is weakened. The credo relates key values and purposes to preferred outcomes and, therefore, gives both guidance and confidence to leaders as they attempt to deal with the ever-changing complexity of the issues with which time and situation confront them. Howard was a classic case of a leader who shifted decisions to one side of the line or the other depending on the exigencies and demands of the case, but who closely consulted the compass of his credo and sailed as close to the compass line as the prevailing wind permitted.

For followers, the existence of a leadership credo makes the leader more understandable and predictable, and thus helps to remove one of the threatening uncertainties of leadership — what will the leader do next? Where is the leader taking us? To the extent that there is a match between the values and beliefs of the leader and the followers, the bond in the relationship is strengthened. Indeed, the credo becomes an important element in the establishment of the leader's authority and, beyond authority, persuasive capacity (Lindblom 1977; Kemp 1988; Heifetz 1998). For the academic such credos enable public leadership to be set in a broader intellectual context. For the practitioner, they can provide that important quality of 'standing for something' or 'vision'.

Credos vary along the dimensions of individual belief systems and some have more policy relevance than others. Some are elaborate and broad in scope, others are narrow, some seem to be little more than statements of lobby group sub-culture, while others approach fully fledged political philosophies. Some are flexible, some are rigid. Perhaps we can talk of 'weak' credos and 'strong' credos, but we need a more sophisticated set of descriptive concepts. Peacock, Crean and Beazley seemingly had weak policy credos and lost their leadership largely as a result. Hewson had a strong policy credo but it was narrow and provided an inadequate 'fit' with the values of the electorate. The inability to articulate a convincing credo becomes a problem for a political leader.

Organisational factors: towards prime-ministerial dominance?

To pursue their policy reform agendas, Australian political leaders have reorganised the institutions of central government to meet their needs: for more sophisticated policy advice, for more flexible means of implementation (and especially for the management of the transition to market approaches), and for more effective political management of the consequences of policies that were often seen as disruptive to existing communities and interests.

A dominant feature of the social and political context of political leadership is continuous change. Leaders, while offering a solution to other people's uncertainties, experience continuing uncertainty themselves, and they are in a good position to do something about it. Leaders are constantly attempting to reduce their own uncertainty in their changing environment. One of the most important ways they do this is by exerting greater control over this environment by improving the skills of their advisers, their co-ordinating capacity, their information flow, and the norms, laws and context governing the behaviour of those causing the most threatening uncertainties. The other major way is by buffering their independence from the pressures upon them by controlling the advisory process and exerting authority. The playing out of these strategies produces continuing evolution in the nature of the institutional environment of leadership and in relations between the major institutions of government (Kemp 1987). The last three decades have been especially fruitful in this regard.

Over the last three decades we have a seen a dramatic evolution in the institutions of central government, both on the political advisory side in ministerial staff arrangements and in the Australian Public Service. In some of this I was directly involved, both in the evolution of the Prime Minister's Office as a distinct and significant element at the centre of government, and as minister responsible for negotiating and securing the passage through the Parliament of the *Public Service Act* 1999.

The democratic idea, in particular, empowered Australian leaders in their reorganisation of government: they saw themselves as leaders with all the legitimacy that comes from having been elected by the people. As such, and within the constraints of the Constitution, they believed they were entitled to have their views prevail. In the course of complex reform, they were entitled to the kind of advice and implementation machinery they felt they needed.

In the first place, they needed a public service expert enough and flexible enough to address the policy demands on it in a way that could deal with the full complexity of the issues. Secondly, they needed political staff who could assist them in their leadership tasks of managing change to obtain the support of the party they led, of the key lobby groups, of the major regions of the country, and of the electorate as a whole.

The dominant issue in relation to ministerial staff was to recognise in the institutional structure that the interests of the political leadership and the public service were not identical, and that there were aspects of political leadership that the public service was not in a position to support. These related to such matters as the setting of priorities, the establishment and communication of the values underpinning policy development, the management of relations with political institutions such as political parties and interest groups and advice on leadership strategies. The theory of the Westminster system had always acknowledged that the public service advised and implemented, but it was the political leader who made decisions. The difficulty was: who would advise the minister on the political aspects of the decisions he was bound to make?

These considerations led Fraser to establish in 1981 a significantly upgraded political staff, of which I was the foundation Director, and an office structure which was largely continued (and further developed) by successive Labor and Coalition governments. As a minister after 1996 I experienced the remarkable capacity to co-ordinate the Ministry which the Prime Ministers Office (PMO) had achieved by that time — a capacity which had not existed twenty years before. Regular discussions were held by the PMO with the staff of ministers and with ministers themselves, within the framework of charter letters in which the Prime Minister set out his annual expectations of ministers in terms of policy priorities. Indeed, by the time of the Howard government, the structures designed to assist the Prime Minister in his leadership role within the government had expanded enormously, embracing not only the PMO but the Cabinet Office (headed up by a political appointee who had become Secretary to cabinet) and a prime minister's department which paralleled the co-ordination role of the PMO within the public service.

The *Public Service Act* 1999 was aimed at greatly increasing the flexibility of leaders in the APS to manage their departments. Senior officers of the service, especially Peter Shergold, later Secretary of the Department of the Prime Minister and Cabinet, led the reforms within the service and with ministers. The greater flexibility assisted in the development of a growing variety of intra- and inter-departmental arrangements as the 'whole of government' approach gathered momentum to better deal with complex problems in areas such as the environment and education.

What are we to learn from this institutional evolution at the centre of Australian government? There is little doubt it led to a strengthening of the dominance of the political leadership in the system of government. This is particularly true of the prime ministership, but it also true of ministers as well within their portfolio areas. It represents, therefore, a lessening of the influence on certain kinds of decisions of the public service. On the other side, however, organisational reform has also produced a level of flexibility in the APS that has empowered it to respond more effectively to policy challenges. The task force on energy policy in 2003-2004 is an example of an innovative approach in which public servants and ministers discussed policy around the cabinet table in a way that would have been unheard of two decades ago.

Conclusion

The policy revolution of recent decades in Australia is not without parallels in other countries, but the Australian example has had a remarkable coherence and continuity from government to government over three and a half decades, despite some partisan differences.

While globalisation provided the context, the effective policy response by Australian political leaders can be linked to several features of the Australian political system. Australian political leadership is exercised in a notably homogenous democratic and rationalist culture to which both major parties responded with policies emphasising equal access to opportunities for the achievement of individual values. The Australian political system confers broad authority on its leaders to reorganise the arrangements for policy advice and implementation as required. The major political parties, operating in an electoral system that encourages competition for the middle ground, produced leaders with developed policy credos that expressed the shared values of the democratic culture, together with a rational approach to policy outcomes that facilitated sophisticated policy analysis and advice from the public service and policy agencies.

References

de Tocqueville, A., 1991, *Democracy in America,* (ed. J. P. Mayer, M. Lerner; trans. G. Lawrence), Norwalk, Conn.: Harper Collins, Easton Press.

Diesing, P., 1962, *Reason in Society: Five Types of Decisions and their Social Conditions,* Westport, Conn.: Greenwood Press.

Errington, W., and P. van Onselen, 2007, *John Winston Howard: The Biography,* Melbourne University Press.

Hancock, W. K., 1961, *Australia,* Brisbane, Jacaranda.

Heifetz, R. A., 1998, *Leadership Without Easy Answers,* Cambridge, Mass.: Belknap Press.

Kemp, D. A., 1973, 'A leader and a Philosophy,' in H. Mayer, *Labor to Power: Australia's 1972 Election*, Angus & Robertson, pp. 48-59.

Kemp, D. A., 1988, *Foundations for Australian Political Analysis: Politics and Authority*, Oxford University Press.

Lindblom, C. E., 1977, *Politics and Markets: The World's Political-Economic Systems*, New York: Basic Books.

Moore, M. H., 1995, *Creating Public Value: Strategic Management in Government*, Cambridge, Mass.: Harvard University Press.

Rae, D., 1981, *Equalities,* Cambridge, Mass.: Harvard University Press:

't Hart, P., and J. Uhr, 2008, 'Understanding Public Leadership in Australia: An Introduction'. Chapter 1, this volume.

Watson, D., 2002, *Recollections of a Bleeding Heart: A Portrait of Paul Keating PM*, Sydney: Knopf.

18. Styles of Conservative Leadership in Australian Politics

Wayne Errington

Introduction

Contemporary political science literature on leadership has sought, primarily, to understand policy innovation and the achievement of goals. For Robert Tucker (1987: 15), political leadership is the act of giving direction to a group or community. Blondel (1987: 25) sees political leadership as action designed to modify the environment. By these measures, leadership is not so much a journey or a relationship as a changing of the social and political landscape for which leaders are the overseers and instigators. Goal-centred approaches to leadership seek to differentiate leadership from office-holding; judging leaders by measuring stated goals against achievements. This interest in the way in which leaders go about achieving their goals has been influenced by management studies (Peele 2005: 188). Yet, conservative leaders tend to be measured by their electoral success rather than their legislative achievements. Conservative leaders can still be measured by their attainment of goals, but the goals of conservative and progressive leaders differ quite markedly. The relationship between leader and followers is a complex one if the goals of the leader are not clear-cut.

Since Weber, the notion of charisma – and personality types more generally – has never been far from the study of leadership. Social psychology has reminded political science that leaders are not simply cogs in the societal mechanism. Burns divided leaders into those with transformational or transactional styles. Again, some notion of goal-setting seems to be explicit since, to Burns, leadership is 'intended change' (1974: 434). More grounded in the experience of conservative leaders is Little's formulation of strong leadership (1988). Strong leadership can lend itself to transformation or to national defence in the face of real or perceived threats. Yet, conservative leadership may be better understood when process-centred accounts of leadership are utilised. Post, for example, stresses the 'mutual purposes' that leaders and followers perceive in their relationship (1991: 102). Indeed, successful leaders tend to be those who can mobilise followers around a set of ideas, rather than simply a set of goals (see Folkertsma 1988).

Conservative leaders tend to defy the labels of leadership theorists or, more to the point, they might suit any of these labels at any given time. Modern political history, particularly in the Anglo-Saxon world, is replete with examples of conservative governments that were activist legislators — self-conscious agents of change. These reformist conservative governments came about for a number of reasons. They had the opportunity (they would argue the duty) to change long-held social compacts within which previous conservative governments had operated. Their opportunities came about because of real and perceived economic problems for which a range of conservative leaders proposed market-oriented solutions. In this environment, conservatives with political ambition promote policy innovation in order to bring notice to themselves and underline their leadership qualities. This is sometimes referred to as 'policy entrepreneurship' (see Mackenzie 2004).

The environment in which leaders govern, then, is crucial to our understanding of both their goals and methods. An economic crisis might convince conservatives that the only way to preserve the social arrangements they value is through policy innovation. This chapter seeks to examine a range of environments and leadership styles that might be appropriate to conservative leaders. It establishes a typology of leadership styles by taking into account goals incorporating, but not limited to, public policy. Those leadership styles are then applied to a number of Australian conservative prime ministers, with the primary focus on the most recent — John Howard.

Making room for conservative leadership

Richardson, Gustafsson and Jordan developed a typology of national policy styles, highlighting a 'consensus' versus 'imposition' approach to implementation on one axis, and an 'anticipatory' versus 'reactive' type of problem-solving on the other axis (1982: 13). These policy styles were adapted by Barton and van Onselen (2004) to leadership styles in Australia, plotting the differences between Australian state premiers Jeff Kennett and Richard Court. Naturally, an impositional style of leadership (that attributed to Kennett by Barton and van Onselen) lends itself to the change-oriented approaches to leadership outlined earlier. One might interpret the more radical style of a Kennett as a desire to maintain a capitalist mode of production. A distinction between classical liberal and conservative goals is nevertheless worth preserving. Either way, leadership literature dealing with goal-oriented policy change can accommodate a style of conservative leadership that sets and achieves policy goals. Other aspects of conservative leadership, though, are not so well served by the dominant paradigm in leadership studies.

Moon (1995), seeking to explain the success of British Prime Minister Margaret Thatcher, developed the concept of innovative leadership to describe leaders with both strong political will and a strong policy capacity (the right environment for change). How, though, do such typologies deal with the conservative leader whose primary goal is to hold office? For Moon, the opposite of innovative leadership is inertia. This might be an apt description of many a political leader, but Moon's typology does not account for a leader whose goals are not specifically policy-oriented. A successful conservative politician such as long-serving

Australian Prime Minister Robert Menzies can hardly be said to have lacked either political will or policy capacity. Yet, Menzies only occasionally sought to be an innovative policy leader as Prime Minister (with a few exceptions, such as extending Commonwealth grants to Catholic schools). Menzies's achievement in fashioning a successful conservative party where others had failed and holding power for 17 years was an impressive feat of leadership.

Achievement of conservative goals, then, may take a good deal of leadership skill. The goals of conservative leaders are not always clear-cut. Successful conservative leaders are adaptive. If they hold office for an extended period, we might expect them to appear in various places on the various diagrams produced by scholars of leadership, depending on the time and the issue in question. Retaining the status quo while being buffeted by exogenous forces such as globalisation, or during a national crisis or disaster, is a feat of leadership too often ignored by the change-merchants. Leadership during a crisis presents an opportunity for a different set of relationships between leaders and followers. Heifetz argues that citizens in democracies too often respond to crises by turning to leaders who offer strength and easy answers rather than those who offer the right leadership qualities to find and implement solutions (1994: 2). A number of Australian conservative leaders have been analysed through the notion of strong leadership. Strong leadership could conceivably be brought to the service of radical goals, but the psychological dimension of this leadership style has been more often associated with the bond between conservatives and their followers.

A simple typology (Table 1) combining the radical or conservative ends of leadership with the impositional or consensus styles described above produces four leadership styles — transformative, strong, reassuring, and conservatorship. The notion of radical or conservative ends does not preclude a range of policy orientations depending on the environment. Strong leadership, for example, might entail stringency measures meant to preserve a set of institutions thought to be under threat (during a war or other crisis) or a set of more radical policies aimed at preserving the social status quo through a new policy orientation (in response to globalisation or declining terms of trade). Conservatorship acknowledges the lack of policy innovation that often defines conservative government without conceding that the political activity involved in the preservation of social institutions does not involve considerable leadership challenges.

Table 1: Goals and methods in political leadership

	Goals	
Methods	Radical	Conservative
Imposition	Transformational leadership	Strong leadership
Consensus	Reassuring leadership	Conservatorship

The notion of transformational leadership is probably the most familiar to scholars of leadership. Combining radical ends with an uncompromising leadership style, transformative leaders run the risk of moving too far ahead of their followers. Kennett sought and failed to be a transformative leader: one with more liberal than conservative goals. However, his failure to win the 1999 Victorian election was a sign that he suffered the fate of many strong leaders: failing to adapt his leadership style to changed circumstance. As the sense of economic crisis that Kennett had exploited faded into the distance, voters turned to the more *reassuring* leadership style of Labor's Steve Bracks.

Contemporary Australian conservative leadership

While Menzies's astonishing record of office-holding success makes him the touchstone of Australian conservative leadership, the environment in which he governed was a largely benign one. His conservatorship was suited to the post-war Keynsian economic management — occupying the political centre ground and painting his opponents as radicals. Mindful of the previous conservative government's failure to win popular support for *laissez-faire* policies and by disposition suspicious of the business lobbies, Menzies used his multiple election victories to win only modest policy changes. The more challenging economic environment of the 1970s was the appropriate environment for a quite different style of leadership exercised by Malcolm Fraser. While the liberal elements of Fraser's ideology have been on display since his retirement from the prime ministership, his relationship with the electorate was based on a willingness to take tough decisions in difficult times. Cuts to expenditure, calls for wage restraint and traditional conservative rhetoric on national security made Fraser an archetypal strong leader (Little 1988).

The Fraser government's failure to reform the Australian economy subsequently became the subject of division within the Liberal Party. While Fraser toyed with monetarism in response to rising inflation (in line with similar efforts elsewhere in the developed world), the ideas that later governments would implement in response to Australia's declining economic fortunes were undeveloped during Fraser's tenure as Prime Minister. Fraser's view of Australia's economic problems was that while difficult decisions were required, the policy prescriptions necessary were those familiar to conservative governments since the end of the war. Strong leadership aimed at radical policy change is a risky political strategy and, therefore, relatively rare. Thatcher's example requires the combination of unusual circumstances and personality types.

One Australian who admired Thatcher's success was Fraser's treasurer, John Howard. As the Labor governments of Hawke and Keating took the difficult decisions to transform the Australian economy (employing the unique combination of Keating's zeal and Hawke's reassurance), Howard battled for supremacy inside the Liberal Party.

Howard started his political career as an unquestioning Menzian, suspicious of change and reform. It was the difficult economic circumstances of the 1970s that caused Howard to question Keynesian economic policy. Howard's conversion to what was fast becoming the neo-liberal orthodoxy coincided with his interest in positioning himself as a successor to Fraser. Howard began to style himself as a reformer during the third term of the Fraser government. He ran into resistance in cabinet for his proposals to deregulate the financial system. Adjusting his policy orientation over the course of his career, Howard constructed an approach to government that defies simple descriptions or labels, and utilised at least two of the leadership styles described in this chapter. He differentiated himself from his major competitor for the Liberal leadership in the 1980s, Andrew Peacock, by advocating policy change more radical than the Hawke government was putting in place. This earned Howard the admiration of many in the press gallery. Promoting reform from opposition, though, proved to be difficult. During his first stint as opposition leader (1985-89), Howard was ahead of both the Hawke government and public opinion on issues of deregulation.

Another of the unsuccessful Liberal leaders during the Hawke-Keating years, Dr John Hewson, took the ideas of liberal transformation of Australian society to its zenith with his *Fightback* package. Unlike most Liberal Party members, Hewson was socially as well as economically liberal. While the recession of the early 1990s should have been ripe for a change of government, the public could not connect with Hewson on any level. His classical liberalism was shared by few voters. His technocratic style lacked the psychological elements of strong leadership that others may have brought to bear in those circumstances. In stark contrast to Hewson, upon his return to the Liberal Party leadership in 1995, Howard attempted to take advantage of the 'reform fatigue' in the electorate.

Conservative by disposition and mindful of the success of Menzies's conservatorship, Howard disappointed many of his most zealous supporters with the caution of his first two terms. The paradox at the heart of John Howard's leadership was his ability to profit from the electorate's fear of change while continually advocating (if not actually delivering) economic reform. He was assisted in this by an environment conducive to strong leadership, especially after the September 11, 2001 terrorist attacks on the United States. While Howard had long since distanced himself ideologically from Fraser, he was a close witness to the effectiveness of Fraser's strong leadership in winning the prime ministership and on issues of national security.

One of Howard's strengths as a communicator was to simultaneously provide reassurance and persuasion. His continual use of talkback radio to justify government policies was a new dimension in Australian politics. The majority of Australians had yet to be convinced that the market-oriented reforms of the last two decades were a good idea. Howard's reply to a journalist's question about his vision for Australia — that he wanted Australians to be 'comfortable and relaxed' summarised the Coalition strategy for the 1996 election.

The Howard Government was the most active legislator in Commonwealth history. This would seem to mark Howard with a different leadership style than Menzies. However, a more active legislature is part of a response to the different government environment that contemporary leaders face. By 1996, the broadsheet press, the public service, both major political parties, and state governments were well versed in making and selling to the public difficult economic and social policy decisions. During and after the 2001 election campaign, Prime Minister Howard was asked one question more than any other: the press gallery wanted to know what his third term agenda was? Similar questions bugged him on the campaign trail in 2004. This constant refrain says something about the expectations of contemporary leaders. Howard's skill in dealing with some of the modern elements of politics — most notably the era of globalisation in which most of his leadership career took place and the demands of the 24-hour media cycle — confounded those critics who assumed that social conservatism was all that there was to his political outlook. It may be counter-intuitive to suggest that a conservative leader was so successful in setting the policy agenda, but Howard — backed by the public relations apparatus of the state — was as successful at this task as any Australian Prime Minister.

Howard's conservatism is underlined by the choices he made as Prime Minister. He was true to those elements of his reform agenda that serve political as well as economic ends — privatisation and labour market reform. His goal with these policies was to undermine social sources of support for the Australian Labor Party. Cuts in public spending, on the other hand, caused the government headaches in this first term for no great economic gain. After 1997, Howard made no serious attempt to rein in public spending. Howard's political goals were about winning — not just keeping Labor out of power but winning battles within his party as well. The extent to which Howard actually believed in the free-market policies he advocated from the 1980s is beside the point. They were only ever a means to an end — making the conservative parties electorally competitive in a changing world.

Howard's reassuring style in his first two terms was assisted by the fact that most of his closest followers had retired by the time he won office in 1996 (or, in the case of Michael Baume, quickly shunted to a diplomatic post instead of a ministry). He could dispassionately assess his own goals and the needs of national governance with fewer demands than the average prime minister to reward allies. His most important attribute in his second stint as opposition leader — in stark contrast to the first — was his ability to reassure key sections of the community that he would take their interests into account when framing policy. The reduction in the immigration intake, his message that Australian history and nationalism was a source of pride, and his willingness to compromise over key elements of his economic program such as privatisation and the Goods and Services Tax all saw Howard treading a difficult path between the demands of elite groups and the voters that Howard saw as crucial to his electoral survival. His stances alienated almost as many constituencies as they impressed, of course, but that is the nature of democratic politics.

On the policy front, then, Howard was selective in the achievement of his goals, subordinate as they always were to his essentially conservative view of Australian politics. His political mission in life was to keep Labor off the treasury benches. He was able to win four elections by keeping up a balance between reassurance and advocacy of further reform. Adherence to the policy orthodoxy of Hawke and Keating (including policies he had earlier opposed, such as Medicare) was important to Howard's relationship with sections of the policy community and the media.

Howard's reassuring style was sufficient to win him the 1996 and 1998 elections, and to stage a comeback from disastrous opinion polling throughout 2001. That comeback depended, in part, in Howard's behaviour during and after the twin events that dominated the 2001 campaign — asylum seekers and the US terrorist attacks. Strong leaders respond to a difficult governing environment. Walter argues that Howard fits the 'strong leader' type due to the uncompromising way he approached factional politics in the Liberal Party, his firm position on social and cultural issues as Prime Minister, and the suitability of his political persona to the 'securitisation' agenda post-11 September 2001 (Walter 2006: 3-4). The first two of these elements of Howard's strong leadership had been in place for some time and did not translate into public perceptions of leadership strength.

In his first two terms, where other senior ministers urged him to take policy packages to a double dissolution election, Howard was satisfied with compromise (Errington and van Onselen 2007: 283). Labor Party advertisements during the 1996 election campaign contrasted public perceptions of Keating's leadership strength with the supposed weakness of Howard. The occasion on which public perceptions of Howard's leadership strength increased dramatically was in the midst of the Tampa affair, where Howard did something that the majority of the public wanted him to do — get tough on asylum seekers. Perceptions of strength were then reinforced by the hostility with which Howard's actions were met in sections of the intelligensia. Until late 2001, one of the characteristics of Howard's prime ministership had been his self-conscious courting of public opinion. Policy 'backflips' were a staple, not an exception, to Howard's strategy. Indeed, the comeback in the opinion polls throughout 2001 was dependent on a number of policy reversals on taxation and welfare policy. It was the 2001 election campaign that crystallised the leadership style that Howard would portray in his final three election contests. His command of the Liberal Party and combative social agenda by that point complemented his leadership style whereas they had caused him problems earlier in this career. It is much easier to be a strong leader as Prime Minister than it is as Leader of the Opposition.

Winning (notional) control of the Senate from 2005 caused Howard to reassess his approach to economic reform. Howard's political success was at its height when his government was forced to compromise with the Senate. Once Howard's leadership was unchallenged by the Senate, Howard felt obliged to live up to the reformist persona he had created over two decades. It was when circumstances allowed Howard to move to an impositional style of leadership that he lost public favour. Whatever the Australian public thought of Howard's strong leadership style on issues of national security, they had no interest in it when it affected in substance an issue close to their daily lives.

We see in John Howard many of the characteristics that political scientists have identified as crucial to our understanding of leadership: he is a fundamentally competitive human being; he liked to win; he enjoyed the tag of strong leader; and he was Prime Minister during a period in which the style (if not always the substance) of strong leadership was valued by the public. However, maintaining a persona of strong leadership would have prevented Howard from fulfilling other political goals. In spite of his protestations that the electorate knew Howard and could take him or leave him, Howard was not prepared to have the electorate judge him on his leadership strengths alone. He was too much of a transactional politician for that. Policy backflips, payoffs to key groups of followers, and compromise was as much a part of Howard's leadership style as strong leadership. Conservative leaders adapt to the times in which they govern. Howard governed in an age of reform and adapted accordingly. He stood firm when it suited, compromised when he had to, and reassured at every step of the way. However, once the strong leader persona came to define him in domestic as well as foreign policy terms, a reassuring Leader of the Opposition was able to defeat him at the 2007 election.

Conclusion

Contemporary Liberal Party leaders judge their success by the founder of their party, Sir Robert Menzies. John Howard looked upon Menzies as his political hero and distanced himself ideologically from the policies of his former boss Malcolm Fraser. Menzies and Fraser embody two important conservative leadership styles — respectively, conservatorship and strong leader. Whatever Howard thought of Fraser's policies, he often sought to portray himself in the strong leader style. Howard was too cautious, though, to govern in that style for his first two terms. Had he kept the mantle of conservator, he may still be Prime Minister.

It may be another conservator who grabs the Menzies mantle next. The fate of Howard's strong leadership may convince future Liberal Party leaders that a style more in tune with popular concerns might be more effective. A nation weary of constant change may look for stability. Alternatively, problems such as global warming may set the stage for another strong leader. In any event, a successful conservative leader will set and achieve goals. Success will be measured by an ability to build and maintain political relationships as much as an ability to achieve lasting policy change. That often involves tailoring leadership style to a changing political environment.

References

Barton, Stephen and Peter van Onselen, 2004, 'Comparing Court and Kennett Leadership Styles: Energy Sector Reform in Victoria and Western Australia', *Policy and Society*, 22:2, p. 120-43.

Blondel, Jean, 1987, *Political Leadership: Towards a General Analysis*, London: Sage Publications.

Burns, James MacGregor., 1974, *Leadership*, New York: Harper and Row.

Errington, Wayne and Peter van Onselen, 2007, *John Winston Howard: The Biography,* Carlton: Melbourne University Press.

Folkertsma, Marvin, 1988, *Ideology and Leadership*, Englewood Cliffs: Prentice Hall.

Goldfinch, Shaun and Paul 't Hart, 2003, 'Leadership and Institutional Reform: Engineering Macroeconomic Policy Change in Australia', in *Governance*, 16:2, pp. 235-70.

Heifitz, Ronald, 1994, *Leadership Without Easy Answers*, New Haven: Harvard University Press.

Little, Graham, 1988, *Strong Leadership: Thatcher, Reagan and an Eminent Person*, Melbourne: Oxford University Press.

Mackenzie, C, 2004, 'Policy Entrepreneurship in Australia: A Conceptual Review and Application,' in *Australian Journal of Political Science*, 39:2, pp. 367-386.

Moon, Jeremy, 1995, 'Innovative Leadership and Policy Change: Lessons From Thatcher', in *Governance*, 8:1, pp. 1-25.

Peele, Gillian, 2005, 'Leadership and Politics: A Case for a Closer Relationship?' in *Leadership*, 1:1, pp. 187-204.

Post, Joseph C., 1991, *Leadership for the 21st Century*, New York: Praeger.

Richardson, Jeremy, Gunnel Gustafsson and Grant Jordan, 1982, 'The Concept of Policy Style', in J. Richardson (ed.), *Policy Styles in Western Europe*, Boston: Allen and Unwin.

Tucker, Robert, 1987, *Politics as Leadership*, London: University of Missouri Press.

Walter, James, 2006, 'John Howard and the "Strong Leader" thesis', paper presented to the John Howard's Decade Conference, Canberra, March.

19. Reinventing Australian Conservatism in the States: New Leadership and the Liberal Revival under Bolte and Askin

Norman Abjorensen

Introduction

The formation of the Liberal Party of Australia in the mid-1940s heralded a new effort to harness the forces of liberalism and conservatism in opposition to Labor Party rule in the latter years of World War II and immediately after. It was not until 1949 that the party gained office at Federal level, beginning what was to be a record unbroken term of 23 years, but its efforts faltered at state level in Victoria, where the party was divided, and in New South Wales, where Labor was seemingly entrenched. The fortunes were reversed with the rise to leadership of men who bore a different stamp to their predecessors, and were in many ways atypical Liberals: Henry Bolte in Victoria and Robin Askin in New South Wales. Their leadership is examined here in the broader context of the post-war liberal revival as well as the ways in which the new Liberal Party sought to engage with and appeal to a wider range of voters than had traditionally been attracted to the non-Labor parties. Above all, this chapter argues that Australian conservatism was revitalised through a concerted effort to promote leaders more readily identified with ordinary Australians than had been the case pre-war. It was the colloquialisation of non-Labor politics.

Political history in Australia, as well as political journalism, has come to mean, almost invariably, a focus on the Commonwealth as the locus of power and the exclusive subject of political interest. This one-dimensional approach to both scholarship and journalism has been correctly characterised as 'doomed to incompleteness and distortion' by its neglect of the two-dimensional system that exists in Australian political life (Galligan 1986: x). To overlook the state dimension is to miss a key dynamic in political life, particularly in regard to parties. The rise of the Liberal Party to its post-war ascendancy was far more than the achievements of Robert Menzies on the national stage.

Conservative politics in crisis

World War II had left its stamp indelibly on the Australian nation; no part of it was left untouched by the experience of mobilisation and the fear of invasion. The characteristics of service life permeated civilian life after the war and the advent of the Cold War, coupled with the considerable tensions generated by the fears surrounding communism at home and ongoing uncertainty in the international situation, ensured that ideas about defence and national security remained prominent in the public mind. Australia's official war historian Paul Hasluck attempted to capture the deep emotions that the war experience triggered, noting in a description of marching troops 'the strong and binding comradeship that a shared grief and pride can bring to men and women' and especially the demeanour of 'the men who had fought, strong, sun-tanned, tight-jawed and fit, swung past with that loose and confident stride that only Australian soldiers have' (Hasluck 1970: 625). It was that 'loose and confident stride' that would define the ethos of post-war Australia. It became, even at a subliminal level, a potent symbol of what Hasluck identified as the 'stronger national consciousness' (Hasluck 1970: 627) that emerged after the war. It would find in its own way an expression in political culture that defined both a character type and a set of attitudes.

As World War II drew to a close in 1945, conservative politics in Australia was in disarray. In the bitter and lingering aftermath of the Great Depression and in the uncertain handling of the war effort in the first Menzies Government (1939-41), the conservative forces were in serious decline and were seen to be increasingly irrelevant, venting what feeble energies they retained on internecine conflict. The resurrection of the 79-year-old Billy Hughes as leader of the United Australia Party (UAP) after the resignation of Robert Menzies was a striking symbol of the lack of vitality in the ramshackle UAP and its cause. Its conservative coalition partner, the Country Party, was also in conflict, having split in 1939 over its relations with the UAP. Later the Country Party saw one of its members cross the floor with an independent to bring down the government, briefly led by Country Party Leader Arthur Fadden in 1941. Furthermore, the Country Party firmly rebuffed invitations to attend the gathering of conservative and liberal organisations in Albury and Canberra in 1944 from which the modern day Liberal Party emerged after the disintegration of the UAP.

In Victoria, the party had been effectively sidelined since 1935 by an alliance between the Country Party and Labor, and this had led to a damaging split and further electoral decline in 1945. In New South Wales the UAP-Country Party government slid quietly into oblivion in 1941 as the ALP shrugged off the influence of J. T. Lang and, under a new and appealing leader in William McKell, surged back into office in what was to be the beginning of a record 24-year term. In terms of the all-important public perception, the UAP had ceased to be 'dinkum'. It was no longer seen as representing popular aspirations; it was perceived as a self-serving and squabbling oligarchy remote from the problems and issues of everyday Australians and lacking the legitimacy to be considered a viable alternative to Labor as the party of government.

Concerns ran deep. Business was worried that the image of private enterprise continued to be tainted in the public mind after the Depression and that greater government involvement in the economy, under both wartime emergency controls and post-war reconstruction, was not only unopposed but appeared to have wide public support. The Institute of Public Affairs was formed precisely to wage such a battle, although the Melbourne and Sydney branches differed in their attitudes to the degree of intervention that was acceptable. Business was also concerned that its interests were not being articulated at the political level. The leading figures behind the formation of the new Liberal Party were keenly aware of the problems the party faced, among them a lack of public credibility, the perception that conservative politicians appeared to be more English than Australian, and that, in the past, conservative politics had failed to reach into the lives of, and appeal to, ordinary Australians. Above all, there had been a failure of leadership.

The general feeling of inadequacy on the non-Labor side, coupled with an air of enveloping crisis, is reflected in the musings of a prominent business figure, F. E. Lampe,[1] about the results of the 1943 Federal election, which he characterised as: 'United they stood, divided we fell' (Lampe 1943: 1). Lampe noted the care taken by the Labor Party not to reveal to the public any sign of dissension in its ranks and contrasted Prime Minister John Curtin's leadership with the lack of leadership in the UAP. He also noted a number of other problems with the non-Labor parties, among them: disagreement between UAP and Country Party leaders on major points of policy; the lack of clear and constructive policy positions; a tendency towards political expediency and lack of organisation; and the 'possibility that the Labor Party is regarded as more Australian than the UAP [and] that the UAP is regarded as being more susceptible to English than to Australian influences'. He identified a widespread belief that Labor offered the best hope of post-war social security and avoidance of depression.

Lampe was concerned that while Labor was focusing on post-war reconstruction, the two non-Labor parties during the 1943 campaign had merely spoken 'more or less vaguely about the need to preserve private enterprise'. They had 'completely failed' to enunciate a policy that would be capable of avoiding depressions and other social evils that followed the 1914-18 war (Lampe 1943: 3). Even the august *Sydney Morning Herald*, generally a supporter on the non-Labor side, was strongly critical of the malaise which had overtaken the emphasise parties, accusing them of representing 'vested interests' which, while not represented directly, were nevertheless organised 'through a clique of professional politicians who close their ranks to new talent' (*Sydney Morning Herald* 1943a).

The UAP was being seen increasingly as irrelevant, both to the demands of the business community and to the so-called 'middle ground' which it needed if it was to achieve electoral success (Lonie 1978: 69). Its ability to match Labor, ideologically or politically, was constantly to be found wanting. The prominent businessman and later Federal President of the Liberal Party, T. M. Ritchie[2] echoed the sentiments of many when he said: 'It is obvious that the weakness of our opposition to the promotion of socialistic political thought and effort arises largely out of our failure to achieve a continuity of political effort by those citizens who do not share the socialistic viewpoints' (Speech to Darlinghurst branch 1945).

There were two recurring themes in the *Sydney Morning Herald's* ongoing critique of the non-Labor malaise — the need to move away from simple anti-socialism and protection of vested interests ('obstructive conservatism') to a broader, more robust liberalism (*Sydney Morning Herald* 1943b) and greater consideration given to the type of candidate needed. The latter contained a prescient insight into the type of Liberal leaders who would emerge in the immediate post-war years and addressed what the *Herald* had long identified as a pronounced lack of practical administrative ability in non-Labor ranks. 'Administrative capacity is obviously needed, but unlike political leadership, it is fairly plentiful in this country. The problem is only how to associate it with politics' (*Sydney Morning Herald* 1943c).

In other words, the pool of talent for leadership was as narrow as it was shallow; the class and social constraints of non-Labor merely churned out more of the same type of politician. If a new start were to be made — and this was the thrust of the *Herald's* argument — then serious attention needed to be given to the encouragement of more diverse talents, an issue that the later influx of ex-servicemen would address and in so doing provide leaders at state level such as Henry Bolte in Victoria and, later, Robin Askin in New South Wales. It was this subtle shift that helped provide the subsequent Liberal Party with the essential ingredient needed to build electoral success on its mass-base organisation — and that was mass appeal.

A sceptical electorate

While the failure at the Federal election in 1946 and the ructions in Victoria were disheartening to many Liberals, there were those in office in the new party who used the occasion to exhort members to even greater efforts to convince the electorate that they were truly what they claimed to be. In a summing up of the party's defeat in 1946, The Victorian president, W. H. Anderson[3] suggested that the electorate remained sceptical of the new party.

> [A]t the last Federal election we nearly won. We had an excellent policy. It was not the policy that lost the Election, and it was not that the people were not getting dissatisfied with the Labor Party. What lost us the election was that the people were not yet satisfied of the bona fides of

the Liberal Party. They were not satisfied that we were dinkum, that we meant what we said, and that we really stood for the people's party representing all sections throughout the country. If they had believed that we would have been in power to-day. You are the only people that can convince them (Anderson 1947: 3).

A new party it might have been, but the past cast a shadow over the present, especially so as many of the names prominent in the new Liberal Party had been equally prominent in the now widely criticised United Australia Party; the people, it seemed, remained unconvinced. Menzies has recounted how he was reasonably pleased with the modest gains in 1946, but that there were also 'plenty of onlookers' who were exceedingly critical, and that his leadership was once more being brought into question (Menzies 1969: 293). Leadership, it seems, was very much part of the debate and resurfaced as an issue early in 1949 when the Institute of Public Affairs, lamenting Australia's poor productivity, especially when compared with the Americans, called for a 'new national outlook and faith'. Leadership was found to be lacking 'at the highest order of political and industrial statesmanship', and what was needed were 'leaders who can bring the nation to a new way of life' ('Triumph or Disaster?' 1949: 13-4).

Sincerity had not been proven, in the words of Anderson; the ordinary Australian had yet to believe these new Liberals were 'dinkum'. Yet at the same time there was correctly perceived to be a rising tide of anxiety about the directions of post-war Australia, and those who had rallied to the call of the new party displayed a 'revived enthusiasm' (Hancock 2000: 88) in setting out to defeat socialism. But just how to harness this need to popular sentiment remained problematic. It was a speech a few months after Anderson's by R. G. Casey[4] that clearly spelled out for the first time just what it was that the Liberals lacked and what they must do. The address, to a Liberal Party Victorian State Council meeting, took the form of a rather blunt *mea culpa*, and spelled out what the Liberals had to do to build on their creation of a mass party. Electoral success would follow only when that foundation was augmented by mass appeal; in other words, the Liberal Party had to reach out beyond the confines of its own membership if it was to become a real political force; it had to be more engaged in the lives of the ordinary people.

> I am one of the many who believe that we Liberals should identify ourselves to the greatest extent possible with the lives of the people. In the past (I am talking of before the war) on our side in politics we tended to live in an ivory tower. We did not have anything like as much contact with the everyday lives of the ordinary average men and women. I am hoping very much that from now on we will increase our efforts to unify ourselves all over Australia with the lives of the ordinary Australian men and women, particularly with those on lower incomes (Casey 1947).

Quite pointedly, Casey, then Federal President of the Liberal Party, was delivering a call to action, a call to go out and become one with 'the ordinary Australian men and women', a call for the Liberal Party to make itself relevant to the everyday concerns of the people and to connect with them; above all, it was a call to talk to the Australian people in a more colloquial voice, a voice that was unambiguously Australian, a voice that spoke to *all* Australians, irrespective of creed or economic or social status.

Getting 'dinkum': enter Bolte and Askin

The Liberals in Victoria pre-Bolte and in New South Wales pre-Askin were poor relations indeed to the successful political machine that Menzies and others had built and with which the Coalition surged to office in 1949. In Victoria, the Liberals had suffered two damaging splits in seven years, and its leadership was inept at best. Tom Hollway, the only Liberal Premier before Bolte, was unable to control tensions within his own party (indeed, he was the cause of many of them), and in any case preferred to govern in consultation with a small circle of advisers outside the party. When Hollway was deposed, the Liberals elected a brooding and intense former prisoner-of-war, Les Norman, who lost his seat without ever making an impact, and then turned to a party veteran, Trevor Oldham, who soon after died in an air crash. When Bolte became leader of a mere cricket team of Liberals in 1953, confronting not only a majority Labor Government and a hostile Country Party, but also a clutch of dissident Liberals under Hollway known first as the Electoral Reform Group and later the Victorian Liberal Party, he faced a very uncertain future. But owing to internecine warfare inside the ALP, he was Premier within two years and held the job, unchallenged, for 17 years. He displayed not only political skills of a high order that maximised his undoubted good fortune, but he brought to the office man-management skills that helped transform a motley rabble into a disciplined government that gave, and received, loyalty. An early supporter of Bolte, even before he became leader, was the party president and a member of the Melbourne business establishment, J. M. Anderson (no relation to W. H. Anderson) who arranged for Bolte to make regular broadcasts on station 3XY, then owned by the Liberal Party.

> We picked on Henry because he showed he had flair. He was shrewd but not cunning. That's what appealed to us. He was a man on the land, in direct contrast to the people we'd been used to. He was always ready to sit down and talk things out (Blazey 1990: 58).

In New South Wales, the non-Labor parties had been in opposition for 18 years by the time Askin was elected to the Liberal leadership after the 1959 election defeat. To many, both in the party and outside it, the Liberal Party in that state was doomed to be a permanent opposition. Four leaders had come and three had gone in as many years: Vernon Treatt, a Rhodes Scholar, barrister and decorated war hero; Murray Robson, a socialite solicitor and former lieutenant-colonel; and Pat Morton, a successful businessman from a political family. Despite a professional party organisation, at the parliamentary level the Liberals were still in many ways a pre-modern party with most members engaged in business and two even ran industry organisations. Askin, a former bank employee and army sergeant, changed all that. He declared himself when he became leader 'a professional politician'. It was a line drawn in the sand that signified a real break with the past and an entirely new approach. The era of Liberals in New South Wales being part-time politicians was over. John Carrick, who served as General Secretary of the Liberal Party 1948-1971 saw Askin as a political pragmatist whose appeal opened up new avenues to potential voters.

> I would give Askin full marks for his policies. He picked the policies out of the grab bag the party had thrown up over a period. He looked at the small shopkeeper kind of show; he looked at the little man who was being picked on with regulations and so on. So he was using things that had irritated people from the end of the war, and he used it and got what he deserved. With Askin we had a person whom we thought would be acceptable to what we called the little voter. That was our campaign theme. It was quite authentic; he was very naturally inclined that way (Carrick 2002).

Interestingly, both Bolte and Askin served as non-commissioned officers in World War II whereas the majority of those who served under them had been officers.

Table 1. The Bolte Cabinet (1955) and Military Service

Name	Military Service	Officer or Ranks
Henry Bolte	Yes	Ranks
Arthur Rylah	Yes	Officer
Arthur Warner	Yes	Officer
Gilbert Chandler	No	
William Leggatt	Yes	Officer
Thomas Maltby	Yes	Officer
Ewen Cameron	Yes	Officer
Wilfred Mibus	No	
Robert Whately	No	
John Bloomfield	Yes	Officer
Horace Petty	Yes	Officer
Keith Turnbull	No	
George Reid	Yes	Officer
Gordon McArthur	Yes	Officer

Table 2. The Askin Cabinet (1965) and Military Service

Name	Military Service	Officer or Ranks
Robin Askin	Yes	Ranks
Charles Cutler	Yes	Officer
Eric Willis	Yes	Ranks
Arthur Bridges	No	
William Chaffey	Yes	Officer
Kenneth McCaw	No	
Philip Morton	No	
Davis Hughes	Yes	Officer
Milton Morris	No	
John Fuller	No	
Thomas Lewis	Yes	Officer
Jack Beale	No	
Stanley Stephens	Yes	Ranks
Harry Jago	Yes	Officer
Wallace Fife	No	
John Maddison	Yes	Officer

There was a knockabout quality to both men who had been active in sport and social groups for many years, and their military experience was also relatively rough-hewn in comparison to their commissioned brothers. It is argued here that it was precisely these qualities that enabled both Bolte and Askin to feel at ease among people; this worked at both a parliamentary level, where keen people management was required and also at the electorate level where a sense of purpose and reliability needed to be communicated. Their public images of beer drinkers who liked a bet on the horses and went to the football resonated with the electorate in a way that no Liberals had managed before and few have since. Two other successful modern Liberal leaders, David Brand in Western Australia and Tom Playford in South Australia, also came from socially modest NCO backgrounds; both men attributed their political success, in part, to their military experiences serving in the ranks.

After an uncertain start, the Liberals, especially at state level, set about demonstrating their *bona fides* to an electorate that had, quite justifiably, developed a lingering scepticism about the capabilities and genuineness of the non-Labor cause, especially as it was represented by the effete United Australia Party. Clearly, a new message had to be devised along with new ways of communicating it, and that involved a new type of leader and style of leadership.

Conclusion: dinkum vs. gravitas in Liberal leadership styles

There are many similarities between Bolte and Askin, the greatest of which is that each was an outsider in terms of the accepted norms of Liberal Party leadership.[5] Neither was from a moneyed background (Askin's was in fact quite poor). Each inherited a party that was deeply divided and presided over a unifying process that was characterised by loyalty. Neither was ever challenged for the duration of their leadership. Each chose the timing of his departure from politics. Why were these apparent outsiders so accepted, so unchallenged, and so successful?

This chapter argues that their differentiation from the norms of their parties was very much a source of their strength and appeal as leaders. They broke the perceived class nexus that had divided parties and their background as NCOs, rather than officers, in the aftermath of World War II, laid an emphasis on teamwork that had been noticeably lacking in previous non-Labor parties. They led rather than commanded. Their demeanour was that of the ordinary person; their habits those of the average Australian. Their immediate appeal cut across fault lines that had previously been defined by an unspoken class affiliation; the language they spoke and the symbols they represented were of the public bar, not the saloon bar.

Each in his own way also represented a type that was in keeping with perceptions of their respective states,[6] especially the capital cities. Bolte, who had religious beliefs (and once even contemplated a career as a preacher) was wary of issues deemed to be in the moral domain, as much from personal conviction as from strategic considerations in keeping the DLP firmly on side. Victoria's laws on censorship, for example, were stringent: Sunday newspapers were forbidden, cinema hours on the sabbath, when they were at last allowed to open, were restricted, and hotels closed at 6:00 pm until 1966.

Askin, very much a Sydney man, professed no religious conviction. He was, like his city, free and easy-going in attitude and politics. His own attitude to authority had a certain cavalier streak. He was, for example, a keen SP (starting price) punter when SP betting was illegal but nonetheless prevalent.

Looming large over any discussion of the history of the Liberal Party, and especially of the issue of leadership, is the glowering shadow of Robert Menzies. Menzies, it is true, came from a position in which he was regarded with scepticism in the eyes of the electorate, to a position of dominance, just as the Liberal Party itself did. Yet did he prove himself to be, as the Liberal founders hoped, *dinkum*?

In a broad sense he did, though not in the same way that ensuing leaders in the field of state politics did, which suggests significant differences in the respective domains: one overarching, so to speak, the other almost personal. Menzies displayed a gravitas that became a trademark. Men such as Bolte and Askin exhibited a folksy earthiness that was almost the opposite, yet dinkum in the strongest colloquial sense. They were, however, no less authoritative as leaders. Indeed, Menzies himself grappled with these distinctions when seeking to explain the appeal of Henry Bolte, noting that Australian people were not interested in 'philosophical disquisitions' by their political leaders, and displayed an 'instinctive resistance' to being talked down to. He continued:

> Whenever Henry Bolte came out with an impromptu observation on some matter presented to him by a Press report, I confess that I used to worry a little. But I was wrong. By the time his observations had been reported in the Press, most people were saying: 'Good old Henry, he speaks what's on his mind'. Now that, properly considered, is a wonderful democratic attribute. It made him familiar to all Victorians and, indeed, to many thousands of people in other States. He was, and is, a man's man (Menzies 1973: *viii*).

In popular parlance, a man's man was to be 'a good bloke'. This was someone who rubbed shoulders with all comers, and was devoid of the airs and graces of those who considered themselves superior. Menzies, who remains *sui generis*, was never in any doubt as to his own superiority. The leavening experience of war service, and the rough and levelling camaraderie that it generates, were never part of his make up. For all his appeal, Menzies lacked the *colloquial* appeal of his more plainspoken state colleagues. This is apparent in his openly paraded attachment to England — 'the locus of Menzies' ideals, the ultimate source of value in his political world' (Brett 1997: 71). It was also apparent in his 'well-modulated voice with its full vowels and clearly enunciated consonants, the sort of voice which conveyed education, confidence and respect for England' (Brett 1992: 15). In the Australia of the time, it denoted a certain class and station in life; it was not the voice of the public bar or the outer at a sporting arena.

To what extent any minister could oppose Menzies is problematic. One junior minister observed in a diary entry: 'He led by dominating, not by team work' (Howson in Aitkin 1984: 203). Menzies' own muted *mea culpa* on his first unsuccessful prime ministership, in which he frankly admitted that his 'knowledge of people, and how to get along with them and persuade them, lagged behind' was only ever partly addressed.

> I was still in that state of mind in which to be logical is to be right, and to be right is its own justification. I had yet to acquire the common touch, to learn that human beings are delightfully illogical but mostly honest, and to realise that all-black and all-white are not the only hues in the spectrum (Menzies 1969: 57).

These criticisms would not be made of the worldly state leaders who would come after Menzies, the men who would lead rather than just command.

References

'Triumph or Disaster?' *IPA Review*, Jan-Feb 1949, 3:1, pp. 13-4.

Anderson, W. H., 1947, Address to Eighth State Council of Victorian Division, 12 August, p. 3. University of Melbourne Archives, Liberal Party records 1/1/2.

Berry, J. W., 1969, 'The Stereotypes of Australian States', *Australian Journal of Psychology*, 21:3, pp. 227-33.

Blazey, Peter, 1990, *Bolte: A Political Biography*, Port Melbourne: Mandarin, p. 58.

Brett, Judith, 1997, 'Robert Menzies and England', in Brett (ed.) *Political Lives*, St Leonards: Allen & Unwin, p. 71.

Brett, Judith, 1992, *Robert Menzies' Forgotten People*, Chippendale: Sun Australia, p. 15.

Carrick, John, 2002, Personal interview conducted by author, 24 May.

Fairfax, Warwick, 1943, *Men, Parties and Politics*, Sydney: John Fairfax and Sons.

Galligan, Brian, 1986, 'Introduction', in B. Galligan (ed.), *Australian State Politics*, Melbourne: Longman, p. x.

Hancock, Ian, 2000, *National and Permanent? The Federal Organisation of the Liberal Party of Australia 1944-1965*, Carlton South: Melbourne University Press, p. 88.

Hasluck, Paul, 1970, *The Government and the People 1942-1945*, Australian War Memorial, Canberra, p. 625.

Horne, Donald, 2000, *Into the Open*, Sydney: Harper Collins, p. 96.

Howson, Peter, 1984, in Don Aitkin, (ed.), *The Howson Diaries. The Life of Politics*, Ringwood: Viking, 1984, p. 203.

Lampe, F. E., 1943, 'Thoughts at Random on the Recent Election,' 30 August. Noel Butlin Archive Centre (ANU), IPA, N136/74, p. 1.

Lonie, John, 1978, 'From Liberal to Liberal: the Emergence of the Liberal Party and Australian Capitalism, 1900-45', in Graeme Duncan (ed.), *Critical Essays in Australian Politics*, Port Melbourne: Edward Arnold, p. 69.

Menzies, Robert, 1969, *Afternoon Light: Some Memories of Men and Events*, Ringwood: Penguin, p. 293.

Menzies, Robert, 1973, foreword in Barry Muir, *Bolte From Bamganie*, Melbourne: Hill of Content, 1973, p. *viii*.

Ritchie, T. M., 1945, Speech to Darlinghurst branch, Liberal Party, 4 July. Ritchie papers, NLA, MS 2555, Box 1, speeches.

Sydney Morning Herald, 15 July 1943a.

Sydney Morning Herald, 2 Sept 1943c.

Sydney Morning Herald, 3 Sept 1943b.

UMA, Liberal Party records, 1/1/2.

ENDNOTES

[1] Frederic Ernest Lampe (1992-1972), retailer and businessman.

[2] Thomas Malcolm Ritchie (1894-1971), businessman and Liberal Party founder.

[3] William Hewson Anderson (1897- 1968), chief accountant Shell Co. of Australia 1935-50. President of the Victorian Division of the Liberal Party 1945-48 and Federal President 1951-56. His role in the formation of the Liberal Party was a significant one as it was in the first decade of its existence. Anderson was among the conservative critics of the UAP and had formed with others the Services and Citizens' Party, one of the splinter parties that later became part of the new Liberal Party.

[4] Richard Gardiner Casey (1890-1976), MHR Corio 1931-40, La Trobe 1949-60; Minister for Works and Housing 1949-50, Minister for National Development 1950-56, Minister for External Affairs 1951-60, Minister in charge of CSIRO 1950-60. Created a life peer as Baron Casey of Berwick. Governor-General of Australia 1965-69.

[5] Even on the verge of Askin's succession to the Premiership, the media proprietor Sir Frank Packer, according to Donald Horne, was concerned that the Liberal Party was not giving their own man 'a fair go'; there was concern that 'he was only a sergeant in the war … not enough rank' (Horne 2000: 96).

[6] For a discussion of these perceptions see Berry (1969).

20. The Retiring Premiers: A New Style of Leadership Transition

Paul Strangio

'I will never resign. They will have to carry me out with my boots on'

(cited in Knight 2003: 244).

Ned Hanlon, Premier of Queensland, 7 March 1946 - 15 January 1952 (died in office)

'I feel I could be premier for 20 years. Ha! Hubris — when we imagine we're gods. In my business you can be wiped out by events, and within a 24 hours news cycle'

(cited in Smith 2006: 496).

Diary entry early 2000, Bob Carr, Premier of New South Wales, 4 April 1995 - 3 August 2005

(resigned)

Leaders who do know when to go

In the introduction to their 2005 edited volume *Yes, Premier: Labor leadership in Australia's states and territories*, John Wanna and Paul Williams point to the 'surprisingly sparse' scholarly literature on sub-national politics in Australia and an associated absence of a 'systematic analysis of state leaders' (pp 25 and 29). The Wanna and Williams study was an admirable attempt to redress that latter omission through a collective study of the (then) current batch of sub-national leaders (all of whom, for the first time since Federation, were from the Labor side of politics). The publication of *Yes, Premier* was preceded by the third edition of *The Premiers of Queensland* (Murphy *et al.* 2003) and has been followed subsequently by collections of biographical essays on the premiers of New South Wales (Clune and Turner 2006) and Victoria (Strangio and Costar 2006). It would be wrong to exaggerate this trend. The famine has not turned into feast — state politics is still the poor cousin of national politics in the attention it receives from scholars, including biographers. Nevertheless, the output of the last few years has afforded an opportunity to augment our understanding of the patterns, both historical and contemporary, of political leadership at the sub-national level.

In the concluding chapter of *Yes, Premier*, Wanna and Williams, joined by Brian Head, isolated such patterns for the purposes of constructing an identikit of the contemporary sub-national leader. They suggest that the features of this archetype are: adaptation to the accountability regimes that have proliferated since the 1980s; 'professional perspectives' which include an interest in national agendas (as opposed to old-style state parochialism); 'resourceful and ubiquitous communicators'; 'transcendence over their section base', particularly trade unions; 'cautious pragmatism'; 'anticipatory and receptive leadership'; the employment of 'participatory and community engagement techniques' such as summits, community cabinet meetings and consultative/advisory committees; and, finally, 'ordinary populism' (Head, Wanna and Williams 2005: 261-3), which manifests in a leadership style that is

> purposely non-elitist, a little mundane, attempting to be 'everyman' or 'everywoman' … They are not classically charismatic; instead, they have a natural common touch. They have cultivated the image of the normal, ordinary, relaxed, accepted leader attuned to his/her community (Head, Wanna and Williams 2005: 258).

The same authors (Head, Wanna and Williams 2005: 263; Wanna and Williams 2005: 18) distinguish this leadership style from that which prevailed in the post-war decades during the age of the so-called 'boss' premiers (leaders such as Henry Bolte in Victoria, Thomas Playford in South Australia, Joh Bjelke-Petersen in Queensland, Charles Court in Western Australia and Eric Reece in Tasmania). They too were populists but of a rough hewn variety, their homespun folksiness mingled with a powerful streak of authoritarianism. By way of comparison, Labor's 'ordinary populists' might also be contrasted with their more immediate predecessors: the earnest technocratic modernists exemplified by John Cain Jnr (Strangio 2006) and Wayne Goss (Wanna 2003).

Since the publication of *Yes, Premier*, there have been elections in each state and territory, but Labor's stranglehold over government at the sub-national level has been maintained. Yet, the leadership landscape has been transformed. While the editors (Wanna and Williams 2005: 15) had speculated that 'many of these leaders will be around for some time — because of their perceived dominance', there has been a changing of the guard in five of the eight jurisdictions. Bob Carr resigned in July 2005 (replaced by Morris Iemma), Geoff Gallop resigned in January 2006 (replaced by Alan Carpenter), Steve Bracks resigned in July 2007 (replaced by John Brumby), Peter Beattie resigned in September 2007 (replaced by Anna Bligh) and Claire Martin resigned in November 2007 (replaced by Paul Henderson). While Gallop resigned because of illness, it has, nonetheless, been a striking sequence: the era of the retiring premiers. At one level, it invites the question of whether the age of the 'ordinary populist' is already passing. Of the premiers and chief ministers discussed in *Yes, Premier*, none better fitted the bill of the congenial, 'everyman' than Bracks and Beattie. Their respective successors, Brumby and Bligh, on the other hand, are of more combative style.

The chief focus of this chapter, however, is on another question: whether timely departure is another trait of contemporary sub-national leadership and a further point of distinction from the 'boss' premiers of the post-war era. If so, what does this suggest about the evolving practices and demands of the office itself? Is it a trend also related to the changed career trajectories of those who rise to occupy high political office? The chapter also contrasts the recent rash of leadership successions at the sub-national level with former Prime Minister John Howard's model of clinging to office to the bitter end. Howard's failure to allow an orderly leadership transition is widely regarded as having been a major factor in the Coalition's election loss of November 2007 and the disorientation suffered by the non-Labor parties since that defeat. Will the example of what has occurred in the state sphere and the disaster that befell Howard and the Coalition in 2007 create an irresistible future impetus for timely departures and planned transitions at the federal level? Finally, the chapter concludes by asking questions about the knock-on effects leadership transitions; in other words, how much is actually transformed within the government that the departing leader leaves behind?

'They will have to carry me out with my boots on'

As exemplified by Ned Hanlon's stubborn response to advice that he relinquish the Queensland premiership due to failing health, timely resignations have not been a common feature of state (or federal) politics. Indeed, one is hard pressed to find examples of successful leadership transitions in Australian politics. Henry Bolte's passing of the baton to Rupert Hamer in Victoria in 1972 is an exception (Abjorensen 2007: 97). Hamer went on to extend the Liberal Party's hegemony over Spring Street politics for nearly another decade and along the way secured three election victories, the first two of which bettered anything achieved by his predecessor (Hannan 1979: 8 and 14-15). Yet, as elaborated below, there is a case to be made that Bolte had stayed too long — something he seemed to grudgingly admit upon resigning: 'Victorian politics will probably improve when I'm gone; get rid of some of the rough edges' (cited in Wright 1992: 205). In New South Wales there was, ostensibly, a sequence of successful transitions during Labor's two-and-a-half-decade unbroken ascendancy between 1941 and 1966 that encompassed the premierships of William McKell, James McGirr, John Cahill, Robert Heffron and John Renshaw. Yet, David Clune and Ken Turner (2006: 10-11) argue this was, in fact, illusionary: 'In none of these cases was it [the transfer of leadership] the result of a carefully planned transition'. Further, writing from a historical perspective, they believe that smooth transitions from successful leaders 'are almost contradictory as a successful premier by definition dominates his government and era and leaves a huge gap to fill'.

The collective record of the 'boss' premiers suggests a predilection not only for clinging to office too long, but of their leaderships taking on a darker, increasingly wilful edge with advancing years. Think, for instance, of Bolte's obduracy over the hanging of Ronald Ryan in 1967. As Mike Richard's compelling study *The Hanged Man* (2002: especially 394-5) convincingly shows, Bolte transformed the issue of the execution of Ryan into a test of his authority: he would not budge in spite of the diverse voices of protest in the community, intense opposition from the major metropolitan press outlets, disquiet within his own cabinet and the consternation of the legal fraternity.

In the same year that Ryan went to the gallows, Tasmanian premier Eric Reece revoked Lake Pedder's status as a National Park as a preliminary to its damming and submergence as part of the Upper Gordon Hydro Electric Scheme. In his second and final term as premier (1972-75), 'Electric Eric', by then in his mid-60s, obstinately proceeded with the flooding, staring down the protests of the burgeoning environment movement and spurning a generous financial offer by Labor Prime Minister Gough Whitlam to preserve Lake Pedder (Bolton 1992: 162-3; Whitlam 1985: 525-30).

Another example is Sir Thomas Playford jnr, whose record breaking 27-year premiership is unlikely to be ever matched. In the phrase of his biographer, a 'benevolent despot', Playford's incapacity to adapt to a changing social and cultural milieu in the 1960s and 'fantasy of indispensability' (he refused to relinquish the reins of government despite his extreme longevity of office and approaching seventieth birthday), ultimately and inevitability resulted in election defeat in 1965 (Cockburn 1991; Blewett and Jaensch 1971: ch. 2).

Then there is the one to trump them all, the 'populist autocrat', Joh Bjelke-Petersen. Following his seventh consecutive election victory in 1986, the septuagenarian Bjelke-Peterson succumbed to a kind of manic grandiosity that climaxed in the delusory and self-destructive 'Joh for PM' campaign (Walter 2003: especially 317-21) which paved the way not for his conquest of Canberra but for his political demise in Queensland.

When surveying these records it is difficult to avoid the conclusion of a direct casual relationship existing between the ageing of the 'boss' premiers and the inflexibility of their later leadership. They were sufferers of the political equivalent of hardening of the arteries. Judith Brett (2007: 10), reflecting upon the predicament of another ageing leader — John Howard in 2007 — might well have been referring to the fate of the boss premiers when she described the hazard for elderly leaders of 'their inevitable disconnection from the social and cultural worlds of people born 20, 30, 40 and even 50 years after them — and from their futures'. Similarly, Angus McIntyre's edited study *Ageing and Political Leadership* (1988) provides a useful conceptual framework for understanding the trajectory of the ageing boss premiers. One of the typologies of ageing outlined by McIntyre, and which he suggests is the most common in politics, is what he terms 'manic ageing'. In essence, this is a denial of the reality of ageing, that is, 'a denial of death', which can manifest in 'a fantasy of immortality or, at the very least, indispensability' (Macintyre 1988: 282-6 and 294). Playford might be categorised as an exemplar of the latter, while there was undoubtedly elements of the former at play in Bjelke-Petersen's tilt for national power.

The contemporary era compared

How, then, do the contemporary sub-national leaders compare? The first point is that, unlike the 'boss' era premiers, they do not constitute a 'gerontocracy'. Since the 1980s there has been a general downward trend in the age at which premiers both obtained and left office. Whereas between the end of World War II and the 1970s the age of those elected as premier across the states averaged in their mid-fifties, that has since declined to the mid-forties. Correspondingly, the average age of exit from office has dropped even more sharply from around 62 to a little over 50.[1] Allied with the trend of premiers becoming younger, the waiting time for office (as measured by the number of years between first entering Parliament and assuming the premiership) has decreased. Clune and Turner (2006: 5) note that during the twentieth century in New South Wales the waiting time for office peaked between 1941 and 1976 when it stretched out to over 23 years, while for the premiers from Neville Wran to Carr the period contracted to eight years. Similar patterns are evident in the other states with the waiting times in Victoria and Queensland, for example, almost halving since the 1980s.[2]

The changing age profile of sub-national leadership conforms to a phenomenon identified some two decades ago by Patrick Weller and Sue Fraser (1987) as the 'younging of Australian politics'. Not surprisingly, Weller and Fraser connected this trend to the changing career patterns of politicians, in particular that for a growing number of parliamentarians, politics was becoming a first rather than second career. Or, to put it another way, the 'younging' of politics (and leadership) can be linked to the growing prevalence of career politicians, those for whom 'their first careers (if they existed at all) were nothing but overtures to the main event' (Weller and Fraser 1987: 76).

Of the group of leaders analysed in *Yes, Premier* this is true at the very least of Beattie, Bracks, Carr and Rann. By the time they were 30 each of these future leaders had flagged an ambition to enter Parliament and/or was operating in a cognate occupation (for example, Beattie as state secretary of the Queensland Labor Party and Rann as press secretary to South Australian ALP leaders from Don Dunstan to John Bannon). Gallop was not far behind. He entered Parliament at age 34, following a brief academic career (Clune 2005; Costar and Hayward 2005; Manning 2005; Phillips and Black 2005; Wanna and Williams 2005a). The irony is that, as leaders, these career politicians were projected as ordinary men who happened to be political masters. Beattie even once likened himself to an 'anti-politician' (cited in Preston 2003: 406). Leaving that aside, the fact that their 'first' careers were in politics, coupled with the relative youth at which they assumed office, was undoubtedly a facilitating factor in their timely retirements.

These Premiers departed politics at an age when they still have the opportunity to construct a post-political career. Indeed, one might also speculate that the predisposition shown by 'ordinary populist' leaders for moving beyond politics is not only about a reversal of the traditional place occupied by politics in an individual's occupational history, but reflects a transformation of politics from being a craft (with its connotations of slowly acquired, abiding skills peculiar to that trade) to a career.

The expectations and demands associated with contemporary leadership at the sub-national level of politics appear also to have played a part in the recent spate of retirements. The notion of premiers being central to the operation of their governments and to the politics of their respective states has long been remarked upon. In his majestic mid-twentieth century study of Australian state governments, S. R. Davis (1960: 3) identified leadership predominance of premiers as an important ingredient in the longevity of many sub-national governments. Yet, the nature of that dominance has changed. Back then, for instance, Henry Bolte was known as the 'pepper and salt' premier because of his reputation for having a hand 'in everything' (cited in Bennett 1992: 144). It was a time when it remained possible for a premier to exercise personal and informal control over the machinery of government, and an era when it was still the norm for premiers to simultaneously hold the Treasury portfolio.

Fifty years on, the exponential growth in the complexity of government (just one measure of which is the rise in the number of ministerial portfolios) has diminished the capacity for premiers to single-handedly dominate government. Premiers are now compelled to delegate to ministers, and are required to operate within intricate and formalised administrative and accountability processes. They are also surrounded by complex and large support structures — over the past quarter of century or so premier's departments have expanded enormously in size as they have assumed greater co-ordinating functions, while the private offices of premiers have also grown dramatically (Clune and Turner 2006: 12-13; Halligan 1988). Shortly after Bracks' resignation, it was revealed that he had had about 70 staff, including around 20 political/policy advisers and 20 media advisers (Austin 2007).

The extraordinary number of media advisers in the Bracks office is a clue to the nature of leadership centrality twenty-first century style. While premiers can no longer operate as a one man band and the scope for ad hoc, informal decision-making has shrunk, their centrality to the performance (and image) of government has arguably never been greater. The template for what Wanna and Williams (2005: 15) describe as the 'the personalisation of leadership' at the sub-national level of politics is usually regarded as having been forged by Neville

Wran, premier of New South Wales from 1976 to 1986. Indeed, it is striking how many of the features of state-level leadership described in *Yes, Premier* were road-tested during the Wran era. Not least of these were the embrace of modern media management techniques (with the leader centre stage to the government's media presentations); transcendence over the party's traditional base; and cautious pragmatism. As Graham Freudenberg (2006: 422) notes, Wran, having learnt from the Whitlam experiment, had an influence over all subsequent Labor administrations through his government's pragmatic balancing of both economic prudence and social progressivism; and anticipatory and receptive leadership. Wran, as well as being an adept 'crisis manager', took the previously rudimentary use of opinion polling by governments to new heights (Chaples, Nelson and Turner 1985: especially 247-50).

Yet, the Wran model was not without its hazards. Ernie Chaples, Helen Nelson and Ken Turner (1985: 250) argued:

> ... the Wran approach to leadership requires a very able politician, with much skill, energy, considerable insight, and probably more than a little luck. The 'man at the top' must operate continuously at peak efficiency ... the demands made by this style are constant and considerable, necessitating a leader who is in the best of form, both physically and emotionally.

Two decades on, those demands have only intensified in the context of the continuing expansion in the breadth and complexity of government. Coupled with this is the mutually reinforcing frenzied relationship that exists between governments engaged in permanent campaigning and constant news cycle management and a media of insatiable appetite. By contrast with the sedate political rhythms of earlier times, it is a climate in which high office is, as Peter Beattie has observed (2007), akin to 'being in the trenches of war', endlessly optimising the next advantage or warding off the next crisis. And, of course, it is leaders who are the chief gladiators in today's remorseless media-focussed political combat.

Do we find here another explanation for the recent run of leadership resignations? In other words, has a leadership model evolved that is unsustainable over the long haul — a model that has an in-built obsolescence date? In the extract from his diary that heads this chapter, Carr confessed to the gnawing anxiety that 'you can be wiped out by events, and within a 24 hours news cycle'. At the times of their resignations, Bracks and Beattie both alluded to the toll of the premiership. Bracks declared he had 'given everything, you know, body and soul, to this job', while his wife, Terry, reinforced the message, commenting: 'It's a relentless job. It's day in, day out. I've seen it first hand' (cited in Austin 2007a). Peter Beattie's wife, Heather, had also worried about the debilitating effects on her husband, complaining on the eve of his resignation that he was a 'tired, exhausted man'. Beattie himself ventured that the increasing demands of the job might mean the time had come to consider imposing a sunset on the tenure of state premiers (Austin 2007a; Parnell 2007). It is Geoff Gallop, however, who has most thoughtfully articulated the wear and tear, both physical and psychological, of contemporary leadership. Not only are the stresses unremitting but, according to the former West Australian premier, the 'trick' performances that accompany high executive office and necessity of reducing complex issues to simple (media friendly) truths, have introduced an aridity, almost soullessness, to the task of modern leadership (Taylor 2006; Gallop 2006; 2007).

Lessons for the federal sphere?

As a procession of state leaders departed the political stage from mid-2005, John Howard chose a very different way to deal with political mortality. This turned out to be less a planned transition than a scorched earth strategy. As questions had grown more insistent about when he would abdicate the prime ministership as he passed his tenth anniversary in office in early 2006, Howard repeated ad nauseam the formula that he would remain leader as long as his party and the voters wanted him to stay. What Brett presciently detected as the 'disingenuousness in this promise' (2007: 10) was to be fully exposed during 2007 as the Coalition government slid inexorably towards electoral defeat. In September, spooked by a continuing succession of poor opinion polls, a majority of the cabinet conveyed to the prime minister that he ought to step aside for his long-time heir apparent Peter Costello, only to have Howard stare them down by making it clear that the party would have to blast him out of the leadership (Kelly 2007).

The end game came two months later at the November election, with the government heavily defeated and Howard losing his own seat. His jilted successor Costello, who subsequently maintained that Howard had never any intention of standing down voluntarily (Costello 2008), now had his own revenge of sorts by announcing that he would not seek the leadership of the severely depleted Liberal Party but would instead leave Parliament. In the words of one commentator, the defeated prime minister 'had incinerated two generations of Liberal leadership on the bonfire of his own vanity' (Milne 2007).

Walter and Strangio (2007: 13-16) have argued elsewhere that the extraordinary dominance exercised by Howard over his government carried the seeds for the Coalition shipwreck of 2007 and disarray on the non-Labor side of politics that has followed. The issue here, though, is less why Howard did not allow a transition, but whether things might be different in the future. In other words, could it be that future prime ministers heed Howard's mistake and seek to emulate the (recent) example of their sub-national counterparts by setting and abiding by a self-imposed de facto limit to their tenure?

Notably, Howard's fate has spurred some soul-searching in the Liberal Party about these matters. In a recent speech to the federal Parliament, Victorian MHR Chris Pearce proposed 'a maximum of three parliamentary terms for any individual prime minister' (Pearce 2008). In doing so, Pearce aligned himself with Peter Beattie, who since political retirement has advocated US-style fixed terms for both prime ministers and premiers (see Berkovic 2007). Meanwhile, the former president of the Victorian Liberal Party, Michael Kroger, has urged his party to learn from the retirements of state Labor leaders about the importance of renewal of governments (Kroger 2008).

Indeed, there are instances where state leadership trends have influenced the federal sphere. For example, Don Dunstan's post-materialism was a path-setter for the Whitlam-led federal Labor Party, and Bob Hawke's leadership approach was undoubtedly influenced by the 'Wran model'. Moreover, if the recent bout of retirements at the sub-national level has something to do with the increasingly taxing nature of the role, then one would expect that imperative to be even more pronounced at the federal level where the demands of office are greater still. Already, doubts are being raised about the sustainability of the ferocious work rate of Howard conqueror Kevin Rudd and the toll that it is exacting on both him and his support staff (Hewett 2007; Murphy 2008).

However, a note of caution — there is a stark difference between sub-national and national leadership. In an era when globalisation and inexorable Canberra-driven centralism are eroding the scope for state autonomy, the gulf between sub-national and national politics is, if anything, widening. Whereas the 'boss' premiers were prone to regard themselves as near equals to the prime minister, today such a view is much harder to sustain. And as state politics becomes the domain for humbler ambitions, it might well be that it likely to produce political leaders more naturally disposed to relinquish office with less fuss. Federal politics, with its continuing seductions of expansive power (and immortality), is quite a different matter. When it comes to prime ministers, it might always be the case that, as Paul Keating has put it, '[they] have got Araldite on their pants ... They want to stick to their seat. And you either put the sword through them or let the people do it' (cited in Brett 2007).

Final thoughts

The sequence of leadership retirements at sub-national level since 2005 opens up further areas of inquiry. At the time of writing, the inheritors of leadership have in one case secured a further term in office (Iemma) or are riding comparatively high in public opinion polls. There is the prospect then for this group of leaders and their governments to be more than mere footnotes or epilogues to those that preceded them. Yet, a question remains about how much has actually been transformed as a consequence of change at the apex of executive government. Has the transition in leadership filtered down into changes in the supporting staff arrangements and into the system of public administration? Has the advent of a new leader precipitated significant policy renewal or have the changes been largely ephemeral — more about a different leadership style than substance? To approach this from another direction: how much does a leadership successor remain captive to the agenda and governing apparatus bequeathed by his/her predecessor? Are the opportunities for a distinctive leadership project and the personalisation of the political executive diminished for successors?

Underlying all this is the fundamental question of how much renewal a leadership transition actually delivers. When Beattie retired he packaged the decision as essential to renewal of the Labor government — 'parties that renew, survive' (Parnell 2007), he declared — and his resignation was, by and large, accepted (and welcomed) in that light. Conversely, as suggested above, Howard's failure to stand aside has been identified as a key reason for the federal Coalition government running out of puff by its fourth term. By this light, leadership transition and renewal are deemed virtually synonymous, with the former a prerequisite for the latter. A study of the current sub-national Labor governments and their second generation leaderships would be an ideal place to investigate whether these assumptions stand up.

References

Abjorensen, N., 2007, *Leadership and the Liberal Revival: Bolte, Askin and the Post-War Ascendancy*, Melbourne: Australian Scholarly Publishing.

Austin, P., 2007, 'Taxpayers pick up the bill for hundreds of advisers', *The Age*, 10 September.

Austin, P., 2007a, 'One eight-year plan that Brumby would do well to adapt', *The Age*, 1 November.

Beattie, P., 2007, 'Calmed after the storms', *Weekend Australian*, 10-11 November.

Bennett, S., 1992, *Affairs of State: Politics in the Australian States and Territories*, Sydney: Allen & Unwin.

Berkovic, N., 2007, 'We need fixed terms: Beattie', *The Australian*, 13 December.

Blewett, N. and D. Jaensch, 1971, *Playford to Dunstan: The Politics of Transition*, Melbourne: F. W. Cheshire.

Bolton, G., 1992, *Spoils and Spoilers: A History of Australians Shaping their Environment*, Sydney: Allen & Unwin.

Brett, J., 2007, 'The Nation Reviewed', *The Monthly*, 21, pp. 10-14.

Chaples, E., H. Nelson and K. Tuner, 1985, 'The Wran model in perspective', in E. Chaples, H. Nelson and K. Turner (eds), *The Wran Model: Electoral*

Politics in New South Wales 1981 and 1985, Melbourne: Oxford University Press.

Clune, D., 2005, 'Bob Carr: The unexpected Colossus', in J. Wanna and P. Williams (eds), *Yes, Premier: Labor Leadership in Australia's States and Territories*, Sydney: UNSW Press.

Cockburn, S., 1991, *Playford: Benevolent Dictator*, Adelaide: Axiom.

Costar, B. and D. Hayward, 2005, 'Steve Bracks: Victoria's "nice guy" who won against the odds', in J. Wanna and P. Williams (eds), *Yes, Premier: Labor Leadership in Australia's States and Territories*, Sydney: UNSW Press.

Davis, S., 1960, *The Government of the Australian States*, London: Longmans.

Freudenberg, G., 2006, 'Neville Kenneth Wran', in D. Clune and K. Turner (eds), *The Premiers of New South Wales, volume 2, 1901-2005*, Sydney: The Federation Press.

Galligan, B. and W. Roberts (eds), 2007, *The Oxford Companion to Australian Politics*, Melbourne: Oxford University Press.

Gallop, G., 2006, interviewed by M. McKew, 'Geoff Gallop: From darkness into light', *Sunday Profile*, ABC Radio, 17 September, <http://www.abc.net.au/cgi-bin/common/printfriendly.pl? http://www.abc.net.au/sunday>

Gallop, G., 2007 interviewed by T. Jones, 'Gallop discusses media's election ambushes', *Lateline*, ABC Television, 1 November, <http://www.abc.net.au/lateline/content/2007/s2079416.htm>

Halligan, J., 1988, 'State Executives', in B. Galligan (ed.) *Comparative State Policies*, Melbourne: Longman Cheshire.

Hannan, T., 1979, 'Electoral and parliamentary patterns in Victorian politics, 1945-76', in P. Hay, I. Ward and J. Warhurst (eds), *Anatomy of an Election*, Melbourne: Hill of Content.

Head, B, J. Wanna and P. Williams, 2005, 'Leaders and the leadership challenge', in J. Wanna and P. Williams (eds), *Yes, Premier: Labor Leadership in Australia's States and Territories*, Sydney: UNSW Press.

Hewett, J., 2007, 'No yawning folks, it's time for work, says Kevin 24/7', *Weekend Australian*, 15-16 December.

Kelly, P., 2007, 'The Defeat', *Weekend Australian*, 15-16 December.

Knight, K., 2003, 'Edward Michael Hanlon: A City Bushman', in D. Murphy, R. Joyce, M. Cribb and R. Wear (eds), *The Premiers of Queensland*, St Lucia: University of Queensland Press.

Kroger, M., 2008, 'Liberals should focus on branch renewal', *The Australian*, 19 February.

Manning, H., 2005, 'Mike Rann: A fortunate "king of spin"', in J. Wanna and P. Williams (eds), *Yes, Premier: Labor Leadership in Australia's States and Territories*, Sydney: UNSW Press.

McIntyre, A., 1988, 'Conclusion', in A. McIntyre (ed.) *Aging and Political Leadership*, Melbourne: Oxford University Press.

Milne, G., 2007, 'PM's hubris leaves the Liberal Party in ruins', *The Australian*, 26 November.

Murphy, D., R. Joyce, M. Cribb and R. Wear (eds)., 2003, *The Premiers of Queensland*, University of Queensland Press, St Lucia.

Murphy, K., 2008, 'Rudd's will to power', *The Age*, 29 March.

Parnell, S., 2007, 'Peter Beattie resigns from politics', *The Australian*, 10 September.

Pearce, C., 2008, Governor-General's Speech: Address-in-reply, http://parlinfoweb.aph.gov.au/piweb/view_document.aspx?id=2788877 &table=HANSARDR, accessed 21 February.

Phillips, H. and D. Black, 2005, 'Geoff Gallop: A new generation Labor man', in J. Wanna and P. Williams (eds), *Yes, Premier: Labor Leadership in Australia's States and Territories*, Sydney: UNSW Press.

Preston, N., 2003, 'Peter Douglas Beattie: The Inclusive Populist', in D. Murphy, R. Joyce, M. Cribb and R. Wear (eds), *The Premiers of Queensland*, St Lucia: University of Queensland Press.

Richards, M., 2002, *The Hanged Man: The Life and Death of Ronald Ryan*, Melbourne: Scribe.

Smith, R., 2006, 'Robert John Carr', in D. Clune and K. Turner (eds), *The Premiers of New South Wales, volume 2, 1901-2005*, Sydney: The Federation Press.

Strangio, P. and B. Costar (eds)., 2006, *The Victorian Premiers, 1856-2006*, Sydney: The Federation Press.

Strangio, P., 2006, 'John Cain jnr: The burden of history', in P. Strangio and B. Costar (eds), *The Victorian Premiers, 1856-2006*, Sydney: The Federation Press.

Taylor, P., 2006, 'Political life so shallow, says Gallop', *The Australian*, 10 June 2006.

Walter, J. and P. Strangio, 2007, *No, Prime Minister: Reclaiming Politics from Leaders*, Sydney: UNSW Press.

Walter, J., 2003, 'Johannes Bjelke-Petersen: "The Populist Autocrat"', in D. Murphy, R. Joyce, M. Cribb and R. Wear (eds), *The Premiers of Queensland*, St Lucia: University of Queensland Press.

Wanna, J. and P. Williams, 2005a, 'Peter Beattie: The "boy form Atherton" made good', in J. Wanna and P. Williams (eds), *Yes, Premier: Labor Leadership in Australia's States and Territories*, Sydney: UNSW Press.

Wanna, J. and P. Williams, 2005, 'The Twilight Zone of State Leaders', in J. Wanna and P. Williams (eds), *Yes, Premier: Labor Leadership in Australia's States and Territories*, Sydney: UNSW Press.

Wanna, J., 2003, 'Wayne Keith Goss: The Rise and Fall of a Meticulous Controller', in D. Murphy, R. Joyce, M. Cribb and R. Wear (eds), *The Premiers of Queensland*, St Lucia: University of Queensland Press.

Weller, P. and S. Fraser, 1987, 'The Younging of Australian Politics or Politics as First Career', *Politics*, 22:2, pp. 76-83.

Whitlam, G., 1985, *The Whitlam Government, 1972-1975*, Melbourne: Penguin.

Wright, R., 1992, *A People's Counsel: A History of the Parliament of Victoria 1856-1990*, Melbourne: Oxford University Press.

ENDNOTES

[1] The author's calculations based on data found in the appendices on state premiers in Galligan and Roberts (2007: 654-5 and 658-66).

[2] The author's calculations based on information in the relevant chapters in Murphy *et al.* (2003); and Strangio and Costar (2006).

PART V

Political Leadership: New Zealand

21. Taming Leadership? Adapting to Institutional Change in New Zealand Politics

Raymond Miller

Introduction

Studies of political leadership typically place great stress on the importance of individual character. The personal qualities looked for in a New Zealand or Australian leader include strong and decisive action, empathy and an ability to both reflect the country's egalitarian traditions and contribute to a growing sense of nationhood. The impetus to transform leaders from extraordinary people into ordinary citizens has its roots in the populist belief that leaders should be accessible and reflect the values and lifestyle of the average voter. This fascination with individual character helps account for the sizeable biographical literature on past and present leaders, especially prime ministers. Typically, such studies pay close attention to the impact of upbringing, personality and performance on leadership success or failure.

Despite similarities between New Zealand and Australia in the personal qualities required of a successful leader, leadership in the two countries is a product of very different constitutional and institutional traditions. While the overall trend has been in the direction of a strengthening of prime ministerial leadership, Australia's federal structure of government allows for a diffusion of leadership across multiple sources of influence and power, including a network of state legislatures and executives. New Zealand, in contrast, lacks a written constitution, an upper house, or the devolution of power to state or local government. As a result, successive New Zealand prime ministers and their cabinets have been able to exercise singular power.

This chapter will consider the impact of recent institutional change on the nature of political leadership in New Zealand, focusing on the extent to which leadership practices have been modified or tamed by three developments: the transition from a two-party to a multi-party parliament, the advent of coalition government, and the emergence of a multi-party cartel. The chapter will conclude by posing three questions. First, is it possible to construct a conceptual framework that captures the impact of institutional change on political leadership in New Zealand? Second, given the importance of managerial competence to the success of coalition government, how transferable are the skills of party leader to those of prime minister? And third, given the constraining influence of an active and engaged public on political parties, should the major party leaders be elected by the MPs, as at present, or by the wider party membership?

Political leadership and institutional change

In his study of ethics in Australian government, John Uhr argues that political leadership can be dispersed and power tamed by a process of institutional checks and balances. Key elements in this process may include: the devolution of power to the state governments, public re-engagement with political parties, a stronger parliament, and ministerial government based on decision-making by consensus (Uhr 2005: 78-87). The resulting 'lattice of leadership' provides an alternative to the concentration of power in the hands of small and self-interested national elites. Although any such proposals are heavily prescriptive, it has been argued that constraining the powers of political leaders and increasing the opportunities for public and community participation produces a more diffused and, therefore, more accountable leadership (Walter and Strangio 2007: 64-85).

During the 1980s and 1990s, politics in New Zealand was marked by growing public opposition to the governing elite, especially over the pace and magnitude of neo-liberal reform. One consequence was the rise in support for small parties — by 1993 almost one third of all voters had begun to cast their votes for the growing array of small parties. A related but even more important consequence of voter disillusionment was the decision by national referendum to replace the existing plurality electoral system with proportional representation (PR). The prospect that National and Labour would be required to share legislative and executive power with the small parties was greeted with alarm by the major party leaders, notably National's Jim Bolger and Jenny Shipley, and Labour's Helen Clark. During the referendum campaign they warned voters that proportional representation would result in legislative paralysis and unstable government. Bolger, who was prime minister at the time, even suggested the alternative of an upper house, an idea that was roundly rejected by the voting public.

Among the subsequent institutional changes that have had a direct bearing on political leadership in New Zealand – offering the prospect that a 'lattice of leadership' would begin to emerge – three stand out.

Proportional representation: leadership through legislative bargaining

One of the most notable features of the new proportional system has been the sheer number of parties winning parliamentary seats. Apart from the occasional presence of a Social Credit MP, throughout the post-war period the only parties holding seats were National and Labour. In contrast, as a result of an electoral system that awards seats in proportion to a party's share of the vote, a total of eight parties sat in the 2005-2008 Parliament. Because this has resulted in minority government, the prime minister has had to keep the lines of communication open with each and every opposition party. This has left Labour in the difficult position of having to turn to its old adversary, National, for support in passing some important legislation, including the Singapore free trade agreement (2000), the controversial anti-smacking legislation (2007), and the NZ-China free trade agreement (2008).

Despite the proliferation of parliamentary parties, the actual number is less relevant to the theme of this chapter than the potential bargaining power each exercises within parliament and government. While some opposition parties are unashamedly opportunistic and pragmatic, others continue to harbour deep ideological and personal grudges dating back to the neo-liberal reforms of the 1980s and early 1990s. Their leaders have even been described as 'political agitators, who thrive on conflict, are often narcissistic and possess an unbending belief in the virtue of their cause' (Miller 2006: 116). These character traits would have little significance were it not for the fact that, in the context of a multi-party parliament, small parties are often veto players, as illustrated by the conduct of the Greens when, in 2002, they threatened to bring the Clark government down the moment it lifted its moratorium on the release of genetically modified corn. While adopting such a hard-line position can bring much-needed media attention, there are some inherent risks: veto players that exceed their powers not only endanger relations with the other parties (as a result of the Greens' decision, Clark decided to exclude them from the next government), but also the voting public.

Coalition government: leadership through inclusion and compromise

A further set of institutional changes impacting on political leadership concerns the transition from a single-party to a coalition government. Unlike Australia's Liberal-National Coalition, which is a permanent arrangement, one or other of New Zealand's two major parties must build a fresh coalition after each and every election. Thus, while the powers of the prime minister have been reduced, the range of strategic and interpersonal skills are much greater than they were when prime ministers enjoyed the benefit of both a guaranteed majority and a full slate of ministerial portfolios with which to reward their MPs. Following the 1993 election, the last under plurality voting, Prime Minister Jim Bolger had the luxury of some 30 executive positions to share amongst his 49 caucus colleagues. In contrast, following the first election under PR, the same prime minister was forced to sacrifice five of his 20 cabinet positions to the junior coalition partner, New Zealand First, with the promise of three additional positions within the term of that government. Lack of ministerial opportunities caused several of Bolger's colleagues to complain that he had 'sold out' to New Zealand First. Within a year, he was replaced as party leader and prime minister.

Successful coalition leadership requires levels of consultation, compromise and inclusiveness barely comprehended a decade or more ago. Although the first coalition failed to survive the fractious personal relationship that existed between Prime Minister Shipley and the New Zealand First leader, Winston Peters, the following three coalitions, all led by Labour, have been remarkably stable and effective. Much of the credit for that success is due to Clark's relentless pragmatism, as well as her skill as a micro-manager. This was especially so during the fraught coalition negotiations process, but is also true in day-to-day relations with the other party leaders — on occasions over a cup of tea, as with the Green co-leader, Jeanette Fitzsimons, and on others more formally. Relations between the coalition partners have been further aided by an agree-to-disagree amendment to the Cabinet Manual. It gives small governing parties the ability to oppose certain cabinet decisions without bringing down the government. This provision was first used by the Alliance in 2000 to oppose the government's free trade agreement with Singapore.

The complex nature of coalition arrangements is best illustrated with reference to the 2005-08 (minority) government. At the 2005 election Labour won 50 seats, 11 seats short of an overall majority. Although the willingness of the Progressive (1) and Green (6) parties to join a Labour-led coalition was assured, this combined centre-left bloc failed to offer Clark the parliamentary majority needed to pass legislation. To complicate matters, the two centre parties, New Zealand First (7) and United Future (3), made it clear that they would not support a government that included the Greens (both argued that the Greens were unreliable and their views extreme). New Zealand First's position was further complicated by the fact that, in the lead-up to the election, Peters had promised voters that his party would not be part of the next government, regardless of whether it was led by Labour or National. Labour's only other possibility was an agreement with the Maori Party (4), an unlikely proposition given the small party's opposition to the government's Foreshore and Seabed legislation. Feelings were mutual, with the prime minister promising during the campaign that, when it came to negotiating a coalition, the Maori Party would be 'the last cab off the ranks'.

The creative compromise to this dilemma was to exclude the Greens from any coalition arrangement, and instead offer both Peters and United Future's Peter Dunne ministerial positions, ostensibly outside of government. In giving Peters the prestigious Foreign Affairs portfolio and Dunne Revenue, Clark provided each party with the barely plausible argument that, while they represented the government (Peters internationally) they were not to be regarded as members of the government (under the terms of their agreement, both party leaders were permitted to oppose the government on all matters outside their portfolios). Having promised that he would not be seduced by the 'baubles of office', Peters was especially vulnerable to the accusation that he had deliberately misled his party's members and voters. To finalise this complex multi-party arrangement, separate agreements had to be reached with each of the coalition and support parties, with the Progressives signing a full coalition agreement, New Zealand First and United Future separate 'Confidence and Supply' agreements, and the clearly disappointed Greens a 'Cooperation' agreement. The speed and effectiveness with which the prime minister finalised these arrangements are testimony to her negotiating and management ability.

The extent to which the prime minister's powers have been curbed by the advent of coalition government can be illustrated with respect to the NZ-China free trade agreement. Shortly before the agreement was signed in April 2008, Dunne reversed his earlier decision to accompany the New Zealand delegation to Beijing in protest at the Chinese government's repression of Tibetan protestors (although his party was prepared to support the agreement in Parliament). Peters went a step further in announcing that his party would vote against the pact on the grounds that it did not provide enough benefits for New Zealand. While successful passage of the agreement was never at risk (it had the support of five parties, including National), the Foreign Minister's announcement provoked calls for his resignation. In response, Labour denied any hypocrisy in having the Foreign Minister publicly oppose New Zealand's most significant free trade agreement. After all, as Clark herself admitted, 'Winston Peters has made it possible for us to govern'.

Cartel parties: leadership through personalisation

A third institutional change that bears on the question of the taming of political leadership concerns the party system itself, specifically the evolution from the mass and catch-all stages of party organisation to that of a cartel (Katz and Mair 1997). While much of the theoretical work on this latter model has focused on the major parties, especially the extent to which they collude over the distribution of the material resources of the state, recent experience in New Zealand points to the existence of multi-layered cartels, with the dispersal of some of the spoils of office to small parties (but only inside parliament), especially those with the potential to keep one or other of the major parties in power. These resources are said to include material support for party (as distinct from parliamentary) activities, including the free use of office space, air travel, staffing, advertising, and professional and consultancy services.

More recent work on cartels (Blyth and Katz 2005) has extended the argument beyond the use of material resources to include anti-competitive measures with respect to the ways the two major parties occupy the ideological and policy space. According to this view, the established parties are less inclined to compete over policy differences, preferring to appeal to the amorphous 'median' voter. Blyth and Katz argue that, through a combination of free market reform and economic globalisation, most of the policy competition has been 'maxed out'. Paralleling developments in the United Kingdom, Australia and elsewhere, New

Zealand is experiencing growing policy agreement. While parties continue to present themselves as bitter and uncompromising rivals during election campaigns, substantial policy disagreement has all but disappeared. In the case of New Zealand, this can be illustrated with reference to the commitment of Labour and National to broadly similar policies on social spending, especially health and education, taxation rates (both support cuts), nuclear power, climate change and the war in Iraq.

In the absence of policy difference, under the cartel model the major parties now stress their 'managerial competence' and 'personal' style of leadership. New Zealand's political leaders were once recruited from the ranks of the farming and small business communities, as well as the unions. During the past two decades these leaders have been replaced by a new generation of highly educated and professionally trained technocrats. Examples of this 'embourgeoisement' of leadership (Kavanagh 1990: 107) include David Lange (lawyer), Geoffrey Palmer (law professor), Clark (university lecturer), Bill English (economist), Don Brash (Reserve Bank Governor), and John Key (currency trader).

Understanding and adapting to institutional change: leadership challenges

Understanding the leadership impact of institutional change

One approach to the study of leadership is the quasi-psychoanalytic method pioneered by James David Barber (1972). While John Henderson's work on New Zealand prime ministers borrows heavily from this model, and makes a number of useful observations about leadership under PR, Barber's highly deterministic and arbitrary schema fails to capture the essence of leadership in a Westminster parliamentary system. One of the most helpful aspects of Henderson's work, however, is his four categories of leader: achievers, power-seekers, reluctants and performers (1992). A second and potentially more useful approach has been offered by Dennis Kavanagh (1990) in his work on British prime ministers. Building on James McGregor Burns' distinction between transformational and transactional leadership, Kavanagh proposes a cyclical typology containing two styles of leadership: mobilising leadership and excessive, or reconciling, leadership. 'Mobilising' leadership may be required in times of national crisis or when there is a need for radical reform. 'Excessive' leadership, on the other hand, comes into prominence when there is need for greater social cohesion and consensus, typically after the destabilising premiership of a mobilising leader. While this model works well in single party governments such as that of the United Kingdom, it has less value when applied to coalition democracies, where the emphasis on co-operation, compromise and consensus is unlikely to be cyclical, but rather continuous.

Combining features of these two models, this chapter proposes a functional model that identifies the three distinct sets of characteristics or leadership styles required of a New Zealand politician. While leaders are called upon to exercise all three functions, the model calls for an overall judgment about the characteristic that most distinguishes that person's style of leadership. *Mobilisers* are the great performers who use the channels of mass communication to inspire and persuade others to be their followers. In a parliamentary system, such politicians must display a range of skills, including extempore public speaking and debating. Examples of mobilising politicians are David Lange and Winston Peters. *Legislators*, on the other hand, are the analytical thinkers who not only have a detailed grasp of public policy, but have the ideological commitment and tenacity to see it enacted. Unlike Mobilisers, Legislators are often prepared to sacrifice personal popularity and ambition for the sake of principle. While Lange was a superb salesman for the government's free market reforms, Roger Douglas, Geoffrey Palmer and David Caygill were its architects.

The third category of leaders, and the one most appropriate to the behaviour of prime ministers in a PR environment, are the *Managers*. Unlike the Mobilisers, who practice the power of mass persuasion, and the Legislators, who achieve transformational change, Managers are the pragmatists who value consultation and compromise, and who appreciate that decisions are forged through hard-fought trade-offs with political allies and adversaries. In short, the Manager 'must balance the needs of a complex array of frequently competing groups, including consultants, advisers, cabinet colleagues, coalition partners, backbench MPs, public servants and the voting public' (Miller and Mintrom 2006: 5). Examples of Managers include some of New Zealand's most successful and long-term prime ministers, notably Peter Fraser, Keith Holyoake and Helen Clark.

From party mobiliser to coalition manager: the new prime ministership

Under the former two-party system, the transition from opposition leader to prime minister was relatively straightforward. As guardians of the party's ideology, party leaders were expected to be highly programmatic and partisan, even dogmatic. Those who became prime minister were able to behave in much the same manner, thanks to a parliamentary majority and absence of veto players, notably the minor parties and independents. Cabinet had to be managed, but there was little need to consult or compromise with the Opposition, thus ensuring that relations remained as robust during the parliamentary term as they had been in the campaign. As McLeay has pointed out, while the role of party leader is largely unchanged, 'MMP [PR] has meant that an effective prime minister can transcend party allegiance in a way that was not possible when leaders and followers were either inside or outside of government, and politics was entirely a zero-sum game' (2006: 109). Within days of an election, competitors morph into allies, and policies once firmly rejected are incorporated into the government's legislative agenda. Because it requires a mixture of guile and good grace, the role of prime minister is quickly transformed from that of mobilising party leader to reconciling coalition manager. This is not to suggest that the leader of a coalition has to be pliant to be effective; in fact, Clark's style of leadership is frequently depicted in the media as strong, unbending, and even ruthless.

Implications for party leadership selection

Defenders of the highly centralised system of leadership selection practised in New Zealand and Australia argue that those closest to the action are best able to assess the relative merits of prospective leaders. They may draw on survey data showing that party delegates and members, and even more so voters, lack knowledge of the internal dynamics of their parliament and government. While they may be well placed to evaluate the mobilising powers of aspiring leaders, especially by observing an election campaign, they are clearly less competent to judge legislative and managerial competence. To accusations of elitism, they are likely to respond that MPs worth their salt will canvass opinion among grassroots party members before voting for the leader.

On the other hand, those who advocate a more democratic selection process argue that ordinary citizens can compensate for any lack of institutional knowledge by bringing a detached and less self-interested approach to their decision. They might also warn against trying to anticipate how people will respond to the challenge of leadership, as illustrated by the selection of Clark as party leader in 1993. At the time she became leader, Clark was in open conflict with the Alliance leader, Jim Anderton, mainly over his split with Labour in 1989. Between 1993 and 1996 relations between the two continued to deteriorate to a point where any prospect of a coalition agreement had all but disappeared. It was this tough, take-no-prisoners approach to leadership that helped make Clark such an appealing prospect as leader. Those MPs who voted for her could hardly have predicted that her reputation as prime minister would be built on an ability to work closely in government with Anderton, for three years her deputy prime minister, as well as with parties as ideologically distant from Labour as United Future and New Zealand First.

Perhaps the most satisfactory outcome to this debate would be to find a compromise similar to that reached by the British Conservative and Liberal Democrat parties. It grants MPs the right to provide a shortlist of potential leaders, with party delegates or members making the final selection.

Conclusion: a robust trend?

As this chapter has argued, leadership practices in New Zealand have been significantly modified or tamed by institutional change. Whilst the prime minister and executive continue to be the pre-eminent political actors, the trend towards minority government has produced a discernible shift in the balance of power towards the multi-party legislature and its increasingly independent select committees. With the emergence of veto players, mainly in the form of the small parties, the role of prime minister is being transformed from that of mobilising party leader to reconciling coalition manager.

Whether these constraints on prime ministerial leadership prove durable is a matter of some conjecture. The currently low levels of public support for small parties point to the possibility of a substantial shrinking in their number and influence in the years ahead. In the event that this occurs, and that there is a return to a single party majority government, will the more consultative and constrained style of prime ministerial leadership prevail, or will there be a return to the leadership practices of the pre-PR era? Only time will tell.

References

Adams, D., 2002, 'The Leadership Contest', in J. Warhurst and M. Simms (eds), *2001: The Centenary Election*, St Lucia: University of Queensland Press, pp. 19-32.

Barber, J. D., 1972, *The Presidential Character: Predicting Performance in the White House*, Englewood Cliffs: Prentice-Hall.

Blyth, M. and R. Katz, 'From Catch-all Politics to Cartelisation: The Political Economy of the Cartel Party', *West European Politics*, 28:1, pp. 33-60.

Capie, D., 2006, 'Constructing New Zealand in the World', in R. Miller and M. Mintrom (eds), *Political Leadership in New Zealand*, Auckland: Auckland University Press, pp. 17-32.

Henderson, J., 1992, 'Labour's Modern Prime Ministers and the Party: A Study of Contrasting Political Style', in M. Clark (ed.), *The Labour Party After 75 Years*, Wellington: Victoria University Press, pp. 98-117.

Katz, R. and P. Mair, 1997, 'Party Organisation, Party Democracy, and the Emergence of the Cartel Party', in P. Mair, *Party System Change: Approaches and Interpretations*, Oxford: Oxford University Press, pp. 93-119.

Kavanagh, D., 1990, *Politics and Personalities*, London: MacMillan.

McLeay, E., 2006, 'Leadership in Cabinet Under MMP', in R. Miller and M. Mintrom (eds), *Political Leadership in New Zealand*, Auckland: Auckland University Press, pp. 92-112.

Miller, R. and M. Mintrom (eds), 2006, *Political Leadership in New Zealand*, Auckland: Auckland University Press, pp. 113-132.

Miller, R., 2006, 'Minor Party Leadership Under Proportional Representation', in R. Miller and M. Mintrom (eds), *Political Leadership in New Zealand*, Auckland: Auckland University Press, pp. 113-132.

Palmer, G., 1987, *Unbridled Power: An Interpretation of New Zealand's Constitution and Government*, 2nd edition, Auckland: Oxford University Press.

Uhr, J., 2005, *Terms of Trust: Arguments Over Ethics in Australian Government*, Sydney: University of New South Wales Press.

Walter, J. and P. Strangio, 2007, *No, Prime Minister: Reclaiming Politics from Leaders*, Sydney: University of New South Wales Press.

22. Comparing Pathways to Power: Women and Political Leadership in New Zealand

Jennifer Curtin

Introduction

There has always been a public fascination with women political leaders, primarily because there have been so few of them; they are indeed exceptional. Because political leadership has primarily been a male domain, arguably one of the last bastions of almost exclusive male power, watching a woman perform this role seems to attract significant interest. Most recently, the focus has been on two aspiring women leaders: Hillary Clinton, whose bid for the Democrat nomination was reported daily in newspapers around the world and, more tragically, the thwarted and fatal campaign by Benazir Bhutto to re-enter the Pakistani government.

In addition to Hillary Clinton, there appears to have been a rush of women political leaders elected to positions of power of late. We can think of Nancy Pelosi (US), Angela Merkel (Germany), Michelle Bachelet (Chile), Cristina Fernández (Argentina) and the thwarted French presidential candidate Ségolène Royal. Over a decade ago, Benazir Bhutto featured alongside Corazin Aquino (Philippines), Mary Robinson (Ireland), Kim Campbell (Canada) and Gro Harlem Brundtland (Norway). Before that it was Margaret Thatcher (Britain), Golda Meir (Israel) and Indira Gandhi (India). While at any one time the number of women prime ministers or presidents may not be high, there has been an increase in the number of countries featuring women political leaders (Reynolds 1999).

There is a small body of work in the form of political (auto)biography that has focused on women political leaders and their entry into executive government. These biographies, and the edited volumes that profile particular women leaders, highlight the difficulties associated with being a woman with political ambition (Genovese 1993; Thatcher 1995; Klenke 1996; Edwards 2001; Clinton 2003). While many such women are portrayed by the media to have experienced a 'meteoric' rise, the reality is that access to the inner leadership group is obtained only with sustained commitment to building a political career.

For any politician, male or female, an enormous investment of time and energy is normally required to build a political career to the point where they have the capacity to influence directly the government's policy agenda, that is, to become part of the leadership group or the executive. Political leadership depends on at least: selection to a safe seat to ensure incumbency over time; professional development through strategic service within party executives and caucuses; practiced performances in parliamentary committees and the debating chamber; party in government; intra-party political or factional machinations; and, possibly, the (in)visibility of one's own 'feminist' positioning. Thus, a mix of factors, individual, structural and politico-cultural, constrain and/or expand the opportunities for women politicians to enter the executive of government where there is arguably considerable potential to act *for* women.

Australia and New Zealand rarely feature in broader cross-national comparisons of women's parliamentary presence (for exceptions see Sawer and Grey 2005; Sawer, Tremblay and Trimble 2006) and New Zealand is more obviously absent than Australia in those that do encompass more than North America and Europe (Commonwealth Secretariat 1999; Outshoorn and Kantola 2007; Haussman and Sauer 2007). Yet both countries have histories of being leaders in areas of women's rights. New Zealand was the first country to give women the vote in 1893, while Australia was the first to give women the right to vote and stand for Parliament in 1902. Australia was a pioneer in the establishing dedicated women's policy machinery while New Zealand's women's policy machinery has become institutionalised despite the election of neo-liberal/conservative governments throughout the 1990s.

New Zealand and Australia are politically and culturally similar but there are some differences in how women's political representation has progressed. Most obviously, New Zealand has had two women prime ministers consecutively since 1997. In that year, Jenny Shipley took over the leadership of the governing conservative National Party to become New Zealand's first woman prime minister. In 1999, New Zealand experienced an election campaign where the two major parties were both led by women and most media reported that the 'gender factor' had been neutralised in New Zealand politics as a consequence (Curtin 1997). Helen Clark won the 1999 election and has gone on to become New Zealand's longest serving Labour leader. By contrast, Australia is yet to elect a woman prime minister. In March 2005, an Australian women's magazine published an article headed with the question 'Will Australia ever have a female Prime Minister?' and there was much pessimism in the feature's response (Loane 2005). Two years later, in October 2007, Australia elected a new Labor government and made history in that it included Julia Gillard as Deputy Prime Minister (who served almost immediately as Acting Prime Minister).

In this chapter I focus on two aspects of the women and political leadership 'question'. First, I explore some of the idiosyncrasies of the New Zealand political system that might account for women's success compared to their Australian counterparts in accessing political leadership positions. Second, I examine what women have 'done' as a result of their attaining executive leadership positions.

There is a burgeoning literature on women and leadership that suggests women have the potential to 'do' leadership differently (Sinclair 1998; Wajcman 1999) but very little of this discusses women's political leadership (for an exception see Rosenthal 1998). There is however, a scholarly interest amongst feminist political scientists in the substantive representation of women, that is, how women politicians act for women, or on behalf of 'women's interests'.

Some would argue that we should not expect women leaders to necessarily act on behalf of women, as if they were a sectional interest.[1] Certainly there have been a number of women leaders who no doubt support this position. But the election of Helen Clark did raise the expectations of many women's groups in New Zealand and shifts in the gender gap in voting behaviour suggest a substantial proportion of women in New Zealand wanted Helen Clark as leader (Aimer 1997; Curtin 2002). So in the second part of this chapter I explore, albeit briefly, whether we can expect to see women leaders acting for women. In doing so, I draw from literature on both representation and leadership in order to reveal the extent to which women political leaders might use their power to make politics and policy more 'women-friendly'.

Accessing leadership

The fact that women achieved national political leadership in New Zealand a decade earlier than Australia may be partly luck or a result of particular electoral fortunes of left-leaning parties, given they are more likely to support women's representation. However, a closer look also reveals the importance of party rules and norms, broader institutional constraints and, in particular, the various 'feminist' support mechanisms behind women's successful recruitment into cabinet.

In an attempt to explain the 'success' of Labour women in getting both elected and selected for cabinet (most often in comparison with Australia), much is made of the lack of formalised factions and the more secular Labour membership in New Zealand (Curtin and Sawer 1996; Sawer and Grey 2005). The New Zealand Labour Party has always had groupings on the left and right, probably mostly obviously evident in the lead-up to, and during, the term of the fourth Labour Government (1984-90), but these are not structured or institutionalised in the same way as in the Australian Labor Party. Moreover, in New Zealand it is quite possible for a Labour parliamentarian from the left group to become Prime Minister (a virtual impossibility in Australia). While trade unions were once the backbone of the New Zealand Labour Party, there was a recognition by some in the Party that this relationship was inhibiting growth and renewal; the Labour Party had become 'elderly, male-dominated and trade-union conservative ... and organisationally sclerotic' (Shields 2001: 125). The Party's reform movement that followed ensured the NZLP opened itself up to a broader membership base with more balanced voting rights at conference. Women in the Party were active supporters of party reform and were able to use it to their advantage. The Labour Women's Council, along with the youth wing, were able to play a more significant role in party policy-making and internal party representation as a result (Wilson 1992; Shields 2001).

But this overshadows an earlier feminisation of the Labour Party created through the initiative of organising separately in order to advance women's political (descriptive) and policy (substantive) representation. When the Labour Party in New Zealand was established in 1916 the first executive of the Party included two women, one of whom was Elizabeth McCoombs, who went on to become the first woman elected to New Zealand's Parliament in 1933. Thus, from the outset, Labour women demanded the opportunity to organise separately, in ways that went beyond the traditional auxiliary function (Nolan 2002). As a result, women-only branches were established throughout the country, and still exist today. In addition, women activists who entered the Labour Party initiated the (re)invention of critical feminist spaces, most significantly the Labour Women's Council in 1975, an earlier version of the which had been disestablished as a result of Party centralisation in the 1930s (Nolan 2002). These two women-friendly initiatives differentiate the New Zealand Labour Party from its Australian counterpart.

The Labour Women's Council (LWC) was comprised of women elected from the Party membership, all women MPs, plus minority group representatives and the Party's Women's Organiser. It reported directly to the New Zealand Party Council, and women from the LWC were also elected to Labour's influential Policy Council. Its brief was to promote and support women into Party executive positions, including the Party Presidency as well as encourage and support women as parliamentary candidates. The issue of a party quota for women was hotly debated by the LWC during the early-mid 1980s but was rejected in favour of softer affirmative action measures that were already employed by the Council and retaining the reserved seats that women had on the Labour Executive.

Academic commentators have noted that by the mid-1980s, the LWC was very influential in its use of 'networking techniques, both to mobilise women outside the party and to coordinate the power of the women's lobby within it' (Gustafson 1992: 280). Michael Cullen (currently New Zealand's Treasurer) has also recognised the 'power' of the LWC to provoke Labour's leaders. 'He [Prime Minister Lange] could say some awful things sometimes about people. His love-hate relationship with the Labour Women's Council was a wonder to behold and gave some of us with similar mixed non-Politically Correct feelings a great deal of pleasure and joy over a number of years' (Cullen cited in Curtin 2008a). Certainly the success of the LWC cannot be underestimated. There have been three women elected as Party President since 1984, all of whom were members of the Labour Women's Council and all have gone on to become politicians. It is not surprising then, that even before the shift to a proportional system in 1996, the proportion of women in Parliament stood at more than 20%; largely a result of the election of Labour Party women (McLeay 2006; Curtin 2008b). After the 2005 election, the proportion of women in the New Zealand Parliament had increased to 33%.

The feminisation of political leadership that has since become a feature of the New Zealand polity began in earnest 1993 when Helen Clark became leader of the opposition Labour Party after having been deputy leader from 1989. Then, in 1997 Jenny Shipley of the conservative National Party became the country's first woman Prime Minister, although she was the only woman in cabinet immediately following her rise to power. At the 1999 election, a Labour-led Government headed by Helen Clark was elected and Clark has been prime minister ever since. In 1999, seven women were given ministerial positions, constituting 35% of Clark's first cabinet (this dropped to 30% in 2006, with one ex-cabinet minister taking the role of first woman Speaker of the House).

Women leaders acting for women?

Those interested in the substantive representation of women have reengaged extensively with the work of Pitkin in order to theoretically extend and from this, empirically examine, the extent to which we can expect and/or see women representatives acting for, or on behalf of, women's 'interests' (Dahlerup 2005; Celis and Childs 2008). Most of this work to date has focused on women as legislators (not surprisingly, given the lack of women as members of the executive). Yet, just as the number of women elected to parliament may not in itself lead to an increase in the substantive representation of women's interests, nor can we assume that an increase in the number of women in political leadership positions, such as cabinet will do likewise.

In a sense, cabinet is equivalent to a 'black box' in our attempts to 'causally' link the descriptive and substantive representation of women. For example, it could be argued that women as backbenchers have some liberty to speak for women as a group, especially if the discourse of women's interests sits easily alongside their party's broader platform. However, once they enter the leadership group of the governing party, that is the cabinet, women come up against one aspect of the 'leadership dilemma'. For political leaders there is usually an imperative to speak for the public interest over private or sectional interests. But the definition of what constitutes the public interest is not an uncontested (or gender-neutral) process, and many have written of the way in which leaders should, or do, aggregate, deliberate, educate, and persuade citizens and/or represent a moral constituency (Ruscio 2004). Moreover, we cannot always 'see' the representation of women by women who are located within cabinet because they are bound by the secrecy and collectively responsibility conventions that bind the inner leadership group.

So, given that New Zealand has experienced a 'critical mass' of women in the executive of a Labour-led government, to what extent have these women leaders been able to capitalise on their leadership posts as progressive stepping stones to greater political influence (Baer 2003: 135-6) on behalf of women? The Clark government's explicit commitment to women's policy and women's interests appears somewhat muted compared to Labour's previous term in government (1984-90; for a more extensive comparison of these two governments see Curtin 2008a). For example, Grey has demonstrated that fewer overt claims were made by female politicians in New Zealand from 2000 to 2005, despite women's representation in the House having increased (Grey 2006).

In terms of policy leadership, in its first term, the Clark government allocated the Ministry of Women's Affairs portfolio to a minister from the junior coalition partner, the Alliance. And although employment equity had been important to both Helen Clark and Margaret Wilson in the 1980s, the Clark government did little to redress the issue during its first term. Subsequently, there was action with the creation within the Department of Labour of a Pay and Employment Equity Unit. However, unlike the fourth Labour Government's legislative initiative in 1990, the policy instrument adopted in 2004 is much more voluntary in nature.

Margaret Wilson initiated labour market reforms which saw a reinstatement of the role of trade unions through the *Employment Relations Act* 2000 (ERA). The ERA did not return New Zealand to centralised wage bargaining but it did enable unions to negotiate collective contracts and required parties to bargain in good faith. In addition, commitments were made to incrementally increase the minimum wage. While union bargaining and minimum wage increases may disproportionately favour the low-paid, and thereby women, neither of these policy initiatives was 'framed' as addressing women's interests in mainstream policy statements.

When 'women's' policy has been implemented by the Labour-led government, the focus has tended to be on women's labour force participation, which is viewed as providing women with economic independence. New policies directed at early childhood services, out of school care, retirement savings reform and paid parental leave have tended to be framed as 'choices' for women (and men) who are temporarily out of the labour market. Moreover, these policies are often couched within a discourse of serving the 'national interest' by the Clark leadership team (including several high profile, left-leaning women ministers such as Ruth Dyson and Lianne Dalziel), that is, contributing to economic growth, prosperity and moving New Zealand 'forward' as a highly skilled, innovative economy (Skilling 2005). Even the Ministry of Women's Affairs reporting requirements under CEDAW (Convention on the Elimination of All Forms of Discrimination against Women), and the various policy commitments that have been promised, have been framed in terms of advancing New Zealand's national interest and identity.

Discussion

So, can we argue that women's increased presence as political leaders in New Zealand has led to anything more than enhancing the symbolic (read passive) representation of women? And does the lack of explicit 'representative claims' constructed by women political leaders on behalf of women voters indicate that women's political leadership does not matter? Part of the answer may lie in an unrealistic expectation that women leaders are able to pursue *openly* (my emphasis) a feminist agenda, when leadership requires the creation and representation of a national constituency. While some groups may be favoured by leaders (business is the oft-cited example), it is unlikely that the high number of 'feminist' women in cabinet would bode well for Labour's leadership had they chosen to vigorously advance the substantive representation of women in the name of women.

Moreover, the broader political context has changed since the 1970s and 1980s. The women's movement is considerably more fragmented than it was in the early 1980s. The Ministry of Women's Affairs had become institutionalised as the vehicle for ensuring gender audits occurred while a broader 'backlash' politics that had been evident elsewhere had begun to take hold in New Zealand – around Maori claims under the Treaty in particular – and was being extended to women. In 2003, the conservative opposition party Leader proclaimed that he did not see the need for a Ministry of Women's Affairs and would not be appointing a spokesperson for the portfolio. During the 2005 election campaign, suggestions were made that Clark's cabinet was part of a broader feminist mafia (Devere and Graham 2005). Thus it is not surprising that we see less 'speaking' for women by women political leaders.

There have been some specific policy gains for women and, while not all women within the leadership group position themselves similarly as feminists, the increased presence of women in parliament and cabinet has been important in embedding women's 'interests' as legitimate in the political and policy arena in New Zealand in a way that is not currently replicated in Australia. However, it is clear that women's policy interests are not always 'framed' in ways that identify women as the core 'interest' group being represented, especially in more recent years. Indeed, the constituency being created is almost purposively not a 'women's' or 'feminist' constituency (Saward 2006). Elsewhere I have argued in more depth that women in the Labour Party have other sites such as the Labour Women's Council where debate about women's policy interests can be freely pursued, while publicly there appears to have been a strategic decision to not 'speak for' women (Curtin 2008a).

Conclusion

In conclusion, we should not read 'silence' in the political domain as a broader silence on women's policy interests and a lack of action for women by women members of the Labour executive. Nor should this silence surprise us. Paul Keating's thanks and commitments to Labor's 'true believers', a category that included women, came back to haunt him after 1993. Now, governing for 'all Australians', rather than specific sectional interests or particular groups within the community, has become a feature of the rhetoric of political leaders everywhere, Helen Clark included. This suggests that as scholars we need to think about the performance of leadership in more than 'transactional' versus 'transformational' terms and in conjunction with ideas about the performance of representation.

References

Aimer, P., 1997. 'Leaders and outcomes: The Clark factor in 1996', in J. Boston, S. Levine, E. McLeay and N. Roberts (eds), *From Campaign to Coalition: The 1996 MMP Election*, Palmerston North: Dunmore Press.

Baer, D. L., 2003, 'Women, women's organisations and political parties', in S. Carroll (ed.), *Women and American Politics. New Questions, New Directions*, Oxford: Oxford University Press.

Celis K. and S. Childs, 2008, 'Introduction: The descriptive and substantive representation of women: New directions', *Parliamentary Affairs*, 61:3, pp.419-425.

Clinton, H., 2003, *Living History: Memoirs*, London: Headline.

Commonwealth Secretariat, 1999, *Women in Politics: Voices from the Commonwealth*, London: Commonwealth Secretariat.

Curtin, J., 1997, *Gender and Political Leadership in New Zealand*, Research Note 14 1997-98, Parliamentary Library.

Curtin, J., 2002, 'Women's voting patterns: Australia and New Zealand compared', in *Women Talking Politics: Newsletter of the Aotearoa/New Zealand Women and Politics Network*, New Issue No. 5, pp. 1-3.

Curtin, J., 2008a, 'Women, political leadership and substantive representation: The case of New Zealand', *Parliamentary Affairs*, 61:3, July.

Curtin, J. 2008b. 'Gendering parliamentary representation in New Zealand: A mixed system producing mixed results' in M. Tremblay (ed.), *Women, Electoral Systems and Legislative Representation*, Palgrave Macmillan.

Curtin J. and M. Sawer, 1996, 'Gender equity in the shrinking state: Women and the great experiment', in F. G. Castles, R. Gerritsen and J. Vowles (eds), *The Great Experiment: Labour Parties and Public Policy*

Transformation in Australia and New Zealand, Auckland: Auckland University Press.

Dahlerup, D., 2005, 'The story of the theory of critical mass', *Politics and Gender,* 2:4, 2006, pp. 511-22

Devere, H. and S. Graham, 2006, 'The Don and Helen New Zealand election 2005: A Media A-gender?', *Pacific Journalism Review,* 12:1, pp. 65-86.

Edwards, B., 2001, *Helen: Portrait of a Prime Minister*, Auckland: Exisle Publishing.

Genovese, M., 1993, *Women as National Leaders*, London: Sage.

Grey, S., 2006, 'Numbers and beyond: The relevance of critical mass in gender research', *Politics and Gender,* 2:4, pp. 491-501.

Gustafson, B., 1992, 'Labour Party', in H. Gold (ed.), *New Zealand Politics in Perspective,* Auckland: Longman Paul, p. 280.

Haussman, M. and B. Sauer (eds), 2007, *Gendering the State in the Age of Globalization: Women's Movements and State Feminism in Post-Industrial Democracies,* Lanham: Rowman and Littlefield.

Klenke, K., 1996, *Women and Leadership: A Contextual Perspective,* New York: Springer Publications.

Loane, S., 2005, 'Will Australia ever have a female Prime Minister?', *Madison,* March Issue, pp. 92-4.

McLeay, E., 2006, 'Climbing on: rules, values and women's representation in the New Zealand parliament', in M. Sawer, M. Tremblay and L. Trimble (eds), *Representing Women in Parliament. A Comparative Study*, Abingdon: Routledge, pp. 67-82.

Nolan, M., 2002, 'Gender and the politics of keeping left: Wellington Labour women and their community 1912-49', in B. Brookes and D. Page (eds), *Communities of Women: Historical Perspectives,* Dunedin: University of Otago Press.

Outshoorn J. and J. Kantola (eds), 2007, *Changing State Feminism,* New York: Palgrave Macmillan.

Reynolds, A., 1999, 'Women in the legislatures and executives of the world: Knocking at the highest glass ceiling', *World Politics*, 51:4, pp. 547-72.

Rosenthal, C. S., 1998, *When Women Lead: Integrative Leadership in State Legislatures*, New York: Oxford University Press.

Ruscio, K. P., 2004, *The Leadership Dilemma in Modern Democracy,* Cheltenham: Edward Elgar.

Saward, M., 2006, 'The Representative Claim', *Contemporary Political Theory,* 5:3, pp. 297-318.

Sawer, M. and S. Grey, 2005, 'Under the Southern Cross: Women's political representation in Australia and New Zealand', in Y. Galligan and M. Tremblay (eds), *Sharing Power: Women in Parliament in Consolidated and Emerging Democracies,* Aldershot: Ashgate.

Sawer, M., M. Tremblay and L. Trimble (eds), 2006, *Representing Women in Parliament. A Comparative Study*, Abingdon: Routledge.

Shields, M., 2001, 'Women in the Labour Party during the Kirk and Rowling years', in M. Clark (ed.), *Three Labour Leaders,* Wellington: University of Wellington Press.

Sinclair, A., 1998, *Doing Leadership Differently: Gender, Power and Sexuality in a Changing Business Culture*, Carlton: Melbourne University Press.

Skilling, P., 2005, 'Trajectories of art and culture policy in New Zealand', *Australian Journal of Public Administration*, 64:4, pp. 20-31.

Thatcher, M., 1995, *The Path to Power*, London: Harper Collins.

Wajcman, J., 1999, *Managing Like a Man: Women and Men in Corporate Management*, St Leonards, NSW: Allen & Unwin.

Wilson, M., 1992, 'Women and the Labour Party', in M. Clark (ed), *The Labour Party After 75 Years,* Wellington: Victoria University Press.

ENDNOTES

[1] This question was asked of me at the 'Public Leadership in Australia and Beyond' Workshop, The Australian National University, 29-30 November 2007.

23. Are Women Leaders Different? Margaret Thatcher and Helen Clark

Marian Simms

Introduction

Untangling the gendered aspects of political leaders' successes provides something of a puzzle. While many studies have demonstrated that gender may be a factor in lack of political success, few studies have examined gender as a factor *in* success. This is in part for methodological reasons — the number of women leaders is very small — hence quantitative approaches do not work well. Of course, the number of successful women leaders — defined as being re-elected to office — is even smaller. This chapter focuses on two very successful such leaders, the UK's Margaret Thatcher and New Zealand's Helen Clark, asking how and in what ways gender was part of their success. It argues that successful leaders operate on three levels: rhetoric or appearance, process, and policy. Gender is relevant to all three. At its clearest and most obvious, gender is integral to image. 'Pretty boy' Tony Blair, or a Spitting Image (British television satire) sketch featuring cigar smoking Thatcher, are cases in point (Carver 2006: 453). Sinclair (2005) maintains that successful women and indigenous leaders utilise their bodies to differentiate themselves from mainstream leaders to increase trust in the particular organisation.

Traditionally, politics has been a gendered occupation in Britain and other Commonwealth countries. Party leaders were seen as the fathers of the nation. It was no accident that the few early women politicians in were depicted as parliamentary 'mothers'. This was in addition to the first women parliamentarians being political widows and or parliamentary daughters.

Research on barriers to political achievement in Australia ascertained that most senior party officials saw the ideal candidate for parliament as: 'tall, dark and handsome, a good father who attends church' (Sawer and Simms 1993: 66). Women were rarely mentioned as first choice candidates. When prompted, one party official suggested 'the local television weather girl' as a possibility. This and other research indicated that women candidates were not valued in a system where candidate selection is highly centralised and firmly based on tightly organised political parties. Body politics are still significant negatives for many women party leaders. For example media research shows significant negative commentary over matters such as clothes choices and marital status and her childless state, with few positive responses.[1] Negative stories have been recently published over women MPs with small children 'neglecting' their political duties (Stanhope 2007).

Studies have shown a dichotomous model of twentieth century public women as either 'monuments' or 'maidens' (Warner 1985). Margaret Thatcher featured in Warner's pioneering study as a successful leader partly because she had become embodied as a contemporary Boudicca after Britain's successes in the Falklands War (1982). The British tabloids featured Thatcher as a statue (monument) of Britannia draped in the union jack. At that point Thatcher had won the first of three successive election victories (1979) — she would later win in 1983 and 1987 — and had already become demonised by British feminists (see Campbell 1984). The Thatcher government's economic agenda was inimical to the feminist social democratic strategy of working through the state. Thatcher's successful management of the 1982 Falkland's conflict was also at odds with the generally pacifist approach of British feminists and indeed many on the British left. Thatcher was also depicted as an enemy of her sex by conservative admirers as was picked up in the 'iron maiden' soubriquet (Cosgrave 1979).

Contemporary leadership studies utilise qualitative methods to provide useful insights. Leaders' images have also come under careful scrutiny in cognate disciplines such as political marketing and political science. The revival of interest in presidentialism is one case in point. Obsession with image, desire to control the political agenda, playing cabinet favourites, down-grading parliament and so on, are all charges laid against former British Prime minister Tony Blair and his presidential style (see Foley 2004). Blair generally stands accused of monopolising power and being obsessed with projecting his own image. In spite of, or perhaps because of, these attributes he was also politically successful and won successive elections.

In reviewing the Blair legacy, studies are also again taking stock of the Thatcher period, and arguing that Blair is a kind of Thatcher in drag. Thatcher — even more than previously (see for example, Moon 1996) becomes viewed as an innovator, not just in policy terms — as with 'Thatcherism' (see Jenkins 2007) — but in process terms. The key features of her process revolution are working above cabinet, micro managing party research and advertising, creating policy, and creating an American style continuous campaign (Scammell 1996).

The development of 'product Thatcher' was also important, in terms of the government's media strategy. One key difference between Blair and Thatcher relates to party tradition. The Conservative party leader is meant to be the font of policy, whereas the Labour party leader is supposed to express the collective will. Blair has taken the British Labour Party considerably further from its roots than Thatcher took her party — although, arguably, the Conservative party revered cabinet more than Labour. The British Labour party always enjoyed links with other sources of opinion, notably the unions. Thatcher's willingness to use friendly peers to oppose her ministers' policies in the House of Lords showed complete cynicism about cabinet conventions (Cosgrave 1979). The downgrading of the cabinet under both Thatcher and Blair has important long-term constitutional implications as well (Foster 2004). In Westminster terms, the leader has taken over the role of cabinet (that 'hyphen and buckle' according to Bagehot 1872: 85), and, equally significantly, taken on the symbolic role of the Monarch, the 'theatrical show of society' (Bagehot 1872: 355).

Turning to New Zealand, successful Labour Prime Minister Helen Clark has also changed important political processes, or the 'way things are done'. Clark rapidly rose to prominence in her 30s during the Labour government of the 1980s, was elected to cabinet in 1987, holding various ministries, was elected as party leader in 1993, and consequently became Prime Minister when the Labour Party was elected to government in November 1999. Her Labour-led government was re-elected in 2002 and 2005.[2] Like Thatcher, Helen Clark reorganised the operations of the machinery of governing. Clark's informal advisory network or 'kitchen cabinet' has been accused of replacing cabinet as a source of political and policy strategy.[3] Clark's role as a politico-constitutional innovator has been partly aided by New Zealand's introduction of Multi-Member Proportional (MMP) representation in the mid-1990s. Designed to better represent minority opinion new parties, MMP has led to coalition government with a major impact on the cabinet, which has become a multi-party body. Since 2005 the New Zealand cabinet no longer observes cabinet solidarity.[4] New policies are sold to the public via extensive government advertising, and the political loyalties of departmental communication chiefs are vetted very closely.

Does image matter? Apart from the growing importance of television during Thatcher's political career, it is arguable that political character is 'created' through repetition. 'Personality' politics is also seen by some (Gaffney 2001; Norton 2003; Foley 2004) as an indicator of presidentialisation. The establishment of 'personality traits' in the minds of voters and the community is created through repetition; and if 'we take Margaret Thatcher, it is probable that throughout the 1980s, the whole United Kingdom population had a notion of her as a person' (Gaffney 2001: 129).

The outlines of the Helen Clark story are well known in New Zealand (James 2005: 5). 'Clark went off to boarding school in Auckland, as brainy rural offspring did … she lived in a frugal household. Clark's father, George, demanded probity'. Clark's father was featured in the favourable biography by Brian Edwards as commending honesty above all: 'When they (Helen and her sister) were young, if they'd sworn at me, it wouldn't have worried me because I swore at the dogs. But if they'd ever cheated or lied, I'd have been down on them like a ton of hot bricks' (quoted in James 2005: 5).

Clark, at crucial points — such as in pivotal debates — would self-reference her strict background: 'later she told the *Herald* she was brought up a Presbyterian went to Sunday school every week … and at Epsom Girls' Grammar walked "in a crocodile" every Sunday morning to … Church' (Young 2004: 1).

Such references could easily be provoked by suggestions that her commitment to mainstream values was less than wholehearted. For example, in 2004, the (then) leader of the centre-right National Party, Don Brash, questioned Clark's commitment to Christianity and to the 'institution of marriage' (Young 2004: 1). Clark has also endured media speculation over whether her marriage is genuine or a smokescreen. Previously, Clark had herself stated that she thought legal marriage was 'unnecessary' and she formalised her partnership with sociology academic Peter Davis on the eve of her first running for Parliament in 1981.

Clark's repetition of her story is consistent with the strategies used by contemporary successful national leaders to normalise themselves, and to demonstrate their individuality and personal character through their proven ability to rise above their circumstances. Another recent example of the repeated storyline is Australian Labor Prime Minister Kevin Rudd's regular references to himself as 'Kevin' 'from country Queensland' an 'economic conservative' who grew up in relative poverty, due to his father's untimely death. In Clark's case she has also had to respond to speculation and comments from others questioning her normalcy, and to make a complex judgment as to what is considered normal for a New Zealand woman. While within her support base in the left wing of the Labour Party, bypassing formal marriage or retaining one's given name would be typical in 1981 when she became an MP, this would not have been the case for most women. For example, marriage rates for women in the general New Zealand community were around 85%.

There are multiple such examples of Thatcher's sex being a factor in her career. According to one biographer (Cosgrave 1979: 226) she generated opposition within the Conservative party in the 1970s not because 'she was a woman', but because of 'the kind of woman' she was. Her election as Conservative Party leader was based on the assumption that she would not dominate — due to her gender. Her strong card was that she was not a feminist. Thatcher's subsequent 'toughness' as measured by pollsters, was a surprise to her party supporters in 1979. The political marketing literature features her makeovers designed to soften and provide a common touch — the visits to chocolate factories and supermarkets (Scammell 1996). These 'softenings' tended to happen after she became Prime Minister rather than before.

Unlike Clark, her personal values — repeated regularly to become part of her character — were not modern, but associated with Victorian values (see Skidelsy 1988: iv). For example, Thatcher opposed the 'permissive society', but introduced few policies to stamp it out (Jenkins 2007: 164). She viewed divorce, abortion and such like with disfavour but introduced no important legislative changes. Thatcher embodied traditional femininity and was happy to be use make up and makeovers.

Ironically these types of situational makeovers for women tended to be sharply criticised by other women politicians of the era, and studies derived from rich interviews pinpoint the attempted feminisation of women politicos as particularly irritating to them. 'Women reported the way in which the media always include the age of women politicians, what they look like, their domestic and family circumstances, their fashion sense and so on' (Sreberny-Mohammadi and Ross 2000: 108).

Thatcher's significance lay in her capacity to utilise features normally associated with weakness and turn them into strengths. Hence being a woman, a mother and of diminutive, even fragile, appearance were turned into political plusses. One study (Jenkins 2007: 165) even suggested that her successful visit to Latin America was due to her Eva Peron-like appearance. George Schultz presented her with a handbag as a sign of achievement. The irony here is that many studies have indicated that most women politicians have complained bitterly about such depictions and wish to be taken seriously by the media and other politicians.

Thatcher's storyline related to her upbringing in Grantham and her sturdy work ethic as instilled by her father. Yet underlying such folksy stories was a carefully crafted sense of public theatre. Her understanding of political marketing was reflected not so much in her image makeovers but in her sophisticated interpretation of qualitative and quantitative polling. Scammell (1996) points out that Thatcher's riding roughshod over polling figures showing widespread opposition was based on her faith in the Party's qualitative polling that was showing the opposite.

Intertwined with discussions of her sex are discussions of her political skills. She was depicted by some as a 'political innovator' (Moon 1995) and as the first great British political marketer (Scammell 1996). It is now widely accepted that innovation — whether of policy or of process — is the creature of key individuals, often operating in small groups (see Childs and Krook 2006). Thus, critical mass theory and other statistical models do not provide satisfactory explanations of policy innovation and social change.

Two further features, however, are striking about Clark's leadership role. First, she has actively carried her reputation as a supporter of women's issues and indigenous politics with her into the top job. Women were and remain an important support base for Clarke, whereas Thatcher's support among women varied. Research has found that women voters rated women party leaders 'more highly' in New Zealand and Canada than in Australia and Great Britain (Banducci and Karp 2000: 820). This may well be reflected in the kinds of images women politicians' project as well as in policies more generally.

Clark has probably sought, and certainly generated, positive media treatment over her recent dealings with other prominent women, and complaints by ordinary women regarding sexual assault by police. Ms Clark took a high profile role in the ceremonial burial ceremony for the deceased Maori Queen in 2006. Photographed with high status relatives of the Queen, this image was relayed to national television news programs and was front-page news throughout the country (Stokes 2006).[5] She established a judicial inquiry into police misbehaviour in 2004 following newspaper allegations of systematic sexual assault on young women by police in the Rotorua district in the North Island of New Zealand, conducted in a culture of cover up. Clark said her 'hair stood on end' at the events outlined by one complainant in a story published in Wellington's *Dominion Post* newspaper in 2004 (Venter *et al.* 2004).[6] Given the lack of credence normally given to sexual assault complainants, the Prime Minister's role was welcomed by feminist organisations and by ordinary women, as reflected in letters to the newspapers and on blogs. One comparable woman leader would be Canada's Kim Campbell, who publicly supported women's issues, but failed to gain re-election.

Clark's public role on women's issues may be related to New Zealand culture where, for example, women's sports enjoy unusually high status — suggesting widespread acceptance of a separate women's culture. Clark is a regular attendee at important netball games. Her own enjoyment of sport, for example squash, skiing and mountain climbing, is well publicised. In traditional Maori society there is also a strong women's culture.

Serious commentators decry the cult of the celebrity that has been fostered by co-dependent media and public relations staff, arguing it has devalued serious political discussion. Yet recent work on leadership (see Collinson 2006, following Burns 1979) reminds us that leaders require followers in whose eyes success is reflected. Deliberately eschewing the so-called leadership traits approach, which specifies a shopping list of attributes for good leadership, 'followership' studies understand leadership in a relational way. Such models are potentially applicable to the public, political arena. They echo existing studies which seek to examine the role of 'gender identity' in responses by voters to leaders.

Second, Clark's long period in office has coincided with a values shift in New Zealand domestic and foreign policies so that, for example, the centre-right opposition party has been forced to adopt a 'no nuclear ships' policy, and has tip toed around the issue of supporting the 'Coalition of the Willing' in Iraq. The Clark government has shifted the role of the state in domestic politics back to the middle after a decade or more of extreme experiments with neo-liberal policies. Remarkably, her government re-nationalised industries, such as the railway track system, oversaw a re-centralisation of the public sector and re-instated a kinder welfare state.

Leaving aside the current debate over whether Thatcherism created real or imagined policy changes (see Jenkins 2007), Clark's policy shifts may be seen as a left wing equivalent of Thatcher's right wing shift. While the term 'Clarkism' is not in common usage, well-known social democratic thinker, Trotter (2008: 15), argues that Clark's 'brand … of social liberalism' has created an exodus of social conservatives from New Zealand.

Centralisation is a common theme under both leaders. Thatcher's re-regulation of the UK public sector compares with Clark's strengthening the work of the New Zealand State Services Commission. Both Thatcher and Clark are well known for their high profiles on the international stage. Thatcher's friendships with Ronald Reagan and Mikhail Gorbachev, and the Falklands war, meant she made a strong mark in foreign policy. Again, as with their differing approaches to neo-liberalism, Clark's foreign policy stamp relates to a more moderate, multi-lateralist policy stance.

Conclusion

Thatcher and Clark have chosen to present themselves as a regal, heroic figures standing for integrity and decency, thus highlighting aspects of women that transcend sexuality. They have turned a media negative — being a female politician — into a positive.

Thatcher's regal status was confirmed during her first term with the Falklands war in 1982. Clark's transition occurred in her third term, with her high profile role at the funeral of the Maori Queen in 2006. Such status transformation has constitutional relevance as the Monarch conventionally has such status under Westminster.

This chapter has also drawn a parallel between Thatcherism and Clarkism. While it has been suggested that Thatcher's real emergence as a conviction politician over the poll tax issue lost her the leadership, it remains to be seen whether Clark will be able to balance pragmatism and conviction through political marketing. Clark's policies on foreign affairs and social welfare have been in a social democratic mode. She has consciously eschewed the triangulation strategies of the likes of Bill Clinton and Tony Blair.

References

Bagehot, W., 1867, *The English Constitution*, London: Dent & son.

Banducci, S. A. and J. A. Karp, 2000, 'Gender, leadership and choice in multiparty systems', *Political Research Quarterly*, 53:4, pp. 815-48.

Burns, J., 1979, *Leadership*, New York: Harper/Collins.

Campbell, B., 1984, *Wigan Pier Revisited: Poverty and Politics in the Eighties*, London: Virago.

Carver, T., 2006, 'Politics of identity' *Government and Opposition*, 41:3, pp. 450-68.

Childs, S. and M. L. Krook, 2006, 'Gender and politics: The state of the art', *Politics*, 26:1, pp. 18-28.

Collinson, D., 2006, 'Rethinking followership: A post-structuralist analysis of follower identities', *The Leadership Quarterly*, 17:2, pp. 179-89.

Cosgrave, P., 1979, *Margaret Thatcher: Prime Minister*, London: Hutchinson.

Foley, M., 2004, 'Presidential attribution as an agency of prime ministerial critique in a parliamentary democracy: The case of Tony Blair', *British Journal of Politics and International Relations*, 6:1, pp. 292-311.

Forster, C., 2004, 'Cabinet government in the twentieth century', *The Modern Law Review*, 67:5, pp. 753-71.

Gaffney, J., 2001, 'Imagined relationships: Political leadership in contemporary democracies', *Parliamentary Affairs*, 54:1, pp. 120-33.

James, C., 2005, 'How come the farmer's daughter and the socialist's son swapped roles?', *New Zealand Herald*, 5 September, p. 3.

Jenkins, S., 2007, 'Thatcher's legacy', *Political Studies Review*, 5:1, pp. 161-71.

Moon, J., 1995, 'Innovative leadership and policy change: Lessons from Thatcher', *Governance*, 8:1, pp. 1-15.

Norton, P., 2003, 'The presidentialization of British Politics', *Government and Opposition*, 38:1, pp. 274-8.

Sawer, M. and M. Simms, 1993, *A Woman's Place: Women and Politics in Australia*, Sydney: Allen & Unwin.

Scammell, M., 1996, 'The odd couple: Marketing and Maggie', *European Journal of Marketing*, 30:10/11, pp. 122-34.

Sinclair, A., 2005, 'Body possibilities in leadership', *Leadership*, 1:4, pp. 387-406.

Skidelsky, R. (ed.), 1988, *Thatcherism*, London: Chatto and Windus.

Sreberny-Mohammadi, A. and K. Ross, 2000, 'Women MPs and the media: Representing the body politic', *Parliamentary Affairs*, 49:1, pp. 103-15.

Stanhope, J., 2007, 'Minister for health attacked for taking maternity Leave', Press release, 14 November.

Stokes, J., 2006, 'Prime Minister pays her respects to monarch', *New Zealand Herald*, 19 August, p. 1.

Trotter, C., 2008, 'Key will not stem the tide', *Otago Daily Times*, 2 May, p. 15.

Venter, N., A. Kelly and J. Gordon, 2004, 'My hair stood on end, says PM', *Dominion Post*, 5 February, p. 1.

Warner, M., 1985, *Monuments and Maidens: Allegory of the Female Form*, London: Picador.

Young, A., 2004, 'Insults get personal between Clark and Brash', *New Zealand Herald,* 16 March, p. 1.

ENDNOTES

[1] Unpublished Labor Party polling indicates that Ms Gillard is a draw card for women voters. There are indications that stories about her private life have been released by the Party to neutralise rumours that she is gay, because she generally wears pants.

[2] Earlier, New Zealand had a centre-right woman Prime Minister Ms Jenny Shipley (1999), and a feminist MP, Dr Marilyn Waring.

[3] This group includes Heather Simpson her adviser and Margaret Wilson, the Speaker of the House and former Labour party president.

[4] New Zealand First party leader, Winston Peters, is Foreign Minister, and his party has guaranteed supply, but Peters has not pledged loyalty to government policies and is a critic of the free trade agreement with China recently signed by Prime Minister Clark.

[5] The Prime Minister was the first woman invited to speak at the 'marae' — Maori community house — during such a ceremony — 'tangihanga'. *New Zealand Herald,* 19 August 2006.

[6] The Report of the Inquiry was released in August 2007.